BASEBALL IS BACK!

And you'll go into extra innings happily browsing through info-packed entries like these:

"$100,000 Infield": The Philadelphia Athletics' famed infield from 1911 to 1914, consisting of 1st baseman Stuffy McInnis, 2nd baseman Eddie COLLINS, shortstop Jack Barry, and 3rd baseman "Home Run" BAKER, helped Connie MACK's A's to three pennants and two championships in four years. The $100,000 referred not to what they were paid but what they would have been worth on the open market (don't think that idea hadn't occurred to Mack, who was notorious for periodic "housecleanings" to raise quick cash). . . .

Wells, Willie "Devil" (shortstop, Negro leagues, 1925–49): Another of the great Negro leaguers who deserved Hall of Fame induction while he was alive, Wells was the greatest shortstop in the black leagues other than "Pop" LLOYD. Wells could hit for average—once leading the Negro National League with a .403 mark—and power—three times leading the NNL in homers. . . .

1876: Inaugural year of the National League of Base Ball Clubs, today known simply as the National League. On April 22, the League played its first game ever, a 6–5 victory by Boston over Philadelphia. The Chicago White Stockings, led by pitcher Albert G. SPALDING and owned by NL co-founder William HULBERT, captured the League's first pennant.

DAVID H. MARTINEZ is a member of the Society for American Baseball Research, which helped him immeasurably in writing this book. He has broadcast baseball games for the University of California (PAC-10 conference) and has hosted a weekly sports call-in/interview radio show. He lives in San Jose, California.

THE BOOK OF BASEBALL LITERACY

DAVID H. MARTINEZ

A PLUME BOOK

PLUME
Published by the Penguin Group
Penguin Books USA Inc., 375 Hudson Street,
New York, New York 10014, U.S.A.
Penguin Books Ltd, 27 Wrights Lane,
London W8 5TZ, England
Penguin Books Australia Ltd, Ringwood,
Victoria, Australia
Penguin Books Canada Ltd, 10 Alcorn Avenue,
Toronto, Ontario, Canada M4V 3B2
Penguin Books (N.Z.) Ltd, 182–190 Wairau Road,
Auckland 10, New Zealand

Penguin Books Ltd, Registered Offices:
Harmondsworth, Middlesex, England

First published by Plume, an imprint of Dutton Signet,
a division of Penguin Books USA Inc.

First Printing, March, 1996
10 9 8 7 6 5 4 3 2 1

 REGISTERED TRADEMARK—MARCA REGISTRADA

LIBRARY OF CONGRESS CATALOGING-IN-PUBLICATION DATA:

Martinez, David H.
    The book of baseball literacy / David H. Martinez.
        p.   cm.
    ISBN 0-452-27426-5
    1. Baseball—Encyclopedias.   2. Baseball—Records.   I. Title.
    GV862.3.M37   1996
    796.357'03—dc20   95–35755
                                                            CIP

Printed in the United States of America
Set in New Baskerville
Designed by Leonard Telesca

BOOKS ARE AVAILABLE AT QUANTITY DISCOUNTS WHEN USED TO PROMOTE PRODUCTS OR
SERVICES. FOR INFORMATION PLEASE WRITE TO PREMIUM MARKETING DIVISION, PENGUIN
BOOKS USA INC., 375 HUDSON STREET, NEW YORK, NEW YORK 10014.

*For Mom and Dad, whose love and support
have made everything in my life possible*

ACKNOWLEDGMENTS

As with any project of this size, I could not have completed this work without the invaluable assistance and guidance of many people. Danielle Perez of Plume has been extremely helpful with suggestions and answers to all my questions; throughout months of work, our respective team allegiances (she with the Yankees, I with the Dodgers) almost never interfered. Jim Pinkston did a fantastic job finding Plume and Danielle, and I will always be grateful to him. My many teachers over the years have all had an indirect influence in making this project possible. In particular, I want to thank Professors David Littlejohn and Maxine Hong Kingston of U.C. Berkeley for their inspiration, and Tom Clarke of Fremont High for turning me on to writing in the first place. Finally, I must mention a number of other people whose contributions to this work and to my life in general deserve special recognition: Anna, Ken, Sara, and Kenny Jacoby; Kevin Mintz; Diane McBurnie; and, of course, Ava Phillips. This is hardly an exhaustive list, and for everyone I missed, you can be sure I'll get you the next time around.

CONTENTS

INTRODUCTION

These are the times that try baseball fans' souls. The labor strife and unabashed greed of the past few years have stained the American pastime, and to hear some members of the media put it, baseball has never been in worse shape.

Wrong.

In 1901, the American League challenged the established National League for its share of the sporting scene. The two leagues battled viciously through player raids and competing publicity. Once the dust settled, baseball embarked on a journey of prosperity. Two decades later, baseball was reeling from the gambling scandal that shook American faith to its core in 1919 and from the on-field death of a popular player, Ray Chapman, in 1920. Baseball—and the nation—flourished. In 1944–45, most of America's able-bodied men were fighting in World War II. Baseball made do with a one-armed outfielder, a one-legged pitcher, and any number of aging veterans coaxed out of retirement. Again, baseball survived. In 1976, the baseball establishment worried about the financial impact of the demolishment of the reserve clause and the advent of free agency. Many predicted impending doom. Instead, attendance exploded, television contracts reached unprecedented heights, and teams miraculously found the money to spend on high-priced players. Then, in 1981, a fifty-day strike split the season in half. Many predicted that baseball's glory days had ended. But baseball came back to post attendance gains for the next decade.

The naysayers came out again in 1994, when, for the first time in ninety years, the World Series was canceled. At that time, a lot of people in the media displayed a surprising lack of knowledge and perspective about the game's history. Their doom-and-gloom predictions dominated magazines, newspapers, and evening broadcasts. I wrote this book partly to increase the overall understanding of the greatest game in the world.

In its pages you'll find the entire relevant history of baseball laid out in different chapters. You want to learn about Honus Wagner and John "Pop" Lloyd? Turn to Chapter 1. Charlie Comiskey and Marvin Miller? Chapter 2. AstroTurf and Ebbets Field? Chapter 5. You want an explanation of slugging percentage? Turn to Chapter 7. You want the titles of some of the greatest baseball books ever written? They're in Chapter 6. Wonder what happened in 1904 to cancel the World Series? Chapter 4. What were the Negro leagues all about? Chapter 3. The origin of baseball rubbing mud? Chapter 8. In short, this book has all the people, places, events, records, statistics, folklore, literature, and other minutiae that all baseball fans should know and care about.

Careful readers will notice a few surprising inclusions—and some purposeful omissions. Amos Rusie, for example. He played a hundred years ago, and he doesn't hold any significant records. Why should the modern fan care about him? Read his entry to find out. And Sol White, Cristobal Torriente, Turkey Stearnes . . . never heard of them? They played before white baseball decided to admit people of color.

After being shunted aside and forgotten by most of mainstream society, they won't be forgotten here.

Of course, this book contains all the greats of the game: Ruth, Gehrig, and Williams. Mays, Mantle, and DiMaggio. Grove, Koufax, and Mathewson. Rickey, MacPhail, and Landis. Smith, Scully, and Angell. But you won't find, for example, every member of the Hall of Fame. Why? Because my purpose was to identify the people who really made a mark on the game, the people without whom a responsible history could not be written. So you're not going to find Joe Medwick, Chick Hafey, Lloyd Waner, and many other Hall of Famers. But you will find some significant non–Hall of Famers, such as Larry Doby and Roger Maris.

I didn't want to simply give you the same old facts and stories you've heard a million times, so throughout the book, you're going to find a lot of opinions—fully supported by the evidence, of course—and some wonderful anecdotes that you probably haven't heard. On the other hand, because I didn't want to cheat you out of baseball's classic lore, I've tried to strike a good balance between old and new.

Because the people are what made baseball great, I've devoted the lion's share of the book to them. Chapter 1 has players and managers, Chapter 2 has everybody else who has influenced the game: executives, broadcasters, writers, commissioners, umpires, and a few other surprises. Unlike some baseball "dictionaries," I provide only those statistics that are significant to understanding the player's contribution to the game. By the same token, I give only those biographical facts that are vital to understanding the person.

The remainder of the book—Chapters 3 through 8—covers all the other parts of the game; the chapter titles give more detail. Again, in my choices, I was aiming for significance. In Chapter 3, you can find brief histories of all the current major league teams, and a few defunct ones, too. There's also information on all but one major league—the short-lived Union Association—as well as a few minor leagues, the Negro leagues, and other groups that aren't easy to classify, such as the Major League Baseball Players' Association.

Chapter 4 was perhaps the toughest. What are the most significant events in baseball history? A hundred different people will give you 110 different answers. But between Chapter 4 and the rest of the book, I think I've covered just about everything. Some events have affected baseball so greatly that their stories are told in more than one entry. The Black Sox scandal, for example, has earned space in Chapters 1, 4, and 6. Everything is cross-referenced. In addition, Chapter 4 also contains brief histories and discussions of recurring events like the All-Star Game and the World Series.

All the current major league ballparks are profiled in Chapter 5. And because no history is complete without a mention of some old classics, I've also included the grand cathedrals of baseball such as the Polo Grounds and Ebbets Field.

Chapter 6 is a catchall covering the lore of the game. You'll find great book titles, games, sayings, poems, songs, eras, baseball-related companies, nicknames, famous stories, and other fun stuff. This chapter included everything from *Bull Durham* to great nicknames to the Rawlings Company.

Chapter 7 is where you're going to find all the statistics fans have come to expect from a baseball book. I've listed all-time leaders in the major offensive and pitching categories, and, for beginners as well as veterans, I've provided explanations of what some stats measure and signify. There are also histories of all the major awards and introductions to advanced statistical measurements.

In Chapter 8, you'll find a sampling of important baseball rules and game terminology, as well as discussions of business-related facts. Not every baseball term is included; that would take its own book (such as Paul Dickson's *The Dickson Baseball Dictionary*). The words and phrases I've chosen should give you a broader understanding of the game, not explain it entirely. Some terms are obvious, such as *double play*, *strike zone*, and *base on balls*. Others, such as *waivers*, *National Agreement*, and *reserve clause*, aren't. In most cases, I've tried to illustrate the meaning of each term with anecdotes, examples, and word origins.

You probably want to get into the meat of the book now, and I don't want to stop you.

HOW TO USE THIS BOOK

Although you can certainly read it cover to cover, this book is meant to be read haphazardly, jumping around to another section when something interests you. For that reason, I've included extensive cross-referencing. Every now and then, you'll notice a name or phrase in SMALL CAPITALS. That means it has its own entry in another part of the book, where you can find more information. But because I didn't want to detract from your reading by drawing attention to every single term in this book, some words and phrases aren't capitalized. Here are the categories of terms I chose to capitalize:

- Names of all people and ballparks
- Significant phrases discussed in Chapter 6, such as "Willie, Mickey, or the Duke?" and *dead ball era*
- Business-related terms defined in Chapter 8, such as *reserve clause* and *free agency*
- League names other than the American and National leagues

- Famous events and dates as defined in Chapter 4
- Several famous Negro league teams
- In Chapter 8 only, all the game terms that are defined in that chapter

Here are the categories and terms I did *not* capitalize in Chapters 1 through 7:

- American League and National League
- MVP Award, Cy Young Award, Gold Glove Award, Hall of Fame
- Names of today's major league teams
- Everyday statistics such as batting average and runs batted in
- Game terminology such as curveball, strikeout

The hope is that, for example, the mention of Frank "Home Run" Baker might lead you to the "$100,000 Infield," which could take you to Eddie Collins, then to the Black Sox scandal, then to Buck Weaver, and so on. The next time you pick up the book, you can follow an entirely different thread of baseball history—and learn some new things along the way.

PLAYERS AND MANAGERS

Aaron, Henry "Hammerin' Hank" (outfielder, 1954–76): One of baseball's true greats and a player of abundant talent, honor, and dignity, Aaron holds numerous baseball records, including career home runs (755), total bases (6,856), and runs batted in (2,297). He was a quiet man who impressed observers not with flashy play, like his contemporary Willie MAYS, but with relentless consistency. He won only a single MVP Award during his career, yet he was among baseball's top players from 1955 to 1974 and appeared in 21 straight All-Star Games. Though he is often denigrated for never having hit 50 home runs in a season, he certainly would have if he had played his peak years in a hitter's park like ATLANTA-FULTON COUNTY STADIUM rather than a pitcher's park like MILWAU-KEE'S COUNTY STADIUM. During his 1973–74 assault on Babe RUTH's career home run record, Aaron received, among the thousands of complimentary fan letters, hundreds of death threats from racists. Somehow he was able to put those out of his mind and do a difficult job—hitting 90-mph fastballs out of the park—in front of sold-out crowds. Now working as an executive with CNN, Aaron still receives those threats.

Abbott, Jim (pitcher, 1989–present): Abbott never played minor league ball after starring at the University of Michigan and on the U.S. Olympic baseball team, and when he hit the majors, he took just two years to develop into an 18-game winner. In 1993 he pitched a no-hitter—all despite having been born with only one hand. Teams today occasionally test Abbott's ability to field grounders, but it doesn't bother him. In one fluid motion, Abbott transfers glove and baseball to his partial right arm, takes the ball out of the glove, and calmly tosses it in time to get the runner. He doesn't let such obvious tests affect him. Courage and determination are the hallmarks of his persona.

Alexander, Grover Cleveland "Old Pete" (pitcher, 1911–30): With 373 career victories and three 30-win and nine 20-win seasons (including one at age 40), Alexander is recognized as one of the greatest hurlers of all time. He had his greatest seasons with the Phillies even though he played home games in the league's most hitter-friendly ballpark, the BAKER BOWL. In 1911, he put together the best season a rookie pitcher ever had, leading the league in wins, complete games, shutouts, and innings pitched. He entered the military in 1918, missing all but three games, and returned from World War I with epilepsy, partial deafness, and alcoholism. Even so, he remained a great pitcher. The Phillies won only a single pennant with Alexander, but after a trade to the Cardinals, he finally contributed to a World Series–winning team. The highlight of his career, as he often liked to say, was when he struck out Tony Lazzeri of the Yankees with the bases loaded in Game 7 of the 1926 Series, preserving the Cardinals' lead and St. Louis's first-ever championship. He fell on hard times after retirement, but his memory was resurrected when he was elected to the Hall of Fame in 1939. Two years later, he died of alcohol-related illnesses.

Allen, Dick (infielder, 1963–77): The focus of attention no matter where he went, Dick Allen (who hated to be called Richie) was one of baseball's most fiercely independent players—as well as one of its most feared hitters. In his rookie year of 1964, he led the league in runs and triples while smacking 29 homers. But he wore out his welcome in Philadelphia five years later, despite great batting numbers. He ended up playing with six different clubs, angering teammates and management everywhere because, among other things, he hated to practice, sometimes arriving at the park just before game time. And with 16 games remaining in the 1977 season, as he was leading the American League in homers, he abruptly announced his retirement, offering no explanations. With a better attitude, he would be in the Hall of Fame, because he was one of his league's top hitters almost every season he was healthy. He topped the 30-homer mark six times, and he won the 1972 AL MVP as a first baseman. But something inside him kept him from performing at the peak of his ability, and only he knows what that was.

Alou, Felipe (outfielder, 1958–74; manager, 1992–present): Part of a prolific baseball-playing family, Felipe and brothers Matty and Jesus had overlapping major league careers. Matty played from 1960 to 1974 and Jesus from 1963 to 1979, and during 1963, they all played on the Giants—an unprecedented feat. Felipe was probably the best of the group. Matty hit for a higher average, but Felipe had more power and has better career stats. Felipe managed for nearly two decades in the minor leagues before finally getting a chance in the majors with the Montreal Expos—and he's made it count. He won 94 games in his first full season at the helm, and in the strike-shortened 1994 campaign, he led the perennially underachieving Expos to baseball's best record and captured the Manager of the Year Award. The battle for baseball supremacy in the Alou family is receiving some tough competition today: Moises, Felipe's son, is among the top players in the National League. Alas, it's too bad Felipe's parents didn't have more sons. Longtime Giants broadcaster Hank Greenwald compiled a list of some possible names for five other Alou brothers: Skip, Bob, Boog, Toot, and Bebop.

Alston, Walter "Smoky" (manager, 1954–76): A virtual unknown at his hiring in 1954—he possessed just one at bat of major league playing experience—Alston nevertheless became one of baseball's most respected managers. For 23 straight years, Alston skippered the Brooklyn and Los Angeles Dodgers, all with one-year contracts. He led his teams to seven pennants and four World Series victories, holds the record with seven All-Star managing victories, and was inducted into the Hall of Fame in 1983, one year before his death at the age of 72.

Anderson, George "Sparky" (manager, 1970–present): Manager of the Cincinnati Reds' "BIG RED MACHINE" of the 1970s and the Detroit Tigers from 1979 to the present, Anderson is the only manager to win World Series in both leagues. The seven-time division winner ranks fifth on the all-time list of games managed, and as soon as he retires, they'll have a bronze plaque waiting for him at Cooperstown.

Anson, Adrian "Cap" (infielder, 1871–97; manager, 1879–98): One of the biggest stars of the 19th century, Anson was an excellent first baseman and a pioneer in the use of such strategies as platooning, the hit-and-run, and pitching rotations. But Anson also helped establish another precedent: He eased the institution of baseball's COLOR LINE when he threatened to forfeit a game against a team that had a black player. Anson was, in fact, a conspicuous example of a sports "hero" who, when he wasn't performing for the crowd, was anything but.

Aparicio, Luis (shortstop, 1956–73): The greatest fielding shortstop in American League history, Aparicio holds league marks for lifetime games, double plays, assists, putouts, and total chances. The 1956 Rookie of the Year won nine straight stolen base titles and nine Gold Glove awards on the way to Hall of Fame induction in 1984. Strangely, although there have been few Venezuelan-born major league players, three have played shortstop for the White Sox: Aparicio, Chico Carrasquel, and, today, Ozzie Guillen. Now living in his homeland, Aparicio named his son Nelson in honor of his longtime double-play partner Nellie Fox.

Appling, Luke "Old Aches and Pains" (shortstop, 1930–50): One of the AL's top shortstops, Appling preceded fellow Hall of Famer Luis APARICIO in the White Sox infield. Though known for his constant complaints (hence his nickname), Appling was actually a very durable player who appeared in at least 130 games 14 times in his career. He is one of only two shortstops ever to win more than one batting title (Honus WAGNER is the other), and he held most of the AL fielding records for shortstops until Aparicio broke them. Playing in an old-timers' game in 1984, Appling returned to the headlines at the age of 77 when he smacked a 350-foot homer off Warren SPAHN.

Ashburn, Richie (outfielder, 1948–62): For many years, Ashburn was probably the best eligible player not in the Hall of Fame, until he was finally selected in 1995. He may be the greatest defensive center fielder of all time—and if he's not the best, he's certainly among the three best. He holds six of the top 10 single-season totals for putouts, and he ranks high in career chances per game and putouts per game. Pete PALMER's complicated "fielding runs" statistic places Ashburn second all-time among outfielders based on defensive skills, behind only the legendary Tris SPEAKER. As a hitter, Ashburn was no slouch either. He led the league at various times in hits (three times), triples (twice), walks (four times), batting average (twice), and on-base percentage (four times). A member of the Phillies, he was selected to five All-Star Games, quite a feat considering he was up against Hall of Famers MAYS, SNI-DER, AARON, MUSIAL, KINER, IRVIN, and SLAUGHTER for the five outfield spots on the NL squad. Look at the numbers and you'll come to a simple conclusion: Ashburn deserved his Hall of Fame selection sooner.

Baker, Frank "Home Run" (third baseman, 1908–22): Baker earned his nickname after smacking home runs in consecutive games of the 1911 World Series, one off Rube Marquard and the other off Christy MATHEWSON—an amazing feat at the time. Baker won four home run titles and two RBI championships to establish himself as a top slugger of the DEAD BALL ERA. It has now become commonplace to ridicule Baker's nickname because his league-leading home run totals were "only" 9, 10, 11, and 12. To do so, however, is to miss the point of baseball's evolutionary patterns and to misunderstand baseball statistics. Baker's slugging percentages were consistently above the norm, and he played on some of the best teams of his age (including the 1911–14 A's teams that boasted the famed "$100,000 INFIELD"). If he played now, he would probably still be among the best sluggers, hitting 30 to 40 homers every year and playing a key defensive position. His selection to the Hall of Fame is well deserved.

Banks, Ernie (infielder, 1953–71): Playing his entire career for the lowly Cubs, Banks nevertheless won back-to-back MVP Awards in 1958–59—the first player to do so in National League history. Active in the time of MANTLE, MAYS, and AARON, Banks hit more home runs from 1955 to 1960 than any player in either league. A solid fielder who won two Gold Gloves at shortstop, Banks moved to first base in the middle of his career after suffering a knee injury. With his trademark expression, "Let's play two today!," he epitomized the type of player who is sorely missed today, a man who plays every game with a smile on his face and a spring in his step. In this regard, only Kirby PUCKETT is on a comparable scale today.

Bell, James "Cool Papa" (outfielder, Negro leagues, 1922–46): One of the greatest of the NEGRO LEAGUES players. Nicknamed for his ability to remain calm under pressure, Bell was an excellent hitter with blinding speed and top-notch defensive skills, on a par with MAYS, DiMAGGIO, and SPEAKER. After the COLOR LINE was broken, Bill VEECK offered Bell a chance to play for the St. Louis Browns in 1951, but the 48-year-old Bell declined. Satchel PAIGE, who played with him, maintained that Bell was so fast he once switched off a lamp and was in bed before the light went out. Unlike most baseball mythology, this story is probably true; Bell has admitted, however, that the switch was faulty. He was inducted into the Hall of Fame in 1974, after the Hall finally agreed to induct a number of Negro league stars.

Bench, Johnny (catcher, 1967–83): The top catcher of his time—many say of *any* time—Bench won two MVP Awards and played in four World Series with Cincinnati's "BIG RED MACHINE." As a hitter, Bench was one of the top offensive players in baseball for several years, and he still owns single-season records for home runs and RBIs by a catcher. As a fielder, he won 10 consecutive Gold Gloves and is now the standard to which all catchers are compared. In 1993, Bench became the victim of the growing controversy over celebrity autograph sales. On a home shopping channel, he sold autographed baseballs at a price substantially higher than true market rates while claiming they were good prices. His image has been tarnished, but not his standing among the greats.

Berg, Moe (catcher, 1923–39): The subject of the immortal phrase "GOOD FIELD, NO HIT," Berg's contribution to baseball came off the field, as he was perhaps baseball's most fascinating character. For starters, he was probably the smartest man ever to play the game, a Phi Beta Kappa from Princeton who spoke several languages (although, the saying went, he couldn't hit in any of them) and earned a law degree from Columbia during off-seasons. When he wasn't dazzling academia with diamond stories, he could be found pursuing another hobby: working as a spy for the U.S. government, which he did both during and after his baseball career. Some recent research—notably in Nicholas Dawidoff's book *The Catcher Was a Spy*—has poked holes in the claim that Berg was a successful spy who helped his country win a war. But the fact that he did actually work for the OSS, the forerunner of the CIA, is enough for me to think Berg was something special. Following his career, Berg led a mysterious, nomadic life that defies description. Unfortunately, he died before he could write his own memoirs; he once fired a potential co-author when the writer confused him with Moe from the Three Stooges.

Berra, Lawrence "Yogi" (catcher, 1946–63, 1965; manager, 1964, 1972–75, 1984–85): One of the greatest catchers of all time—and one of the most amusing—Berra is as renowned for his numerous World Series records as for the malaprops, mixed metaphors, and mangled musings he has uttered (*see* YOGI-ISM). But it is as a catcher that he should be remembered. He won three MVP Awards, but he had at least five other seasons that were equal to the MVP years. Flawless defensively, with excellent power, Berra was the anchor of the most dominant dynasty in baseball history as his Yankees captured 14 pennants in Berra's 19-year career. After his career, Berra embarked on a successful career of managing, coaching, and celebritydom that has included two pennants and countless commercials.

Boggs, Wade (third baseman, 1982–present): One of the top 10 third basemen of all time, one of the best hitters of his time, and a fine defensive player as well, Boggs didn't play his first major league game until the age of 26, so he may never reach the 3,000-hit plateau. Even so, his credentials for the Hall of Fame will be pretty hard to dismiss: seven consecutive 200-hit seasons (1983–89), nine times batting over .320, seven times with 100-plus runs, nine straight All-Star Games, three division titles. Those numbers should more than make up for his lack of power and speed—which are what Boggs's critics have used against him throughout his career.

Bonds, Barry (outfielder, 1986–present): The son of Bobby BONDS, Barry was far and away the best player in baseball in the early 1990s, a Gold Glove outfielder with power, speed, and game-breaking ability; he's still among the top five. His single-season statistics compare favorably with all-time greats such as WILLIAMS, MUSIAL, MAYS and MANTLE, and it's only a matter of time before he cements his position among the true greats. For the first few years of his career with the Pirates, Bonds was all promise and little production, the subject of frequent trade talks. Through hard work, he busted out in 1990 and rapidly ascended to greatness, winning MVPs in 1990, 1992, and 1993 and finishing second in 1991. Returning to his hometown team in 1993, free agent Bonds signed the richest contract in history with the Giants—then promptly earned every penny and more with one of the 10 best seasons in the last 35 years: .336 average, .458 on-base percentage, .677 slugging percentage, 46 home runs, 129 runs scored, 123 RBIs, 365 total bases, 29 steals. Now 31 years old, it's possible that Bonds's best years are behind him, but considering the good shape he keeps himself in, he could still become the first player in history to capture four MVPs.

Bonds, Bobby (outfielder, 1968–81): A star in the 1970s, Bonds is perhaps more famous for having been traded nine times and being the father of the best player of the 1990s (Barry BONDS) than for having achieved five 30 home run–30 stolen base seasons and winning three Gold Gloves. Bobby's career remains an enigma; the fact that such an obviously talented player was traded so often is one of baseball's charming puzzles.

Boudreau, Lou (shortstop, 1938–52; manager, 1942–50, 1952–57, 1960): Rarely remembered today, Boudreau is one of the 10 best shortstops of all time. A boy wonder who became player-manager of the Indians at age 24, he had his greatest season in 1948 when he batted .355 with 98 walks and only nine strikeouts. While leading the Indians to their last World Series victory that year, he also won the MVP Award.

Bouton, Jim (pitcher, 1962–70, 1978): Though he won 21 and 18 games in consecutive seasons with the Yankees, Bouton is best known as an iconoclastic troublemaker who, it must be acknowledged, was way ahead of his time. In contrast to most players of his era (or any era), Bouton was a literate man who actually read books and believed that he was entitled to be treated with dignity and respect by the team that employed him. While still pitching in the majors, Bouton angered the baseball community with his tell-all book *BALL FOUR*, the book that forever changed the public perception of professional athletes. Years later, he attempted an unsuccessful comeback with the publicity-hungry Braves at age 39. He says now that he never gets invited to old-timers' games.

Branca, Ralph (pitcher, 1944–56): The Brooklyn Dodger who surrendered Bobby THOMSON's "SHOT HEARD 'ROUND THE WORLD" that won the 1951 pennant for the Giants. Though his name will live in infamy, Branca was actually a pretty good pitcher, a 20-game winner and a quality pitcher in several other years. But he was never the same after Thomson's home run. An off-season injury and the constant reminders of his famous failure limited him to just 12 wins before retiring from baseball in 1956. Dodger die-hards wish he'd retired on October 2, 1951.

Bresnahan, Roger (outfielder/catcher, 1897–1915): A member of the Hall of Fame, Bresnahan is most known for having popularized shin guards and a chest protector for catchers— which were soundly jeered and criticized until everybody in the league adopted them. The Hall of Fame and many publications have credited Bresnahan with actually *inventing* those tools. In fact, other players in other leagues had been using them for several years before Bresnahan started wearing them on a regular basis in the majors.

Brett, George (infielder, 1973–93): A member of the 3,000-hit club, Brett is the only player to win a batting title in three different decades. In his best season, 1980, Brett flirted with the .400 mark for much of the year before finishing at .390. Playing his entire career with the Royals, he led the team to seven division titles, two pennants, and Kansas City's only World Series victory, in 1985. A classy player to the end, Brett retired at the end of the 1993 season when he determined that his play was not up to his high standards, even though he was still a fine player. In the view of many baseball historians (including myself), Brett ranks behind only Mike SCHMIDT and perhaps Eddie MATHEWS—but ahead of Brooks ROBINSON—as the greatest third baseman of all time.

Brock, Lou (outfielder, 1961–79): A leadoff hitter extraordinaire, Brock batted .293 lifetime with 3,023 career hits, had a good amount of power, and excelled in two World Series for the St. Louis Cardinals. But it was the stolen base that propelled him to fame. Brock held the two big stolen base records, career and single-season, until Rickey HENDERSON shattered both marks. His single-season mark of 118 was Brock's most impressive statistic, since it came when he was a supposedly over-the-hill 35 years old.

Brouthers, "Big Dan" (first baseman, 1879–96, 1904): Though he smacked just 106 career homers, Brouthers (pronounced BREW-thers) was one of the top sluggers of the 19th century, having led the National League in slugging six years in a row on the way to a Hall of Fame induction in 1945, 13 years after his death. A .342 career hitter with a .520 slugging average, Brouthers is credited with originating the phrase "Keep your eye on the ball."

Brown, Mordecai "Three-Finger" (pitcher, 1903–16): Brown earned his nickname after he lost his forefinger in a corn-grinder accident at the age of seven. With the mangled right hand giving his pitches an unnatural break, Brown fashioned a Hall of Fame career that included six straight 20-win seasons for the Chicago Cubs. When New York Mets pitcher Bob Ojeda sliced off part of the index finger on his pitching hand in the 1980s, there was hope among many baseball fans that he would parlay the accident into a renewed career as "Three-Finger" Ojeda, but that sentiment never caught on.

Buckner, Bill (first baseman/outfielder, 1969–90): Buckner was an excellent hitter throughout the 1970s and mid-1980s with the Dodgers, Cubs, and Red Sox, the winner of a batting title and possessor of a .289 career average who played on two pennant winners. But he will forever be remembered for the error he committed with two outs in the 10th inning of GAME SIX in the 1986 World Series to help the Mets beat Buckner's Red Sox. Made to be the scapegoat for continuing Boston's string of 78 years without a Series title, Buckner was traded in midseason the following year. He lasted several more seasons with declining effectiveness before finally (mercifully) retiring in 1990.

Campanella, Roy (catcher, 1937–57 [including the Negro leagues]): The great catcher for the Brooklyn Dodgers, whose powerful bat, unparalleled fielding skills, and principled leadership helped his teams to five pennants and one World Series championship. "Campy" was known for his cheerful demeanor and once said, "You have to be a man to play professional baseball, but you have to have a lot of little boy in you, too." But that disposition didn't keep him from dominating opposing pitchers on the way to three MVP Awards. In fact, had it not been for the COLOR LINE—which stalled the beginning of Campanella's career in the major leagues—and for the tragic auto accident that paralyzed him in 1958, there would be no doubt as to who was the greatest catcher of all time: not BENCH or BERRA or COCHRANE or DICKEY; it would be Campanella.

Canseco, Jose (outfielder, 1985–present): Canseco has made almost as many headlines for what he's done at the plate as for what he's done everywhere else. He busted onto the scene in 1986 to smack 33 homers and win the Rookie of the Year Award. In 1988, he captured MVP honors while becoming the first player in history to hit 40 homers and steal 40 bases. He helped his A's to three straight pennants from 1988 to 1990, and he was as feared by pitchers as any batter in the game. Meanwhile, off the field, he had a number of run-ins with the law for speeding and possessing a weapon, and his squabbles with his wife made news when she crashed her car into his. He even made the tabloids after being seen coming out of Madonna's New York City apartment. After being traded to the Rangers in 1992, his career took a turn for the worse. Never known for stellar fielding, he starred in any number of highlight reels when a fly ball bounced off his head and over the fence for a home run. Later in the 1993 season, he convinced his manager to let him pitch a game in relief. The experiment was a pathetic failure. Not only did Canseco allow two hits, three walks, and three runs in one inning, but he also blew out his arm so badly that it required surgery. He came back in 1994 to put together a fine season until the strike cut it short. It's too bad the arm injury forced him into a permanent DH role. With Canseco, every fly ball was an adventure. He was much more fun to watch back when he was stationed in right field.

Carew, Rod (infielder, 1967–85): The winner of seven batting titles, including a spectacular .388 in 1977, Carew was the prototype of the "pure hitter," a player who took a scientific approach to hitting and could bang a hit to all fields. A member of the Twins and Angels, Carew studied pitchers and was one of the few players who adjusted his batting stance based on the pitcher's strength, reasoning that you can't hit the same way against a fastball pitcher as against a curveball pitcher; he would even adjust his stance mid–at bat. Never one to hog the limelight, he joined the 3,000-hit club on the same day in 1985 that Tom SEAVER notched his 300th victory.

Carlton, Steve (pitcher, 1965–88): The top left-handed pitcher of the post-KOUFAX era and winner of a record four Cy Young Awards, Carlton is perhaps best known for winning 27 games in 1972 for a Phillies team that won only 59 total games. Throughout his career, "Lefty" didn't speak to reporters but let his pitching talk for him: 329 career victories, 4,136 career strikeouts–including 4,020 in the NL, a league record. At the end of his career, Carlton bounced around four different teams despite having completely lost his effectiveness as a pitcher, thus tarnishing the image of one of the all-time greats. His 1993 Hall of Fame induction has helped restore the luster.

Carter, Gary (catcher, 1974–92): The top catcher of the post–Johnny BENCH era, Carter starred for the Expos and Mets in the late 1970s and 1980s, combining top-flight catching skills with a potent bat. He slugged 20 or more homers nine times to become the only catcher other than Yogi BERRA and Bench to achieve such consistency, and he drove in 100 runs four times. An excellent handler of pitchers with a great throwing arm at his peak, Carter was selected for 10 All-Star Games and played on three division winners and one World Series champ. His friendly, outgoing personality earned him the nickname "The Kid," and it may have also helped him hang on at the end of his career as an aging backup who could tutor the younger players.

Cepeda, Orlando "The Baby Bull" or "Cha Cha" (first baseman, 1958–74): Cepeda became a popular Hall of Fame candidate in 1984 and came pretty close to being elected in his last few years of eligibility, but ultimately didn't make it. Next the VETERANS COMMITTEE will have a crack at him, and he'll probably make that cut. He illustrates the chasm between the two distinct opinions about the Hall: Is the shrine designed to reward true greatness or just overall excellence? There's no doubt Cepeda was an excellent performer. He was a valuable part of four pennant-winning teams in San Francisco and St. Louis and won the 1967 MVP unanimously. He slugged 379 career homers, including 20 or more in 11 different seasons, and he drove in more than 95 runs 9 times. But was he a true great? The numbers don't suggest that he was. He had only a couple of seasons when he was considered among the best players in the game. When you put him next to the other Hall of Fame sluggers of his day—such as MAYS, AARON, Frank ROBINSON, McCOVEY, KILLEBREW, and YASTRZEMSKI—Cepeda falls short on both career and single-season comparisons. Statistically, Cepeda looks more like fellow first basemen Gil Hodges and Norm Cash, neither of whom may ever get elected to the Hall. So does Cepeda belong? He's a good player, but I don't think he's Hall of Fame material.

Chance, Frank "The Peerless Leader" (first baseman, 1898–1914; manager, 1905–14, 1923): Chance's most lasting accomplishment was player-managing the 1906 Cubs to a major league record 116 wins. His most lasting *fame*, meanwhile, came as the third member of the TINKER TO EVERS TO CHANCE double play combination immortalized in the poem "BASEBALL'S SAD LEXICON" and elected to the Hall of Fame as a group in 1946. Chance was a respected player in his day, an excellent hitter and player-manager. The biggest knock on him is his short career. He played only six seasons as a full-timer and managed only 11 years. He reached a pretty good peak as a player but for a very short period. It's unlikely he would have been elected to the Hall if the poem had never been written. (The same can be said for Joe TINKER, but not, in my opinion, for Johnny EVERS.)

Chapman, Ray (shortstop, 1912–20): A popular star shortstop for the Indians, Chapman was in the midst of a career that might have taken him to the Hall of Fame when he was accidentally beaned in the skull with a fastball from Carl MAYS—the only on-field death in major league history. Following the tragedy, umpires began to keep fresh baseballs in play—rather than re-use every ball, *even ones fouled into the stands*—to increase the ball's visibility. That innovation, combined with the outlawing of the spitball the previous season, was most responsible for the advent of the LIVELY BALL ERA. *See also* AUGUST 16, 1920.

Charleston, Oscar (outfielder, Negro leagues, 1915–50): Generally regarded as the greatest NEGRO LEAGUES ballplayer of all time, Charleston was a strong hitter, great fielder, and legendary baserunner who would today be remembered with COBB, RUTH, DiMAGGIO, MANTLE, and MAYS if he had been white or born fifty years later. Instead, his accomplishments were largely ignored by fans and the media because he was black. In exhibition games against white major leaguers, research shows Charleston batted .318 with 11 homers in 195 at bats, including one off Walter JOHNSON to give Smoky Joe WILLIAMS a 1–0 victory. "Charleston could hit that ball a mile," said Dizzy DEAN. "When he came up, we just threw and hoped like hell he wouldn't get hold of one and send it out of the park." Like Tris SPEAKER, Charleston played a shallow center field, able to cut off singles that might otherwise drop in front of him but also able to outrun any drive over his head. After his peak years had ended, Charleston played a major role in integrating the major leagues by encouraging Branch RICKEY to sign Roy CAMPANELLA. Charleston died in 1954, 22 years before the baseball Hall of Fame got around to honoring him.

Chase, Hal (first baseman, 1905–19): A fascinating, charismatic figure, "Prince Hal" was by all accounts an enormously talented infielder—the best defensive first baseman of his era and perhaps of all time—and an above-average hitter, once leading the league in batting average. He was also universally regarded as a crook. Throughout his career, his managers accused him of purposely trying to lose games, and he was brought up on charges before the National League president in 1918. Though he was acquitted due to lack of evidence on that charge, he was suspended by his own team a year later for the same reason. Every now and then, you may read ill-informed baseball fans and writers claiming that Chase was one of the greatest first basemen of all time. They're wrong. Let's put aside the allegations of "laying down"—charges for which there is little proof and which he denied but that followed Chase wherever he went. If we look only at the statistics, it's hard to see why people might believe that. We're talking about a .291 career hitter with no power and an abnormally low on-base percentage. He never drove in or scored 100 runs, and he led the league in only three categories: home runs (FEDERAL LEAGUE) in 1915 and hits and batting average in 1916. As far as fielding, he never led the league in fielding average, which, of course, is not the only measure of fielding excellence but is a pretty good one. On the other hand, he did lead the league in errors five times, not the kind of production you want from a first baseman. You could argue that Chase's skills transcended statistics, much like Jackie ROBINSON and Roberto CLEMENTE. But the way to measure such a claim is through pennant victories. How many pennants did Chase's alleged talents win for his teams? Zero, and there's no doubt he was partly to blame. Certainly you could make a pretty good all-star team of players who never won a pennant, such as Ernie BANKS, Rod CAREW, Ferguson JENKINS, Ralph KINER, and others. But Chase wasn't as good as any of those guys, and when you're discussing the true greats, you have to take into account the entire record. I would rather have Stuffy McInnis, Mickey Vernon, Vic Power, Jake Daubert, Jack Fournier, Norm Cash, or almost any other first baseman on my team before I would want Hal Chase.

Cicotte, Eddie "Knuckles" (pitcher, 1905–20): An excellent pitcher, one of the best of his era, Cicotte accepted money from gamblers to throw two games of the 1919 WORLD SERIES.

He confessed and was kicked out of baseball with seven other members of what would be called the Chicago BLACK SOX. Cicotte's story is tragic because he was a generally honest, dignified ballplayer. And it's pretty obvious that the whole affair could have been avoided if Sox owner Charles COMISKEY had considered his players more important than his profit. Cicotte had a legitimate complaint. In 1919, he had a clause in his contract calling for a $10,000 bonus if he won 30 games. He was benched inexplicably for two weeks, apparently on orders from Comiskey, and he finished the season with just 29 victories—thus losing the bonus. Cicotte said he took the money from the gamblers to provide for his family what legitimate means of money-earning could not. Later in life, he became philosophical about the scandal. "I've tried to make up for it by living as clean a life as I could," he would tell reporters. "I'm proud of the way I've lived, and I think my family is, too." *See also* BLACK SOX SCANDAL.

Clemens, Roger (pitcher, 1984–present): The best pitcher of his time and among the greatest of all times, "The Rocket" has captured a number of both team and personal honors: He has led his Red Sox to three division titles and a pennant and has won three Cy Young Awards. He holds the record for strikeouts in a nine-inning game—20—and he once notched a 1.93 ERA in FENWAY PARK, an amazing total for such a great hitters' park. If he were to retire today, he would be immediately enshrined in the Hall of Fame. But he would probably trade it all if he could deliver a World Series victory to Boston.

Clemente, Roberto (outfielder, 1955–1972): Possessor of perhaps the best outfield arm of all time, Clemente also excelled at the plate, lashing line drives in droves on the way to four batting titles, 13 seasons over .300, and exactly 3,000 career hits. He also won an MVP Award and helped his Pittsburgh Pirates to two World Series victories. Most long-time fans can tell stories about the amazing things Clemente could do in the outfield, like throw out a runner at home from the warning track on one bounce, or gun a runner at third on the fly from the right field corner. He was that good. During his career, he fought to help Latin ballplayers gain acceptance into the major league fraternity, but his dedication and valor didn't end on the field: His death on New Year's Eve 1972 occurred while he was aboard a mercy mission carrying supplies to earthquake-ravaged Nicaragua. He once said, "I want to be remembered as a ballplayer who gave all he had to give." He is.

Cobb, Ty "The Georgia Peach" (outfielder, 1905–28): Among his many accomplishments—11 batting titles (if you count the disputed 1910 BATTING RACE), almost 4,200 hits, and three seasons over .400, to name a few—the one that should stand out most is that he led all vote-getters in the first Hall of Fame balloting, ahead of RUTH, YOUNG, JOHNSON, WAGNER, MATHEWSON, et al. In addition to his tremendous batting prowess, he was also a terror on the base paths, stealing bases and otherwise creating tremendous havoc. He held the single-season record for stolen bases until Maury WILLS broke it in 1962 and the mark for career steals until Lou BROCK surpassed him in the 1970s. Though not a great fielder, Cobb was fast enough to catch up to most of his mistakes and competitive enough to work hard. And with the wood in his hands, he had no superiors and few equals. Playing in a time when home runs were rare, Cobb led the league in slugging percentage eight times and won a Triple Crown. The one honor that eluded him was a World Series victory; his Tigers captured three pennants early in Cobb's career but couldn't win the big one. The big blot on Cobb's legend is that he was, without question, the meanest man who ever played baseball—a racist, anti-Semitic bully who would kick, spit, spike, punch, or shoot anything that got in his way. He once tore into the stands during a game to beat up a heckler, not even stopping when he discovered that the man had no arms or legs. And it wasn't the murder of his father by his mother when Ty was 18 that put the demons into his soul; as Cobb himself would have said, he was an SOB before that and an even bigger SOB afterwards. After baseball, he led the life of a bitter old man, estranged from his ex-wives and children. Lucky for him he invested in Coca-Cola when that company was just starting, so he was able to retire a wealthy man. But at his death in 1962, he had kept few friends in baseball, and only three former players showed up at the funeral.

Cochrane, Mickey (catcher, 1925–37; manager, 1934–38): The greatest catcher of his era, Cochrane won two MVPs and played on five pennant winners with the A's and Tigers—player-managing two of them. He could hit like few other catchers, batting over .320 seven times with good power and excellent strike zone judgment. A remarkably consistent fielder who appeared in 120 to 135 games for 10 straight seasons, Cochrane's career came to an end after he was beaned in the head on a pitch from Bump Hadley of the Yankees in 1937; he remained unconscious and near death for 10 days before he finally pulled through.

Collins, Eddie "Cocky" (second baseman, 1906–30; manager, 1924–26): A superb fielder, baserunner, and hitter, as well as a player-manager for many years, Collins is without a doubt one of the two or three greatest second basemen of all time. He was a model of consistency throughout his career, batting around .340, scoring 100 runs, stealing 50 bases, and playing flawless defense year in and year out. A member of the Athletics' famed "$100,000 INFIELD," Collins later went to Chicago and played with the 1919 BLACK SOX team that threw the World Series. Collins, however, was so above reproach as a player and a gentleman that the gamblers never even thought to approach him. It also didn't hurt that his generous contract with Philadelphia was honored by the White Sox after he came over in a trade. He finished his career with 3,312 hits and a career average of .333, in addition to six pennants.

Conigliaro, Tony (outfielder, 1964–71, 1975): A young, popular Red Sox slugger, Conigliaro was in the prime of his career in 1967 when he was struck in the face and nearly killed by a fastball. Having smacked 104 homers before the age of 23, "Tony C" was on pace to become one of the greats. Although he came back in 1969 for two more good years, he was out of baseball after a sad 1971 season, only to return for an ill-fated 1975 comeback. His post-sports career led him into broadcasting, but then a heart attack felled him, and he died in 1990.

Cronin, Joe (shortstop, 1926–45; manager, 1933–47): A top shortstop of his era, Cronin was a highly intelligent man who rose up the ranks to become player-manager at the ripe age of 26, general manager at 42, and American League president at 53. Cronin is also the answer to an obscure trivia question: Who's the only player to be traded away by his father-in-law? (Cronin was married to the daughter of Senators owner Clark Griffith when Griffith dealt Cronin to Boston in 1935.)

Cummings, Candy (pitcher, 1872–77): A member of the Hall of Fame not for his stellar career (six major league seasons), but because he claimed to have invented the curveball. Candy (which was 19th-century slang for "best") said he was "inspired" by watching a clamshell curve in the air when thrown; he claimed he threw his first curveball in an amateur baseball game in 1867. However, several of Cummings's contemporaries—such as Harry WRIGHT and Henry CHADWICK—maintained that curves had been around since the 1850s. But for some reason, the Hall of Fame's voters chose to believe Candy's story. It's not the only time the Hall would be guilty of such action (*see also* DOUBLEDAY MYTH).

Dandridge, Ray "Hooks" (third baseman, Negro leagues, 1933–55): "I saw all the greats—Brooks ROBINSON, Graig Nettles," said Hall of Famer Monte IRVIN, "but I've never seen a better third baseman than Ray Dandridge." Like Honus WAGNER, Dandridge was built funny, with horseshoe-shaped legs that kept him low to the ground. He was also famous for the screaming line drives that jumped off his bat. Unlike many

NEGRO LEAGUES greats, Dandridge was only a step away from the white major leagues but never made it. Signed by the New York Giants in 1949, management sent Dandridge to Triple-A Minneapolis. There, the 36-year-old played in 99 games and batted .362, missing the AMERICAN ASSOCIATION batting title by two points. He had another stellar season in 1950, leading the league in at bats and hits while batting .311 with 24 doubles and 11 homers. He was named MVP of the league, but the Giants still didn't call him up. He played two more good seasons in Minneapolis, then moved to the Pacific Coast league with Oakland and Sacramento. In 1987, he was elected to the Hall of Fame by the VETERANS COMMITTEE (rather than the Special Committee on the Negro Leagues, which selected most of the other Negro league greats).

Day, Leon (pitcher, Negro leagues, 1934–50): Day was a fast-balling righthander who was regarded as the most consistent pitcher of his time. He didn't have the flash of Satchel PAIGE or the blazing speed of Smoky Joe WILLIAMS, but he was smart on the mound and he knew how to win: According to available records, Day posted such win-loss records as 13–0, 7–1, 12–1, and 13–4. When needed, he could play the outfield or second base and was billed as "the most versatile and outstanding player" on a Newark Eagles team that included Hall of Famer Monte IRVIN. Day died in 1995, just a week after receiving word that he had finally achieved his dream of joining his friends in the Hall of Fame.

Dean, Dizzy (pitcher, 1930–47): The Sandy KOUFAX of his time, Dean was one of the two or three best pitchers in baseball for four years until a line drive broke his toe during the 1937 All-Star Game. A member of St. Louis's "GAS HOUSE GANG" and the last NL pitcher to record 30 victories in a season, Dean was also the game's most colorful character. He once boasted that he and his brother, Paul, whose nickname was "Daffy," would win 45 games in a season. When they won 49, Dizzy noted, "It ain't braggin' if you can do it." A great baseball story is the one about Dean getting hit with the ball while sliding into second; the newspaper headline the next day read, "X-Ray of Dean's Head Shows Nothing." After his playing days ended, Dean enjoyed a long career as a broadcaster, where he was able to get away with expressions like "He slud into third" and "The runners return to their respectable bases." (In that respect, he is the model for every other poorly educated jock to make his way onto television or radio, where he's given free rein to "adapt" the rules of English grammar and usage.) Despite his short playing career, Dean is one of a handful of players who left a lasting impression on the sport. That qualifies him for any Hall of Fame—an opinion shared by Hall voters in 1953.

Delahanty, "Big Ed" (outfielder, 1888–1903): One of five major league baseball–playing brothers, Delahanty was a great hitter, one of the top sluggers of his era, but he is remembered more for how he died than how he played: the notorious drunkard fell into the Niagara River and tumbled over the Falls after getting booted from his team's train in the middle of the 1903 season. He was obviously elected to the Hall of Fame on his stats, not his character, because the numbers are excellent: a lifetime .346 average, three seasons over .400, two batting championships, two home run titles, and 2,597 career hits.

Dent, Bucky (shortstop, 1973–84; manager, 1989–1990): Dent was a "GOOD FIELD, NO HIT" shortstop who etched his name into the history books with, surprisingly, his bat. He batted just .247 in 12 seasons with the White Sox, Yankees, Rangers, and Royals. But it was one swing of the bat with the Yankees that made him a household name. His moment of fame came in the 1978 PLAYOFF between New York and Boston to decide the American League East championship. Leading 2–0 in the seventh, Red Sox pitcher Mike Torrez allowed first baseman Chris Chambliss and outfielder Roy White to reach base. Dent was up next. Torrez was obviously tired, but manager Don

Zimmer left him in, fully believing that his big right-hander could retire weak-hitting Dent. Big mistake. On the second pitch of his at bat, Dent smashed a looping fly ball that barely cleared the GREEN MONSTER, giving the Yankees a lead they wouldn't relinquish en route to a 5–4 victory. Dent played six more seasons, and in 1989 and 1990 managed the Yankees for 89 games.

Dickey, Bill (catcher, 1928–46): For the first half of the century, Dickey and Mickey COCHRANE were considered the greatest catchers of all time. Because of BERRA, CAMPANELLA, BENCH, and FISK, Dickey has dropped out of contention for the top honor, but he's still among the 10 best. Dickey appeared in 11 All-Star Games and eight World Series with the Yankees, hitting for average and power on a star-laden team. Dickey, in fact, still holds the record for highest batting average achieved by a catcher, .362, in 1936. As a Yankee coach, he tutored his successor, Berra, to greatness.

Dihigo, Martin "El Maestro" (infielder/outfielder/pitcher, Negro leagues, 1923–45): Cuban-born Dihigo was a master of versatility. Men who saw him play, from Cumberland POSEY to Buck LEONARD to Johnny MIZE, hailed Dihigo as the greatest all-around player in history. He hit from both sides of the plate. He pitched with great skill. He stole bases. He had perhaps the best outfield arm of his time, yet he could play any position. He hit for average and power. He managed for many years. He also played almost anywhere organized baseball existed: the United States, Cuba, Mexico, Puerto Rico, Venezuela, you name it. The Hall of Fame here in the U.S. isn't the only Hall to honor Dihigo; he is also a member of the Cuban and Mexican Halls of Fame.

DiMaggio, Dominic (outfielder, 1940–53): Though remembered more for being Joe's little brother, Dominic was an excellent ballplayer in his own right; Red Sox fans even used to sing an homage to him: "He's better than his brother Joe /

Do-min-ic Di-Maggio." Not quite, but pretty good nonetheless: He had four seasons with 100-plus runs and a .298 career average, and he played in seven All-Star Games—most alongside Joe. One of the first non-pitchers to wear glasses in the field, DiMaggio was nicknamed "The Little Professor," a moniker he earned. Once, after having been called out on strikes, Di-Maggio yelled at the umpire from the dugout, "I have never witnessed such incompetence in all my life!"

DiMaggio, Joe "The Yankee Clipper" (outfielder, 1936–51): A near-flawless ballplayer, DiMaggio won three MVP Awards, had a major league record 56-game hitting streak, played in 10 World Series during 13 major league seasons, was immortalized in a Simon and Garfunkel song, and has received almost every other accolade a player can get. It is not an overstatement to say that he towered over the American League nearly every year he played, leading the league at various times in homers, RBIs, batting average, and slugging percentage. Known for playing every inning just as hard as the last, DiMaggio was once asked why he was so intense on the field. DiMaggio's answer: "Because there might be somebody out there who's never seen me play before." The American icon led a near-storybook life: The son of poor Italian immigrants, he made it big in New York City, where his famous hitting streak captured the heart of America; after his career ended, he married the nation's most famous movie star, Marilyn Monroe, and when that ended painfully, it was said, "It just proves that a man can't be a success at two national pastimes." His life would make a fascinating subject for a movie, if only he would allow one to be made. Now known to a generation as Mr. Coffee, he is perhaps the most recognizable former ballplayer in the country. *See also* 56; 1941 SEASON; STREAK, THE; "JOLTIN' JOE DiMAGGIO."

Doby, Larry (outfielder, 1942–59 [including Negro leagues]): Signed by Indians owner Bill VEECK soon after Jackie ROBINSON broke baseball's COLOR BARRIER, Doby integrated the

American League on July 5, 1947. Unlike Robinson, Doby jumped straight from the NEGRO LEAGUES to the majors without the benefit of seasoning in the white minor leagues. Still, Doby took only a year to become one of the top players in the league—a slugging center fielder with excellent strike zone judgment and great fielding skills, basically a midcentury version of Dale MURPHY. He led the league in homers twice, RBIs and runs once each, and played on seven All-Star teams and two pennant winners. He has never received much support for the Hall of Fame, and it's hard to understand why. His career totals in the majors aren't that impressive—253 homers, 970 RBIs, .283 batting average—but he deserves some credit for the extra burden placed on him as one of baseball's sometimes forgotten pioneers. The Indians recently retired his number, and it's about time the VETERANS COMMITTEE enshrined him.

Drysdale, Don (pitcher, 1956–69): When Dodgers manager Walter ALSTON once ordered Drysdale to intentionally walk a batter, Drysdale responded by hitting the batter with his first pitch. "Saved three pitches" was Drysdale's logic—an attitude that typified his pitching style and explains why he is the all-time leader in hit batsmen. From his six-foot-five frame, he whipped the ball toward the plate sidearm, frightening most right-handed hitters (except Hank AARON, who slugged 17 homers off Drysdale during his career, the most against any single pitcher). He won a Cy Young Award in 1962, tossed a then-record 58⅔ consecutive scoreless innings in 1968, captured three strikeout crowns, and, joining Sandy KOUFAX in a lethal one-two punch, helped his teams to three World Series appearances. Following his career, Drysdale worked for many years as a broadcaster who delighted in downgrading the modern ballplayer: "If the game gets any more namby-pamby," he once said, "they'll be hitting off a tee." In 1993, Drysdale died suddenly of a heart attack at the age of 54. He'll be missed.

Durocher, Leo "The Lip" (shortstop, 1925, 1928–41, 1943, 1945; manager, 1939–73): A scrappy shortstop with St. Louis's "GAS HOUSE GANG," among other teams, before embarking on a five-decade career as manager, Durocher is best known for asserting that "nice guys finish last." In fact, as he notes in his excellent autobiography, called *NICE GUYS FINISH LAST*, when he spoke those words, he was referring to a specific group of nice guys—the New York Giants of the mid-1940s, *not* to nice guys as a whole. Durocher, on the other hand, prided himself on being unpleasant and even downright mean while on the field, and his career can be charitably described as controversial. At any given point in his career, he could have been found feuding with owners, players, other managers, and league officers—enough to warrant a one-year suspension in 1947. But he was worth the controversy: his 2,008 managerial victories for the Dodgers, Giants, Cubs, and Astros ranked him sixth on the all-time list. After years of being snubbed, Durocher was finally named to the Hall of Fame in 1994, two years after his death.

Eckersley, Dennis (pitcher, 1975–present): Perhaps the greatest relief pitcher of all time, Eckersley has had two distinct major league careers. From 1975 through 1986, he worked as a quality starting pitcher, posting double-digit win totals nine times with the Indians, Red Sox, and Cubs. Then, in 1987, when his career seemed finished as a starter, he was traded to the Oakland A's, which turned out to be the best move of his life. He quickly became baseball's premier closer, converting 45 saves in his first full year out of the bullpen. For the next four years, Eckersley redefined relief pitching with his live fastball and pinpoint control. In 1989, he allowed just 32 hits and 3 walks in 57 innings. In 1990, at the age of 36, he was even better: 73 innings, 41 hits allowed, 4 walks, 0.61 ERA, 48 saves. Then, in 1992, he captured the Cy Young and MVP awards while posting 51 saves and a 1.91 ERA as the A's captured their fourth division title in five seasons. Slowed down for the past few years by aging muscles, Eckersley will pose a tough question to Hall of Fame voters five years after he retires. There's no question that he reached and sustained a peak of ability unmatched by any previous relief pitcher. But is that enough to get him in the Hall of Fame? You could compare Eck with Sandy KOUFAX and Dizzy DEAN, who had similarly brief moments of greatness. However, then you have to ask if relief pitching is worth as much as starting pitching. Eck may not make it to the Hall on the first ballot, but I think he should make it eventually.

Evans, Dwight "Dewey" (outfielder, 1972–91): Evans's 2,484 hits, 385 home runs, 1,384 RBIs, lifetime .272 batting average and .373 on-base percentage, and three All-Star selections may not be enough to get him into the Hall of Fame. But for 20 years—all but one with the Red Sox—Evans was the standard-bearer for excellence in right field. Flawless defensively, he captured eight Gold Gloves. And he could hit some. When he left Boston after the 1990 season, he left a void that has been hard to fill.

Evers, Johnny "The Crab" (second baseman, 1902–29): When you look only at the statistics, you may come to the conclusion, as many have, that the only reason Evers is in the Hall of Fame is because of the famous TINKER TO EVERS TO CHANCE poem by Franklin P. Adams, "BASEBALL'S SAD LEXICON." In fact, Evers was an excellent second baseman, a top fielder and capable hitter who put together some pretty good offensive seasons. Awarded one of baseball's early MVP Awards in 1914, Evers was an intelligent player who led his Cubs and Braves to four pennants and was mostly responsible for causing the controversial 1908 PENNANT RACE to end in a tie. Owing to his reputation as a scrappy winner, he probably would have received Hall of Fame induction poem or no poem.

Ewing, Buck (catcher, 1880–97): Though the statistics don't seem to bear this out, Ewing is often called the greatest player of the 19th century. He played just about every position on the field and also managed for several years, but he was best known as a catcher, where he was the first player to throw from the crouch and one of the first to use a big mitt. Although you can be unimpressed with the stats—a .303 career average with little power—you can't discount the fact that he was the biggest star in the game before Honus WAGNER, and Connie MACK and many others called him the greatest catcher they ever saw. And when the Hall of Fame was still in its infancy, Ewing was chosen for the honor in 1939, well ahead of such other eligible greats as Ed DELAHANTY, Rogers HORNSBY, King KELLY, and many others.

Feller, Bob "Rapid Robert" (pitcher, 1936–56): The greatest strikeout pitcher of his era, Feller was a star by the age of 17, when he struck out 15 batters in his first major league start and tied the major league record with 17 Ks a few weeks later. He possessed a fastball that was clocked at 100 mph, but he wasn't always able to control it, totaling 100-plus walks in nine different seasons. In spite of the walks, Feller led the league in victories six times. Had it not been for World War II, which robbed Feller of four peak seasons, he would have finished with over 340 victories and 3,400 strikeouts. As it was, he totaled an impressive 266 wins and 2,581 Ks—all with the Indians—in a Hall of Fame career.

Fingers, Rollie (relief pitcher, 1968–85): The best reliever of his era, Fingers was equally known for his trademark handlebar mustache as for his career total of 341 saves, which was tops on the all-time list until 1993. Unlike most modern-day relievers, Fingers had a remarkably long career as an effective player. In the early 1970s, he helped his A's to five straight division titles and three straight World Series victories by averaging nine wins and 20 saves per year. Then, in 1981, two trades later, he won an MVP and Cy Young Award with a 6–3 record, a league-leading 28 saves, and a 1.04 ERA. At the end of his career, the only team that offered him a contract was the Cincinnati Reds, which has a team policy forbidding facial hair. Rather than shave off his trademark, Fingers retired.

Fisk, Carlton "Pudge" (catcher, 1969–93): One of the greatest catchers of all time, Fisk holds career records for games caught (2,499) and home runs by a catcher (351 as a catcher, 376 overall). He joins Yogi BERRA and Johnny BENCH as the only catchers with 300 career homers and 1,000 career RBIs. A native New Englander, Fisk came up with the Red Sox and won the 1972 Rookie of the Year Award unanimously with a 22–home run season and an All-Star appearance. Though injured for much of 1975, he helped the Red Sox to the World Series, where his 12th-inning home run won the thrilling GAME SIX. He left Boston in 1981 as a free agent and finished his career with the White Sox, whom he led to the Western Division crown in 1983. Two years later, the 37-year-old nearly won a home run title with 37 dingers. Known for his great handling of pitchers and on-field leadership, Fisk retired in the middle of the 1993 season at the age of 45.

Flood, Curt (outfielder, 1956–71): Flood is the All-Star outfielder who sued baseball to achieve free agency after being traded in 1969 from St. Louis to Philadelphia. For the previous ten seasons, he had starred as a good-hitting, great-fielding center fielder for three pennant winners. But the shock of being traded suddenly and remorselessly—after he had established a successful photography business in St. Louis—proved too much for him to take. Choosing to sacrifice his career and his $90,000 salary to achieve better treatment for players, Flood challenged the legality of baseball's RESERVE CLAUSE and took his case *(FLOOD V. KUHN)* all the way to the Supreme Court, where he lost a mind-bogglingly idiotic decision. Despite the setback, his defiance helped usher in the free agency era. Every athlete in every major sport today owes Flood a huge debt.

Ford, Whitey (pitcher, 1950–67): The New York Yankees star left-hander who holds most World Series pitching records, including career victories (10), losses (8), games (22), innings pitched (146), and strikeouts (94). Ford won a Cy Young Award and retired with a record of 236–106 for a .690 winning percentage, the highest among 20th-century pitchers with long careers. He and Mickey MANTLE were inseparable during their days with the Yankees, so it was only fitting that they were inducted into the Hall of Fame together in 1974.

Foster, Andrew "Rube" (pitcher/outfielder/manager/executive, Negro leagues, 1898–1926): Part John MCGRAW, part Christy MATHEWSON, part "Ban" JOHNSON, part P. T. Barnum, Foster himself was a true original. He earned his nickname when he outpitched major league star Rube WADDELL in a 1904 exhibition game. Often player-managing, he led his teams to a crop of NEGRO LEAGUES pennants. One club won 110 out of 120 games, another, 123 of 129. Throughout his career, he acted as player and promoter, manager and executive. He formed the Negro National League in 1920 and ruled as Ban Johnson did the American League—with strength and vision. To maintain competitive balance, he shifted players from team to team, and he lent money to failing franchises to keep them afloat. Ultimately, however, the stress was too much: In 1926, he succumbed to mental illness and died four years later in an institution. The Hall of Fame recognized him in 1981.

Foxx, Jimmie "The Beast" (first baseman, 1925–45): In an era of exceptional hitters, this A's and Red Sox star outclassed almost everybody. He was, for example, the first American Leaguer to challenge RUTH's record of 60 homers, finishing with 58 in 1932; he might have broken the record if he hadn't injured his wrist in a household accident with several weeks remaining in the season. He was also the first player to capture three MVP Awards. Additionally, he won a Triple Crown and led his teams to three pennants. A huge, broad-shouldered man who possessed muscles atop muscles, Foxx was a nimble first baseman who could also fill in at third base (135 career games), catcher (109), and even on the mound (10). Among the all-time greats, Foxx ranks behind only Lou GEHRIG as the greatest first baseman of all time.

Gaedel, Eddie (pinch hitter, 1951): The 65-pound, three-foot-seven-inch midget hired by St. Louis Browns owner Bill VEECK to bat during a game as a publicity stunt. It happened on August 19, 1951, against the Tigers; Detroit pitcher Bob Cain tossed four pitches but none could penetrate Gaedel's one-and-a-half-inch strike zone, and Gaedel—wearing jersey number 1/8—walked. Gaedel had wanted to swing at a pitch, but Veeck ordered him not to: "Eddie," Veeck had informed him, "I'm going to be up on the roof with a high-powered rifle . . . If you so much as look as if you're going to swing, I'm going to shoot you dead." The day after the stunt, Veeck received a telegram from AL president Will Harridge condemning the action, but Veeck's purpose had already been achieved, and Gaedel's 15 minutes of fame cemented.

Gehrig, Lou "The Iron Horse" (first baseman, 1923–39): The greatest first baseman of all time, Gehrig was a quiet, humble man who let Yankee teammates Babe RUTH and Joe DiMAGGIO garner most of the headlines and the big salaries. Gehrig instead led by example, combining tremendous power, clutch hitting, and great strike zone judgment and never missing a game beginning in 1925 until a fatal disease (amyotrophic lateral sclerosis, a disease that, of course, now bears his name) forced him out of the lineup in 1939. Gehrig grew up in relative poverty in New York City, a child of German immigrants who wanted nothing more than that their son graduate from college with a good career ahead of him. He spent two years at Columbia on a football scholarship, but because his father needed an emergency operation, Gehrig signed with the Yankees to pay the medical bills. The rest of the story is movingly detailed in the Gary Cooper film *PRIDE OF THE YANKEES*. *See also* 2,130; "LOU GEHRIG'S FAREWELL SPEECH"; MAY 2, 1939.

Gehringer, Charlie "The Mechanical Man" (second baseman, 1924–42): The top second baseman of the 1930s, Gehringer was known for consistency and durability: He turned out 200-hit seasons like clockwork, drove in 100 runs seven times, won two MVP Awards, led his Tigers to three World Series, and played near-flawless second base for nearly two decades. A University of Michigan graduate, Gehringer also served the Tigers as general manager for two years and vice president for seven. His Hall of Fame induction in 1949 was merely a formality.

Gibson, Bob (pitcher, 1959–75): About Gibson it was once said that he "always pitches when the other team doesn't score any runs." Such was certainly the case in 1968 when Gibson, an accomplished power pitcher for the St. Louis Cardinals, fashioned an ERA of 1.12 with 22 victories in what has been called the greatest season by a pitcher in history. (*See also* 1968 SEASON.) The five-time 20-game winner was dominant in other years as well, winning two Cy Young Awards. Great performances in the 1967 and 1968 World Series—including a Series-record 17 strikeouts in one game—firmed his reputation as one of the most intimidating hurlers of all time. His Hall of Fame induction in 1981 merely made it official. Today, as the debate rages over whether athletes should act as role models, Gibson's comment from 1970 has gained new meaning: "Too many people think an athlete's life can be an open book. You're supposed to be an example. Why do I have to be an example for your kid? *You* be an example for your kid."

Gibson, Josh (catcher, Negro leagues, 1930–46): Those who saw him play—including fellow Hall of Famer Walter JOHNSON—said Josh Gibson was the greatest catcher of all time, a slugger who could hit a ball farther than anyone and could throw out speedy baserunners from his knees. For part of his career, he teamed with the flamboyant Satchel PAIGE to form perhaps the greatest battery in NEGRO LEAGUES history, if not all time. Gibson was just 33 years old, already a 16-year veteran, when the Dodgers broke the COLOR BARRIER with Jackie ROBINSON, and Gibson was reportedly bitter that he had been passed over. Certainly Bill VEECK or Branch RICKEY or another forward-thinking owner would have signed Gibson in short order, but a brain hemorrhage took his life in 1947. The Hall of Fame recognized him in 1972.

Gibson, Kirk (outfielder, 1979–95): A former All-American receiver at Michigan State, Gibson approached baseball with the ferocity of a football player and helped his Tigers and Dodgers to three division titles and two World Series victories. Most importantly, however, Gibson starred in one of the greatest moments in baseball history. It was Game One of the 1988 World Series, the overmatched Dodgers facing mighty Oakland. The A's went to the bottom of the ninth leading 4–3 as Gibson stood in the trainer's room, practicing his swing. His ailing knees had forced him to sit out that game, but he shot himself full of cortisone so that if the situation presented itself, he could come out for one at bat. Gibson had been the Dodgers' spark all season, and he would win the league's MVP despite underwhelming statistics. On the mound for the A's in Game One stood Dennis ECKERSLEY, the league's best reliever, who'd notched 45 saves that season. Eck got the first two outs quickly. Then pinch hitter Mike Davis worked Eck for a walk, and Gibson strode slowly to the plate, pinch-hitting for reliever Alejandro Peña. The crowd erupted. He worked the count to 3–2, including one ground ball foul that forced Gibson to limp to first base and another foul that nearly brought him to his knees, à la Roy Hobbs in the movie THE NATURAL. Then Eckersley tried a back-door curveball, and Gibson swung. The ball sailed high into the Los Angeles night, finally landing 10 rows into the right field bleachers. The game was over, the Dodgers had won, and Gibson's place in baseball history was secured. Even though Gibson didn't play the rest of the Series, his spirit was there as the Dodgers went on to beat the A's in five games.

Gooden, Dwight "Doc" (pitcher, 1984–present): A sad case of talent wasted, Gooden started his career with more than a bang—it was a nuclear explosion. His rookie campaign in 1984, which won him the Rookie of the Year trophy, was one of the best first years ever by a pitcher, and it came before Gooden was even old enough to drink. The next year, he won a Cy Young Award with an even more amazing season. He followed that up with a 17–6 season that helped his Mets win the World Series. In 1987, it began to fall apart. That year, he missed a month of the season while being treated for cocaine addiction. Two years later, an arm injury felled him. For the next four years, he posted progressively worse seasons, and in 1994, he received a one-year suspension for failing a drug test, putting his future in jeopardy. Here's something odd: Gooden and Darryl Strawberry both came up with the Mets around the same time, both achieved wealth and fame at a young age, and both later experienced severe personal and drug-related problems. You have to believe that living and performing under the constant glare of the New York media had something to do with it.

Gossage, Rich "Goose" (pitcher, 1972–94): Relief pitcher extraordinaire, Gossage helped redefine the role with his menacing stare, goofy mustache, and 100-mph fastball. He saved games through pure intimidation, daring hitters to stand in the box against him. Few ever felt comfortable. Gossage totaled 310 saves with nine teams, so it'll be interesting to see how the Hall of Fame treats him. At his peak, he was the best in the game, and in his 1981 strike-shortened season—0.77 ERA, 20 saves in 32 games—is one of the top 10 seasons ever posted by a reliever. I doubt that's enough to get him into the Hall. But with relief specialization a recent phenomenon in baseball, Gossage will be a good test case as to how the shrine will treat the current generation of relief aces.

Gray, Pete (outfielder, 1945): Having lost his right arm at the age of six, Gray nevertheless worked to become an exceptional minor league outfielder—batting .333 with only six errors in 1944—before joining the defending AL champion St. Louis Browns in 1945. Gray's promotion to the majors symbolized the dearth of baseball talent in America while most able-bodied men were fighting World War II. Although his story is inspiring, it doesn't have a happy ending: Gray batted just .218 in 234 at bats and never appeared in a major league uniform after that season.

Greenberg, Hank (first baseman, 1930–47): One of the dominant hitters in an era of great hitters, Greenberg's star shone brightly in almost all of the nine seasons he was a regular. Leading the league at various times in home runs (four times), RBIs (four times), runs (once), doubles (twice), and walks (twice), he helped his teams win four pennants while himself capturing two MVP Awards. After making his name with the Detroit Tigers, at the end of his career he joined the lowly Pittsburgh Pirates, who thought enough of Greenberg to make him baseball's first $100,000-per-year player. The first Jewish superstar, Greenberg faced prejudice wherever he went, but he handled the difficulties with class and grace. Injuries and World War II limited his career totals to 331 homers and 1,276 RBIs—but his greatness can't be measured by statistics alone.

Griffey, Ken, Jr. (outfielder, 1989–present): Griffey joined the American League with much fanfare in 1989: a 19-year-old kid with loads of talent, called the second coming of Willie MAYS et cetera. For his first four seasons, "Junior" dazzled fans with spectacular catches, deep home runs, and youthful exuberance. But his stats—25 home runs on average, a .515 slugging percentage—didn't seem to show his true potential. Then, in 1993, he busted out with a 45–home run campaign that quieted any skeptics. In strike-shortened 1994, he continued to cement his reputation as one of today's greats by smacking 40 home runs in just 433 at bats—at the age of 24. Since he came up so young, he has a good chance to break some big records before he retires, especially Hank AARON's mark of 755 career home runs. The only question is, will he want to? To surpass Aaron, a player would have to slug 34 home runs every year for 22 years. With the money today's players are making, they're financially secure for the rest of their lives by the time they're 28. Is *anyone* going to want to play 22 years?

Grove, Lefty (pitcher, 1925–39): A surly man renowned for his hatred of losing, Grove fed off that demeanor to fashion a pitching career that can arguably be called the greatest of all time. Strictly a fastball pitcher in the beginning, Grove got his professional start with the minor league Baltimore Orioles, where Babe RUTH also began. During Grove's five seasons there, the team captured five INTERNATIONAL LEAGUE pennants. The New York Giants offered $75,000 for Grove, but Orioles owner Jack Dunn held out for $100,000, which is what the Philadelphia Athletics ended up paying. It was the wisest move of A's manager/owner Connie MACK's career. Pitching in the hitting-rich 1920s and 1930s, Grove led the league in ERA a record nine times, in winning percentage five times, and in strikeouts for each of his first seven seasons. Plus he won 20 games eight times and pitched in three World Series. He finished with a career record of 300–141 for a .680 winning percentage—the highest among 300-game winners. He shares the American League record with 16 straight victories; after he lost potential win number 17 by a score of 1–0 on a misjudged fly ball, Grove showed his temper by tearing up the locker room, his uniform, and anything else he got his hands on. Amazingly, Grove suffered only two injuries during his career, one a sore arm in 1934 and the other a mysterious ailment that stumped doctors in 1938: He says they couldn't find a pulse in his pitching arm. Somehow, he still led the league in ERA.

Gwynn, Tony (outfielder, 1982–present): The National League's premier "pure hitter," Gwynn averaged 189 hits over his first 10 full seasons in the majors and, through 1994, captured five batting titles. Never a power hitter, the lifelong San Diego Padre could steal bases when he was younger, reaching a high of 56 in 1987, when he also batted .370 with a .447 on base percentage. In 1994, he was batting .394 when the strike hit, robbing us of the chance to see whether he could become the first .400 hitter in more than 50 years. A probable Hall of Famer.

Hamilton, "Sliding Billy" (outfielder, 1888–1901): The premier base stealer and leadoff hitter of the pre-1900 era, Hamilton finished his career with 912 steals, which would have ranked him ahead of Ty COBB except that scoring rules of Hamilton's time credited a player with a steal for taking an extra base on a hit. Even so, Hamilton was a great player, leading the league in steals, RBIs, and on base percentage five times each, batting twice, and runs scored four times— including an incredible 192 in 1894.

Hartnett, Gabby (catcher, 1922–41): Hartnett, a standout catcher who ranks as one of the top 10 of all time at his position, starred in what is perhaps the greatest moment in the history of the Chicago Cubs. He'd player-managed the Cubs in 1938, leading a surge from six and a half games out of first to just one and a half behind the league-leading Pirates. In the opener of the final weekend series, Hartnett came to bat in the bottom of the ninth with the score tied and darkness falling. Pittsburgh pitcher Mace Brown got ahead 0–2 to Hartnett, but the catcher smashed the next pitch over the fence and into the night, assuring his fame with the now-famous "homer in the gloamin'." The rest of his career wasn't too shabby either: 1,790 games, .297 average, 236 home runs, 1,179 RBIs, and the best throwing arm in his league. The Hall of Fame honored him in 1955.

Henderson, Rickey (outfielder, 1979–present): The greatest leadoff hitter of all time, Henderson has combined power, speed, excellent strike zone judgment, and high-average hitting like no player in history. In a gentler time, his coliseum-sized ego could be considered a charm. To fans in Oakland, who have had to endure Henderson's yearly tirades and complaints during three stints with the A's, it has been an annoyance. But there is no disputing Henderson's greatness as a player. When he retires, the Hall of Fame will accept him graciously, and Henderson will have the opportunity to atone for the tactlessness he showed Lou BROCK when he broke Brock's all-time stolen base record: "Lou Brock was a great base stealer," Henderson announced to the crowd that day in 1991, "but today *I am the greatest!*" (Brock, who was on hand, ignored the affront.)

Hernandez, Keith (first baseman, 1974–91): The best-fielding first baseman of his time—and perhaps all time—Hernandez played his best years with the Cardinals and Mets, winning the 1979 MVP (shared with Willie STARGELL) and starring in two winning World Series. He captured a position-record 11 Gold Gloves and holds the all-time record for assists by a first baseman. An on-field leader throughout his career, Hernandez is an "on-the-bubble" player when it comes to the Hall of Fame. If he wants to improve his chances, he should go into managing or broadcasting to keep his memory alive. Without that extra push, it's possible that the voters may forget his contributions to the game, which came not through outstanding stats but through quiet excellence.

Hornsby, Rogers (second baseman, 1915–37): The best-hitting second baseman of all time, Hornsby averaged over .400 for a five-year period, slugged 20-plus homers seven times, won two Triple Crowns, and led the league in a multitude of categories throughout the 1920s (his *BASEBALL ENCY-CLOPEDIA* entry is half boldface). And for his career, he batted .358, second highest of all time, earning him the title of baseball's greatest right-handed hitter. Of his fielding, praise is harder to come by. Ty COBB once wrote, "Hornsby couldn't catch a pop fly, much less go in the outfield after them, [and] could not come in on a slow hit ..." An angry, moody man, Hornsby alienated teammates and management wherever he played. He was traded five times, once after the 1926 season, during which he had player-managed the Cardinals to a World Series victory, then again a year later, after he'd led the league in runs, walks, slugging, and on base percentage—and then again a year after that. That, to me, is a strange but insightful footnote to an otherwise great career.

Hoy, William "Dummy" (outfielder, 1888–1902): With a .287 career batting average, an excellent batting eye, and great speed, Hoy toiled for six teams over 15 years. His effect on the game is legendary: a deaf-mute, Hoy was responsible for forcing umpires to use hand signals to indicate balls and strikes; prior to 1888, umpires shouted every call. Today, his nickname—Dummy—seems insensitive and cruel. Hoy, however, liked it and considered it a term of endearment. He died in 1961 at the age of 99.

Hubbell, Carl "The Meal Ticket" (pitcher, 1928–43): The top National League left-hander of his time, Hubbell earned his nickname with a trademark screwball that carried the Giants to three pennants. His accomplishments are many: 46 consecutive scoreless innings, five 20-win seasons, three ERA championships. But his most famous feat came in the 1934 All-Star Game, when he struck out five future Hall of Famers in a row—Babe RUTH, Lou GEHRIG, Jimmie FOXX, Al SIMMONS, and Joe CRONIN.

Huggins, Miller "The Mighty Mite" (second baseman, 1904–16; manager 1913–29): Huggins managed the New York Yankees to their first six pennants and first three World Series titles, laying the foundation for the Yankee dynasty that ruled baseball for nearly five decades. Most of the credit for those championships goes rightfully to Babe RUTH, but Huggins played a role nearly as significant: He had to control Ruth, no easy task. They clashed often. Huggins once fined Ruth the unheard-of sum of $5,000 for staying out late, causing Ruth to consider quitting the Yankees. For his part, Ruth once hung Huggins over the rear platform of a moving train. But when Huggins died of blood poisoning in 1929, Ruth cried. Elected to the Hall of Fame in 1964, Huggins is also honored with a monument in center field of YANKEE STADIUM.

Hunter, Jim "Catfish" (pitcher, 1965–79): A Hall of Famer with 224 career victories and five 20-win seasons, Hunter helped lead his A's to three World Series titles in the early 1970s. He earned his nickname not because of any real predilection toward fishing, but because A's owner Charlie FINLEY, always seeking publicity, wanted his prodigy to have a country nickname. Hunter and Finley had a strained relationship during the player's tenure with the club. But when Finley reneged on Hunter's 1974 contract by failing to pay $50,000 to an insurance annuity, the Players Association filed a grievance on behalf of Hunter asserting that as a result of the violation, Hunter should be released from his contract with the A's. An independent arbitrator agreed, and Hunter became baseball's first free agent. He signed a multimillion-dollar contract with the Yankees and helped them to three pennants before retiring in 1979.

Irvin, Monte (outfielder, 1938–56 [including the Negro leagues]): An excellent outfielder who played eight seasons in the white major leagues with the Giants, Irvin is in the Hall of Fame more for his 11 years in the NEGRO LEAGUES, where he was one of the best players. When Branch RICKEY was deciding who to select as the man to break baseball's COLOR LINE, most people believed Irvin would be the choice. But Rickey picked Jackie ROBINSON, and Irvin had to wait an extra two years before getting his chance in the majors.

Jackson, "Shoeless" Joe (outfielder, 1908–20): A top player of his time and any time, Jackson was one of the eight players thrown out of baseball following the BLACK SOX SCANDAL. He averaged .356 for his career, third best of all time, but that's because he was kicked out before his career could enter a normal "decline" phase. The subject of numerous books, including W. P. Kinsella's excellent novel *SHOELESS JOE* (upon which the film *FIELD OF DREAMS* is based), Jackson was an illiterate South Carolina mill worker who earned his nickname when he played a minor league game barefoot. He batted .400 once and slugged over .500 six times in an era when home runs were hard to come by—all with one of baseball's sweetest swings, so sweet that Babe RUTH claimed to have copied it. Despite the taint of the scandal, Jackson made a good life for himself after baseball, raising a family and becoming a successful businessman (and learning how to read). "I have read now and then that I am one of the most tragic figures in baseball," he said a few years before his death. "Well, maybe that's the way some people look at it, but I don't quite see it that way myself." He never fought his suspension because he said he had enjoyed a good career, accomplished a great many things, and "there wasn't much left for me in the big leagues." And he still deserves a place among the greats, even if it's just in the record books and not the Hall of Fame.

Jackson, Reggie, "Mr. October" (outfielder, 1967–87): The greatest World Series performer in the past 30 years—hence the nickname—Jackson was a 14-time All-Star who smacked 563 home runs, struck out a record 2,597 times, and led his teams to the postseason 11 times. The controversial Jackson, who was as loved and hated as any player in history, was fond of making grandiose claims such as, "The only reason I don't like playing in the World Series is I can't watch myself play." There was no question he could talk a good game, but it's equally evident that he delivered. Between 1970 and 1983, no American League team *without* Jackson in the lineup won the World Series, while Jackson's teams—the 1972–74 A's and

1977–78 Yankees—captured five championships. Additionally, he was one of baseball's first high-priced free agents, who before the 1977 season turned down a higher salary from Montreal to play for the Yankees because, Jackson said, "If I play in New York, they'll name a candy bar after me"—which, of course, they did. In 1992, he was justifiably elected to the Hall of Fame.

Jenkins, Ferguson (pitcher, 1965–83): A top pitcher of his era, Jenkins compiled a record of 284–226 while playing mostly for second division teams such as the Cubs and Rangers and is one of the best players never to appear in a World Series. The 1991 Hall of Fame inductee made headlines in 1992 after his girlfriend, suffering from mental illness, killed both herself and Jenkins's young daughter. Jenkins's strength in confronting that tragedy eclipsed anything he did on the baseball field.

Johnson, Walter "The Big Train" (pitcher, 1907–27): Perhaps the greatest pitcher of all time, Johnson recorded 417 victories with 12 seasons of 20-plus victories, 5 ERA titles, 12 strikeout crowns, and a record 110 shutouts—among many outstanding achievements. He possessed the best fastball of his time as well as magnificent control, and he was among the biggest stars in the game almost every year he pitched. Saddled with mediocre-to-poor teams most of his 21-year career, the Washington Senators ace had to wait 17 years before he was able to showcase his enormous talents in the World Series. But he made the most of his opportunity, winning the final game of the 1924 Series against the Giants with a clutch four-inning relief performance. He finished his career with 3,508 career strikeouts, considered an unbreakable record until the 1980s. A consummate gentleman, Johnson never questioned an umpire's authority and hated to throw inside pitches for fear of injuring opposing hitters—a character "flaw" that Ty Cobb, among others, exploited to great success by crowding the plate. Such knowledge makes Johnson's statistics even more impressive.

Johnson, William "Judy" (third baseman, Negro leagues, 1921–38): A 1975 Hall of Fame inductee, Johnson was a steady performer who performed well in the clutch and was an excellent glove man—basically, the George BRETT of the NEGRO LEAGUES. Johnson was also a player-manager for many years and after his on-field career worked as a scout; his greatest post-playing achievement was the signing of Dick ALLEN.

Joss, Addie (pitcher, 1902–10): In his first major league start, Joss tossed a one-hitter; in his next, he lost a no-hitter in the ninth. With that auspicious debut, one of baseball's tragic stories was born. Joss fashioned four 20-win seasons, threw a perfect game in the heat of a tight pennant race, and had won 160 games by the age of 30 despite an injured elbow. But in 1911, a bout of tubercular meningitis took his life at the age of 31. He was elected to the Hall of Fame in 1978.

Kaline, Al (outfielder, 1953–74): The youngest-ever batting champ when he hit .340 at the age of 20, Kaline starred in Detroit for 22 years, winning 11 Gold Gloves, smacking 399 home runs, tallying 3,007 hits, and appearing in 14 All-Star Games. Consistency, not flashy play, was his hallmark. With Kaline, you could pencil in a .300 average, 25 homers, and 85 RBIs—and more often than not over his career, he delivered. When it really counted, he was a terror, and in his only World Series appearance, in 1968, he was Detroit's hitting star, batting .379 with two homers and eight RBIs as the Tigers beat the Cardinals.

Keefe, Tim (pitcher, 1880–93): One of baseball's least-remembered superstars, Keefe won 342 games—including a record 19 in a row at one stretch—and posted an all-time low ERA of 0.86 in 1880. The first pitcher to use a change-up effectively, "Sir Timothy" had a 42–20 record in 1886—

with a league-leading 62 complete games and 535 innings pitched—at a time when teams employed two- and three-man pitching staffs and played 85 games per season. Despite the impressive number of career victories, the Hall of Fame didn't induct Keefe until 1964.

Keeler, Wee Willie (outfielder, 1892–1909): The five-foot-four-and-a-half-inch, 140-pound Keeler is most famous for having described his batting style with the immortal words, "I HIT 'EM WHERE THEY AIN'T"—a philosophy that he put to good use. With 2,962 career hits for the Dodgers, Orioles, Giants, and Yankees, Keeler compiled a .345 career average, including a high of .424, won two batting titles, and shares the National League record with a 44-game hitting streak in 1897. A skilled bunter, Keeler played most of his career when fouls were not counted as strikes, so he could remain at bat bunting foul balls until he got one in; the rule was changed partly in an effort to negate his success.

Kelly, Mike "King" (outfielder/catcher, 1878–93; manager, 1887–91): A stylish star, perhaps the most popular player of his day. Kelly's statistics, while impressive, do not show his true greatness. He played all nine positions and helped revolutionize catching by becoming one of the first to use finger signals to call pitches. He stole as many as 84 bases in one season as the inventor of the hook slide, led his teams to six pennants, and was purchased by a rival team in 1887 for a record $10,000—$5,000 of which went to Kelly himself for the use of his photograph for team promotions. Tragically, he died of pneumonia, penniless, at the age of 36.

Killebrew, Harmon (infielder/outfielder, 1954–75): A hulk of a man, "Killer" did one thing well on the baseball field—hit home runs—and he did it better than almost anybody who ever played. With eight seasons over 40 homers, including six home run titles, he belted 573 for his career, sixth most of all time. His weaknesses were many: he batted just .256 for his career and was a notoriously poor fielder. Nevertheless, the devastating offensive performer for the old Senators and Twins was elected to the Hall of Fame in 1984.

Kiner, Ralph (outfielder, 1946–55): Perhaps the greatest home run hitter this side of Babe RUTH, Kiner led the NL in that category for the first seven years of his career—an amazing feat. The homers propelled him to become baseball's highest-paid player, even though his Pirates, Cubs, and Indians never contended for the pennant. But after he reached a peak of 54 homers with an average of 37 per season, a back sprain ended his career after just 10 seasons. Kiner now broadcasts baseball games for the New York Mets, where his ability with his mouth falls far short of his ability with his bat. Here's a few examples: "All of his saves have come during relief appearances"; "He's going to be out of action the rest of his career"; "We'll be right back after this word from Manufacturers Hangover."

Klein, Chuck (outfielder, 1928–44): An MVP and Triple Crown winner, Klein was helped immensely during his peak seasons by playing for the Phillies in the tiny BAKER BOWL, which artificially inflated his stats. Still, Klein was one of the top all-around players in the league for many years: five straight seasons over 200 hits, four home run championships, two RBI titles, a stolen base title, and an all-time record 44 outfield assists in one season. His Hall of Fame induction in 1980—22 years after his death—was well deserved.

Koufax, Sandy (pitcher, 1955–66): The most dominant pitcher of his era, Koufax began his career as an erratic fastballer with control problems and compiled a record of 36–40 during his first six years with the Dodgers. But before the 1961 season, on the advice of coaches, Koufax changed his pitching motion. The rest is history: five consecutive ERA titles; three 20-win seasons; four strikeout crowns, including a league-record 382; three Cy Young Awards and one MVP; four no-hitters, including a perfect game; six All-Star appearances;

three pennants; and two World Series championships. But following his stupendous 1966 season, which cemented his reputation among the baseball gods, the 31-year-old Koufax did the unthinkable: He retired from the game, blaming chronic arthritis caused partly by a 1964 injury. The Hall of Fame welcomed him on the first ballot in 1972 as its youngest-ever inductee.

Lajoie, Napoleon "Larry" (second baseman, 1896–1914): Perhaps the American League's most popular player during his entire career—popular enough that his Cleveland team was actually known as the "Naps" in his honor for several years—Lajoie was also one of its best overall performers. He could hit, hit for power, field, and throw; the only thing he lacked was speed. Though coming against inferior competition (*see* 1901 SEASON), Lajoie set a 20th-century record for batting average with a .426 mark in the AL's inaugural campaign. One of the focal points of the AMERICAN LEAGUE WAR, Lajoie began his career with the Philadelphia Phillies in 1897 before joining the AL's Athletics in 1901. To circumvent a Pennsylvania Supreme Court decision prohibiting Lajoie from playing with the Athletics, AL President "Ban" JOHNSON transferred Lajoie to Cleveland beginning with the 1902 season, where Lajoie would play until 1914, winning two batting titles (not counting the disputed 1910 BATTING RACE) and leading the league at various times in hits, doubles, RBIs, and slugging percentage. He finished his career playing two years for the Athletics. The final totals: 3,242 hits, 1,599 RBIs, a .338 average, and a 1937 Hall of Fame induction. Recent statistical analysts have called Lajoie baseball's greatest second baseman. With competition coming from three other immortals—Eddie COLLINS, Rogers HORNSBY, and Joe MORGAN—it's certainly a disputed title. But it's hard to argue with Lajoie's numbers.

La Russa, Tony (infielder, 1963, 1968–71; manager, 1979–present): One of the top managers of recent times, La Russa epitomizes today's highly intelligent, analytical field generals.

A marginal major league player over six seasons, La Russa earned a law degree during off-seasons in case his major league career didn't work out. But now that he has become a two-time Manager of the Year—with the White Sox and the A's—La Russa says he will never have to resort to practicing law: "I'd rather drive a bus in the minors than be a lawyer."

Lasorda, Tommy (pitcher, 1954–56; manager, 1977–present): The ebullient manager of the Los Angeles Dodgers since 1977, Lasorda won pennants in his first two full seasons as manager and went on to capture two more pennants and two World Series titles. Not a bad accomplishment for a guy who never won a game as a pitcher in parts of three major league seasons. Claiming to "bleed Dodger blue" and believing in "the Great Dodger in the sky," Lasorda is widely proclaimed as a great manager and motivator.

Leonard, Buck (first baseman, Negro leagues, 1933–50): A 1972 Hall of Fame inductee, Leonard was one of the NEGRO LEAGUES' most feared sluggers, teaming with Josh GIBSON on the Homestead Grays to form a 1–2 punch equal to the RUTH–GEHRIG tandem that then existed in the "other" league. Leonard played an intelligent first base but was known better for his high-average power hitting. By the mid-1940s, Leonard was one of the league's most popular players, and he was probably the third-highest-paid player in his league, earning $1,000 per month during the season—just below Gibson and Satchel PAIGE.

Lloyd, John Henry "Pop" (shortstop, Negro leagues, 1905–31): Lloyd was called "the Black Wagner" while active, and Honus WAGNER said he felt honored to have been compared to him. Lloyd was probably the NEGRO LEAGUES' most popular player during his career, a slugging shortstop known—like Wagner—for scooping up part of the infield when fielding grounders. An active player until the age of 58, Lloyd missed by 40 years the chance to play in the white major leagues. But he seemed to accept his fate: "I do not consider that I was born at the wrong time," he said in 1949, two years after Jackie ROBINSON's major league debut. "I felt it was the right time, for I had a chance to prove the ability of our race in this sport, and because many of us did our very best to uphold the traditions of the game and of the world of sport, we have given the Negro a greater opportunity now to be accepted into the major leagues with other Americans." Lloyd died in 1965, seven years before the Hall of Fame dedicated part of its shrine to Negro league stars and 12 years before he was selected for the honor.

Lynn, Fred (outfielder, 1974–90): Lynn—at his peak, when healthy—was really something special: a flawless outfielder with range and a great arm, a devastating offensive performer with power and great bat control. Alas, with Lynn, the phrases "at his peak" and "when healthy" rarely applied at the same time. Injuries robbed him of between 20 and 40 games per season throughout his career—many due to reckless outfield play. His career started with loads of promise: He was the first player to win the MVP and Rookie of the Year awards in the same season as he guided his Red Sox to the 1975 pennant. He posted another great season in 1979, hitting 39 homers with 122 RBIs. But after that, he never could stay healthy enough to approach those numbers. After bouncing around with the Angels, Orioles, Tigers, and Padres, Lynn retired in 1990 and now works as an analyst for ESPN.

Mack, Connie (owner/manager, 1894–1950): From the team's inception in 1901 and for the next 50 years, Connie Mack—born Cornelius McGillicuddy—owned and managed the Philadelphia Athletics. Always dressed in a suit and tie, even while on the field, Mack oversaw the development of some of baseball's all-time greats, including Eddie COLLINS, "Home Run" BAKER, Mickey COCHRANE, Jimmie FOXX, and Lefty GROVE. But because he was also a part owner, winning pennants was only Mack's second-greatest concern; profits were always number one. And so Mr. Mack—as everybody always called him—often sold his stars while at the peaks of their careers to raise cash for his struggling bottom line. Still, he remained one of the best-loved figures in the game for most of his six decades in baseball, renowned for his gentle manner and always respectful attitude toward players and umpires. Because a man generally will not fire himself from a job, Mack continued to own and manage the Athletics until the age of 88, establishing unbreakable records for games managed (7,878), victories (3,776), and losses (4,025).

Maddux, Greg (pitcher, 1986–present): The best National League pitcher since Sandy KOUFAX in terms of consistent greatness, Maddux captured consecutive Cy Young Awards in the mid-1990s and has posted five other fine seasons—all in the two toughest parks for pitchers in the league, WRIGLEY FIELD and ATLANTA-FULTON COUNTY STADIUM. Like his teammate Fred MCGRIFF, Maddux doesn't always get mentioned when the talk turns to the Hall of Fame. I don't know why. How many other pitchers have won at least three Cy Youngs? CARLTON, Koufax, SEAVER, PALMER, CLEMENS—all in the Hall or sure to be in. And how many other players have won three or more major awards? FOXX, DiMAGGIO, MUSIAL, CAMPANELLA, BERRA, MANTLE, SCHMIDT, and BONDS—same story as above. Here's the real question: Will Maddux win 300 games? Probably not. Today's pitchers don't follow four-man rotations like those in the past. That cuts about 6 to 10 starts off their season totals, which means the loss of between 90 and 150 starts over the course of a 15-year career. Conservatively speaking, a good pitcher wins 55 percent of those starts; consequently, today's five-man rotations knock between 50 and 80 wins off a pitcher's career totals. In fact, it's doubtful anybody will ever win 300 again.

Mantle, Mickey (outfielder, 1951–68): When it comes to raw talent, nobody in baseball history can top Mickey Mantle. Undoubtedly the greatest switch-hitter of all time, a case can be made that at his peak he was also the greatest center fielder of all time, with apologies to MAYS, DiMAGGIO, and COBB. Only Cobb was faster, and only Mays was a better fielder. None had more power, none judged the strike zone better, none played on more pennant winners, and none could hit from both sides of the plate. During his 18-year career, "The Mick" won three MVP Awards, slugged 536 homers, won the 1956 Triple Crown, and led his Yankees to 12 World Series. Ah, but the injuries ... Over the course of his career, Mantle's countless ailments cost him thousands of at bats and, conservatively, 100 home runs. Compounding the injuries, he now admits, was his refusal to care for his body—an attitude that probably stemmed from his knowledge that Hodgkin's disease had taken the lives of nearly every male member of his family by middle age; Mantle believed he would never live past 40. Following his premature retirement at the age of 36, Mantle became haunted by the idea that he could have been better: a better player on the field and a better father to his children. The stress he put on himself led to alcoholism, and in 1994, the 62-year-old Mantle checked into the Betty Ford Clinic, resolving to overcome his disease and to exorcise the ghosts inside him. Only weeks after finishing his treatment, tragedy struck: His 36-year-old son died of a heart attack after earlier battling Hodgkin's and a drug addiction. In 1995, the years of alcohol caught up to him. He was diagnosed with cancer and underwent successful liver transplant surgery. But the cancer spread too quickly. Weeks later, the disease took Mantle's life, and an entire nation mourned the loss.

Maranville, Rabbit (shortstop, 1912–35): Only once surpassing the .300 level despite playing much of his career during the hitting-rich 1920s and 1930s, Maranville nevertheless hung around for 23 years, mostly with Boston and Pittsburgh, on the strength of his defense. The inventor of the basket catch, he dazzled fans, players, and managers alike with tremendous range and a strong arm, and he still holds the all-time record for putouts (Ozzie SMITH is still a few years away from breaking it). Acknowledging that baseball is about more than just hitting, the Hall of Fame inducted Maranville shortly after his death in 1954.

Marichal, Juan (pitcher, 1960–75): A dominant pitcher of his era, Marichal played in the shadows of Giants teammate Willie MAYS and pitching rivals Sandy KOUFAX and Bob GIBSON, which is why his image as an all-time great may have faded with time. He never won a Cy Young or MVP Award despite six 20-win seasons—which is one more than Gibson and three more than Koufax, who captured seven postseason awards between them. Possessing an exaggerated leg kick as well as the major leagues' best control, Marichal finished his career with 243 victories on the way to Hall of Fame induction in 1983. But he will perhaps always be remembered for an incident in CANDLESTICK PARK in 1965 during a game against the hated Dodgers. Believing Dodger catcher John Roseboro had tried to hit him with a return toss to the pitcher, Marichal took his bat and began to club Roseboro on the head until he was restrained by other players. The league fined Marichal $1,750 and suspended him for nine days, the equivalent of two starts; when the pennant race was over, the Dodgers had beaten Marichal's Giants by two games.

Maris, Roger (outfielder, 1957–68): A quiet, retiring, intelligent man, Maris will forever be remembered for a single feat: smashing 61 homers in 1961 to break Babe Ruth's single-season record (*see* 61). The pressure placed on him during that momentous year by the fans, the media, teammates, opposing players, and the league officials helped extinguish the light of a player who was turning into one of baseball's brightest stars. Even before that momentous season, the Yankee right fielder had led the league in RBIs and slugging percentage to win the 1960 MVP Award. After 1961, however, he wouldn't top 33 homers or 100 RBIs—although he was still in his twenties. Even so, at his peak, he was a complete ballplayer, with good defensive skills to go along with his dead-pull hitting. Though he passed away in 1985 after a battle with cancer, Maris's memory continues to live among baseball fans not just because of the record but because of the larger question the record begs: Does Maris belong in the Hall of Fame? There are two easy ways to argue this: Yes—because he was a better player than a lot of guys already in the Hall; and No— because he didn't do much else of consequence besides break the record. The answer here refutes both of those arguments: It makes no sense to compound one mistake by making another, which would occur if the Hall inducted Maris *simply because* he was a better player than, say, Lloyd Waner; the issue of who was better is moot when considering Maris's qualifications. On the other hand, Maris broke arguably baseball's most famous and revered record. Add to that the fact that during his 12-year career he played a key position on seven pennant-winning teams (though not all those years as a regular). Although Maris is ineligible under current Hall of Fame rules, my guess is that in a few years those rules will change, as they often do, and the VETERANS COMMITTEE will select him.

Martin, Billy (infielder, 1950–61; manager 1969–88): A scrappy but truly average infielder during his playing days, Martin made his name on the basis of two things: his managing skills and his temper. Growing up on the streets of Berkeley, California, Martin evidently learned at an early age what his fists were for. And throughout his career as both a player and manager, Martin seemed to keep finding himself in situations where that training came in handy. "Lots of people look up to Billy Martin," said Jim BOUTON. "That's because he just knocked them down." It was his hotheadedness that got him hired and fired as manager nearly a dozen times—including five times with George STEINBRENNER's Yankees. Martin's destructive behavior finally caught up with him in 1989 when his truck skidded off the road and crashed, killing himself and injuring a friend. Both Martin and his friend were drunk at the time, and the friend was supposedly in better shape to drive.

Martin wasn't wearing his seatbelt. Occasionally there is talk of inducting Martin into the Hall of Fame. I don't think he belongs. While he was a resourceful manager who won four division titles and two pennants, he was not an all-time great. His career won-loss totals don't measure up to the real Hall of Fame managers, such as DUROCHER, ALSTON, McCARTHY, or McGRAW. When you factor in Martin's boorish behavior off the field and the fact that he couldn't keep a job, does that spell Hall of Fame? It doesn't to me.

Mathews, Eddie (third baseman, 1952–68): The top power hitter among third basemen until Mike SCHMIDT arrived, Mathews teamed with fellow Brave Hank AARON from 1954 through 1966 to slug a combined 863 homers—all-time best for a pair of teammates. Though he never won an MVP Award, Mathews did capture two home run crowns, drove in 100 runs five times, appeared in nine All-Star Games, and finished his career with 512 homers. Though average defensively, Mathews nevertheless deserves to rank among the top five third basemen of all time—with Schmidt ranked number one and numbers two through five taken by, in any order, MATHEWS, George BRETT, Brooks ROBINSON, and "Home Run" BAKER.

Mathewson, Christy (pitcher, 1900–16): Mathewson was perhaps the most admired baseball hero of his time, a college-educated, clean-cut gentleman in an era dominated by scrappy, dirty, uneducated athletes. And the New York Giants star could pitch a little, too: 12 seasons of 20-plus victories, including four of 30 wins or more; five ERA crowns; five strike-out titles; four pennants; and 373 career victories to place third on the all-time list. His greatest performance on the mound came during the 1905 World Series, when Matty tossed three shutouts against the Athletics in six days. Famous for a "fadeaway" pitch, now called a screwball, Mathewson was the master of control and intelligent pitching, once going 68 consecutive innings without issuing a walk. In 1936, Mathewson was chosen as one of the first five players to enter the Hall of Fame—an honor shared with RUTH, JOHNSON, COBB, and WAGNER. Alas, Mathewson was the only member of the "Immortal Five" not in attendance at the induction. He had died in 1925 of tuberculosis stemming from exposure to poison gas in France during World War I.

Mattingly, Don (first baseman, 1983–present): Mattingly won a batting title in his first full season with the Yankees, then captured the MVP Award the next year after driving in 145 runs. He could hit for power and average, perform well in the clutch, and field his position better than anybody. A painful back injury slowed him in the early 1990s, but he has come back to have several more fine seasons. Among the most respected players in the game, he spoke for all Yankees when he blasted team owner George STEINBRENNER for the boss's treatment of his players: "The players get no respect around here," he said. "They give you money, that's it. Not respect. We get constantly dogged. And players from other teams love to see that. That's why nobody wants to play here." He patched things up with Steinbrenner, but his message was heard.

Mays, Carl (pitcher, 1915–29): A lot of people, including the pitcher himself, have said that if it were not for a fateful afternoon in August 1920, Carl Mays would be in the Hall of Fame. He was an outstanding pitcher, a five-time 20-game winner who ranked among the league's best pitchers for much of his career, mostly with the Red Sox and Yankees. Of course, he will always be remembered for one thing: throwing the underhand fastball—not a spitball, as some have suggested—that killed Indians shortstop Ray CHAPMAN. But that's not the only reason he's not in the Hall of Fame. Fred LIEB, a member of the Hall of Fame's VETERANS COMMITTEE, said that during discussions of Mays, the Chapman incident never came up. What actually kept him out were the allegations—never proven but convincing to many—that Mays threw a game in the 1921 World Series. In all, the picture of Mays is not a pretty one. He was a bitter, resentful man who was already one of the least-liked players in the league before the Chapman incident and angered managers and teammates with a "troublemaker" attitude that probably curtailed his career, and who, sadly, wished he could make the world forget that one of his pitches accidentally killed a fellow major leaguer. *See also* AUGUST 16, 1920.

Mays, Willie "The Say-Hey Kid" (outfielder, 1948–73 [including the Negro leagues]): Mays is another baseball player whose legend seems to transcend sports. First, the numbers: 660 career homers, third on the all-time list; two MVP Awards; two seasons of 50-plus homers; 10 seasons of 100-plus RBIs; 20 All-Star Game appearances—the list could go on forever. He could steal bases, leading the league four times. And he could field: His 440-foot, back-to-home-plate catch in dead center field in the 1954 World Series is one of baseball's most famous moments—and Mays always said it wasn't even his best grab (*see* CATCH, THE). He played his first professional years in the NEGRO LEAGUES just as major league integration began to take hold. In 1951, he came to the Giants and immediately went into a horrible slump. But after receiving a vote of confidence from manager Leo DUROCHER, Mays began to hit; his first homer came off of the best left-hander in baseball at the time, Warren SPAHN. Following his Rookie of the Year campaign, Mays then lost two years to the Korean War, seasons he wished he could have back at his retirement because he came within only 55 of breaking Babe RUTH's career home run record. He returned from the war in 1954 to slug 41 homers, win the batting title, and capture MVP honors while helping his Giants to the championship. For the rest of his career, baseball fans stood in awe of his fantastic play—enough so that many fans and writers have called Mays the greatest player in the history of the game. I lean toward Ruth for that honor, but I can understand their point. As a player, Mays could literally do it all. As a cultural icon, he was nearly the equal of Ruth, for he seemed to represent all that was good in America. With his joyous enthusiasm and always-smiling face, he seemed to embody a passion for life that all Americans could aspire to. And, like Jackie ROBINSON's, Mays's acceptance as a national hero certainly helped the civil rights movement.

Mazeroski, Bill (second baseman, 1956–72): The greatest fielder among second basemen in baseball history, Maz holds nearly every fielding record at that position, so it would be pointless to include a listing here. While not impressive offensively, Mazeroski was the kind of player who, as baseball people like to say, didn't hurt his teams with his bat. Ironically, however, it was as a hitter that he achieved his most lasting fame. In the 1960 WORLD SERIES, with the score tied in the bottom of the ninth of Game Seven, Mazeroski belted a dramatic homer off Ralph Terry to give the championship to Maz's Pirates. Snubbed by the Hall of Fame on countless occasions, Maz is currently ineligible for that honor, owing to a pointless rules change barring players who never achieved a 60 percent vote from the BBWAA. If and when Maz becomes eligible again, he has a good chance of getting in now that he's facing the very forgiving VETERANS COMMITTEE, which just inducted Phil RIZZUTO—not as good a player as Mazeroski.

McCarthy, Joe (manager, 1926–50): A Hall of Fame manager with baseball's all-time highest winning percentage (.614), McCarthy skippered the Cubs, Yankees, and Red Sox during his 24-year career. His greatest fame came as manager of the Yankees, whom he guided to eight pennants and seven World Series titles in 15 years. Blessed with the good fortune to fill out a lineup card that included the likes of RUTH, GEHRIG, and DIMAGGIO, the strict, often dour McCarthy was the most respected manager of his day.

McCovey, Willie "Stretch" (first baseman, 1959–80): Baseball history is dotted with men who earned the admiration and respect of fans, teammates, and opposing players not just for their stellar work on the field but also for their quiet grace and dignity off it. Honus WAGNER, Stan MUSIAL, and Lou GEHRIG are members of this fraternity. So is Willie McCovey. Beginning and ending his 22-year career in San Francisco, McCovey remains the most popular player in *San Francisco* Giants history. And every year, the Giants honor one player who exemplifies sportsmanship and service to the community with the "Willie Mac Award." Of course, it was his play on the field that carried McCovey to the Hall of Fame: 521 career home runs, an NL-record 18 grand slams, three home run titles, the 1959 Rookie of the Year Award, and the 1969 MVP Award. Today, the Alabama-born McCovey makes his home in the San Francisco area, appearing frequently at the ballpark and still looking as if he could belt one out of the park.

McGinnity, Joe "Iron Man" (pitcher, 1899–1908): Famous for pitching both ends of doubleheaders—including three twin-bill victories in one month—McGinnity's nickname originally stemmed from his work in an iron foundry but perfectly applied to his pitching abilities. In addition to the doubleheaders and two 30-win seasons, the 1946 Hall of Famer compiled a superficially amazing 246 victories during just 10 seasons in the majors, mostly with the Giants. The reason he is included in this book is that he is a good example of how much pitching has changed since the turn of the century. McGinnity played in an era when pitchers could conserve their energy against some batters because the threat of the home run was virtually nonexistent. He and his contemporaries could therefore rack up 350-plus innings and 30-plus victories in the same way today's pitchers throw 250 innings with 20 victories. In their own context, McGinnity's stats are really no better than those of Ferguson JENKINS or "Catfish" HUNTER, whose numbers don't seem as impressive.

McGraw, John "Muggsy" (third baseman, 1891–1906; manager, 1901–32): Feisty, combative, scrappy—three words often used to describe McGraw, whose nickname, fittingly, was "Little Napoleon." During his playing days as third baseman of the rough-and-tumble Baltimore Orioles, McGraw was known for a good batting eye and a fierce desire to win that included such actions as tripping baserunners, spiking fielders, and baiting umpires—and his punching hand was always at the ready. But it was as a manager that McGraw achieved baseball immortality. During his 30 years at the helm, McGraw's New York Giants captured 10 pennants and three World Series. Hailed as a managerial genius by contemporaries and historians, McGraw helped mold the careers of a dozen Hall of Famers, including Christy MATHEWSON, Carl HUBBELL, and Bill TERRY.

McGriff, Fred "Crimedog" (first baseman, 1986–present): A quiet man with a booming bat, McGriff is perhaps the least talked about great player in the game today. He hasn't won an MVP, but he bangs out 30 home run/100 RBI seasons every year and has played on two division winners in Toronto and Atlanta. Since he keeps himself in such good shape all the time, he has a good chance to slug 500 home runs, which will guarantee his election to the Hall of Fame. Maybe then people will talk about how great he was. I think we should appreciate him now, while he's still around to wow us.

McLain, Denny (pitcher, 1963–72): The answer to the question, Who was the last pitcher to win 30 games in one season? Actually, McLain had a much more interesting life than his record indicates. The immensely talented pitcher won back-to-back Cy Young Awards (in 1968 for his 31–6 season and the following year in a tie with Mike Cuellar) and led his Tigers to the 1968 World Series. But his career took a fast downward spiral after that. First he was suspended for bookmaking and consorting with gamblers. Then he got caught illegally carrying a gun—another suspension. And he dumped buckets of ice water on sportswriters to earn yet another suspension. Such activities, of course, affected his playing ability—and just three years after being on top of the baseball world, not even 30 years old, he was out of baseball. But his troubles didn't stop there: He filed for bankruptcy. He suffered a mild heart attack. He was caught smuggling cocaine. Finally, in 1984, he was convicted of a number of charges, including racketeering and extortion, and was sent to jail. The conviction was overturned on a technicality after McLain had spent 29 months in prison, but he later pleaded guilty to the charges and received probation in addition to the time served. In today's debate over whether athletes are role models, McLain serves as a strong argument for "no."

McNally, Dave (pitcher, 1962–75): While "Catfish" HUNTER was baseball's first bona fide FREE AGENT, McNally and Andy MESSERSMITH were the two men who actually pioneered the system for free agency in use today. Like Messersmith, McNally was one of the top pitchers in baseball for several years, a 4-time 20-game winner with the Orioles. But in 1975, unhappy with the Montreal Expos' contract offer after an off-season trade, McNally began the season with the team but without a contract. By the middle of the year, an injured wrist began to bother him, and he decided to retire. Knowing McNally's contract situation, Marvin MILLER of the Major League Baseball Players' Association (MLBPA) asked him to help in their test case against baseball's RESERVE CLAUSE; Messersmith, for different reasons, also volunteered to be part of the test. The MLBPA believed that not having signed the contract made the two men free agents at the end of the year. In a stunning decision, arbitrator Peter Seitz agreed with the MLBPA and granted Messersmith and McNally the right to negotiate with any club. Although Messersmith was the focal point of the case, McNally's role should not be forgotten: The Expos offered him a 1976 contract for over $100,000—in effect trying to buy him off to avoid the suit against baseball—but the 33-year-old McNally remained firm. He turned down a lucrative offer in order to help future ballplayers.

McPhee, John "Bid" (second baseman, 1882–99): An oft-forgotten player, McPhee was indisputably baseball's greatest fielding second baseman until Eddie COLLINS appeared, and some old-timers (all dead now) never strayed from their choice of McPhee as number one. "Bid" played most of his career before gloves were introduced, so his fielding statistics look terrible on the surface (career .944 fielding percentage, where today's best field at a .980 clip). While active, however, the Cincinnati star was every bit as respected as Roberto Alomar is today and Bill MAZEROSKI was years ago. It's interesting that the Hall of Fame will induct players like Fred Lindstrom and Tony Lazzeri, who put up glossy but ultimately unremarkable hitting stats, while ignoring fabulous glove men like Mazeroski, McPhee, and Nellie Fox.

Messersmith, Andy (pitcher, 1968–78): Messersmith was one of baseball's top pitchers for several years in the early 1970s, earning as much as $90,000 per year. Before the 1974 season, he'd been traded from the Angels to the Dodgers, where he enjoyed his most productive season. So in 1975, he asked Dodgers owner Walter O'MALLEY to include a no-trade clause in his contract. O'Malley refused and renewed the contract without Messersmith's signature, as clubs were allowed to do because of the RESERVE CLAUSE written into every player's contract. Messersmith, along with Dave McNALLY, played the entire season without signing the contract—an action that, according to the Major League Baseball Players' Association (MLBPA), would automatically make the two players free agents at the end of the season. The owners contested the assumption, and the case went to arbitration, where Peter Seitz ruled in favor of the players in a momentous decision. Although McNally chose to retire, Messersmith signed a multiyear contract with the Atlanta Braves worth $1 million but failed to live up to the big money. Traded twice again, he returned to the Dodgers, a shadow of his former self. Ironically, as MLBPA president Marvin MILLER points out in his memoir, *A Whole Different Ballgame*, O'Malley fought to keep Messersmith a Dodger forever by binding him to the reserve system; what Messersmith wanted was a no-trade clause that *would* *have* kept him a Dodger forever. Instead, O'Malley's short-sighted action accelerated the free agency era.

Minoso, Minnie (infielder/outfielder, 1946–64, 1976, 1980 [including the Negro leagues]): A few years ago, the commissioner's office halted what it considered a travesty: the White Sox's plan to suit up Minnie Minoso for a game to continue his streak of playing a game in every decade since the 1940s. The Sox had pulled the stunt twice before, in 1976—when the 53-year-old Minoso became the oldest player ever to get a hit in the major leagues—and again in 1980. These antics have unfortunately altered the image of a man who, when young and healthy, was one of baseball's most exciting players. Though he didn't play in the majors full-time until age 28 because of baseball's COLOR LINE, Minoso stayed around long enough to lead the league at various times in hits, stolen bases, doubles, and triples while tallying 1,963 hits and a career average of .298—mostly with the White Sox. In the current debate over players who are worthy of the Hall of Fame but not in it, Minoso's name often arises. Does he belong? Look at it this way: Minoso didn't play in the majors full-time until he was 28. Give him back six of those years and he probably ends up with close to 3,000 hits and a higher batting average—definitely Hall of Fame material. The case for Minoso is different from the case of someone like Pete REISER or Herb SCORE or Tony CONIGLIARO, who might have made it to the Hall if not for devastating injuries. It was the color of his skin that kept Minoso from enjoying a more productive career. It shouldn't keep him out of the Hall of Fame, too.

Mize, Johnny "The Big Cat" (first baseman, 1936–53): At his peak, Mize was one of the most feared hitters in the National League, the winner of four home run crowns, a batting championship, and three RBI titles. A 10-time All-Star, he was traded by the Cardinals to the Giants in 1941, one season before St. Louis began its run of four pennants in five seasons. Then he played on the underachieving Giants for the next four years. But Mize didn't miss out on the World Series entirely, as he played a small but important role in the Yankees' juggernaut that won championships from 1949 through 1953.

Molitor, Paul (infielder/designated hitter, 1978–present): A variety of devastating injuries sidetracked what should have been an easy track to the Hall of Fame for this versatile player. But late in his career, when his skills were supposed to be declining, Molitor posted some impressive offensive seasons, won his first World Series, and reestablished his claim to the Hall. A superlative hitter, smart baserunner, and team leader, Molitor came up with the Milwaukee Brewers but joined Toronto in 1993 as a free agent. The only knock against him now is that, owing to the injuries, he posted his best seasons as a designated hitter, not as a complete player. It'll be interesting to see how long it takes the Hall of Fame voters to elect him.

Morgan, Joe (second baseman, 1963–84): "Little Joe" stood just five-feet-seven, but among baseball's best second baseman, no one ever stood taller. The winner of back-to-back MVPs in 1975 and 1976, Morgan excelled in every facet of the game. At the plate, he hit for a high average with a great batting eye and good power—enough that he is the all-time leading home run hitter among second basemen (Ryne SANDBERG was on pace to break that record until he retired suddenly in 1994). On the base paths, Morgan combined speed with brains to compile an 81 percent stolen base success rate and 689 career steals. And in the field, he won five Gold Gloves. He ignited Cincinnati's "BIG RED MACHINE" to two World Series victories during his MVP years, refusing to be overshadowed by illustrious teammates Pete ROSE and Johnny BENCH. In 1982, his home run on the last weekend of the season for the Giants knocked the hated Dodgers out of the pennant race. The following year, he helped Philadelphia's "Wheeze Kids" win the NL pennant. Inducted into the Hall of Fame in 1990, Morgan now makes his living as a businessman and broadcaster whose name arises frequently as a candidate to be a club manager or a league president; Morgan has declined all offers because of his numerous business interests.

Morris, Jack (pitcher, 1977–95): Nobody won more games in the 1980s than Jack Morris, the intimidating split-fingered fastball expert who made his name and reputation with the Tigers. The three-time 20-game winner was a workhorse, averaging about 35 starts, 250 innings, and 11 complete games per year for most of his career. His ERAs were never great, but that's probably because he's played most of his career in hitters' parks: TIGER STADIUM, the METRODOME, and the SKY-DOME. With 254 career victories, he's no cinch for the Hall of Fame, but I think he'll eventually get in.

Munson, Thurman (catcher, 1969–79): Grouchy and proud, enigmatic and immensely talented, Munson continued the New York Yankees string of superstar catchers—Bill DICKEY, Yogi BERRA, Elston Howard, and Munson—who among them won five MVPs and countless pennants. Munson could hit for power and average and he could even run a little. Behind the plate, he had no superiors. He was, in fact, in the midst of a Hall of Fame–caliber career when tragedy struck. On August 2, 1979, the 32-year-old Munson was flying his private plane home to be with his family, as he often did, when he lost control and crashed. His death cast a pall over YANKEE STADIUM, where Munson had endeared himself to the fans with his consistently gritty performances. In this era of pampered superstars, it's unlikely that the likes of Munson will be seen again.

Murphy, Dale (outfielder, 1976–93): At his peak, Murphy was among the most feared offensive players in the National League. And he achieved that peak for seven seasons—a fact that many fans may forget since Murphy's final six seasons amounted to a steady progression from average to bad to worse. He came up originally as a catcher, but he developed a strange mental block that kept him from making routine throws, even tosses back to the pitcher. He was no more successful at first base, but once they gave him some room to move, he blossomed. When Murphy was winning back-to-back MVPs in 1982–83 and leading his Braves to their first postseason play in two decades, he possessed a deadly combination of speed, power, and excellent center field play. He finished his career with 398 home runs, despite sticking around fruitlessly trying to reach the 400 mark. And unlike most players who reach Murphy's level of superstardom, he never changed. He remained the polite, smiling, autograph-signing gentleman from beginning to end.

Murray, Eddie (first baseman, 1977–present): "Steady Eddie" is a nickname that never caught on for Murray, but it should have. Excepting the strike-shortened 1981 (when he led the league with 78 RBIs) and 1994 (when he had 76) seasons, Murray has driven in at least 84 runs every year of his career and has topped the 100 mark seven times. For most of his career, he was a manager's dream. Playing every day, he could be counted on year after year for a .290 average with 30 home runs, 75 walks, 90 RBIs, and 90 runs scored—if not more. The switch-hitting Murray, who played his best years in Baltimore, never astounded the fans or media with flashy stats and so never earned an MVP award, but he earned more MVP votes than any other American Leaguer in the 1980s and finished among the top five vote-getters five different times. He has earned a place in the Hall of Fame, MVP or no.

Musial, Stan "The Man" (first baseman/outfielder, 1941–63): They love Stan Musial so much in St. Louis that they built a statue of him to stand guard in front of Busch Stadium. Such is a fitting tribute to a man who was a rock of consistency throughout his 22-year career. Durable and strong, he never missed more than 20 games in a season nor batted below .300 until he was 38 years old—a full 17 years straight. He led the league 46 times in various major offensive categories, won three MVPs, helped his teams to four pennants, and appeared in 24 All-Star Games—where he holds career records for All-Star home runs (6), extra-base hits (8), and total bases (40). At his retirement in 1963, he held almost every National League career batting record, including hits (3,630), runs (1,949), doubles (725), and RBIs (1,951). A fan favorite wherever he went, Musial earned his nickname in Brooklyn, where fans grew fond of saying, "There's that man again" whenever Musial stood at the plate in his patented "peek-a-boo" batting stance that looked as if he were peering around a corner. For his career, Musial rarely struck out, showed excellent power, never got hurt, and played every inning, every at bat as if it were the seventh game of the World Series. Musial was, in fact, a near-flawless ballplayer who earned the respect of everyone from opposing players to reporters to rival fans, and he belongs in a select group of superstar players—along with the likes of WAGNER, MATHEWSON, JOHNSON, and GEHRIG—who exemplified true sportsmanship and excellence. If you were picking a player for your all-time all-star team, you could do no better than Stan Musial in left field.

Newcombe, Don (pitcher, 1944–60 [including Negro leagues]): At his peak, "Newk" was one of the National League's most feared pitchers. Coming up with the Dodgers, he was the major leagues' first black star pitcher, winning the Rookie of the Year Award in 1949. And in 1956, his 27–7 record won him baseball's first Cy Young Award in addition to the NL MVP, making him the first pitcher to capture all three of the major awards. But he could never win in the clutch: His World Series record was 0–4 with an 8.59 ERA, and he was the starter in the 1951 playoff game against the Giants won on Bobby THOMSON's famous home run (*see* "SHOT HEARD 'ROUND THE WORLD"). A victim of alcoholism, Newcombe was never the same after his phenomenal 1956 season, and he was out of baseball four years later. But he fought his disease and eventually overcame it. Now he works in the Dodgers' front office, counseling players against the evils of alcohol abuse, giving back to the game some of what it gave him.

Newhouser, Hal (pitcher, 1939–55): A left-hander who had the bad fortune to reach his peak as a pitcher during the war years, Newhouser's career is routinely denigrated by ill-informed fans. He remains the only pitcher to win back-to-back MVPs, capturing the awards in 1944 and 1945 with outstanding 29–9 and 25–9 records and ERAs of 2.22 and 1.81. It is true that the best players were in the service during those years, while Newhouser was a 4-F with a bad heart. But look at his records after the war: 26–9, 1.94 ERA in 1946; 17–17, 2.87 in 1947; 21–12, 3.01 in 1948; and 18–11, 3.36 in 1949—all with mediocre Detroit Tiger teams. He lost most of his effectiveness after that, but he hung around long enough to compile a 7–2 record as a relief pitcher with the 1954 Indians, who won an all-time record 116 games. For many years, he was the subject of a Hall of Fame dispute, but the question was put to rest in 1992 when the VETERANS COMMITTEE selected him.

Nichols, Charles "Kid" (pitcher, 1890–1906): A Hall of Fame hurler who excelled both before and after the pitching mound was changed from 45 feet to 60 feet 6 inches from home plate, Nichols won 360 career games to place him seventh on the all-time list. He led Boston to two pennants, and he won 30 or more games seven straight years, a record that will never be broken. Of course, we have to remember that it was an entirely different time for pitchers: Without the threat of the home run, pitchers could afford to conserve their energy for important points in the game. Pitching today, he would never achieve 360 wins—but he would still be a star.

Niekro, Phil (pitcher, 1964–87): Niekro didn't become a regular starter until the age of 28, but he still was able to win 318 games (14th place all time) and lose 274 (5th). The secret to his success was the Niekro knuckleball, which he perfected while toiling for the then lowly Atlanta Braves. By employing a pitch that puts little strain on the arm, Niekro was the National League's preeminent workhorse throughout the 1970s, leading the league in innings pitched and complete games four times each. He also led the league in victories twice and in losses a record four straight times—including a serendipitous season when he led in both wins and losses with a 21–20 record. He was an effective pitcher until the age of 48—121 of his victories and 103 of his losses came after he turned 40. Combined with his brother Joe, who knuckled his way to a 22-year career of his own, the Niekro brothers totaled 539 career victories, 10 wins more than Jim and Gaylord PERRY for the all-time lead among major league siblings. While not a first-ballot Hall of Famer, Phil Niekro will get in eventually.

Nuxhall, Joe (pitcher, 1944, 1952–66): When the World War II draft took most able-bodied men, major league baseball was forced to make do with what was left. Fifteen-year-old Joe Nuxhall was too young for war, but not too young, according to the Cincinnati Reds, to pitch in the majors. In his only appearance of 1944, the nervous Nuxhall faced nine batters, getting two outs, surrendering two hits, and walking five. He then went to the minors and resurfaced in 1952 to start his real career as a productive if unspectacular hurler, finishing his career with a 135–117 record over 16 seasons. The funny thing is, the Reds originally asked Nuxhall's father to try out for the club, but Joe, who accompanied his father by chance, impressed the Reds more. When the club signed him, he was believed to be the youngest-ever major leaguer; later research has discovered that a 14-year-old named Fred Chapman pitched for Philadelphia's American Association club in 1887.

Oh, Sadaharu (outfielder, Japanese leagues, 1959–77): With 868 career homers, Oh qualifies as the world's all-time home run champion. When he first came up with the Yomiuri Giants, however, his greatness was hardly evident. Formerly a pitcher, Oh batted just .161 as a rookie. But when he began studying martial arts, he learned to attain total control over his physical and spiritual self. Baseball success soon followed, and the stats are amazing: nine MVP Awards, 15 home run titles, five batting championships, back-to-back TRIPLE CROWNS, and nine Golden Glove awards for fielding excellence. Possessing a distinctive, exaggerated leg kick that reminded observers of a dog doing business at a hydrant, Oh smashed his 868 dingers in just 9,250 at bats—a better percentage than Henry AARON or Babe RUTH. But during a famous 1974 home run hitting contest, Aaron bested Oh 10–9 before 50,000 fans in Tokyo. How would Oh have done in the U.S.? Clete Boyer, who had a 20-plus-year career as a player and coach in the majors, saw Oh at his peak and said he had the strength of Aaron and the eyesight of Ted WILLIAMS.

O'Neil, Buck (first baseman, Negro leagues, 1937–55): An excellent performer in the NEGRO LEAGUES, O'Neil became the first black coach in major league baseball when he joined the Cubs for the 1962 season. Most of his contributions to baseball, however, have come off the field. He's currently the head of the NEGRO LEAGUES HALL OF FAME and has become a tireless ombudsman for the sport as a whole. We all got to know him pretty well in Ken Burns's epic baseball documentary; out of all the experts Burns featured, O'Neil was the most eloquent, most sincere, most engaging of all.

Ott, Mel (outfielder, 1926–47): Ott joined the New York Giants at the age of 17 because manager John MCGRAW didn't want to send him down to the minors for fear that a coach might "ruin" him. McGraw obviously knew what he was talking about, as Ott became a regular at age 19 and smashed 42 homers at 20, the youngest ever to reach that mark. The five-foot-nine, 170-pounder generated his power from a high leg kick that helped him capture six NL home run crowns during his 22-year career. He became adept at jerking the ball into the short right-field porch at New York's POLO GROUNDS, so two-thirds of his 511 career homers came at home. But whether home or away, Ott was one of the most feared hitters in the league, drawing at least 80 walks in 16 different seasons. He also played a flawless right field and was talented enough to log substantial time at third base when the Giants needed it. He led his teams to three pennants, appeared in 12 All-Star Games, and became one of the most popular players in Giants history. Less successful as a manager, Ott was the subject of Leo DUROCHER's famous edict that "nice guys finish last." He was elected to the Hall of Fame in 1951.

Paige, Leroy "Satchel" (pitcher, 1926–53, 1965 [including Negro leagues]): The most famous player in NEGRO LEAGUES history, Paige was its preeminent showman in addition to perhaps its best pitcher. Locked out of major league ball until he was well past his prime, he pitched against white players often enough during winter barnstorming trips that Dizzy DEAN, Joe DiMAGGIO, and Charlie GEHRINGER, among others, called Paige the best pitcher they ever saw. Other Negro league experts place Smoky Joe WILLIAMS above Paige in terms of skill, but there can be no doubting Paige's ability to draw fans. For much of his career, he was the biggest gate attraction in the league; huge crowds would gather to watch whether he fulfilled his promise to strike out the side on nine pitches, and he usually came through. His salaries were good—probably as high as $40,000 per year—though not as good as they should have been. When Cleveland owner Bill VEECK finally brought Paige to the majors in 1948, the pitcher was 42 years old, the oldest rookie in major league history. Still, he could fill the seats. His first three starts drew over 200,000 fans to set night-game attendance records in Cleveland and Chicago. His major league stats seem undistinguished—28–31, 3.29 ERA—until you remember his age, which Veeck tried to say was higher than it was (to generate publicity, Veeck claimed his "team of detectives" had determined Paige was born in 1899 when in fact Paige always knew he was born in 1906). In another publicity stunt, the Kansas City Athletics hired Paige to pitch a game in 1965; the 59-year-old tossed three shutout innings, allowing only one hit. By the time he was finished, Paige estimated that he and his overpowering fastball (known variously as his "bee ball," "trouble ball," and "Long Tom")

had seen action in more than 2,500 games, winning 2,000 of
them, against Negro league and semipro teams; other esti-
mates include 100 no-hitters, 22 strikeouts in one game, and
as many as 153 games pitched in one calendar year. Aside
from his dominance on the mound, Paige's unique brand of
wit and charm has entered American folklore. In his much-
quoted "How to Stay Young," Paige offered these suggestions:
"Avoid fried meats, which angry up the blood. Keep the juices
flowing by jangling around gently as you move. Don't look
back. Something might be gaining on you." Despite his out-
ward reputation as a showboat, Paige was keenly aware of his
standing in society. When the Hall of Fame decided to honor
a number of stars with a special wing for Negro leaguers in
1972, Paige observed, "The only change is that baseball has
turned Paige from a second-class citizen to a second-class immortal." Paige's life story is uniquely American, and any fan
would benefit from a reading of his autobiography, *Maybe I'll
Pitch Forever*, or one of his several biographies.

Palmer, Jim (pitcher, 1965–67, 1969–84): Perhaps more famous now for his seminude underwear ads, Palmer was one
of the greatest pitchers of recent years. Playing his entire career with the Baltimore Orioles, Palmer is one of just three
AL pitchers to have won 20 games in eight different years,
and he also captured an AL-record 3 Cy Young Awards.
Palmer finished his career with 268 victories and a 2.86
ERA—fifth among pitchers with more than 3,000 innings
pitched—making him a first-ballot Hall of Famer in 1990. But
perhaps tempted by the riches being handed out to even jour-
neyman pitchers, Palmer attempted a comeback one year after his induction to the Hall. The comeback failed, of course,
but probably for the best: A successful return would have
jeopardized Palmer's feat of never having allowed a grand
slam.

Perry, Gaylord (pitcher, 1962–83): Perry won 314 games and
is the only pitcher to capture Cy Young Awards in both

leagues, but he will always be remembered for the illegal pitch he did or did not throw: the spitball. Actually, the question of whether he threw the spitter has long been answered; he even titled his autobiography *Me and the Spitter*. But throughout his career, which began with San Francisco in 1962 and ended seven teams and 22 years later, opposing managers, batters, and umpires tried to catch him with incriminating evidence—Vaseline, K-Y Jelly, a nail file—and found nothing. That is, until August 23, 1982, when umpires finally ejected Perry for throwing an illegal pitch. But as Perry himself would admit, it was the *threat* of the spitball that scared hitters, not the pitch itself. He threw it perhaps once or twice a game, perhaps not at all. He didn't make his living off it. So those who might claim that Perry cheated his way to five 20-win seasons and 3,534 strikeouts are wrong. Hall of Fame voters never doubted his credentials, electing him in 1991.

Pipp, Wally (first baseman, 1913, 1915–28): People like Wally Pipp are destined to be remembered as losers by those who don't know better. It was Pipp who, as a member of the New York Yankees in June 1925, asked for the day off ostensibly because of a headache but probably because he just wanted to go to the racetrack. Manager Miller HUGGINS took the opportunity to take a look at a young slugger just recruited out of Columbia University named Lou GEHRIG. The rest, of course, is history: Gehrig would set a major league record by playing 2,130 consecutive games; Pipp would be traded the next season. Certainly Pipp's life and career encompassed more than that fateful summer day. He had been a slick-fielding, good-hitting first baseman for a dozen years, leading the league in homers twice and triples once. Nevertheless, his name lives in infamy. Even today, fans and players warn of the "Wally Pipp syndrome" when a player removes himself from the lineup due to illness and a young phenom takes his place.

Plank, "Gettysburg Eddie" (pitcher, 1901–17): The Gettysburg College graduate won 326 games in his career to put him number one among all left-handed pitchers until Warren SPAHN came along. Although he was among the league's best pitchers almost every year he pitched, winning 20 games in 8 different seasons and helping his Philadelphia A's to four pennants, he never led the league in any of the major categories. Like Spahn, Plank's hallmark was his durability—for which Plank was recognized by the Hall of Fame in 1946.

Posey, Cumberland (outfielder/owner, Negro leagues, 1911–46): A Negro league giant, Posey was part Connie MACK, part Branch RICKEY, part William HULBERT. The college-educated Posey led the legendary HOMESTEAD GRAYS almost from their inception, as a player, manager, and owner. During that time, the Grays established a great dynasty, winning more than 80 percent of their games most years, against both white semipro teams and Negro league competition. Posey was an excellent judge of talent, discovering or developing many of the biggest stars in the leagues, such as Smoky Joe WILLIAMS, "Cool Papa" BELL, Buck LEONARD, and Josh GIBSON. Posey ambitiously tried to establish a tightly controlled league system similar to the major leagues, with schedules and stable franchises. But this was in the 1930s, when business conditions were hardly favorable to new ventures. His East-West League failed, so Posey went back to leading the Grays through the loose-knit system of league games combined with barnstorming, continuing as a Negro leagues power broker until his death in 1946.

Puckett, Kirby (outfielder, 1984–present): Kirby Puckett is a member of an endangered species: a player who plays every day, every inning with a smile on his face and a spring in his step. He truly loves the game. He's also one of the biggest stars of the past decade, a high-average line-drive hitter who has led the league in hits four times and batting average once. A perennial All-Star, Puckett has also played on two championship teams, the 1987 and 1991 Twins. In the latter World

Series, Puckett's leadoff homer in the bottom of the 11th won Game Six to send the Series to Game Seven, which the Twins won in 10 innings. He has put up good enough numbers and made enough friends throughout baseball that five or so years after he retires, he'll almost certainly receive induction to the Hall of Fame.

Radbourn, Charles "Ol' Hoss" (pitcher, 1880–91): Radbourn pitched in a era when pitchers threw underhand from 50 feet way and a team's pitching staff usually consisted of two or three men. These facts should go a long way toward explaining why Radbourn's 1884 season is so amazing: a 59–12 record (some record books credit him with 60 wins), 678 innings, and 441 strikeouts—all league-leading figures and major league records that will never be broken. That season, his Providence Grays won the National League pennant and faced the American Association's New York Metropolitans in the first postseason championship to be known as a "World Series" (*see* 1884 WORLD SERIES). "Hoss," who earned his nickname not because he was built like a horse but because he had the stamina of one (at least for that one season), lasted in baseball just 11 years, putting together only three really good seasons, so his 309–195 record is deceiving. Still, Hall of Fame electors honored Radbourn in 1939 among one of the first groups of inductees, more than 40 years after his death.

Reese, Pee Wee (shortstop, 1940–42, 1946–58): For much of his career, Reese was the National League's most respected shortstop, a 10-time All-Star who helped his Brooklyn Dodgers to seven pennants through flawless fielding, consistent hitting, and superb leadership. Among his other accomplishments, the Kentucky-born Reese also helped ease Jackie ROBINSON's entry into the majors simply by treating Robinson like any other player. "You know," Reese once told Robinson after their careers had ended, "I never went out of my way to be nice to you." "Maybe that's what I always appreciated most," Robinson replied, "that you didn't." Somehow, Reese was passed over for the Hall of Fame until 1984, when the VETER-ANS COMMITTEE selected him.

Reiser, Pistol Pete (outfielder, 1940–52): The Herb SCORE of hitters, Reiser had a lasting effect on baseball despite an abbreviated career. In 1941, his first full season, he led the league in batting average, slugging percentage, doubles, triples, and runs scored while playing a mean center field. His Dodgers won the pennant for the first time in over 20 years, and Reiser finished second in MVP voting. The 22-year-old's promise seemed boundless. Then came the injuries. Reiser played the outfield with such abandon that the walls didn't seem to matter. In 1942, he slammed into the EBBETS FIELD fence with such force that he had to be taken off the field on a stretcher. He did the same in 1947. He weathered broken bones, beanings, and dislocations and came back for more. But the injuries took their toll, and Reiser's stats reflect his deteriorating physical condition. When he retired in 1952, his true legacy was beginning to appear: outfield warning tracks and padded fences.

Rice, Jim (outfielder, 1974–89): At his peak, the Red Sox star was a top offensive performer whose best season came in 1978, when he won the MVP by leading the league in homers, RBIs, hits, triples, and slugging percentage. He even amassed 406 total bases, which hadn't been done since the 1930s. For his career, he slugged 20 or more home runs 11 times, reaching a peak of 46, and drove in at least 100 runs in eight different seasons. After the 1986 season, when he contended for the MVP, his skills eroded quickly. He was finished by 1989, just 18 home runs short of 400. His strength, meanwhile, was near-legendary. Author/umpire Ron Luciano says he once saw Rice break his bat on a checked swing. Rice may not be a first-ballot Hall of Famer, but he'll get in eventually.

Rice, Sam (outfielder, 1915–34): No discussion of Sam Rice can occur without the mention of two significant facts. One is that Rice finished his career just 13 hits shy of the magical 3,000 mark. Hardly anyone paid attention to statistics like that until around the 1940s, but the oversight probably delayed Rice's entrance to the Hall by several years. Rice said that if he'd known what the numbers were, he would have stayed around long enough to get his 3,000th. The second interesting fact concerns the famous catch he may or may not have made to save Game Three of the 1925 World Series for Rice's Washington Senators. On a long drive by Pittsburgh's Earl Smith, Rice caught up with the ball just in front of the fence and caught it as he fell into the stands. Ten seconds later, he emerged with the ball held prominently in his glove, and the umpire signaled out. Pirate players protested that Washington fans had placed the ball in his glove, and Pirates fans in the bleachers offered affidavits to that fact. For the rest of his life, Rice would answer questions about the catch with a smile, saying, "The umpire called him out." He promised to reveal the truth in a letter to be opened after his death. In 1974, the issue was put to rest: In a letter to the curator of the Hall of Fame, he maintained that the umpire had made the right call, writing, "I had a death grip on [the ball]." Of course, these two stories shouldn't overshadow Rice's record as a player, which included 14 seasons batting over .300, a .322 career average, and three World Series appearances despite playing for the usually lowly Senators.

Ripken, Cal (shortstop, 1981–present): A great player, among the greatest at his position of all time. A career-long Oriole, Ripken is a big man—six-four, 215 pounds—which is rare for a position that demands quickness and range. Nevertheless, he is a superb fielder who has excelled because he knows how to position himself against opposing hitters. Also anomalous for a shortstop, Ripken is a slugger; averaging 20 to 30 homers a year, he holds the career record for home runs by a shortstop. He captured a Rookie of the Year Award and two MVPs, played on a World Series champion his third season, and has been elected to the All-Star Game 12 straight years. But what drove him to superstardom was his quest for the all-time record for consecutive games played, which, of course, was held by Lou GEHRIG (*see* 2,130) until Ripken broke it in September 1995—though not without controversy. Even a cursory examination of his statistics showed that Ripken's offensive numbers declined as the streak grew longer, and many in baseball and the media called for him to take a rest. But as the total grew higher, it was too late for that. The streak became bigger than Ripken himself, and to give up when he was so close would have been ridiculous. And in any case, even at his worst, Ripken was and continues to be better than 90 percent of the shortstops around. When he retires, he'll be a lock for COOPERSTOWN.

Rizzuto, Phil "Scooter" (shortstop, 1941–42, 1946–56): Recently selected to the Hall of Fame by a sympathetic VETERANS COMMITTEE, Rizzuto was a good but not great shortstop. In a 13-year career, during which he played on nine Yankee pennant winners, Rizzuto batted .273 with decent speed and good strike zone judgment. He scored 100 runs twice, had a 200-hit season, and won an MVP in 1950 with a tremendous season. Not true Hall of Fame numbers, in my opinion. Since retiring, Rizzuto has spent more than 30 years as a Yankees broadcaster, so some have argued that his Hall of Fame induction is for his total contribution to baseball.

Roberts, Robin (pitcher, 1948–66): A six-time 20-game winner, Roberts employed a pitching style that was characterized by great control, lots of innings pitched, and lots of home runs allowed. He led the league in wins four years in a row, with a high of 28, despite playing for mostly bad teams—and he qualifies as the third-best pitcher in Phillies history, behind Pete ALEXANDER and Steve CARLTON. An early leader in the

Players Association of the 1960s, Roberts was elected to the Hall of Fame in 1976.

Robinson, Brooks (third baseman, 1955–77): The greatest fielder among third basemen of all time, "Hoover" won a record 16 straight Gold Gloves and set career records for assists, putouts, double plays, and fielding average. He played in 15 consecutive All-Star Games and led his Orioles to five division titles and four pennants. At the plate, he possessed medium-range power, usually slugging 20 to 25 homers a year, with batting averages around .270. His only MVP came in 1965, when he led the league in RBIs and smashed 28 homers in addition to his stellar play at the hot corner. His play during the 1970 World Series cemented his reputation as an all-time great when he made a number of spectacular catches and throws to nail disbelieving Cincinnati hitters. He's the most popular player in Baltimore history, where it's heresy to claim that there was ever a better third baseman than Brooks. But let's look at Mike SCHMIDT: 10 Gold Gloves, eight home run titles, three MVPs, 548 career homers, and six division titles. Robinson was a great player. Schmidt was simply better.

Robinson, Frank (outfielder, 1956–76): Two decades after retiring as a player, Robinson works in the front office of the Orioles and maintains a high profile around the game. He was major league baseball's first black manager, and his name often surfaces when executive openings occur. Somehow, though, his stature off the field has overshadowed his greatness on it, for one rarely hears stories about what a great player he was. And he was a great one. The only man to win MVPs in each league, Robinson slugged 30 or more homers 11 times, played in 11 All-Star Games, and led his teams to five pennants. After the 1965 season, the Reds considered Robinson "an old 30" and traded him to the Orioles. Bad move: Robinson tore up the American League to win the Triple Crown with a .316 BA–49 HR–122 RBI season and led Baltimore to its first-ever World Series victory. He finished his career with 586 home runs, fourth on the all-time list.

Robinson, Jackie (infielder, 1945–56 [including Negro leagues]): Jackie Robinson was a true American hero who had a greater impact on baseball—and on society—than any other player in history. The story of his signing has become part of American folklore and is recounted briefly here: When Dodgers general manager Branch RICKEY went looking for the "right kind of man" to break major league baseball's 60-year-old COLOR BARRIER, he selected Robinson, a UCLA-educated Army officer. Rickey knew the story of how Robinson had refused to bow to the military's Jim Crow laws and was court-martialed for insubordination—a trumped-up charge of which he was acquitted. In 1945, while a member of the NEGRO LEAGUES' KANSAS CITY MONARCHS, Rickey offered the shocked Robinson a minor league contract. During the signing meeting, Rickey informed Robinson that opposing teams and many fans would resist the attempt to integrate the game, but that Robinson was not to retaliate against any of the taunts, beanballs, and spikings he would inevitably face, lest Robinson give baseball's racist powers any reason to halt the "great experiment." To this, Robinson reportedly asked Rickey, "Are you looking for a man without the guts to fight back?" Shouted Rickey: "I want someone with guts enough *not* to fight back!" And so against the teeth of criticism from league officials, opposing players, and even mainstream publications such as *The SPORTING NEWS*, Robinson's journey began. In 1946 with the Dodgers' Triple-A farm club in Montreal, Robinson dominated the league. Then in 1947 in Brooklyn, he won baseball's first Rookie of the Year Award despite playing first base for the first time in his life. Robinson basically repeated his 1947 performance in 1948, but by 1949, with all restraints lifted, he broke loose. By that time, black players had joined other major league clubs, and the "experiment" was deemed a success. Robinson enjoyed his greatest season, leading the league in batting and stolen bases, playing a stellar second base, helping his team to the World Series, and winning the MVP. Aside from integrating the game, Robinson also helped bring to baseball a new level of excitement. He would dance and dart off the base, trying to rattle the pitcher; he'd go from first to third on an infield hit; he'd steal home—the kind of baseball that had existed in the Negro leagues but that most major league fans and players hadn't seen since the days of COBB and SPEAKER. To the Dodgers, meanwhile, Robinson brought a winning attitude. Brooklyn had finished a close second or third in four of the previous five seasons before Robinson arrived. With Robinson as their catalyst, however, the Dodgers captured six pennants in 10 years as well as Brooklyn's only World Series victory. He called it quits prior to the 1957 season at the age of 36, but even in retirement, he couldn't avoid the spotlight: Not when he publicly campaigned for Richard Nixon's presidential bid in 1960. Not when he received criticism for his vocal opposition to the war in Vietnam. Not when his son put him on the front pages again after being arrested on a drug charge in 1968, after which Robinson became a tireless spokesman against drug abuse. And not when he denounced major league baseball for its lack of black baseball managers and executives. On October 24, 1972, the diabetic Robinson suffered a heart attack and died at his home in Connecticut. Close friends suggested that the constant pressure and responsibility of being a cultural icon conspired to take his life away at the age of 53. What Robinson did for baseball can be easily documented. What he did for society at large is still being measured. Eric F. Goldman's study of the postwar period, *The Crucial Decade*, acknowledges the debt owed to Robinson: "Jackie Robinson's triumph, so widely publicized and admired, enormously furthered acceptance for the Negro in many fields of American life. . . . [He] was the flashing symbol of an era in the national life when, for all minority groups, for all lower-status Americans, the social and economic walls were coming tumbling down." Baseball's color barrier, then, wasn't the only wall Robinson helped destroy.

Robinson, Wilbert "Uncle Robby" (catcher, 1886–1902; manager, 1902, 1914–31): A Hall of Famer, Robinson led the Brooklyn Dodgers to their first two 20th-century pennants. The rotund and affable manager was so popular in Brooklyn that the team was even named the "Robins" in his honor for much of his career.

Rose, Pete "Charlie Hustle" (infielder/outfielder, 1963–86; manager, 1984–89): It's impossible to talk about Rose without mentioning the scandal that ended his career. But in fairness to him, let's look at his on-field performance first, because the bottom line of his career is that he helped his teams win. He could play just about any position on the field, whatever was needed. He batted from both sides of the plate, so he was never at a platoon disadvantage. He never got hurt. And he always ran out every ground ball, every pop-up, even every base on balls. The results are phenomenal: three batting titles and 10 200-hit seasons, while leading the league variously in runs (four times), hits (seven times), and doubles (five times). In terms of career records, the numbers are equally amazing. He is baseball's all-time leader in hits (4,256), games (3,562), and at bats (14,053), and he is among the top 10 in runs, doubles, and total bases. But baseball isn't just about numbers; it's about winning, and Rose was hardly deficient in that area, either. From 1970 through 1976, his "BIG RED MACHINE" captured five division titles, four pennants, and two championships. After he joined the Phillies as a million-dollar free agent in 1979, it took only one year for the team to win its first-ever World Series. The 1983 team also won the pennant, but lost the Series. In 1984, he rejoined the Reds as a player-manager, where he was less successful on the field and where his real troubles began. Actually, the commissioner's office had known about Rose's problem—gambling—since around 1970, but did nothing about it. In 1989, however, assisted by an IRS investigation into income tax evasion against Rose, commissioner Bart GIAMATTI hired a special prosecutor to examine charges that Rose was not only a compulsive gambler who consorted with known bookmakers and drug dealers but, more important for baseball's sake, that Rose had bet on baseball games, including games his own team had played. Regardless of the fact that Rose was accused of betting on his teams to *win* (as opposed to the BLACK SOX, who threw the World Series in exchange for money from gamblers), such actions violated one of baseball's most sacrosanct policies. Throughout the proceedings (and to this day), Rose steadfastly denied he ever bet on baseball. During the tumultuous summer of 1989, Rose filed suit against the commissioner seeking to stop the investigation on various legal grounds. Rose was roundly criticized in the press for dragging out the ordeal, and in August, he agreed to a settlement: He would accept a lifetime ban from baseball if the agreement signed by both Rose and Giamatti would make no mention of Rose's alleged baseball gambling. Then Rose could apply for reinstatement after one year. However, Rose's troubles continued in 1990 as he pleaded guilty to tax evasion and served five months in an Illinois federal prison. He has been trying to rehabilitate his image with the public in order to gain acceptance to the Hall of Fame, from which he is now barred. He has admitted to having a "gambling disorder," and he appears frequently on TV shopping shows hawking signed memorabilia. All of which brings up the question of whether he *has* to prove anything more to us. Although he was an average *talent*, he holds several important career records, and he won a lot of ball games for his teams. Rose himself wants us to look at the record when we're considering him for the Hall. On that basis, of course, he deserves immediate induction. The Hall is filled with rapscallions and racists, dirty players and greedy executives who unscrupulously exploited their employees. Nothing Rose ever did, for example, was as shameful as the deeds of Kenesaw Mountain LANDIS, "Cap" ANSON, and the many others in the Hall who barred an entire race from playing in the majors. On the other hand, Rose signed an agreement barring himself from the game, and it is ludicrous to enshrine a man who isn't even allowed to connect himself with major league baseball. If we do induct Rose, what kind of example are we setting for future generations? It's a tough issue, one with no simple answer.

Rusie, Amos (pitcher, 1889–95, 1897–98, 1901): Rusie had a tremendous, legendary effect on the game of baseball: He was partially responsible for the pitching mound being moved from 50 feet to its current distance of 60 feet 6 inches from home plate in 1893. Nicknamed "The Hoosier Thunderbolt," Rusie pitched with such blazing speed that his catcher even had to put a thin sheet of lead in his catching mitt to protect his hand. Rusie won 30-plus games four years in a row for the Giants, led the league in a variety of categories throughout his career, and became the standard to which all fastballers were measured for decades after his retirement.

Ruth, Babe (pitcher/outfielder, 1914–35): There seems to be a growing movement these days to assert that Babe Ruth was *not* the greatest ballplayer of all time. Such an idea is patently ridiculous. Ruth was easily the greatest on several different levels. First, he had a tremendous effect on the game by almost single-handedly reintroducing the home run as an offensive weapon. Until Ruth came along, baseball games were played and won with singles, stolen bases, the hit-and-run, and occasional extra-base hits. By showing the baseball world that an uppercut swing could produce home runs on a regular basis, Ruth changed the sport forever. And it wasn't because of a new "RABBIT BALL," as some revisionists have claimed; he did it with the same "dead" ball as was already being used (*see also* DEAD BALL ERA, LIVELY BALL ERA). Ruth deserves the title of "baseball's greatest" on a second level as well: that of a cultural icon. He was American sports' most famous athlete, known and loved by children and adults everywhere. Around the globe, Ruth *was* America, and stories have been told of Japanese soldiers during World War II shouting epithets about Babe Ruth to the Americans, trying to anger them. Additionally, Ruth was the highest-paid athlete in the world, reaching a peak of $80,000 per season at the beginning of the Depression—a sum that exceeded the president's salary, which prompted Ruth to say, "Why not? I had a better year than he did." Third, Ruth dominated the game on the field to an unbelievable extent. His entry in the BASEBALL ENCYCLO-PEDIA is almost entirely boldface (signifying a league-leading performance). I won't recount all his totals, but here's a few: 12 times leading the league in homers, six times in RBIs, eight in runs scored, 12 in slugging percentage, and so on. He is responsible for six of the top 10 offensive seasons of all time. And he didn't do all of this in a vacuum, either. He led his teams to 10 pennants, both as an outfielder and a pitcher. Speaking of pitching, Ruth was also the best pitcher in the league before he shifted to the outfield in 1919. He led the league in ERA, shutouts, and complete games at various times during his two 20-win seasons in 1916 and 1917. All of this, however, isn't enough for some people. Some argue for Willie MAYS as baseball's greatest player because Mays could do it all: hit, hit for power, run, field, and throw. But baseball isn't about specific skills; it's about *creating runs* for your team, and Ruth did more of that than anyone—just look at the numbers. And anyway, the Bambino was a fine defensive player for much of his career, and in the beginning, he was an aggressive, if often reckless, baserunner. When you factor in his pitching, it's no contest as to who was greater. Ruth's teams won pennants, he dominated the game, and he rewrote history. If he's not the greatest, then no one can claim that honor.

Ryan, Nolan (pitcher, 1966, 1968–93): The Babe RUTH of strikeout pitchers, Ryan is a biological marvel. No one in major league history ever threw harder—101 mph was his top measured speed—or longer—27 major league seasons—than Ryan. He struck out (5,714) and walked (2,795) more batters than anyone, he allowed the fewest hits per nine innings (6.55) ever, he holds the major league record with 383 strikeouts in one season, and he led the league in those categories throughout his career with the Mets, Angels, Astros, and Rangers. He also tossed a major league–record seven no-hitters, the last two when he was over 40 years old. He attributed his success to excellent conditioning, which kept him injury-free almost throughout his career. He finished with 324 wins (tied for 12th all-time) and 292 losses (third). And when he comes up for induction to the Hall of Fame in 1999, he may be the first-ever unanimous inductee.

Sandberg, Ryne (second baseman, 1981–94): Despite starting his career as a third baseman, Sandberg has earned the distinction of being one of the five best second basemen of all time. He was the complete ballplaying package, combining power, speed, fielding skills, strike zone judgment, and leadership like no second sacker before him except Joe MORGAN. Sandberg captured nine Gold Gloves and an MVP, and he was the only second baseman other than Rogers HORNSBY to win a home run title. He also led his Cubs to division titles in 1984 and 1989, their only postseason action since World War II. Playing home games in WRIGLEY FIELD inflated his batting totals somewhat but didn't diminish his greatness. He shocked the baseball world in June 1994 by announcing his sudden and immediate retirement, claiming that injuries and age had taken their toll and he couldn't continue to collect a paycheck when he considered himself a subpar ballplayer. A year and a half later, Sandberg changed his mind and announced his unretirement to rejoin the Cubs, therefore postponing for several years his inevitable Hall of Fame induction party.

Santo, Ron (third baseman, 1960–74): The greatest third baseman who is eligible but is not in the Hall of Fame, Santo was perhaps the top fielder in his day other than Brooks ROBINSON—and Santo possessed the home run sock Robinson lacked. Santo had excellent strike zone judgment and led the league in walks four times while slugging 17 to 33 home runs for 13 straight seasons—all while diagnosed with diabetes, which he kept secret from the public during much of his career. Playing mostly with the lowly Cubs, Santo never made it to the postseason, never won an MVP, and never led the league in any major category—facts that Hall of Fame voters have held against him.

Schmidt, Mike (third baseman, 1972–89): The greatest third baseman of all time and a consummate gentleman on and off the field, Schmidt nonetheless enjoyed a tumultuous relationship with his "fans" in Philadelphia, where he played his entire career. Blamed for Philadelphia's playoff losses in 1976, 1977, and 1978, Schmidt was regularly booed even while winning his eight home run championships and three MVP Awards. In fact, on the very day the club announced that fans had voted him the Greatest Philly Ever, the boo-birds came out when Schmidt made a second-inning error. Still, he turned in amazing—if unappreciated—performances throughout his 18-year career. Defensively, he won 10 Gold Gloves and holds the single-season record for assists by a third baseman. Offensively, he smashed 548 career homers, including 30 or more 13 times, and led the league in slugging percentage five times and in RBIs four. Additionally, he led his Phillies to the postseason six times and delivered the club's only World Series victory in 1980. Those fans who still believe Brooks ROB-INSON or Pie TRAYNOR or anyone else is baseball's greatest third baseman are ignoring mountains of evidence to the contrary.

Score, Herb (pitcher, 1955–62): For two seasons in the mid-1950s, Score was perhaps the top pitcher in baseball, a left-handed fireballer who led the league in strikeouts his first two years while winning 16 and 20 games with the Indians. But in early 1957, a line drive off the bat of Yankees' Gil McDougald changed everything. It struck Score in the face and ended his season after only five games. He tried pitching again the following year, but lasted only 12 ineffective games. And though he hung on until 1962, the promising talent of his first two seasons appeared only in brief flashes. Since retirement, he has remained in the game by working as Cleveland's play-by-play broadcaster.

Seaver, Tom (pitcher, 1967–86): "Tom Terrific" was, above all, a winner. In his rookie season, 1967, he recorded a 16–13 won/loss mark with a Mets team that lost 101 games. Two years later, his 25 wins led the "AMAZIN' METS" to their first and most improbable World Series title and earned him his first of three Cy Young Awards. Atypical of a pitcher with his control, he notched 200 or more strikeouts for nine straight seasons and holds the National League record with 19 whiffs in a single game. Throughout the 1970s, Seaver averaged 18 wins per year and pitched mostly .600 ball on mostly sub-.500 teams. Traded to the Reds in midseason 1977, he still won 21 games and, a year later, led the Pete ROSE–less Reds to the division title. He returned to the Mets in 1983, ostensibly to finish out his career, but a clerical error placed him on waivers, and he ended up with the White Sox a year later. He played three seasons in the AL, and on the same day Rod CAREW got his 3,000th hit, Seaver recorded his 300th victory in YANKEE STADIUM, just a few miles from where his career began. Elected to the Hall of Fame on his first try in 1992, Seaver remains a true gentleman, admired by fans, other players, and the media.

Sewell, Joe (shortstop, 1920–33): Sewell took over the Indians' shortstop duties following the death of Ray CHAPMAN in 1920 and batted .329 over 22 games to help Cleveland win a closely contested pennant race. He basically repeated that performance for the 1921 season, but in 1922, he "slumped" to .299 with 20 strikeouts. He would never strike out as often again, for Sewell was the king of the contact hitters. During his career, he struck out 114 times, never reaching double figures in a season from 1925 until his retirement in 1933. He had a lifetime batting average of .312, great defensive skills, and doubles power, but it was his ability to make contact that made him famous and put him into the Hall of Fame in 1977.

Simmons, Al (outfielder, 1924–43): "I hated pitchers," said Simmons after his career was over, and it showed. He won two batting titles, smacked 253 hits to set an all-time single-season record for right-handed batters, drove in 100-plus runs—with a high of 165—for the first 11 seasons of his career, and batted cleanup on the 1929–31 Athletics that won three American League pennants and is widely recognized as one of the most dominant teams in history. They called Simmons "Bucketfoot Al" because when he swung the bat, his left foot stepped so much toward third base that it looked as if it was headed toward the water bucket at the end of the bench. On a lesser hitter, such a batting motion would have indicated that he was afraid of the pitcher; it would have been a sure ticket to the minors. With Simmons, it was his ticket to the Hall of Fame.

Sisler, George (first baseman, 1915–22, 1924–30): By 1922, Sisler's star was on the rise. After batting .407 and .420 to win two batting titles, Sisler was the second-best player in the American League, next to Babe RUTH. He was baseball's finest fielder at first base, he had enough speed to lead the league in steals three times, and he nearly brought his St. Louis Browns their first pennant. Then fate intervened: a sinus infection damaged Sisler's optic nerves, forcing him to miss the 1923 season and permanently affecting his skills. He came back for 1924, but he wasn't the same. According to author/statistician Bill JAMES, Sisler before the injury was on track to finish his career with 4,000 hits and a .362 career average. After the injury, Sisler put together some fine if undistinguished seasons and still tallied around 2,800 hits and a .340 average. Although the stats look good by today's standards, even Sisler said, "I didn't consider that real good hitting." As James has pointed out, a strong case can be made that, in terms of peak performance, Sisler was the greatest first baseman of all time. In fact, you could make a pretty good all-star team of legitimately great players whose careers were cut dramatically short by injury or disability. KOUFAX, DEAN, GREENBERG, and Sisler would be the big stars.

Slaughter, Enos "Country" (outfielder, 1938–59): A hustling outfielder with above-average batting skills, Slaughter achieved baseball immortality during 10 seconds of the 1946 World Series. With the score tied and two outs in the bottom of the eighth inning of Game Seven, the Cardinals' Slaughter stood on first base. Harry Walker smashed a single to left center as Slaughter took off running. After a long run, center fielder Dom DiMAGGIO retrieved the ball and threw to shortstop Johnny Pesky. Slaughter should have stopped at third, but he ran through a stop sign from his coach and headed for home. According to the actual game film, Pesky turned and fired to the plate with only a split second of hesitation, but the throw was just up the line and Slaughter slid in safely with the run that put the Cards ahead to stay. After the game, news stories hailed Slaughter as a hero. A few days later, however, Pesky got blamed for the loss as writers, fans, and other observers began to claim that he had held on to the ball too long before throwing it. While the play would forever brand Pesky as a goat, Slaughter got the opposite treatment: lifetime adulation and Hall of Fame induction.

Smith, Lee (pitcher, 1980–present): Tall and intimidating, with a frightening glare and 95 mph fastball, Smith is a rarity: a top closer who avoided the plague of reliever burnout. Most closers last only a few years at the top; Smith spent more than a decade among the league's best. That alone should earn him induction to the Hall of Fame. His all-time record 434 saves (through 1994) for the Cubs, Cardinals, Red Sox, Orioles, and Angels are just icing on the cake.

Smith, Ozzie (shortstop, 1978–present): Perhaps the greatest fielding shortstop of all time, Smith is also one of baseball's most popular players. He plays the game the way purists believe it should be played: with attention paid to the small but important things such as fielding, baserunning, bunting, contact hitting, hitting behind the runners, and so forth. Smith is, in fact, a modern-day Rabbit MARANVILLE with better batting skills. (Their statistics are actually pretty similar, but Maranville played much of his career when batting averages were inflated, which means Rabbit's .258 career average would be about .230 today.) The call Ozzie "The Wizard of Ahs," and his amazing plays for the Cardinals and Padres were a staple of highlight shows throughout the 1980s and into the 1990s. Forty-one years old as the 1996 season approaches, Smith has lost a few steps, but he has kept himself in such good shape that he can still play.

Snider, Duke (outfielder, 1947–64): The third member of the famed "WILLIE, MICKEY, OR THE DUKE?" power-hitting, great-fielding triumvirate that patrolled center field for the three New York teams during the 1950s, Snider is not as famous as his illustrious colleagues. But consider this: During the 1950s, nobody hit more homers or drove in more runs than Snider. He smacked 40-plus home runs five straight years, a feat no other National Leaguer has ever accomplished, and he had 90 or more RBIs in nine consecutive seasons. As a member of the Dodgers, first in Brooklyn, then in L.A., Snider led his teams to eight World Series and performed brilliantly throughout. He is the NL's lifetime leader in Series homers and RBIs, and he is sixth overall in total bases (as well as third in strikeouts). He finished his career with 407 career homers, a final tally some say was helped by being the only left-handed hitter in the Dodgers' right-handed offensive juggernaut—which included Roy CAMPANELLA, Jackie ROBINSON, Pee Wee REESE, Gil Hodges, and Carl Furillo—and teams hesitated to pitch lefties against them. Nonetheless, you have to be able to hit those pitches. Many modern fans believe Snider would often take himself out of games when lefties did pitch. But they should look at Snider's yearly games played totals: from 1949 to 1956, he never missed more than 10 games per year.

Spahn, Warren (pitcher, 1942, 1946–65): Basically the Hank AARON of pitchers, Spahn, like Aaron, had only a few years in which he was considered baseball's very best at his position. But, also like Aaron, his sheer number of excellent seasons is absolutely staggering. Because of World War II, Spahn didn't win his first game until the age of 25, but once he got on a roll, he was unstoppable. From 1946 through 1963 (18 seasons), he won 20 games 13 times, led the league in at least one major category (wins, ERA, strikeouts) 13 times and made the All-Star team 15 times. His career totals are phenomenal: 363 victories, the most by any left-hander, and 13 20-win seasons, which ties the NL record held by Christy MATHEWSON and is only one fewer than Steve CARLTON, Tom SEAVER, and Roger CLEMENS combined. During the Braves' pennant-winning 1948 campaign, Spahn joined fellow 20-game winner Johnny Sain in an otherwise poor rotation, causing fans to cry, "Spahn and Sain and pray for rain." By 1957, when the Braves made it back to the World Series, Sain was retired and Spahn was 36, which meant he had only six more good years left in him. Three years after that, Spahn pitched a no-hitter, and a year later, at the age of 40, he tossed another one. And when he retired from major league baseball after 1965, he pitched two more seasons in the minors. He finally sat still long enough for the Hall of Fame to induct him in 1973.

Speaker, Tris (outfielder, 1907–28): Speaker combined power, speed, smarts, and fielding skills like almost no one before or since. "The Grey Eagle" revolutionized the center field position by playing so close to second base that he sometimes participated in infield double plays and received catcher throws on steal attempts. He reasoned that playing shallow could allow him to cut off balls hit in front of him and his blazing speed could catch up with balls hit over his head. Of course, he got away with the strategy because he played most of his career during the DEAD BALL ERA, when few batters could regularly hit a ball 400 feet. Speaker, in fact, was one of those few.

Though he only smacked 117 homers during his career, he did slug an all-time record 792 doubles—many of which undoubtedly would have been homers if he'd played during the 1930s. He won only a single batting title because he played when COBB and then SISLER were at their peaks, but his career average is a phenomenal .345 and he collected 3,514 hits. Another great accomplishment was that he player-managed Cleveland to the 1920 pennant while batting .388 with a league-leading 50 doubles and a .483 on-base percentage (which, amazingly, didn't lead the league). In the late 1920s, however, he was involved in a scandal that nearly got him kicked out of baseball. As recounted in Fred LIEB's book *Baseball as I Have Known It*, Speaker, Ty COBB, and Joe Wood were implicated in a plot to fix a game between Speaker's Indians and Cobb's Tigers in 1919. The prime evidence against them was a letter by Wood to Detroit pitcher Dutch Leonard strongly suggesting that Cleveland had thrown a ball game that would have helped Detroit capture second place ahead of New York. But when commissioner Kenesaw Mountain LANDIS held a hearing to settle the charges, Leonard refused to appear, and Landis had no choice but to acquit Cobb, Speaker, and Wood. Hall of Fame voters had all but forgotten the taint by 1937 and elected Speaker by acclamation.

Stargell, Willie "Pops" (outfielder/first baseman, 1962–82): A beloved man and fan favorite, Stargell slugged his way into the Hall of Fame. In many National League ballparks, there is a spot somewhere in the outfield seats, usually 470 feet or more from home plate, where Stargell parked one. And he's the only man ever to hit a ball out of DODGER STADIUM, which he did twice. During his greatest offensive season in 1973, he led the league in doubles, homers, RBIs, and slugging percentage. But his greatest *overall* season came in 1979, when Stargell captained his Pirates to the World Series with a 32-homer, 82-RBI season that captured for him the regular season, LCS, and World Series MVP trophies. He retired with career totals of 475 homers and 1,540 RBIs, and he was elected to the Hall of Fame in 1988.

Staub, Rusty (outfielder, 1963–85): An impressive hitter who played much of his career in terrible hitters' parks, Staub amassed 2,716 hits and 1,466 RBIs over his 23-year career with the Astros, Expos, Mets, and Tigers. He was a fan favorite wherever he went and earned the nickname "Le Grande Orange" in French-speaking Montreal—"the big redhead," which wasn't too far off, since he must have weighed 240 when he retired. During his final seasons, he specialized in pinch-hitting and became one of the few players to notch 100 career pinch hits. He now operates a restaurant in New York City.

Stearnes, Norman "Turkey" (outfielder, Negro leagues, 1921–41): A great outfielder and slugger, Stearnes is one of many NEGRO LEAGUES greats who aren't in the Hall of Fame but would undoubtedly be if they'd been born white or years later. Research has found that Stearnes ranks in Negro league annals among the top home run hitters of all time, behind Josh GIBSON but ahead of other sluggers such as Oscar CHARLESTON and Mule Suttles. But Stearnes says he never counted his long-balls: "I remember one year, my first season with Detroit, 1923. I think I hit about 50-some. But after I was up here about a year, I hit so many that that's the reason I didn't count them." Why hasn't the Hall of Fame recognized him? Probably because he wasn't colorful like Gibson or "Cool Papa" BELL or Satchel PAIGE. There are no stories about Stearnes scoring from second on a ground out or hitting a 650-foot home run out of YANKEE STADIUM. Bell always believed Stearnes belonged in the shrine: "If they don't put Turkey Stearnes in," he once said, "they shouldn't put *anybody* in." Stearnes died in 1979.

Stengel, Casey (outfielder, 1912–25; manager, 1934–65): Through six decades in baseball, Stengel was known as both

clown and genius, prankster and innovator. During his playing days, he once doffed his cap to let a bird fly out. Another
time, he disappeared into an outfield drainage hole, only to
reappear in time to make a play. He talked in a mangled English known as STENGELESE that delighted and confused all
around him. When he became a major league manager, he
was saddled with lowly teams in Boston and Brooklyn, and he
never got out of fifth place with those clubs. But when George
WEISS was named the Yankees' general manager, one of his
first moves was to hire Stengel—prompting scoffs and chuck-
les among baseball men. Stengel, meanwhile, set out to prove
everybody wrong. He weaved his magic to earn 10 pennants
in 12 seasons, and it wasn't just the talent of the players that
did it. Stengel had to deal with injuries and egos and
mediocre-to-good pitching. Despite the appearance of a be-
fuddled old man, he was always in total control of his team.
But he couldn't control his owners, and the 1960 pennant
would prove to be his last. "I was fired," he told reporters.
"I'll never make the mistake of being 70 years old again." In
a move typical of the corporate Yankees, they fired Weiss for
the same reason. The two joined forces in 1962 with the expansion Mets, with Stengel as its rumpled field leader. The
72-year-old had the perfect demeanor to sit through four consecutive dreadful seasons: patient, intelligent, grandfatherly,
and above all, possessing a good sense of humor. A year after
his retirement, the Hall of Fame inducted him, and Stengel
then became a gracious and lovable ambassador for the game
until his death in 1975. Author Robert Creamer wrote his definitive biography, *Stengel: His Life and Times.*

Terry, "Memphis Bill" (first baseman, 1923–36): The last National Leaguer to hit .400, Terry starred for the New York
Giants during the time of McGRAW, OTT, HUBBELL, and
Frisch. He never batted under .300 for a full season, and he
holds the NL record for hits with 254 during his .401 season in
1930. He took over the reins of the Giants when John McGraw
retired in 1932 and guided them to two pennants as a player-

manager and another just from the dugout. Also a graceful fielder, Terry finished his career with a .341 average en route to Hall of Fame induction in 1954. Although you can discount Terry's .400 season because the entire National League batted .300 that season, you can't discount it by much. Hitting 100 points above the league average is still an impressive feat; how often does a player bat .365 these days? Occasionally, sure—but not every year.

Thomas, Frank "The Big Hurt" (first baseman, 1990– present): Winner of the 1993 and 1994 MVP Awards, Frank Thomas is, quite simply, baseball's best pure power hitter since Ted WILLIAMS and Mickey MANTLE. That may sound like hype, but it's supported by evidence. Let's compare him to some other contenders. He hits for a better average than Reggie JACKSON, Mike SCHMIDT, or Harmon KILLEBREW. He has better strike zone judgment than Frank ROBINSON, Jim RICE, or Willie MAYS. And he hits home runs longer, higher, and more frequently than Dale MURPHY, Dave WINFIELD, or Barry BONDS. He's not a great fielder and he's not fast, but with the wood in his hands, there's nobody better. The only question is, how long can he keep it up? Big men like Thomas generally don't have long careers; their bodies break down earlier than usual. I'm definitely rooting for him, because not only is he an exciting player, but he's also a polite, good-hearted human being. Baseball needs more like him.

Thompson, Sam (outfielder, 1885–98, 1906): Thompson was so good that the Tigers coaxed him out of retirement to play the final eight games of the 1906 season when he was 46 years old. It didn't matter—Detroit still finished sixth. At his peak, however, Big Sam was one of the most feared players in the National League, a slugging outfielder who starred for the Detroit and Philadelphia clubs. Over his 15-year career, Thompson batted .331, slugged .505, and drove in 1,299 runs in just 1,407 games—the highest ratio of RBIs to games played of all time. And his 127 career home runs ranked him second on the all-time list, behind Roger Connor, until Babe RUTH came along. He was elected to the Hall of Fame in 1974.

Thomson, Bobby (outfielder, 1946–60): Thomson gained lasting fame because of a 280-foot line drive that happened to win the 1951 pennant for the Giants. The "SHOT HEARD 'ROUND THE WORLD," as it came to be called, culminated the Giants' furious pennant chase against the Dodgers, which couldn't have been won without Thomson's regular-season contributions: He batted .293, drove in 101 runs, and smacked a career high 32 homers. Though mostly remembered for that one moment, Thomson was a six-year veteran of the big leagues by then, a power-hitting outfielder who had already appeared in two All-Star Games. After 1951, Thomson enjoyed a productive if unspectacular career, but he never made it back to the postseason—although he came close. He was traded from the Giants before the 1954 season, missing out on New York's pennant that year. And in 1957, he was dealt by the Braves in midseason as Milwaukee went on to capture that pennant. Thomson's second major claim to fame occurred involuntarily: In 1954, he broke his leg at the beginning of the year, opening a spot on the Braves roster for Hank AARON. Thomson isn't in the Hall of Fame, but the bat he used to beat the Dodgers is.

Tinker, Joe (shortstop, 1902–16): Elevated to immortality (and the Hall of Fame) by Franklin P. Adams's famous poem "BASEBALL'S SAD LEXICON" celebrating the TINKER TO EVERS TO CHANCE double play combination, Tinker was a capable hitter and base stealer who impressed with fabulous defense. Except for Honus WAGNER, Tinker may have been the best defensive shortstop of his day. He played on four Cubs pennant winners, including the 1906 team that won an all-time record 116 games. And while neither his hitting nor fielding statistics look formidable by today's standards, we have to remember that he played in an entirely different period. For one thing, league averages back then hovered around .245, which makes Tinker's .262 average look like .285 today—good for a shortstop. Also, fielding hadn't progressed to where it is now, so Tinker's career fielding average of .938 was an impressive total for his time. In addition, he was respected enough to be named player-manager for the last four years of his career. I don't think any of this qualifies him for the Hall of Fame, but he's not the worst player in there.

Torriente, Cristobal (outfielder, Negro leagues, 1914–32): Cuban-born and heavily muscled, Torriente was a slugger who starred on half a dozen NEGRO LEAGUES clubs. He was good enough in 1918 to force the great Oscar CHARLESTON from center field to left on the famed American Giants club. A teammate said Torriente would have been signed by the New York Giants if it weren't for his hair. "He was a light brown," said Jelly Gardner, "and he would have gone up to the major leagues, but he had real rough hair." A number of light-skinned Negro league players, in fact, played in the majors while the COLOR LINE was still in place, most of them of Latin origin, including two-time ERA leader Dolf Luque and 17-year veteran catcher Mike Gonzalez.

Traynor, Pie (third baseman, 1920–37): Regarded as the greatest third baseman of all time many years ago, Traynor batted .320 with doubles and triples power through 17 years with Pittsburgh. He drove in 100 runs seven times and played on two pennant winners. Defensively, he had great range and a good arm and was considered the top fielder at his position. Certainly, Traynor's batting totals lose some impressiveness, since he played at a time when all hitting statistics were inflated. And today, with SCHMIDT, MATHEWS, BRETT, ROBINSON, SANTO, and BOGGS in the historical picture, Traynor isn't even in the top five all-time at the position. Until those guys came along, however, Traynor was considered number one, and that deserves respect.

Uecker, Bob (catcher, 1962–67; broadcaster): "Anybody with ability can play in the big leagues," says Uecker. "But to be able to trick people year in and year out the way I did, I think that's a much greater feat." The lifetime .200 hitter for the Braves and Cardinals, known to a generation as "Mr. Baseball" from beer commercials, has parlayed his great sense of humor into a successful broadcasting career for the Milwaukee Brewers. He's even gotten a few acting jobs, his most famous as the dad in the sitcom *Mr. Belvedere*, which, as a reviewer also noted about Uecker's autobiography, was every bit as good as his playing career.

Vance, Dazzy (pitcher, 1915, 1918, 1922–35): A 1955 Hall of Fame inductee, Vance's oft-told life story is a tribute to perseverance. In the minors, he'd injured his arm while pitching five complete games in seven days. When he came up to the majors in 1915, he went 0–4 and allowed 47 baserunners in 30⅔ innings. Another trial in 1918 ended with similar lack of success. Four years later, Dodgers manager Wilbert ROBINSON gave him another look, and this time Vance stayed. Beginning in 1922, when he was 31, until the early 1930s, Vance was one of the best pitchers in the game. With a blazing fastball— hence his nickname—he notched three 20-win seasons and captured a record seven consecutive strikeout crowns and three ERA titles. He also tossed a one-hitter and no-hitter in consecutive games. In 1924, his best season, he went 28–6 with 30 complete games, 262 strikeouts, and a 2.16 ERA—all league-leading totals—only to see his Dodgers lose the pennant by 1½ games to the Giants. In MVP voting that season, Vance beat out more than a dozen other future Hall of Famers, including Rogers HORNSBY, who hit .424 with power, and Frankie Frisch, who sparked New York's pennant victory. An impressive accomplishment.

Vander Meer, Johnny (pitcher, 1937–51): "The Dutch Master" wasn't a great pitcher. His top win total was 18, he only won in double figures six times, and he finished his career with a record of 119 wins and 121 losses. He also walked 100-plus batters six times. But for two games in 1938, Vander Meer was literally unhittable, and therein lies his fame. On June 11, the Reds pitcher shut down the Boston Braves without allowing a hit, and he came back four days later to no-hit the Brooklyn Dodgers in the first night game ever at EBBETS FIELD. This, to me, is the one *potentially* breakable record that never will be broken. By comparison, some records aren't even *potentially* breakable because the game has changed so much. For example, all of "Cy" YOUNG's marks, including his 511 career victories and 749 complete games, are way out of reach, as is Ed WALSH's 20th-century record for innings pitched in a single season, 464. They pitched in the DEAD BALL ERA, when pitchers could conserve their pitching energy knowing home runs were rare. Babe RUTH's superhuman .847 slugging percentage is equally anomalous because no one has come within 100 points of the mark since the 1930s, when slugging totals were at an all-time high. But Vander Meer's record for consecutive no-hitters will stand forever because a person would have to pitch *three* straight no-nos—a feat which is possible but absolutely improbable.

Vaughan, Arky (shortstop, 1932–43, 1947–48): one of the 10 best shortstops of all time, Vaughan was a perennial .300 hitter with medium-range power and good fielding skills, and he played on nine straight All-Star teams while with the Pirates and Dodgers. He was also a man of great integrity and loyalty. In 1943, he threatened retirement in midseason to protest a shameful suspension meted out by manager Leo DUROCHER against one of his teammates. At the end of that season, despite superb offensive statistics, Vaughan did retire because he didn't want to play for Durocher anymore. He came back three years later, when Durocher was suspended by the league, and played well in a part-time role, finally making it to his first World Series. He drowned in a boating accident in 1952 and was elected to the Hall of Fame in 1985.

Waddell, Rube (pitcher, 1897–1910): A stellar talent, Waddell could have been one of the greats. Branch RICKEY once said, "When Waddell had control—and some sleep—he was unbeatable." He had a blazing fastball and led the league in strikeouts six straight seasons—with a high of 349, which was 110 more than the second-place finisher. His greatest season was 1905, when he led the league with 27 wins, 287 strikeouts, and a 1.48 ERA. Except for the strikeout totals, however, his other seasons were good but not great; he won 20 four times, but because it was an era of three-man pitching staffs, 20 wins was not a standard for great pitching as it is today. Waddell's problem, as Branch Rickey implied, was that he was absolutely unreliable, and he may have been developmentally disabled in addition to alcoholic. Making it to the ballpark was always a challenge. Being in condition to pitch was another. Opposing players and managers used to try to break his concentration by giving him little toys. He loved to chase fire engines. He played marbles with kids. He drank. After years of putting up with him, A's manager Connie MACK finally got fed up with him and shipped him to baseball Siberia, the St. Louis Browns. After a couple of undistinguished seasons with the Browns, Waddell died in 1914 from tuberculosis, which he contracted while trying to help residents of a Kentucky town brace against a flood. He was elected to the Hall of Fame in 1946 by an apparently sympathetic Old-Timers Committee. The voters must have based their judgment on Waddell's talent alone, rather than his production, which was so-so; Dave McNALLY had as good a career:

	W	L	W%	ERA	20-win seasons	Best season
Waddell	193	143	.574	2.16	4	27–10, 1.48 ERA, 287 Ks
McNally	184	119	.607	3.24	4	22–10, 1.95 ERA, 202 Ks

The only real difference between the two is the ERA, but Waddell played in a time when league ERAs were in the 2.00s, whereas league ERAs in McNally's time were in the 3.00s. In my mind, the ERA advantage is negated by McNally's higher winning percentage and the fact that even though it was much easier to win 20 games in Waddell's time, they each had the same number of 20-win seasons. Waddell may have been better, but I think you'd have a hard time proving it definitively. Meanwhile, Rube is in the Hall and McNally will never be. Some things don't make sense.

Wagner, Honus (shortstop, 1897–1917): "If I had a choice of all players who have played baseball," long-time Yankee boss Ed BARROW, who guided Babe RUTH's career, once said, "the first man I would select would be Honus Wagner." Wagner came up as an outfielder with the National League's Louisville franchise but moved to Pittsburgh when the other club folded after 1899. A few years later, he shifted to shortstop, and though already a star, Wagner blossomed. The numbers themselves are amazing: eight batting titles, nine 100-RBI seasons, five stolen base crowns, six times leading the league in slugging, and on and on. But they don't tell the whole story. He loved to play the game, he loved to win, and he would and could do whatever it took to win. As a fielder, he was the greatest of his time. As a hitter and baserunner, only Ty COBB was better. As a positive clubhouse influence, he was unmatched. He was more beloved by fans than anybody until Ruth. He was friendly with rookies and veterans alike, and he maintained his humility despite his fame. Legendary manager John McGRAW said: "I consider Wagner not only as the number one shortstop, but had he played in any position other than pitcher, he would have been equally great at the other seven positions. He was the nearest thing to a perfect player no matter where his manager chose to play him." Wagner refused to sign a 1918 contract with Pittsburgh when owner Barney Dreyfuss demanded to cut his salary, citing "war conditions." Wagner was 44 anyway and ready to quit, and Dreyfuss decided he had no use for him anymore. The hard feelings between the two lasted, resulting in Wagner's near banishment from the game. By the Depression, Wagner was living in poverty with his wife and two daughters. His sporting goods business had failed, and he was too proud to ask for any charity. An article by Hall of Fame sportswriter Fred LIEB describing Wagner's plight changed all that. Wagner got a job with the Pirates as a coach and gate attraction, and he spent the remaining years of his life with the game he loved. He was one of the first five men elected to the Hall of Fame in 1936. And when you're talking about an all-time all-star team, there's no doubt about who belongs at shortstop. (*Baseball Digest* recently ran a series choosing baseball history's top 10 players at each position, and for shortstop, they selected Ozzie SMITH number one. While I've agreed with their other selections, the choice of Smith over Wagner is absolutely ill-informed. Wagner was as good a fielder as Smith—though perhaps not as flamboyant—and he was a much better hitter and leader. What more do you want?)

Waitkus, Eddie (first baseman, 1941, 1946–55): If you've read the book or seen the movie *THE NATURAL*, you know part of Waitkus's story. He was an All-Star first baseman with the Cubs and Phillies, a good hitter who'd batted .292 in 1947 and .295 in 1948. He had many fans, but none more devoted than 19-year-old Ruth Ann Steinhagen from Chicago. Right after the first time she saw Waitkus play in 1947, she became so obsessed with him that she attended just about every Cubs game and talked about him incessantly, to the dismay of her parents, who never liked baseball. She clipped out newspaper articles and photographs and built a shrine to Waitkus in her room, sometimes carrying on conversations with the photos. Every man in her life—from her father to her boss to actors in movies—seemed to resemble Waitkus. When Waitkus was traded to Philadelphia before the 1949 season, she became despondent and had to leave her job. Waitkus knew nothing about this because she'd never tried to contact him, and if he walked by her after a game, she would back away and once almost fainted. Early in 1949, the obsession caused her to buy a rifle from a pawnshop. "[I]f I couldn't have him," she told a court psychiatrist after she'd been caught, "neither could anyone else." When the Phillies came to Chicago she checked into the team's hotel, and that night, she sent him a note asking him to come to her room. He arrived at her door just before midnight on June 14, 1949. "What do you want to see me about?" he asked. Telling him she had a "surprise" for him, she turned and took the rifle out of her closet. "For two years you have been bothering me," she told him, "and now you are going to die." Calmly, she pulled the trigger and shot him in the stomach. She had planned to kill herself next but she said she lost her nerve. Instead, she called the hotel operator and asked for a doctor. Arrested and diagnosed as a schizophrenic, she spent three years in a state mental hospital. Waitkus's recovery, meanwhile, was miraculous. He missed only the rest of the 1949 season and came back to play a full schedule in 1950, helping the "WHIZ KID" Phillies to the National League pennant with a .284 average and 102 runs scored. He lasted five more seasons and retired with a career batting average of .285.

Walker, Moses Fleetwood (catcher, 1884): Jackie ROBINSON was not, technically, the first black man to play in the major leagues. He wasn't even the second. Those honors go to two brothers named Moses Fleetwood Walker and Welday Wilberforce Walker, both of whom played in 1884 for the Toledo club of the American Association, which was then considered a major league. "Fleet," as Moses was nicknamed, was a rarity among ballplayers: college educated, highly intelligent, and black. However, neither brother performed impressively that season: Moses, an excellent defensive catcher, batted just .263 in 42 games, while Welday, an outfielder, played in just six games with a batting average of .182. Both were released from the team at the end of the season. Both encountered overt racial harassment from opposing fans and players throughout the season, but neither accused their club of racism. And they continued their baseball careers with teams in other professional (minor) leagues. Blacks playing alongside whites was, in fact, an occasional if uncommon occurrence until 1894, when the COLOR LINE became entrenched.

Walsh, "Big Ed" (pitcher, 1904–17): Though Walsh was just six-one, that was big in his day. He was a workhorse who both started and relieved throughout his career—never better than during his great 1908 season, when Walsh almost single-handedly kept his White Sox in the pennant race. He pitched seven games over the last nine days of the season, including three complete games in two days. Relieving in another game, he struck out Nap LAJOIE with the game on the line. He won 40 games that season as he set the major league "modern" record for innings pitched with 464. ("Modern" is usually defined as going back to 1893, when the pitching mound was moved to its current distance.) Walsh also holds the record for lowest career ERA—an untouchable 1.82. All those innings took their toll, and by 1913, after leading the league in games and innings pitched numerous times, his arm was pretty much shot. From then until he finally retired in 1917, he appeared in just 31 games.

Waner, Paul (outfielder, 1926–45): Not only was Waner a terror at the plate and in the outfield, he could also attack the bottle. There is a famous story that he quit drinking one year at the request of his manager. By midseason, however, he was batting just .240, so the skipper brought him some liquor, and Waner's batting stroke returned. One of the few men to win a batting title in his rookie season, Waner was a hitting machine who finished his career with 3,152 career hits, which ranked him fourth on the all-time list when he retired. He could have had 3,153 hits, but on the occasion of his 3,000th, he asked the official scorer to change an infield hit to an error so that he could truly earn the hit. Playing for the Pirates in spacious FORBES FIELD, he didn't have home run sock, but his doubles and triples totals and his yearly slugging percentages in the .500s indicate he had excellent power. Brooklyn

Dodger fans nicknamed Waner "Big Poison," which didn't refer to a giant deadly concoction but rather, according to Red SMITH, was Brooklynese for "Big Person." Since Waner was only five-eight and 150 pounds, one can only assume the term was meant figuratively. Waner had a brother Lloyd, who, like Paul, is in the Hall of Fame (but unlike Paul, doesn't belong). Poor Lloyd had a tough act to follow, and fans didn't help by nicknaming him "Little Poison" even though he was an inch taller than his brother.

Ward, John Montgomery (pitcher/shortstop, 1878–94; manager, 1884, 1890–94; labor leader): Ward owns perhaps the most impressive résumé in baseball history. A graduate of Penn State, he came up to the National League in 1878 as a pitcher, compiling his greatest season a year later when he led the league in victories (47), winning percentage (.712), and strikeouts (239) while guiding Providence to the pennant. When not on the mound, he also played the outfield and the middle infield. His arm went bad in 1884, so he moved full-time to shortstop and became the league's top fielder as well as an excellent baserunner, stealing as many as 111 bases in a season. Meanwhile, he was elevated to manager and was perhaps the most innovative of his era. He helped popularize the hit-and-run and railed against the sacrifice bunt, both positions contrary to the accepted wisdom of the time. He also wrote one of the first books teaching baseball strategy, called, simply, *Ward's Baseball Book*. During nights and off-seasons, he earned a law degree at Columbia, which prepared him for the next set of duties: those of labor leader. He helped form the short-lived PLAYERS' LEAGUE, which was the first real challenge to the baseball establishment and helped institute a number of reforms that restricted some of the owners' control over the players. He was elected to the Hall of Fame in 1964, which was about 25 years after he should have made it.

Weaver, Buck (third baseman, 1912–20): Poor Buck Weaver. In 1920, he was only 30 years old and having the greatest season of his career when he was suspended and later banned from baseball for knowing about the plot to throw the 1919 WORLD SERIES. It's possible that, with the LIVELY BALL ERA just around the corner, Weaver would have fashioned a Hall of Fame career. But instead, he had chosen to protect his teammates and didn't divulge the knowledge that other White Sox players were conspiring with gamblers to fix the championship. Weaver always maintained that although he knew about the plot, he always played his best, and the numbers seem to back him up. For the Series, he batted .324 with four doubles, a triple, and no errors (on the other hand, he had no RBIs despite batting third in the lineup throughout the games). After the banishment, he applied for reinstatement every year until his death in 1956. The commissioner's office denied his requests every time.

Weaver, Earl (manager, 1968–1982, 1985–1986): A great, innovative manager who led Baltimore to six division titles, four pennants, and a World Series victory. He also had six second-place finishes, and he didn't finish lower than fourth until his final season at the helm, when the Orioles brought him out of retirement for one last go-round. Combative and often abusive toward umpires, Weaver was ejected from games a league-record 91 times. But he was also perhaps the most innovative manager of his time. He was the first to keep detailed records of batter–pitcher matchups to help him in determining pinch hitters and relievers. He helped develop the best pitching staffs of his era, with almost two dozen 20-game winners and 10 Cy Young Award winners. And, among other things, he took platooning to new heights. Soon he'll have a plaque at COOPERSTOWN.

Wells, Willie "Devil" (shortstop, Negro leagues, 1925–49): Another of the great Negro leaguers who deserved Hall of Fame induction while he was alive, Wells was the greatest shortstop in the black leagues other than "Pop" LLOYD. Wells could hit for average—once leading the Negro National League with a

.403 mark—and power—three times leading the NNL in homers. In the field, he had great range, good hands, and an accurate arm. He died in 1989 at the age of 81.

White, James "Deacon" (third baseman/catcher, 1871–90): A remarkable player and man, White was one of professional baseball's first great stars. He could play anywhere in the field, and he could hit—twice leading his league in batting and three times in RBIs. Respected and admired by just about everybody, White earned his nickname because he reputedly never smoked, drank, caroused, or cursed, and he carried his Bible on road trips. A true visionary, he was among the first players to complain about their shoddy treatment by owners; he threatened to test the reserve clause in the courts, and he helped in the PLAYERS' LEAGUE revolt of 1890. When White was sold from Buffalo to Pittsburgh, he refused to report unless he received some payment: Pittsburgh ownership relented and handed over about $1,500. In explaining his bold action, White spoke for all ballplayers who had ever been treated like property: "No man can sell my carcass," he declared, "unless I get at least half."

White, Sol (infielder/manager/executive/historian, Negro leagues, 1887–1926): With many NEGRO LEAGUES players, writers often like to use white major leaguers as comparable reference points: they'll write that "Pop" LLOYD was the black Honus WAGNER, for example, or Josh GIBSON was the black Babe RUTH, or Buck LEONARD was the black Lou GEHRIG, and so forth. But with Sol White, there really is nobody comparable to him. Though no stats were kept during his playing days, White was a star performer who played on or managed some of black baseball's dominant teams, including the CUBAN GIANTS, Cuban X Giants, and Philadelphia Giants, as well as over half a dozen other teams, including a few other Giants. He also played an important role in the formation of the early organized Negro leagues, and he wrote *The History of Colored Base Ball* in 1906, the first book of its kind and an important reference even today. He's been dead since 1948, so it may not make sense to induct him into the Hall of Fame now, but he really should have been elected years ago.

Wilhelm, Hoyt (pitcher, 1952–72): The first relief pitcher elected to the Hall of Fame, Wilhelm didn't get to the majors until he was 28 but still managed to last 21 seasons. How? The knuckleball, of course. Wilhelm perfected his delivery to put as little strain as possible on his arm, allowing him to pitch in an all-time record 1,070 games for nine different teams. He led the league in ERA during the only two years in which he qualified for the title—once when he was a rookie and pitched 159 innings, the other when his team converted him to starter. During other years, he posted ERAs mostly in the ones and twos and racked up a then-record 227 career saves and a still-record 123 relief wins. On offense, he achieved another measure of notoriety: He slugged a home run in his first major league at bat, then managed to get just 37 more hits, none of them homers, for the rest of his life while compiling a .088 batting average.

Williams, Billy (outfielder, 1959–76): Sweet-swinging Billy Williams starred for the Cubs for nearly his entire career, which means, of course, that he had to wait until he left Chicago for Oakland to make it to the postseason. Remarkably consistent, Williams played in 1,117 consecutive games, fifth on the all-time list, and his typical season consisted of a .290 average with 28 homers and 95 RBIs. He finished his career with 2,711 hits, 426 home runs, and 1,470 RBIs—enough to earn him Hall of Fame induction in 1987.

Williams, Smoky Joe (pitcher, Negro leagues, 1897–1932): People who have studied the issue often call Williams the greatest NEGRO LEAGUES pitcher ever. Even Satchel PAIGE, Williams's only rival for that distinction, said, "Smoky Joe could throw harder than anyone." And one manager, the great Cumberland POSEY, said Williams was as fast as Walter

JOHNSON and Lefty GROVE. In fact, Williams pitched exhibition games against Johnson, Pete ALEXANDER, Chief Bender, and two other white Hall of Famers—and beat them all. Legend has it that Williams struck out 25 batters in one 12-inning ball game and 27 in another 12-inning contest, although the latter was played under some rickety portable lights. Considering his stature among Negro leagues scholars, it is a mystery why Williams is not in the Hall of Fame.

Williams, Ted (outfielder, 1939–60): Ted Williams was a mediocre fielder and baserunner who had trouble staying healthy. He led his team to only a single pennant and flopped in his only World Series. He could be moody, curt, arrogant, and opinionated. Still, Williams is one of the greatest players of all time because he was arguably the greatest hitter of all time. Throughout his career, Williams led the league at least twice in *every* major offensive category except hits and triples. He won two Triple Crowns, seven batting titles, and four RBI and home run championships—all with the greatest batting eye in history, as evidenced by this amazing fact: From his sophomore season in 1940 until he retired in 1961, he led the league in on-base percentage *every single season he was eligible*, three times surpassing the .500 mark and five other times over .490. Alas, despite his greatness, he won just two MVP Awards when he really should have won four. In 1941, when he batted .406 and led the league in runs, homers, walks, on-base percentage, and slugging, he lost the award to Joe DiMAGGIO and his 56-game hitting streak. The Yankees won the pennant, DiMaggio led the league in RBIs, and he was a better fielder, which are three points in his favor. But consider this: DiMaggio batted .408 during his streak and .357 overall, which means that during the other 83 games he batted just .321. Williams, on the other hand, batted .406 *over the entire season* with more homers and 13 more runs scored, although with 15 fewer RBIs. But Joe was the media darling who played in the Big City with the glamorous Yankees, while Ted played with the also-ran Red Sox. The following season, Williams won the

Triple Crown with a .356–36 HR–137 RBI season but lost another MVP, this time to Yankee second baseman Joe Gordon. Williams finally captured the MVP in 1946 when his Sox won the pennant. But in 1947, when he won his second Triple Crown, he lost the MVP by a single point when a Boston writer who hated Williams left him off his award ballot entirely. Ted won his second MVP in 1949, but the following season he broke his elbow in the All-Star Game and his hitting was never the same. Even with the bad arm, he still managed to win three more batting titles, but his power and run-producing abilities were diminished, as he topped the 30 mark in homers and the 100 mark in RBIs only once each during his final 11 seasons. Williams missed five seasons to fight in World War II and Korea, which cost him his chance at 3,000 hits and 650 home runs. As it was, he finished with 2,600 hits and 521 total homers—the last home run coming in the final at bat of his career, a great moment that is described movingly in John Updike's famous essay "HUB FANS BID KID ADIEU." Williams's life story, meanwhile, has been the subject of several recent books, none better than Williams's own autobiography, called *My Turn at Bat.* It belongs in every baseball library.

Wills, Maury (shortstop, 1959–69): The man who got all the credit for bringing back the stolen base as an offensive weapon, Wills set the then-record for steals with an amazing 104 in 1962. His great season almost propelled the Dodgers to the pennant and it won Wills the MVP Award against some tough competition. He captured four other stolen base titles and stole 586 for his career, which at the time of his retirement ranked him 10th on the all-time list; he has since fallen to 17th. Later, he became the second black manager in baseball history when he took over the struggling Mariners in midseason 1980. The pressure evidently got to him. When he was fired 24 games into 1981, he went into a depression. "I had no reason to go to bed at night and no reason to wake up," he told interviewers. "I was that close to death." Police arrested him twice for cocaine possession and once for auto theft, but Wills was never convicted on any charge. He went through drug rehab and has turned around his life. He is today a popular candidate for Hall of Fame induction, and the thinking here is that he deserves it. He was 27 by the time he hit the majors and he still managed more than 2,000 hits. He helped his teams to four pennants, played Gold Glove–caliber shortstop, and profoundly affected the game by reminding people that stolen bases can score runs if used effectively. Those are all criteria for Hall of Fame induction.

Wilson, Hack (outfielder, 1923–34): A five-foot-six 200-pounder with power is not everyone's choice to play center field. But that's where Wilson played during most of a 12-year career with the Cubs, Giants, Dodgers, and Phillies in which he was much better known for his bat. Though he led the league four times in home runs and twice in RBIs, he's in the Hall of Fame for a single season—1930. During the famous "Year of the Hitter," Wilson slugged a National League record 56 homers and drove in a major league record 190 runs. Wilson was then 30 years old and on top of the baseball world, but liquor seems to have taken it all away. He played four more years with declining ability, finally finishing with 244 career homers and 1,062 RBIs. Pretty good numbers, to be sure, but all compiled in an era when high run totals were common, so Wilson's accomplishments aren't really as impressive as they seem.

Winfield, Dave (outfielder, 1973–present): Even considering Bo Jackson, Deion Sanders, and any other two-sport star who might come along, it's clear that Dave Winfield is the greatest all-around athlete to play baseball in the last 40 years. He was drafted by teams from each major sport, choosing baseball partly because the Padres guaranteed him a starting spot right out of college. A slugger with good speed and fielding skills, he became one of baseball's most consistently impressive players throughout the 1970s and joined the Yankees with much fanfare in 1981 after signing a free agent contract worth between $16 and $23 million (depending on cost-of-living escalators), the highest ever at the time. Remarkably injury-free throughout most of his career, he missed the entire 1989 season with a back injury that required surgery. But he came back to post several more slugging seasons and won his first World Series title with the Blue Jays in 1992. Still active through 1995, he has banged out more than 3,000 hits and is closing in on the 500 mark in home runs, which is moot toward his selection to the Hall of Fame. He earned that years ago.

Wright, George (shortstop, 1871–82; manager, 1879): The best player in the country at his peak, Wright starred on the legendary 1869 CINCINNATI RED STOCKINGS, along with his brother Harry WRIGHT. While Harry was the brains of the team, George was the offensive force: During Cincinnati's undefeated season, he batted .629 with 49 homers in 60 games. He also made the most money, earning $1,400 to his brother's $1,200. When the National Association came together in 1871, higher salaries enticed the brothers to jump to the Boston team, where they won four of the five pennants in NA history. But when pitchers started throwing curves regularly, Wright's batting prowess dwindled to nothing. He tried managing but lasted only a season. Instead, he focused his energy on the burgeoning sporting goods market, where he made a good living. He died at age 90 in 1937, just after he'd been elected to the Hall of Fame.

Wright, Harry (outfielder/pitcher, 1871–75; manager, 1871–93; pioneer): A newspaper of his day called Wright "a baseball Edison. He eats base-ball, breathes base-ball, thinks base-ball, dreams base-ball, and incorporates base-ball in his prayers." All of which may be true, but baseball wasn't even his first love. Wright played CRICKET in his native England before coming to the States. Once he picked up the new game, Wright saw its potential. After earning raves as an innovative player and manager, he organized the 1869 CINCINNATI RED STOCKINGS, the first openly all-professional baseball club—an accomplishment that earned Wright the title of "Father of Professional Baseball." As a pitcher, Wright was a top junkballer, capable of retiring batters with trick pitches rather than heat. He managed in the National Association and the National League until 1893, during which time he remained a respected and influential baseball figure. Among his many managerial innovations, Wright initiated the practice of fielders backing up one another. As far as rules changes, Wright suggested that pitchers throw overhand instead of underhand and sidearm. He was selected to the Hall of Fame in 1953.

Yastrzemski, Carl (outfielder/first baseman, 1961–83): Now that the numbers are in the books, it would be easy to denigrate Yaz's career. We think of him as a slugger, but he hit fewer than 20 homers in 15 of his 23 seasons. We think of him as a high-average hitter, but he batted under .285 more than half his career. We think of him as a good fielder—and in fact he did win seven Gold Gloves—but he played first base and DH for most of the second half of his career. Yet despite all that, he was one of baseball's most respected players and most feared hitters throughout the 1960s and 1970s. Maybe it was because he played for the Red Sox that his negatives are so easy to bring up; such is what has happened to almost every other Red Sox star, from Ted WILLIAMS to Jim RICE to Dwight EVANS to Roger CLEMENS. Boston fans are probably the most knowledgeable, most passionate, yet most disappointed fans in American League history. And because none of the aforementioned players were (or have yet been) able to deliver a championship, they've chosen the most visible players as their scapegoats. Modern Red Sox history is the story of perennial promise but ultimate failure, so it's easy to identify and highlight the failure of their heroes. Yastrzemski was a hometown boy who fulfilled a boyhood dream by starring with the Sox. His best years came in the 1960s, especially 1967, when through clutch hitting and great defense, he practically carried the team to Boston's first pennant in 20 years, earning Yaz a Triple Crown victory (.326 BA–44 HRs–121 RBIs) and MVP Award. By the 1970s, he had lost some of his batting stroke, but he was still a consummate team leader who led by example. However, personal and team disappointments continued for Yaz as the Sox lost another Series in 1975 (*see* 1975 WORLD SERIES) and a thrilling pennant race in 1978 (*see also* BOSTON MASSACRE). When he retired, Yaz was the only American League player who had tallied both 3,000 hits and 400 homers. He was elected to the Hall of Fame on the first ballot in 1989.

Young, Denton "Cy" (pitcher, 1890–1911): The man for whom the prestigious pitching award is named, Young holds nearly every significant career pitching record: wins (511), losses (316), innings (7,354), games started (815), and complete games (749); he's also pretty high up there in games pitched (906, seventh place) and shutouts (76, fourth). He could amass such amazing numbers because he played in a time—the DEAD BALL ERA—when pitchers didn't have to throw hard every pitch, so teams could employ three-man staffs and good pitchers could throw 350 to 450 innings and get 40 to 50 decisions every season. But that shouldn't denigrate Young's accomplishments because, even though pitching was so different back then, Young was among the best at his craft for nearly all of his 22 seasons in the majors. Pitching the bulk of his career with the Red Sox and Cleveland Spiders, he led the league in victories four times, ERA twice, shutouts seven times, and a bunch of other categories numerous times as well. Fans today know him by a familiar nickname, but many don't realize that "Cy" itself is short for another nickname, "Cyclone," which was bestowed upon Young when he was pitching for a minor league club in his hometown of Canton, Ohio, in 1890. "I thought I had to show all my stuff," recalled Young, "and I almost tore the boards of the grandstand with my fastball. One of the fellows called me 'Cyclone,' but finally shortened it to 'Cy,' and it's been that ever since." Despite all the pitching records, Young was not in the first group of enshrinees to the Hall of Fame in 1936. It's not because he was undeserving, however. Hall voters in those early days were split into two groups, one selecting players from the 19th century and the other players from the 20th. Since Young's career straddled both eras, he didn't receive enough votes from either faction to make it. He was instead elected a year later.

Yount, Robin (shortstop/outfielder, 1974–93): A first-round draft pick in 1973, Yount was a major league regular for the lowly Brewers at the age of 18, just a year out of high school. After a few years of stress-filled on-the-job training, he developed into one of the best players of his generation—a consistent offensive threat with great natural ability in the field and impressive leadership skills. He won MVP Awards at two positions, becoming the only player other than Hank GREENBERG to accomplish such a feat. During his 1982 MVP campaign, he took his Brewers to the World Series while leading the league in hits, doubles, and slugging percentage; driving in 114 runs and batting .331; and playing a mean shortstop. A couple years later, back and arm problems forced him out of the infield and into center field, where he returned to previous form as one of the league's top players. Milwaukee never won another title, but Yount won a close MVP Award vote against RBI leader Ruben Sierra in 1989. After that, however, the injuries caught up with him. He played four more seasons as a more or less ordinary player, long enough to reach 3,142 hits, before retiring after 1993. He should be in the Hall of Fame before you know it.

Zwilling, Dutch (outfielder, 1910, 1914–16): Zwilling was a pretty good hitter who led the FEDERAL LEAGUE in homers in 1914 and RBIs in 1915. But his real claim to fame is that he comes last in any alphabetical listing of major league ballplayers.

EXECUTIVES, MEDIA, AND OTHERS

Adams, Daniel "Doc" (pioneer): An early "Father of Baseball" who helped influence and standardize baseball rules during the middle of the 19th century. Recent research has credited Adams with a much larger role than was previously thought. *See* CARTWRIGHT, ALEXANDER.

Allen, Lee (historian): Author Bill JAMES, who has studied the issue for decades, gives Lee Allen a lot of credit for the growth and quality of baseball research over the past 40 years. Allen took the job of Historian at the Hall of Fame in 1958 after years of job-hopping. There he spent thousands of hours compiling detailed biographical data about every major league ballplayer. He built up the Hall's library to what it is today—the largest and best baseball library in the world. It was Allen's idea to create the *BASEBALL ENCYCLOPEDIA*, the first comprehensive statistical record of the major leagues. When he died in 1969, his effect on the sport was only beginning to be realized. Today, the literature of baseball is rich with fascinating biographies, analytical histories, statistical studies, and more. And not a few of these books owe their existence, whether directly or indirectly, to Lee Allen. Quite a legacy.

Allen, Mel (broadcaster): TV and radio voice of the New York Yankees from 1939 until 1964 (when he was inexplicably fired) and now the host of TV's *This Week in Baseball*, Allen was one of baseball's most influential broadcasters, who popularized baseball on the radio during its early years. When you hear somebody say "How about that!" or "That ball is going, going, gone!" you're hearing Mel Allen.

Angell, Roger (writer): Angell appeared frequently on Ken Burns's *BASEBALL* documentary, but he is better known for the beautiful articles about baseball that he contributes to *The New Yorker* magazine a few times a year. Baseball fans should own at least one of his five baseball books: *Season Ticket, Late Innings, Five Seasons,* and *The Summer Game* contain reprints of his *New Yorker* pieces, and *Once More Around the Ballpark* is a "greatest hits" collection. What makes Angell so great is that his writing combines charming, eloquent prose with a philosophy that can be summed up simply: He just loves the game. And as ugly cynicism in baseball grows at an alarming rate, Angell's words can provide just the tonic we need. One reading of an Angell book will remind you why you fell in love with the game in the first place.

Barber, Red (broadcaster): The voice of the Brooklyn Dodgers, Cincinnati Reds, and several other teams, Barber was one of the pioneers of baseball broadcasting on radio, beginning his career in the mid-1930s first with the Reds and later as the first baseball broadcaster in New York City. He was known for his unique expressions, many of which come from his southern roots, such as "They're tearin' up the pea-pod," "It's brewing up into a real rhubarb," and "The bases are FOB— full of Brooklyns." After retiring from broadcasting, Barber enjoyed a successful writing career, penning books on such subjects as the breaking of the COLOR LINE (*1947: When All Hell Broke Loose in Baseball*) and sports broadcasting (*The Broadcasters*). Barber died in 1993.

Barrow, Ed (executive): The general manager of the Yankees from 1921 to 1945, Barrow is largely responsible for creating the dynasty that would rule baseball until the 1960s. Before taking over the Yankees, he managed the Red Sox, where he approved shifting Babe RUTH from .the pitcher's mound to the outfield (although, as Robert Creamer points out in *BABE: THE LEGEND COMES TO LIFE*, Barrow and Ruth argued vehemently about the move). Even before that, Barrow discovered Honus WAGNER. In New York beginning in the 1920s, he signed Lou GEHRIG, Tony Lazzeri, Bill DICKEY, Lefty Gomez, Joe Gordon, and Joe DiMAGGIO, among others. Like most general managers of his day, Barrow was infamous for underpaying his employees. In 1938, for example, DiMaggio asked Barrow for a $45,000 salary; Barrow responded by noting that the great Gehrig earned only $41,000. "Mr. Gehrig is underpaid," DiMaggio said. DiMaggio held out but finally relented and signed for $25,000 when his "greed" angered the Depression-era public. Meanwhile, Barrow's employers were millionaires.

Beckett, Dr. James (publisher): The guru of the baseball card market, Beckett publishes books and magazines featuring price guides for baseball and other sports cards. Beckett, a Ph.D. in statistics, was the first person to stabilize the baseball card market when he instituted the first national statistical price survey for the cards in 1976. Beginning in 1979, he oversaw the publication of the *Sport Americana* guidebooks, which provided the first comprehensive price guide to the entire history of baseball cards. Since 1984, when *Beckett Baseball Card Monthly* was first published, the card-collecting "hobby" has skyrocketed into a $3 billion industry, and Beckett Publications has kept pace with magazines devoted to basketball, football, and hockey cards. Beckett himself, meanwhile, remains *the* authority in the market, and it's no mere coincidence that the card market exploded around the time his authoritative guides were published. He wasn't the sole reason for the astonishing growth, to be sure, but his contributions can't be dismissed.

Boswell, Thomas (writer): An excellent sportswriter who works for the *Washington Post*, Boswell has written extensively on baseball, including the books *Why Time Begins on Opening Day*, *How Life Imitates the World Series*, and *The Heart of the Order*, and he even invented a statistic called TOTAL AVERAGE. Boswell's prose is at once eloquent, funny, and opinionated. As some of his book titles suggest, baseball to him transcends what happens on the field. He seems to have a unique grasp on the undefinable quality about the game that keeps Americans riveted to the intermittent, even slow, action. At the same time, he doesn't forget that what baseball is really about, deep down, is fun.

Carey, Harry (broadcaster): The radio voice of the Cardinals, Athletics, and, more famously, the Chicago Cubs, Carey has broadcast baseball since the 1950s. A fan favorite, his trademarks include the phrases "It might be . . . it could be . . . it is!" and "Holy cow!" (a phrase borrowed by Phil RIZZUTO). He also leads the crowd in singing "TAKE ME OUT TO THE BALL GAME" during the seventh-inning stretch. Broadcasting is apparently genetic in the Carey family: son Skip broadcasts Atlanta Braves games and grandson Chip is a pro basketball and college football announcer.

Cartwright, Alexander (pioneer): A bank teller by trade, Cartwright is recognized as one of the founders of modern baseball. However, newly discovered evidence suggests that, like Abner DOUBLEDAY, Cartwright has been erroneously credited with a greater role than he actually deserves. According to author John Thorn, Cartwright *was* among those responsible for

founding the first organized baseball club—the NEW YORK
KNICKERBOCKERS—that played with a set of official rules (*see
also* KNICKERBOCKER RULES). One of those rules was the establishment of foul territory, whereas ROUNDERS and CRICKET—
baseball's precursors—have no foul ground. But contrary to
what his Hall of Fame plaque says, Cartwright *did not* set the
bases 90 feet apart nor establish nine innings per game and
nine players per lineup. Those innovations would come as
much as a decade *after* the year (1845) when Cartwright allegedly wrote the rules. In fact, Thorn's exhaustive research credits Daniel "Doc" ADAMS as the originator of many of those
rules. While president of the New York Base Ball Club, Adams
played the same game as the Knickerbockers—using Cartwright's alleged rules—*in 1840*. And that game, known as
"base ball," was essentially the same as one played as early as
1832 (though not by Adams himself)—which means that
Cartwright's game was being played for nearly 15 years before
he supposedly invented it. From 1848 through 1862, while
Cartwright was mining for gold in California, Adams served as
the Knickerbockers president and then as presiding officer of
the NATIONAL ASSOCIATION OF BASE BALL PLAYERS, during
which time Adams, not Cartwright, helped refine the game
further by fixing the bases 90 feet apart and the pitching box
45 feet from home plate. Under Adams's guidance, the rules
were also changed to declare the winner of a game to be the
team leading after nine innings—not, as the original Knickerbocker rules dictated, the first team to score 21 runs (which
was possible because pitching and defense hardly existed).
What was Cartwright's role in all this? As stated earlier, he
did help form the first organized baseball club with a written
constitution that set some rules of the game, such as the
diamond-shaped field (actually a square), the idea of foul territory, and the change in the rounders rules that called for retiring baserunners by throwing the ball at them. Baseball
historians and writers alive at the time of baseball's development, such as Henry CHADWICK, never claimed that baseball
had a spontaneous creation, and probably neither did Cart-

wright. They always wrote that baseball was an evolutionary descendant of those British games. The truth is, the game of baseball doesn't have a distinct starting point—not 1845 or 1839 or even 1832—nor does it have a single "Father of Baseball." What started Americans believing that baseball had a Divine Creator was Albert G. SPALDING's infamous MILLS COMMISSION REPORT in 1907.

Chadwick, Henry (pioneer): The first reporter to cover the sport regularly for major newspapers, Chadwick developed the box score and the first scoring system, and wrote the first books and guides on the sport. Many called him "Father of Baseball" because he had strong ideas about how the game should be played, preferring "scientific" baseball—spray hitting, aggressive baserunning—over slugging; these strategies dominated baseball until the 1920s. Additionally, Chadwick was largely responsible for popularizing the game among fans with his writings. To illustrate the evolution sportswriting has experienced, here's a sampling of Chadwick's prose describing a game in 1869: "On October 26th the Red Stockings returned to New York from Troy, after defeating the strong nine of the Haymakers of that village by a score of 12 to 7, and on the afternoon of that day played the first game of a new series of contests with the Mutual Club. The Saturday previous they had opened play in the east with a noteworthy triumph over the Athletics in Philadelphia by a score of 15 to 8, and therefore they entered upon this contest flushed with two victories, that at Troy being the most creditable display." Wow.

Chandler, A. B. "Happy" (commissioner, 1945–51): The one-time senator and governor of Kentucky, Chandler was elected baseball COMMISSIONER following the death of Kenesaw Mountain LANDIS in 1944. Though surviving just six years in the high office, Chandler oversaw the sport's most lasting change: the breaking of the COLOR LINE. Chandler defied the ownership by publicly supporting integration—a surprising position from a Southern politician. Though his role in Jackie ROBINSON's signing was probably not as big as he liked to take credit for, the fact is that his predecessor never would have allowed it. Justifiably or unjustifiably, Chandler was proud of his accomplishment.

Comiskey, Charles (owner): The founder of the Chicago White Sox, Comiskey was instrumental in the formation of the American League. Before that, he had a 13-year career as a player and manager, during which he pioneered the strategies of shifting fielders for different hitters and having the pitcher cover first base on balls hit to the right. Later, under Comiskey's leadership, the White Sox won four pennants and two World Series. It might have been three if Comiskey's notorious parsimony hadn't forced eight members of the 1919 team to accept money from gamblers to throw the Series. *See also* BLACK SOX SCANDAL; 1919 WORLD SERIES.

Conlon, Jocko (umpire, 1941–64): For 24 years, Conlon was the standard by which umpires were judged. Famous for his quick thumb, he ejected 26 men in his first full year as an umpire. "I demanded respect on the field from managers and players," he once said. "To me, that's seventy-five percent of umpiring." He was elected to the Hall of Fame in 1974.

Dedeaux, Rod (college baseball coach): Perhaps the greatest coach in college baseball history, Dedeaux headed the University of Southern California's baseball program from 1958 until 1978, during which he captured 10 national championships. Dedeaux played for the Brooklyn Dodgers in 1935 after graduating from USC years earlier. While coaching at his alma mater, he recruited a number of major league stars, including Tom SEAVER, Dave Kingman, Fred LYNN, Ron Fairly, and Don Buford. Today, USC's baseball park is called Dedeaux Field, a fitting tribute to the man who built college baseball's most successful program.

Doubleday, Abner (Civil War veteran): "The only thing Abner Doubleday started," said one writer, "was the Civil War." Indeed, Captain Doubleday fired the first Union shot at Fort Sumter. Later, he commanded Union troops at the beginning of Gettysburg. But he did not start the game of baseball—that is 100 percent myth. Nowhere in his diaries or memoirs does he even *mention* the sport he supposedly invented in the spring of 1839 in COOPERSTOWN, New York. In fact, it's doubtful he was even *in* that part of the state, since he was a student at West Point at the time. But Albert G. SPALDING's infamous MILLS COMMISSION REPORT gave Doubleday sole credit for the game's invention, and the Hall of Fame is now located in the city of its supposed birth. The Hall itself, forced to toe the party line, does admit that "various critics have challenged the speculation on Doubleday. . . . Many of these contradictory theories have been well-documented by their proponents. . . . If Baseball was not actually first played here in Cooperstown by Doubleday in 1839, it undoubtedly originated about that time in a similar rural atmosphere." Why do they even bother?

Eckert, William "Spike" (commissioner, 1966–68): Baseball's worst commissioner, "The Unknown Soldier"—as he was dubbed immediately after his hiring—was wholly unfit for the post. The retired Air Force general hadn't sought the job and knew nothing about baseball but was selected by a group of owners who wanted a patsy as commissioner. With the Major League Baseball Players' Association beginning to grow in strength, the choice of Eckert proved embarrassing to the owners. What they needed was a business professional who had some sort of relevant experience. The owners realized their mistake and ousted him in 1968, ending Eckert's two-year "reign."

Fehr, Donald (union leader): Fehr has headed the Major League Baseball Players' Association since 1984, having previously worked under Marvin MILLER as the MLBPA's general counsel. Combining Miller's tough negotiating stance with the dogged persistence of a good lawyer, Fehr has led the Association through two strikes and a lockout. During the 1994 STRIKE, he was probably as hated by the general public as his adversary Bud SELIG, but Fehr and the MLBPA had a more defensible position. After all, the players were fighting to keep the owners from taking away something that had been given to them by the owners themselves. Where Fehr and the players went wrong was that they underestimated the owners' collective resolve. The owners were itching for some kind of victory over the players after 25 years of defeats. Fehr has turned off a lot of people with his seeming aloofness, and late in the strike, writers and other observers called for Fehr to take himself out of the negotiations because it was feared that the personal animosity between Fehr and owners' negotiator Richard Ravitch was getting in the way of a settlement. In fact, the obstacle wasn't the personalities but rather the reluctance on either side to change its views. It's easy to resent the players for their huge salaries: They're getting paid millions to play a kids' game. But the players didn't steal that money— they earned it through their hard work and the work of Miller and the union. You can't expect the players to give that away without a fight.

Finley, Charles O. (owner): The controversial owner of the Oakland A's in the 1960s and 1970s, Finley helped institute the designated hitter, night World Series games, and colorful uniforms. To his fellow owners' chagrin, however, he also helped usher in the FREE AGENCY era when he reneged on his contract with "Catfish" HUNTER; the consequent union grievance resulted in Hunter being declared baseball's first free agent. A master of promotion and a great judge of baseball talent, Finley was much less successful managing his employees. Although his A's own three straight World Series from 1972 to 1974, they did it with feuds, fights, and two different managers. Once, Finley fired, rehired, and refired manager Alvin Dark within a 24-hour period. Charitably described as cheap, Finley sold his team and got out of baseball rather than succumb to the demands of free agents seeking high salaries.

Frick, Ford (executive, 1934–65): National League president from 1934 to 1951 and baseball commissioner from 1951 to 1965, Frick is best known as the man who put an ASTERISK next to Roger MARIS's record 61-homer season because it occurred in 162 games, not the 154 that Babe RUTH played in (*see* 61). A onetime sportswriter who was associated with baseball for 43 years, Frick also helped ease Jackie ROBINSON's entry into baseball by issuing this ultimatum to players threatening to strike rather than play against Robinson: "I don't care if half the league strikes. Those who do will . . . be suspended, and I do not care if it wrecks the NL for five years. This is the United States of America, and one citizen has as much right to play as another." During Frick's reign as commissioner, baseball underwent several sweeping changes: four major franchise shifts, including the WESTWARD EXPANSION by the Braves, Dodgers, and Giants; the addition of four new teams, changing the dynamics of baseball for the first time since the AL was formed in 1901; and the explosion in television and radio revenues during the 1950s. The Robinson matter notwithstanding, however, Frick was a notorious yes-man who himself took little part in any of the monumental events that shaped his tenure. He let the real power brokers—the owners—have nearly free rein over the game; in those preunion days, he was just what the owners needed.

Giamatti, Bart (executive, 1986–89): Onetime president of Yale University, Giamatti fulfilled a lifelong dream by becoming NL president in 1986 and baseball commissioner two years later. His joyous enthusiasm for the game kept his reign focused on what he believed was best for baseball and made him popular among owners, fans, and the media. The players may have had a different opinion after Giamatti, in the most lasting decision of his short tenure, handed Pete ROSE a suspension for allegedly betting on baseball. Although investigators never fully resolved those allegations and Rose continues to deny them, the suspension has stood, and Rose today remains barred from the Hall of Fame. Just nine days after announcing that momentous decision and 154 days after taking the office, Giamatti, a chain smoker, died from a heart attack at the age of 51.

Gowdy, Curt (broadcaster): Radio voice of the Red Sox from 1951 through 1965, Gowdy made his lasting mark on broadcasting as the TV voice of NBC's national baseball coverage through 1975—including the *Game of the Week*, All-Star Game, and World Series. Known for a basic, natural style of speaking, the Wyoming native also hosted *The American Sportsman* for two decades.

Harwell, Ernie (broadcaster): A six-decade veteran, Harwell is one of the deans of baseball announcing, a 1981 recipient of the Ford C. FRICK Award for excellence in broadcasting. He got his start as a fill-in with the Brooklyn Dodgers when, in 1948, he was traded by the minor league Atlanta Crackers to Brooklyn for catcher Cliff Dapper—making Harwell the only broadcaster so honored. He has worked for the Dodgers, Giants, and Orioles, but it is with the Tigers that he has made his name. And when the Tigers ownership unceremoniously fired him in 1992, there was such an uproar that he had to be brought back after one season.

Honig, Donald (author): Baseball literature's most prolific writer, Honig has edited or written more than two dozen books on the sport. Some of his best are the oral histories: *Baseball When the Grass Was Real*, *Baseball Between the Lines*, *The October Heroes*, and *The Man in the Dugout*. Another excellent one is called *Baseball America*; in an entertaining way, it looks at the game's history from a sociological perspective. He has also written a number of team and league histories, and many other works. It's not a baseball season without at least one new book by Donald Honig.

Hulbert, William (executive, 1876–82): Hulbert owned the Chicago franchise of the NATIONAL ASSOCIATION, a loosely run league notoriously devoid of discipline that lasted only a few years. Hulbert wanted to create a league with schedules and rules, so he and a few other team owners formed the National League in 1876. Though he was not the first NL president—Morgan Bulkeley, a figurehead, was—Hulbert took over the reins of the league when Bulkeley failed to show up for an important league meeting. Under Hulbert's tight control, the fledgling league prospered. Hulbert, known for a time as "The Savior of the Game," died in 1882. Somehow, Bulkeley—who lasted less than one season as head of the league and had zero power—has been in the Hall of Fame for 50 years while Hulbert, who masterminded the whole deal, wasn't honored until 1995.

James, Bill (author): The most influential baseball writer in recent times, James is largely responsible for revolutionizing the way people approach baseball statistics. Through his *Baseball Abstracts*, which he published from 1978 through 1988, James examined and analyzed countless statistical questions, such as the true value of the stolen base and the importance of walks, and he has introduced new methods of judging ballplayers through the practice of SABERMETRICS, a term coined by James himself. Among his other body of work, he wrote what I and many others consider the quintessential baseball history book—*The Bill James Historical Baseball Abstract*; every fan should own a copy. You could say James is responsible for the explosion in statistics you see during a game: "Batting average on Tuesday afternoons," "Home runs against lefthanders in day games after night games," and so forth. But that would be an injustice to James. In fact, his precedent-setting statistical analyses and general approach to the game have positively influenced—directly or indirectly—an entire generation of baseball fans and writers, myself included.

Johnson, Bancroft "Ban" (AL president, 1901–26): The founder of the American League, Johnson was working as a sportswriter when he and Charles COMISKEY took over the Western League in 1893. Seven years later, Johnson decided to take on the baseball establishment by changing the league's name to the American League and a year later proclaiming the AL to be a "major league"—touching off the AMERICAN LEAGUE WAR (*see also* 1901 SEASON). When the truce was called, Johnson emerged as the big winner: He wielded the greatest influence over the three-man National Commission that ruled baseball until the commissioner's office was established in 1920. Stern and unyielding, Johnson always did what he felt was best for the league. For example, he banned liquor from ballparks and meted out harsh penalties against players engaging in "rowdyism." To enforce the rules, he backed his umpires vehemently at a time when on-field officials often received little support or protection from league offices. When Kenesaw Mountain LANDIS was installed as baseball's autocratic commissioner, Johnson's power disappeared. Without the control he was accustomed to, Johnson retired from the game in 1926.

Klem, Bill (umpire, 1905–40): "In my heart," Klem once said, "I never missed a call." With this attitude, Klem excelled at an always-tough job—made even tougher by the fact that when Klem broke in, only one umpire officiated a game. A pioneer in the use of hand signals, he was inducted into the Hall of Fame in 1953.

Kuhn, Bowie (commissioner, 1969–84): The much-despised Kuhn presided during one of baseball's most dramatic and controversial periods: the free agency era. At his election, Kuhn was working at the New York law firm that served the National League. As commissioner, his legal training would be called upon often. The dismantling of the RESERVE CLAUSE, caused partly by the landmark Supreme Court case *FLOOD V. KUHN*, defined his tenure, as did the 1981 players' strike that canceled 52 games. He made lots of enemies: He suspended Willie MAYS and Mickey MANTLE from participating in any baseball-related functions because of their associations with Atlantic City casinos; he made several shortsighted decisions that helped facilitate the downfall of the reserve clause; he handed down suspensions to powerful owners George STEINBRENNER and Ted TURNER; he allowed the TV networks to schedule all World Series games at night; and he created a controversial playoff system for the 1981 strike-torn season that angered fans and owners. His tenure was, in fact, marked by more losses than victories, and the owners ousted him in 1984 when they decided they wanted a businessman-CEO to lead a restructured baseball "corporation" into the future—which led to the selection of Peter UEBERROTH as commissioner. One of his frequent adversaries, Charlie FINLEY, had this to say when Kuhn resigned: "If Bowie Kuhn had a brain in his head, he'd be an idiot."

Landis, Kenesaw Mountain (commissioner, 1921–44): Only a handful of men influenced major league baseball more than Kenesaw Mountain Landis. Baseball's first commissioner, he had worked previously as a federal judge who vaulted to fame through a number of antitrust decisions—many of which were outrageous enough to get overturned by higher courts. But when baseball needed an authoritarian figure to preside over the game in the wake of the BLACK SOX SCANDAL and the death of Ray CHAPMAN, the owners turned to the man who had refused to make a ruling in the FEDERAL LEAGUE case against major league baseball several years earlier. Wanting to provide fans with the appearance of total propriety, the owners granted Landis nearly absolute power—a decision the owners would soon come to regret. Landis's first act was to reaffirm the expulsion of the eight members of the 1919 BLACK Sox who conspired to fix the World Series. He banished many more players for illegal or alleged illegal acts, suspended Babe RUTH for barnstorming, and granted free agency to several hundred minor league ballplayers who were being crushed under the weight of the oppressive farm system. And despite public denials, he silently supported baseball's execrable policy of denying blacks entry into major league baseball. When Landis died in 1944 after 23 years on the job, the owners were publicly sad but privately relieved. They then promptly rewrote the bylaws to limit the commissioner's power. To many owners' dismay, Branch RICKEY took advantage of Landis's death to open the national pastime to people of all races.

Lanigan, Ernest J. (historian): The 20th century's most influential *unknown* baseball figure, Lanigan set the stage for modern statistical analysis. Working in the 1910s and 1920s, he invented or popularized such statistics as runs batted in, slugging percentage, ERA, and others. He was the first man to compile career statistics of all major league players. He helped create the BASEBALL WRITERS ASSOCIATION OF AMERICA, and he wrote or edited countless articles and books on baseball statistics and history. In 1946, when he was 73, Lanigan became director of the Hall of Fame, a post he held for only two years, when he was shifted to the position of "historian." During his tenure, Hall of Fame attendance increased dramatically.

Lau, Charlie (coach): Widely proclaimed as baseball's foremost hitting guru until his death in 1984, Lau's theories have influenced a generation of players. Lau played 11 seasons as a catcher for six teams, only once appearing in more than 100 games and never batting .300 for a full season. But he was a hard-working student of the game who developed his successful theories through countless hours of analyzing the best hitters. Lau emphasized a balanced stance, an aggressive forward motion, and a slight downswing on the ball. Ted WILLIAMS and others who disagree with Lau's theories have argued that they rob a player of his power—and indeed, none of Lau's direct disciples has ever hit 40 homers. But it's hard to argue with a batting theory that strongly influenced, among its most talented progeny, George BRETT, Wade BOGGS, and Hal McRae, who among them have led the league 37 times in various offensive categories. Lau's classic book, *The Art of Hitting .300*, is still in print fifteen years after it hit the bookstores.

Lieb, Fred (writer): One of the baseball-writing fraternity's most talented scribes, Lieb covered the game for seven decades beginning in 1910. Among his many books, he wrote a marvelous account of his experiences called *Baseball as I Have Known It*, in which he discusses the players and personalities—from WAGNER through STENGEL—who shaped the game he loved. He died a few years after being chosen for the Hall of Fame's writer's wing in the early 1970s.

MacPhail, Larry (executive/owner): A true visionary and power broker, MacPhail left a legacy to professional sports that will continue as long as games are played. Among his innovations: night games, radio broadcasts, air travel, and old-timers' days. In addition, he built pennant winners for three different franchises—Cincinnati, Brooklyn, and the Yankees—all while apparently trying to suppress a volatile temper that got him fired from two jobs. MacPhail rests at the top of a baseball dynasty that continues today: Son Lee MacPhail served as AL president from 1974 until 1983, and grandson Andy MacPhail has worked as the general manager for the Twins and Cubs. It's unlikely, however, that anyone will ever exert more influence over the business of professional sports than Larry MacPhail.

Miller, Marvin (union leader, 1966–84): With few notable exceptions, no man did more during the last 50 years to revolutionize American sports than Marvin Miller. A longtime officer with the United Steelworkers' Union, Miller was elected head of the Major League Baseball Players' Association (MLBPA) in 1966, when the burning issue on players' minds was their pension plan. They didn't care that the RE-SERVE CLAUSE kept their salaries ridiculously low while the owners made exorbitant profits. And they didn't care that baseball's pathetic system of resolving players' grievances was illegal and immoral. Marvin Miller *taught* them to care, and in so doing, he gained for all professional athletes higher salaries and overall equitable treatment. Miller's excellent memoir, *A Whole Different Ballgame*, gives a complete and honest explanation of all the events that marked his tenure: the 1972 and 1981 players' strikes, the numerous collective bargaining agreements he helped negotiate, the renowned *FLOOD V. KUHN* Supreme Court battle, the landmark 1975 arbitration case that granted free agency to Andy MESSERSMITH and Dave MCNALLY, his seemingly weekly fights with commissioner Bowie KUHN, and other historic events. Miller also tells a funny story that illustrates the players' naiveté with labor-related matters: After they chose Miller as their head, the players said they wanted him to balance the political scale by choosing a conservative as chief legal counsel; they suggested that Miller consider an out-of-work politician who was known to be a big sports fan. His name was Richard Nixon. Needless to say, Miller made it a condition of his appointment that he be allowed to choose his own counsel. Many fans probably would have liked to have seen Nixon, who was no friend to labor, serve as a union leader rather than president. Not only wouldn't Watergate have occurred, but players today probably wouldn't be as rich and aloof as they are and the game may not have reached the brink of financial ruin, as many claim it has right now. But Miller can't be faulted for that. If the players weren't earning that money, the owners would be. And it's the owners who've shelled out the multimillion-dollar, long-term contracts to undeserving players. Miller simply gained the same freedom for baseball players that the rest of us have in our daily jobs: the right to work elsewhere if we're unhappy in our present job.

Murphy, Robert (labor leader): A former lawyer with the National Labor Relations Board, Murphy led a short-lived movement in the 1940s to improve working conditions for baseball players. After forming the American Baseball Guild (ABG), he came close to organizing a strike by the Pittsburgh Pirates to demand more equitable treatment. But it fell apart because not enough players—many of whom were anti-union and afraid of the owners—supported the efforts. The ABG died soon after, but not before effecting some important changes. It established a pension plan for retired ballplayers, got the owners to provide meal money while on the road and during spring training (still called "Murphy Money"), helped raise the minimum major league salary to $5,000, and set the stage for the more successful Major League Baseball Players' Association that would be headed by Marvin MILLER two decades later.

O'Malley, Walter (owner): The most hated man in the history of Brooklyn, O'Malley was responsible for airlifting the Dodgers from the New York borough to Los Angeles, a maneuver the Brooklyn faithful have never forgiven. The bankruptcy attorney rose to power in the Dodgers organization in the 1940s and took over completely by 1952 after a power struggle with co-owner Branch RICKEY. A true visionary with a sixth sense for making money, O'Malley was one of the first owners to recognize the potential of television, making the Dodgers perhaps the most watched team in America in the 1950s. He saw the untapped potential of the West Coast and convinced fellow owner Horace Stoneham of the Giants to join him in a WESTWARD EXPANSION. And he wielded tremendous influence over league officials during a time of a weakened commissioner's office. When he came to L.A., he demanded and received a sweet deal that included 300 acres of choice land just a few miles from downtown. There he built DODGER STADIUM using his own money—the better to make a profit from concessions and parking, but also the better to create a first-class ballpark where a family could enjoy an inexpensive, clean day out. After O'Malley's death in 1979, control of the club shifted to his son, Peter O'Malley, who continues at the helm to this day. The biggest difference between O'Malley and most of the other owners was always the fact that O'Malley made his living from baseball while his brethren treated baseball as a hobby. This put O'Malley a step ahead at all times and helped him cement a huge legacy that includes (but is not limited to) the extremely profitable team that plays ball in front of three million paying fans every year.

Palmer, Pete (author/statistician): Palmer has been involved in baseball statistical analysis since the 1960s, joining Bill JAMES as the two men who have done the most in recent times to redefine people's approach to baseball stats. Palmer has served as a consultant to the official statisticians of the American League, but his *magnum opus* is *The Hidden Game of Baseball,* in which he introduces a revolutionary method of evaluating ballplayers called "Linear Weights." The system involves a complicated formula of weighting a player's contributions—in the field, on the mound, and at bat—and comparing them to the league average player at that position. Such a methodology theoretically allows for an unbiased comparison of players from all eras and all ballparks. The formula has some flaws—especially when it comes to evaluating fielding—but overall, it offers a very illuminating view of what it takes to win ball games. *The Hidden Game* is an intriguing work, and if you can find it in the stores, it's worth buying. Palmer's ideas also appear in abbreviated form in TOTAL BASEBALL, the great reference he co-edits with John Thorn.

Povich, Shirley (writer): Sports editor of the *Washington Post* at the age of 21, Povich wrote about baseball and other sports for that paper beginning in 1924. He was one of the first writers to disdain the hero-worshipping and cliché-driven prose employed by so many of his brethren. He helped usher in the practice of in-depth, analytical sportswriting, covering not just the whos and whats but the whys and hows. When you learn from the local sportswriter *why* your team lost the game—

because, say, a baserunner had been faked out by the opposing shortstop during a critical play—you're learning that partly because of Shirley Povich.

Prince, Bob (broadcaster): A broadcasting legend, Prince did Pirates games for four decades and became an institution in Pittsburgh. He helped redefine sportscasting with his unabashed boosterism, giving Pirates followers a fellow fan in the booth. He claimed to have originated the phrase "How sweet it is!" and he would often declare after a come-from-behind victory, "We had 'em all the way." Years after he was fired from the Pirates, he hooked up with the Astros for one season. A Houston player reported that Prince wasn't popular there because he spent too much time reliving the old days with the Pirates. Today, there are any number of "homer" announcers—and they all owe a debt to Prince for making such a practice fashionable.

Rickey, Branch (executive): Rickey revolutionized baseball in two huge ways. As general manager of the Cardinals, he invented the farm system, a collection of minor league teams owned by a major league team for the purpose of providing talent for the big club. Rickey believed that there is "quality in quantity," and he turned out to be right. By 1940, the Cardinals controlled 33 different minor league teams and would win nine pennants from 1926 through 1946. A magnificent judge of talent, Rickey's system produced some of the greats of the game, including Rogers HORNSBY, Dizzy DEAN, and Stan MUSIAL, as well as fellow Hall of Famers Joe Medwick, Jim Bottomley, Chick Hafey, and others. If a measure of genius is how soon others copy you, it's clear that Rickey qualifies, because soon after the Cardinals achieved success, every other team began to create its own farm system. By the 1940s, Rickey had joined the Brooklyn Dodgers, where he would make his second great impact on the game of baseball, affecting American society in the process. It's hard to speculate on a person's true motives when he does a good deed, so I won't even try to explain exactly why Rickey risked his career to sign Jackie ROBINSON, thus breaking major league baseball's 60-year-old COLOR BARRIER. While certainly a noble move, some have argued that it was really about money. Rickey wanted to increase Dodger attendance, they argue, by appealing to the growing black population in New York City. Or, they say, he wanted to use the untapped talent of the NEGRO LEAGUES to win pennants for the Dodgers and earn money for himself. Maybe it was simply because he wanted to right an injustice. We'll never know the real answer, of course, but it almost certainly encompasses everything. Either way, the point is that Rickey fought to open up major league baseball to an entire race of people, which, according to a number of social historians, helped accelerate the civil rights movement. On a smaller scale, Rickey turned the Dodgers into real winners. With Robinson and a succession of other talent of all races, Brooklyn became the National League's most successful franchise in the immediate post-war era. Forced out of the Dodger's front office in a power struggle with Walter O'MALLEY, Rickey joined the Pittsburgh Pirates, where he built a winner out of a lowly franchise in less than a decade. After leaving Pittsburgh, Rickey challenged the baseball establishment again by becoming the point man for the CONTINENTAL LEAGUE in the early 1960s. That league failed, but it did force the baseball powers into their first expansion since the turn of the century. Rickey died in 1965 at the age of 84.

Rothstein, Arnold (gambler): Rothstein was running a gambling parlor in New York, dealing mainly with horse racing, when he became involved in the scam that would cement his reputation forever: the throwing of the 1919 WORLD SERIES by eight corrupt players. Rothstein was the money man, fronting cash to pay off the players. Although only a portion of the payroll made it to the players, Rothstein hit the jackpot, adding to his already considerable fortune. The effects of the actions of the BLACK SOX, and Rothstein by extension, were great and far-reaching: the creation of the commissioner's office; the lifetime expulsion of eight members of the team, including "Shoeless" Joe JACKSON; and a general loss of American innocence (*see* BLACK SOX SCANDAL). In 1928, hours after winning $600,000 on the presidential election, Rothstein was shot to death during a poker game.

Scully, Vin (broadcaster): A broadcaster giant, Scully has been the voice of the Dodgers since the 1950s. The Fordham University graduate took over broadcasting duties when Red BARBER quit (or was fired, depending on what you read) in a contract dispute, and Scully continues today as probably the most recognizable voice in baseball. Scully has an easygoing delivery and great command of the language, and, unlike most broadcasters, he usually works alone, without a color commentator. He has a great eye for the nuances of the game, and while some may argue that he says and describes too much, most in baseball will agree that there's no finer broadcaster doing baseball today.

Selig, Bud (owner): A used car salesman by trade, Selig purchased the bankrupt Seattle Pilots in 1970 and moved them to Milwaukee to become the Brewers. There, in a small-market setting, he invested in a good farm system and produced such stars as Robin YOUNT, Paul MOLITOR, Pete Vuckovich, Ben Oglivie, and others, resulting in a 1982 World Series appearance. Since then, however, the Brewers have rarely contended for a division title and have lost some high-priced stars to the free agent market. According to Selig, the team now loses millions of dollars every year. Selig blamed his misfortune on the sport's existing labor structure, so when he got the chance to take the helm of the baseball ship, he grabbed it. He reigned as "acting commissioner" during the 1994 STRIKE, earning a $1 million salary in that capacity, which was almost 50 percent higher than any previous commissioner. What did he do to earn that money? He got all of baseball to believe that the future of the sport hinged on the success or failure of its small-market franchises. Because his

Brewers and a handful of other teams lost money, Selig helped shut down baseball (*see* SEPTEMBER 14, 1994). He got the *profitable* teams to buy his argument because they knew that they could make even *more* money under the labor plan Selig envisioned—and they were desperate for a labor victory over the players. "Buddy" wasn't alone, of course. He had some greedy and power-hungry allies throughout ownership circles, especially White Sox owner Jerry Reinsdorf and Marlins boss Wayne Huizenga. Whenever another owner tried to suggest a more reasonable course of action than to jam an unfair labor agreement down the players' throats, Selig and the gang would shut him up. Selig is the master of the conference call, a consensus-builder extraordinaire (when the consensus revolves around money), and, as we all will remember him, the man who did what world wars and natural disasters couldn't: cancel the World Series.

Seymour, Dr. Harold (author): Seymour was the first scholar to treat baseball history as part of American history. His famous two-volume examination of the game, *Baseball: The Early Years* and *Baseball: The Golden Age*, pioneered the study of sports history at a time when "serious" academia considered such a topic frivolous. He says that when he first decided to write about baseball in a historical context, his peers at Cornell University in 1941 were skeptical, and Seymour had to convince them of baseball's legitimacy as a subject for serious scholarship. Seymour's books are universally regarded as the best starting points for baseball researchers who want to learn more about the game's origins, its early stars and controversies, and so on. Seymour is, in fact, known as "Baseball's Biographer" to today's researchers.

Smith, Walter "Red" (writer): A true sportswriting great, Smith started writing in 1927 and kept it up until his death in 1982. He was the most respected sports journalist of his time and in 1979 became the first sports columnist to win the Pulitzer Prize. Equally renowned for his wit and his opinions, he used his columns in the *New York Herald Tribune* and the *New York Times* to celebrate, disparage, or eulogize several generations of sports heroes and villains. He attacked pomposity, personified by Smith's favorite target, Bowie KUHN. And he supported the underdog, backing Marvin MILLER and the Players' Association, for example, when most in baseball saw the labor movement as somehow harmful to the game. Smith, who saw everybody in baseball from RUTH to Reggie, led a fascinating life, described movingly in Dave Anderson's biography *Red.*

Spalding, Albert Goodwill (pitcher, 1871–77; executive/businessman): A true pioneer and entrepreneur in the grand American spirit, Spalding made several important contributions to baseball. First, he was a great pitcher, probably the greatest of his time. From 1871 through 1875 in the National Association and 1876 in the National League, he topped all pitchers in victories. Second, he played a large role in the formation of the National League by writing its constitution and by lending needed credibility to the upstart venture. Third, when his arm gave out, he started the sporting goods company that continues to bear his name, and he began to issue the first yearly baseball guides. The business, which supplied balls and other equipment to the major leagues, made him one of baseball's wealthiest and most powerful men, as did his tenure as president of the Chicago franchise, probably the NL's most popular. Fourth, he helped save the National League during the PLAYERS' LEAGUE revolt by launching a public relations campaign attacking the motives and financial resources of the rebels, which effectively doomed the new league. And fifth, he was chiefly responsible for creating the myth that Abner DOUBLEDAY invented baseball. It was Spalding who ordered the formation of a commission to study the origins of the game, and it was Spalding who made sure the MILLS COMMISSION REPORT said that baseball was invented by an American and was *not* adapted from the British games ROUNDERS and CRICKET. Today, the SPALDING SPORT-

ING GOODS COMPANY is a billion-dollar enterprise, and so is the sport Spalding helped popularize.

Steinbrenner, George (owner): "We plan absentee ownership," said Cleveland shipbuilding magnate George Steinbrenner in 1973 as the group headed by him purchased the Yankees from CBS. If only Yankee fans had been so lucky, for Steinbrenner loved to bask in the yellow glow of the New York tabloids and quickly became the most meddlesome owner in recent times. He began his tenure auspiciously: suspended for two years after his conviction for making illegal contributions to Nixon's 1972 reelection campaign. He returned to plunge the Yankees into the new free agent market by signing "Catfish" HUNTER, Reggie JACKSON, and "Goose" GOSSAGE to bring the Yankees their first pennants in over a decade. Later, he signed Dave WINFIELD to the richest free agent contract in history, a 10-year contract worth $15 million—plus some cost-of-living escalators that could increase the deal to about $23 million. That extra $8 million nearly proved to be Steinbrenner's undoing, for he immediately began to despise Winfield and his agents. Throughout the 1980s, while Winfield was building his Hall of Fame career, Steinbrenner fought with and belittled Winfield and even broke the part of the contract that ordered Steinbrenner to donate $3 million to the ballplayer's charitable foundation. Steinbrenner then went a step too far, according to the commissioner's office: On claims from a gambler named Howard Spira who said that Winfield had given him money to pay off his debts to mobsters, Steinbrenner began to have private detectives investigate the player and his foundation. As it turned out, the foundation was on shaky financial and ethical ground, and Winfield was publicly humiliated. But the investigation would haunt Steinbrenner. Spira began to extort money from the Yankee boss, threatening to go public with the owner's actions in digging up dirt on Winfield. Steinbrenner gave Spira $40,000 to keep him quiet, then Spira spilled his story to the commissioner's office. The investigation and hearing that followed were as one-sided and prejudicial as one could imagine; for example, Steinbrenner's lawyers weren't allowed to depose or cross-examine many important witnesses. The results were predictable: Commissioner Fay VINCENT banished Steinbrenner for two years in 1990. According to John Helyar's account of the affair in his book *Lords of the Realm*, it's pretty apparent that the baseball establishment was out to get Steinbrenner for his many other sins—from outrageous free agent signings to boorish behavior off the field. You might say now, however, that the tables are turned, for Steinbrenner is back in baseball, older and quieter, while Vincent is not.

Stevens, Harry (entrepreneur): An English immigrant steelworker, Stevens came upon the idea of improving ballpark scorecards in the early 1880s. He approached owners all over professional baseball with his new version, and many of them let his company sell the scorecard in their ballparks. Stevens branched out into food sales, and soon his business was the largest around. Among his many innovations, Stevens invented the most popular ballpark treat: the hot dog. And even today, his name adorns the shirt backs of ballpark vendors across the country.

Turner, Ted (owner): The heir to a billboard company, Turner transformed his father's modest advertising firm into a powerful all-media conglomerate through marvelous foresight and manic energy. He purchased the downtrodden Atlanta Braves because they were the mainstay of his new cable TV channel; he kept them from moving out of town. Flamboyant and opinionated, Turner immediately set out to buy a winner. In the aftermath of the Andy MESSERSMITH free agency decision, Turner was the only owner to make a serious offer to the star pitcher, signing him to a $1 million multiyear deal. In a feat of promotional bravado, Turner issued Messersmith jersey number 17 and "nicknamed" the player "Channel." What a coincidence that Turner's cable station was Channel 17! The league president put an immediate halt to the blatant commercialism. Turner broke a great many other rules and traditions, angering the stolid baseball men who'd reigned for decades and earning Turner a one-year suspension at one point (which allowed Turner to skipper his yacht *Courageous* to an America's Cup victory). It was Turner who, along with George STEINBRENNER, received most of the blame for escalating baseball's salary structure by offering huge contracts to free agents. Turner still keeps a high profile among baseball owners, through not only his successful corporation but also his marriage to actress Jane Fonda.

Ueberroth, Peter (commissioner, 1984–89): Ueberroth built his fortune in the travel agency business and his reputation as the leader of the most successful Olympics in history. Then, fresh off the 1984 Los Angeles games, Ueberroth succeeded Bowie KUHN as baseball commissioner. *Time*'s Man of the Year immediately negotiated a liberal settlement to end an umpires strike that threatened the World Series, and the owners got a glimpse of the CEO they'd just contracted. He knew how to lead and how to make money. As he did with the Olympics, he priced corporate sponsorships much higher than ever before, he increased revenue from merchandising, and he negotiated the largest TV contracts in history, filling the owners' coffers like never before. He also preached "fiscal responsibility" to the owners, which, according to an independent arbitrator, was code for "Don't sign free agents to large, multiyear contracts." The resulting collusion ruling cost the owners hundreds of millions of dollars. Ueberroth's other pet project was getting rid of the drug problem that was consuming baseball in the early to mid-1980s. He meted out harsh penalties to players caught with drugs, and he even tried to unilaterally institute a drug testing policy, which got shot down by the union. Ueberroth lasted only five years on the job, apparently unable to put up with "the twenty-six idiots," in his words. The owners were also eager to get rid of the man who'd made them carloads of money; one owner would later say that Ueberroth was "more interested in his own image and where *he* was going." Where was that? There was much talk that Ueberroth was going to run for the senate, the governorship, or even the presidency, but none of that has happened. Yet.

Veeck, Bill (owner): Whenever you read Bill Veeck's name in a book or article, the word "maverick" is almost always nearby: "Bill Veeck, the maverick owner of the St. Louis Browns . . ." And it's not a misnomer. Veeck was always an innovator, always ahead of his time. During his long career, he owned three different teams—the Indians, Browns, and White Sox (twice)— and he brought his unique brand of leadership to each one. In Cleveland, he integrated the American League with the signing of Larry DOBY in 1947 and, later, Satchel PAIGE, helping to secure a pennant in 1948 and drawing over 2.6 million fans, the most ever at the time. With the Browns, he sent midget Eddie GAEDEL to the plate in a grand publicity stunt, but he couldn't revive that moribund franchise. As White Sox owner, however, he delivered the team's first pennant since the BLACK SOX SCANDAL and introduced the first exploding scoreboard. Most of his tactics were frowned upon by his fellow owners, who felt baseball should remain classy and dignified. Veeck, on the other hand, saw baseball as entertainment for the masses. He staged stunts and promotions almost daily, like pregame circus acts, postgame fireworks, the time he let fans manage a game from the stands, or his "Disco Demolition Night," which caused his team to forfeit when marijuana-stoned fans stormed the field. Veeck learned his trade firsthand, as the son of a Chicago sportswriter who went on to become the Cubs' president. The young Veeck, in fact, came up with the idea of planting ivy along the outfield walls in WRIGLEY FIELD. A law school graduate, he urged the commissioner to do something about the RESERVE CLAUSE built into every player's contract—in 1940. A few years later, he tried to buy the lowly Phillies and stock the club with NEGRO LEAGUES stars—half a decade before Branch RICKEY and Jackie ROBINSON broke the COLOR LINE. Veeck, who died in 1986, told his life story in VEECK AS IN WRECK, universally regarded as one of the finest sports autobiographies ever.

Vincent, Fay (commissioner, 1989–92): Vincent's three-year reign as commissioner is best described as "tumultuous." He took over the post following Bart GIAMATTI's death just seven days after the most momentous decision of a commissioner since the days of LANDIS: the banishment of Pete ROSE. Vincent immediately introduced himself to the American public when an earthquake interrupted Game Three of the 1989 WORLD SERIES. Vincent was a calm voice of reason during the hysteria that surrounded the tragedy. A lawyer by trade, Vincent, in fact, made a specialty of taking over during crises: he had been named CEO of Columbia Pictures after the famed movie company was embroiled in a number of scandals. As baseball commissioner, he suspended George STEINBRENNER for a variety of illegal and unethical acts and tried to realign baseball in the name of geographical correctness—both moves he considered "in the best interests of baseball." The Chicago Cubs challenged the latter move in the courts, arguing that the commissioner couldn't intervene when business interests were involved, and won. But the threat of an activist commissioner made the owners nervous. It was 1992, and they didn't want Vincent messing with the upcoming labor negotiations. Many owners wanted him out. At first Vincent stood firm, backed by the bylaws of the NATIONAL AGREEMENT that seemed to state that a commissioner could not be fired. But four days after a September vote of "no confidence," Vincent resigned. Considering the state of baseball after he left, Vincent had the last laugh.

Weiss, George (executive): Along with Ed BARROW, Weiss pieced together the Yankee dynasty that ruled baseball for five decades. Weiss ran the Yankees' farm system from 1932 until 1948, when he took over the general manager duties from Larry MACPHAIL, who had earlier replaced Barrow. Following in his predecessors' footsteps, Weiss was stingy with his bosses' money. Just one example of many: When Mickey MANTLE followed his Triple Crown season of 1956 with another spectacular, MVP award–winning year, Weiss actually tried to cut Mantle's salary on the grounds that his home run total had dropped from 52 to 34, ignoring all the other areas in which Mantle had improved (Mantle stood firm and actually eked out a small raise). In 1960, Weiss experienced the same ruthlessness he had perpetuated on his players: he was fired unceremoniously because he was "too old." He joined the expansion Mets and promptly hired Casey STENGEL—who'd been Weiss's first hire with the Yankees in 1948—and together they began to build the team that would win the championship in 1969 while the Yankees were wallowing in mediocrity. In 1971, Weiss was elected to the executives' wing of the Hall of Fame.

Yawkey, Tom (owner): Yawkey's Hall of Fame induction came in 1980, three years after he had passed away, but the team he owned for 44 years—the Red Sox—still hasn't been able to deliver him or his memory a World Series championship. Yawkey earned his fortune through the lumber and mining industries and funneled a lot of his cash into making the Sox a respectable, popular sports franchise. They used to say Yawkey robbed his players of the hunger to win the championship because he was too generous with their salaries. More likely, it was because the Yankees played in the same league. Yawkey's wife, Jean, currently owns the club.

TEAMS, LEAGUES, AND OTHER GROUPS

A, AA, AAA: The three levels of minor league baseball, also referred to as SINGLE-A, DOUBLE-A, and TRIPLE-A.

All-American Girls Professional Baseball League: The AAGPBL was a World War II–era alternative to major league baseball. With most young men, including the best ballplayers, fighting the war, Cubs owner/chewing gum king Philip K. Wrigley worried that fans might not want to see minor league 4-Fs in major league uniforms. He recruited former ballplayers to act as managers, among them Jimmie Foxx, and invited women from all over the country to try out for the new league. It began play in 1943 with just four teams, and to most fans, it was just a novelty. The teams had flowery-sounding nicknames such as the Daisies, Chicks, and Belles, and the players wore short dresses instead of baseball pants. "In the beginning," says star shortstop/catcher Lavone "Pepper" Davis, "a lot of people came out to laugh and the guys to look at the legs." But the league gained an enthusiastic following, and it gradually increased to 10 teams. Salaries also increased from $50 to $75 per week to as much as $600 per month, which was close to what some major leaguers of the time made. Unlike their male counterparts, however, the women had to follow strict rules of conduct. Makeup was to be worn at all times. No drinking or smoking was allowed in public. A chaperone joined them at any public engagement. And they had to attend charm school. On the other hand, they acted like major leaguers in at least one key way: says Davis, "I had a boyfriend in every town." By 1954, however, interest had waned and the league folded. Women's professional baseball remained all but forgotten until the release of the box office smash *A League of Their Own* in 1992 and the 1994 formation of the Colorado Silver Bullets, a women's team that plays men's minor league and semipro teams throughout the country.

American Association (old): A major league from 1882 to 1891. The AA was the most innovative league of its time, if you look at it from a player's and fan's perspective (as opposed to an owner's perspective). To entice National League players, AA owners rejected the NL's restrictive RESERVE CLAUSE, and the AA was the first league to hire full-time umpires, allow beer sales, and schedule games on Sundays. The AA and NL coexisted peacefully for 10 years, and even played several postseason series against each other. But the poorly managed AA couldn't keep up with the powerful, established NL. Following the 1891 season, the NL absorbed four AA clubs, effectively disbanding the rest of the Association. *See also* 1884 WORLD SERIES.

American Association (new): The American Association is currently a minor league at the TRIPLE-A level. The AA has teams in Indianapolis, New Orleans, Nashville, Louisville, Omaha, Buffalo, Oklahoma City, and Iowa.

American League: Also known as the JUNIOR CIRCUIT, the AL was founded in 1901 by "Ban" JOHNSON, a former sportswriter who gathered for the new venture several prominent players, managers, and executives from the long-established National League. The new league was not, however, embraced immediately by the baseball "powers." Instead of recognizing the value of a two-league system, the haughty NL owners saw the AL as a threat to their bank accounts, leading to two years of feuds and roster raids, a skirmish known as the AMERICAN LEAGUE WAR. By 1903, the two leagues had declared peace by signing the NATIONAL AGREEMENT. Since that time, of course, the two-league system has become a standard practice, and the AL has thrived. Thanks in part to the dominant Yankee teams of 1920 through 1964, the AL has won more than 56 percent of the World Series. The AL, however, was slower than the NL to promote racial integration and didn't have a black MVP until 1963, compared to 1949 for the NL. But the AL was the first league to expand when it added two teams in 1961; the NL embraced expansion a year later. With the demise of the Yankee dynasty after the 1964 season, the AL experienced a crisis: Owing to the earlier integration, the NL boasted most of baseball's best players—MAYS, McCOVEY, CLEMENTE, GIBSON, AARON, and others—while the AL was losing fans. To liven up games and increase fan interest, the league implemented the DESIGNATED HITTER rule in 1973, which had the effect of adding about one run per game per team. The ploy worked and attendance began to boom, so, in 1977, the AL decided to expand again by adding Seattle and Toronto. This gave the AL 14 teams versus 12 for the NL—a disparity that lasted until 1993, when the NL added the Colorado Rockies and Florida Marlins.

Atlanta Braves (also Boston, Milwaukee): National League East team. Having set up shop in 1871, the Braves are the only franchise to have fielded a team in every season of professional organized baseball. They began their history as the Boston Red Caps and were also known as the Red Stockings and Rustlers before settling on Braves in 1912. The new nickname proved popular with fans, especially when the 1914 "MIRACLE

BRAVES" captured the pennant and World Series after languishing in last place as late as July 4. Alas, postseason play eluded the team for the next 34 years, during which time the perennial last-place finisher even changed its name to the Bees in a futile attempt to stimulate foundering attendance. In 1948, after the Braves name was restored, the team reached the World Series—but fell to the Indians in a six-game championship. Failing to attract enough fans in a city with two teams, the club moved to Milwaukee in 1953, in effect beginning baseball's WESTWARD EXPANSION that would also include the Dodgers and Giants moving to California. From 1957 through 1959, led by Henry AARON, Eddie MATHEWS, and Warren SPAHN, the Braves would win two pennants, come close on a third, and beat the powerhouse Yankees in a thrilling World Series. Flagging attendance again forced a move in 1966, this time eastward to Atlanta, where media mogul Ted TURNER purchased the team in 1976. Due to cable television, the Braves are one of baseball's richest and most popular teams, and in 1995 the team finally brought a World Series title to Atlanta—the first championship in any sport for that city.

Baltimore Orioles (new): American League East team. In 1953, the St. Louis Browns moved to Baltimore because the owners realized they couldn't make money in a two-team city, where the Browns always played bridesmaid to the Cardinals' bride. The club's new owners changed its nickname to pay homage to the old National League Orioles of the 1890s, and it wasn't long before a thorough rebuilding process built a pennant contender worthy of John MCGRAW's old club. From 1960 until the mid-1980s, the O's contended more often than not. And in the late 1960s, led by feisty manager Earl WEAVER, they put together one of the greatest teams in history. With a succession of 20-game winners on the mound, the Orioles had the league's best pitching staff. In the field, Brooks ROBINSON anchored the league's best defense. And at the plate, sluggers like Frank ROBINSON and Boog Powell followed Weaver's "BIG

BANG" THEORY. The club won pennants from 1969 through 1971 and again in 1979 and 1983, plus two more division titles. Alas, the great Orioles won just two World Series, and only one during Weaver's tenure, in 1970. The second championship came in 1983, when a new crop of stars—led by MVP shortstop Cal RIPKEN, and steady slugger Eddie MURRAY—beat Philadelphia's aging "Wheeze Kids" (see "WHIZ KIDS") in five games. Injuries and ill-advised forays into the free agent market decimated the club, and in 1988, the club hit rock bottom, losing a record 21 straight games to start the season. Since moving to their new home, Oriole Park at CAMDEN YARDS, in 1992, the Orioles have become baseball's most profitable team. They continued to sell out almost every game and, while most clubs were posting modest $4–$8 million profits in the early 1990s, the Orioles earned as much as $28 million in profits. When financially strapped owner Eli Jacobs sold the club in 1992, a bidding war lifted the purchase price to $173 million—a record for any American pro sports franchise.

Baltimore Orioles (old): The old Orioles came into being in 1892 and disappeared when the National League reorganized in 1900. During their first two years, they won just 106 out of 277 games, a .383 winning percentage. For five of the six years in between, however, they dominated baseball, becoming the game's most storied franchise until Babe RUTH transformed the Yankees. With six future Hall of Famers, the Orioles captured three pennants with two second place finishes, and in the postseason Temple Cup series—which pitted the league's top two finishers—the Orioles won twice. The Hall of Fame roster: Wee Willie KEELER in right field, Joe Kelley in left, Dan BROUTHERS at first, Hughie "Ee-Yah" Jennings at short, John McGRAW at third, and Wilbert ROBINSON behind the plate. They supposedly popularized "inside baseball"—the hit-and-run, squeeze, double steal, sacrifice, etc.—which dominated the game until the 1920s (actually, all those strategies were in use long before the Orioles, but when the legendary McGraw claimed his Orioles invented or popularized them, people believed him). What the Orioles can rightfully claim is that they were the dirtiest team in history. McGraw used to brag about cutting from first to third behind the umpire's back, about holding a runner on third by grabbing his belt loop, about berating and spiking umpires, about vicious, bloody brawls. Owned by the same "syndicate" that had purchased the Brooklyn team, the Orioles saw all their good players move to Brooklyn in 1899, and the Orioles were gone a year later. The American League placed a franchise in Baltimore in 1901, but when AL President "Ban" JOHNSON desired a club in New York, he ordered Baltimore transferred north. That team became the Yankees, and Baltimore would be deprived of major league baseball until 1954.

Baseball Writers Association of America (BBWAA): The union of newspaper and magazine journalists who cover baseball was established in 1908 to improve travel conditions for writers and promote uniform scoring standards. Today, the organization has grown into a powerful force: Members vote on the major postseason awards—the MVP, CY YOUNG, and ROOKIE OF THE YEAR AWARDS—and HALL OF FAME selections.

Boston Red Sox: American League East team. A charter member of the American League, the Red Sox (alternately known as the Americans, Pilgrims, Puritans, or Somersets) were, until 1920, one of baseball's proudest franchises. They won World Series in 1903, 1912, 1915, 1916, and 1918, and they boasted such stars as "Cy" YOUNG, Tris SPEAKER, Harry Hooper, and Smoky Joe Wood. The latter three championships came partly because of a young pitching phenom named Babe RUTH. Then-owner Harry Frazee needed to raise cash for his latest Broadway musical production. He sold all his stars until Ruth was the only one remaining—then he sold Ruth, at that point the single-season record-holder for home runs, for $100,000 cash and a $300,000 mortgage on Fenway Park. It was the worst move in baseball history. Not only did Ruth become the greatest player in the game, but the Red Sox fell out of contention for 25 years. The club went through two ownership changes, the last a young, wealthy logging magnate named Tom Yawkey. Whether it was the "Curse of the Bambino" or perennial lack of pitching that kept Yawkey's Sox from winning is hard to say. It certainly wasn't for lack of trying. When Yawkey took over the team in 1933, the Sox had reached absolute rock bottom: They'd finished the 1932 season 43–111, 64 games out of first. Within five years, Yawkey had purchased or traded for some of the AL's brightest stars—including Lefty GROVE, Jimmie FOXX, and Joe CRONIN—and the Sox had joined the first division. But the Yankees proved too strong until 1946, when the Sox finally put it together during the regular season only to lose a seven-game World Series to the Cardinals. Later, they put together some devastating offensive clubs; the 1950 team—with only a half-season from Ted WILLIAMS—scored 1,027 runs. The 1948 and 1949 teams weren't far behind offensively, yet none could bring the pennant home to FENWAY PARK. Carl YASTRZEMSKI took over for Williams in left field in 1961 and almost single-handedly delivered a pennant six years later. But another seven-game Series loss kept Boston fans wanting more. The 1975 club, sparked by Rookie of the Year/MVP Award winner Fred Lynn and fellow rookie Jim RICE, captured the pennant, but by this time, a pattern was established: a pennant followed by a seven-game World Series loss. In 1978, after leading by seven and one-half games in late August, they lost the division on the final game of the season, a one-game playoff against the hated Yankees (*see also* BOSTON MASSACRE). The pattern returned in 1986, when Bill BUCKNER got the blame for a near-tragic GAME SIX loss. Loyal Red Sox fans continue to wait for an end to the Curse.

Cactus League: Nickname for the SPRING TRAINING league that plays in Arizona, as compared to the league that plays in Florida, which is called the GRAPEFRUIT LEAGUE. While teams have been training in Florida and other parts of the Southeast since the 1880s, Arizona spring training is a relatively new phenomenon. Currently, eight teams play in the Cactus League: the Angels, Cubs, Brewers, A's, Padres, Giants, Mariners, and Rockies.

California Angels (originally **Los Angeles**): American League West ball club. An expansion team created in 1961, the Angels are different from nearly every other expansion team in that they took only a single year to field a pennant contender, finishing third in 1962. Their first year was played at Wrigley Field in Los Angeles, formerly a minor league ballpark, followed by three years in DODGER STADIUM, which was called Chavez Ravine when the Angels were in town. They moved to ANAHEIM STADIUM and became known as the *California* Angels in 1965, but it's worth repeating that they don't really represent all of California. Notorious for never having appeared in a World Series despite coming close in 1979, 1982, and 1986 (*see* 1986 POSTSEASON), the Angels have a distinctly Southern California flavor: They play just a few miles from Disneyland, and they're owned by actor-cowboy Gene Autry.

Central Division: As of the 1994 SEASON, the Central Division is one of three divisions in each league of major league baseball. The AL's Central Division consists of Cleveland, Chicago, Milwaukee, Minnesota, and Kansas City. The NL Central consists of Cincinnati, Chicago, St. Louis, Houston and Pittsburgh.

Chicago Cubs: National League Central team. A charter member of the National League, the Cubs have represented Chicago since the 1870s, at first calling themselves the White Stockings. From 1880 to 1890 and 1901 to 1918, the team perennially challenged for the pennant and won nine of them. Their biggest success came in 1906, when the team, led by the TINKER TO EVERS TO CHANCE double play combination and a great pitching staff, won an all-time record 116 games. World Series victories in 1907 and 1908 and pennants in 1910 and 1918 followed, and the club moved into brand-new WRIGLEY FIELD in 1916. The team then slumped until 1929, when a

high-powered offense led by Hack WILSON and new arrival
Rogers HORNSBY drove the team to the pennant. They
reached the World Series again in 1932 and 1935 but lost the
championship for the fifth straight time. Since then, returning to the postseason has been a rare and celebrated event; a
1945 pennant, in the midst of World War II, has proved to be
their last. But they have come close: in 1969, they led the NL
East for much of the season before falling to the "MIRACLE
METS"; in 1973; they finished just five games out after leading
for much of the season; in 1984, now owned by the Chicago
Tribune Co., which purchased the club from the Wrigley family in 1981, the Cubs lost the NLCS after winning the first two
games of a five-game series; and in 1989, another NL East title
was wasted in an NLCS loss to the Giants. You'll often hear
Cubs fans referred to as "long-suffering Cubs fans." Under-
standable, considering the Cubs haven't won a championship
since 1908, an American professional sports record.

Chicago White Sox: American League Central team. In 1900,
crafty owner Charles COMISKEY challenged the incumbent National League Cubs for the attention of baseball-crazy Chica-
goans when he moved his American League team from St.
Paul to Chicago. It was an unqualified success. The White
Stockings, as they were first known, won the AL's first two
pennants, slumped, then captured the 1906 pennant to challenge the crosstown Cubs on the field. Despite a pathetic offense, the White Sox (as the name was shortened to) used
their dominant pitching to best the Cubs, who won a record
116 games during the regular season, four games to two. The
Sox wouldn't win another pennant until 1917, as recent arriv-
als Eddie COLLINS and "Shoeless" Joe JACKSON led the club to
100 victories and a World Series championship. The title
would prove to be their last. In 1919, the Sox dominated the
American League but lost a stunning World Series upset to
the Reds. Throughout the Series, rumors abounded that gamblers had gotten to the Sox, and afterward the rumors turned
out to be true (*see also* 1919 WORLD SERIES). The BLACK SOX

SCANDAL rocked the game, leading to numerous reforms, including the formation of the commissioner's office. More than that, it shattered the White Sox franchise because eight Chicago players were kicked out of baseball. They didn't recover to post a pennant winner—or even a serious contender—until the 1950s. In March 1959, Bill VEECK purchased controlling interest in the club from the Comiskey family. On the field, the club celebrated the change as the "Go-Go Sox," led by the double play combination of Luis APARICIO and Nellie Fox and outfielder Minnie MINOSO, captured their last AL pennant, only to lose to the now-Los Angeles Dodgers in a six-game Series. Veeck sold the club, then repurchased it in 1976, but they didn't win another division until after he sold it to financiers Jerry Reinsdorf and Eddie Einhorn in 1981. The Sox won division titles in 1983 and 1993 with first baseman/MVP Frank THOMAS, baseball's best all-around slugger since Mickey MANTLE. But in neither year did they make it to the Series.

Cincinnati Reds: National League Central team. Professional baseball came out of the closet in Cincinnati in 1869 (*see* CINCINNATI RED STOCKINGS) with a club that went undefeated. They approached those heights again in 1882 as the Reds, now members of the American Association after five years in the National League, captured the AA pennant by 11½ games. Thirty-seven years passed before another pennant, and this time the club captured the World Series. But it was a tainted title, as the 1919 WORLD SERIES would best be remembered for the scandal that erupted a year later: The expulsion of eight Chicago players accused of fixing the Series (*see also* BLACK SOX SCANDAL). A decade later, Larry MACPHAIL took over the club presidency, introducing night baseball and hiring Red BARBER as a full-time radio play-by-play man. The combative MacPhail lasted only a few years, but he'd done his job. Attendance soared, and so did the club. They won pennants in 1939 and 1940, capturing the latter World Series with the pitching of 1939 MVP Bucky Walters and the hitting of

1940 MVP Frank McCormick (probably the two least-known MVP winners ever). No Reds team made another pennant run until the late 1950s. They did make big news, however, when they succumbed to the McCarthyism that was sweeping the nation: the team removed the word "Reds" from home jerseys—where it had been for 45 years—and changed the name to "Redlegs"; the dumb move lasted until 1961. After the "Reds" name was restored, the club captured a pennant in 1961, then went dry for the rest of the decade. The move into modern RIVERFRONT STADIUM in 1970 seemed to spark the Reds to new heights. Led by Pete ROSE, Johnny BENCH, Joe MORGAN, Tony Perez, and manager Sparky ANDERSON, the "BIG RED MACHINE" won six division titles, four pennants, and two championships, including the thrilling 1975 WORLD SERIES. Free agency and retirements dismantled the team, but in the mid 1980s, Rose returned to his home to break the all-time record for hits and to player-manage. The team finished second several times and seemed poised to break out in 1989, but that was the year Commissioner Bart GIAMATTI investigated charges that Rose had broken a long-standing rule by betting on baseball. The Reds' title hopes disappeared when Rose was booted out of the game. Under new manager Lou Piniella in 1990, however, the Reds streaked to the pennant and swept a stunned A's team in four straight to win the Series. Today, the club has been a frequent victim of injuries, and hometown hero Pete Rose remains an outcast from the game.

Cincinnati Red Stockings, 1869: It has long been accepted as fact that these Red Stockings were baseball's first professional team—and by extension, *America's* first professional sports team. Major league baseball teams even put patches on their uniforms in 1994 commemorating the "125th Anniversary of Professional Baseball." But as this book points out in many other places, such a notion is simply baseball mythology, not fact. Men were getting paid to play the game for a decade prior to the advent of the Red Stockings. Most were members of ostensibly "amateur" teams and were forced to take the cash under the table, but published reports do exist of games played as early as 1864 where proceeds from ticket sales were divided among the players. What the 1869 Red Stockings can rightfully claim is that they were the first team to *openly* recruit players with generous cash payments. In an era of ubiquitous free agency, the team hired players for between $600 and $1,400 for a 10-month schedule of games against clubs from New York, San Francisco, and just about everywhere in between. Led by brothers Harry and George WRIGHT, the Red Stockings dominated the nation with a 60–0 record, beginning a strong tradition of Cincinnati baseball that continues today.

Cleveland Indians: American League Central team. Today, we think of the Indians as a historically pathetic franchise, a perennial loser that played in a big ugly stadium and traded away all its good players and couldn't draw fans and had movies made about how bad they were. But until the late 1960s, the Indians were one of the American League's winningest teams—not in terms of pennants, because they only won three, but in terms of total victories. They started out as the Cleveland Blues, filling the void left in that city when the NL's Cleveland Spiders disbanded after the horrific 1899 season (*see* WORST TEAMS OF ALL TIME). In 1902, the club received Nap LAJOIE as part of the spoils of the AMERICAN LEAGUE WAR, but couldn't win a pennant with arguably the game's greatest second baseman. They did change their name to "Naps" in honor of their star, but when Lajoie left after the last-place 1914 season (the team's only last place finish until the 1970s), fans voted to change the team's name to Indians. The new nickname purportedly paid homage to slugging outfielder Lou Sockalexis, an American Indian, who'd starred briefly for the Spiders in the 1890s before drinking himself out of baseball and into the grave in 1913. A trade for Tris SPEAKER began the rebuilding process, and by 1917, the club returned to pennant contention. They finally reached the

World Series in 1920, overcoming the tragic death of short-stop Ray CHAPMAN to capture a stunning pennant race. That Series provided two events never before seen in baseball's ultimate stage: an unassisted triple play by Bill Wambsganss and a grand slam by pitcher Elmer Smith. Even more unlikely: a Cleveland championship, something the city wouldn't see again for 28 years. By 1948, all of baseball's stars had returned from the war, and ace pitcher Bob FELLER was at the top of his game. With shortstop Lou BOUDREAU playing and managing, the Bill VEECK-owned Indians captured the pennant after beating the Red Sox in a one-game playoff. In the Series, Cleveland topped the Boston Braves in six games behind the great pitching of another Bob, future Hall of Famer Bob Lemon. With the best pitching staff in baseball, the Indians won another pennant in 1954—this time besting the Yankees with an American League record 111 victories. But the Giants swept them in the Series, and Cleveland hasn't returned since. The Indians earned their "lovable loser" tag in the 1970s because of 20 straight seasons of second-division finishes. The movie *Major League* and its sequel did nothing to enhance the team's image. It took general manager John Hart and a revolutionary personnel strategy to do that: Hart signed his young players—Albert Belle, Carlos Baerga, Sandy Alomar, Jr., Jim Thome, and Kenny Lofton—to long-term contracts, in most cases before they became stars. And as the Indians moved into their beautiful new stadium, JACOBS FIELD, they were poised to return to the top tier of American League teams.

Colorado Rockies: National League West team. In part to keep Congress from enacting antitrust legislation against major league baseball, and in part to mine the virgin western territory of Colorado, National League owners in 1991 awarded two expansion franchises to the cities of Denver and Miami. Rockies owners Jerry McMorris and John Antonucci paid $95 million for the privilege. In the expansion draft prior to the 1993 season, the Rockies focused on putting together a team that could compete soon. "We wanted to be competitive just as fast as we can," said executive VP John McHale, Jr., after the draft, "and we wanted guys who will stay with us for a number of years." They selected several major league veterans and even signed a free agent: first baseman Andres Galarraga, late of the Cardinals. The signing of Galarraga proved a stroke of genius. Coming off two injury-plagued seasons, the former .300 hitter regained his batting stroke and, after flirting with the .400 mark, captured the batting title with a .370 average while adding 22 homers and 98 RBIs in just 120 games. Don't be surprised if Rockies players come to dominate the league's hitting categories. The city of Denver is, of course, more than 5,000 feet above sea level, and batted balls just rocket out of there. And the fans love it; in their first season, the Rockies drew over four million fans, a major league record. With baseball's realignment in the 1994 season, the Rockies vaulted into contention for the NL West title, the earliest an expansion team has ever contended for a division title or pennant (except the Angels). COORS FIELD, their new home, opened in 1995, ending the days of four million fans because the new ballpark doesn't hold as many fans as Mile High Stadium.

Continental League: An attempted "third major league" proposed by Branch RICKEY in the early 1960s, the Continental League was formed in response to major league baseball's philosophy of slow growth and limited expansion, which effectively shut out most of America. The New York Mets and Houston Colt .45s were to be Continental League franchises, but Rickey's inability to receive the necessary financial backing doomed the league, and the two clubs instead entered the National League.

Cuban Giants: The first salaried black team, the Cuban Giants, like their white counterparts the 1869–70 CINCINNATI RED STOCKINGS, dominated early black baseball. In 1885, as Jim Crow was beginning to take over white organized baseball, the club was formed by the headwaiter at a Long Island summer resort, who gathered other black waiters to provide entertainment for the hotel's guests. When the resort closed for the winter, the Athletics, as they were then called, went on a barnstorming tour against amateur, semipro, and even some major league teams, winning most contests. Later that season, the club took on some new players and a benefactor, who financed the team, shifted their home base to Trenton, New Jersey, and changed the name to the Cuban Giants. According to a famous story, the players didn't want fans and opposing players to think of them as simply a bunch of waiters, so they pretended they were foreigners, Cubans, and spoke gibberish on the field to seem authentic. They chose "Giants" because the National League's New York Giants were the most popular white club. Sol WHITE, an early player, executive, and historian of black baseball, says the Cuban Giants weren't considered a novelty act: "Their games attracted the attention of the base ball writers all over the country, and the Cuban Giants were heralded everywhere as marvels of the base ball world. They were not looked upon by the public as freaks, but they were classed as men of talent. . . . They closed the season of '86 with a grand record made against National League and leading college teams." The club joined a number of Negro leagues during the early years, but they refused an opportunity to join the all-white Eastern League in 1887 because the move would have cost them money. Still, the Cubans remained at the top of the black baseball world until the end of the century. The team that replaced them on top was the Cuban X Giants, who actually had no affiliation to the originals; they simply usurped the name to capitalize on the popularity of the originals, who then became known as the *Genuine* Cuban Giants.

Detroit Tigers: American League East team. This club has been known by a single nickname—the Tigers—since its inception in 1901, making it the only longtime major league team that can claim such a distinction. In the beginning, the Tigers had trouble winning games and drawing fans, but the arrival of Ty COBB in 1905 began to turn things around. By Cobb's first full season in 1907, when he led the league in almost every offensive category, the Tigers had won their first pennant—a close race decided by just a half a game because Detroit never made up two rainouts. They won the pennant again in 1908 by the same margin because of a rainout that was never made up; under today's rules, of course, they would have to play those missing games. In 1909, there was no dispute as Detroit captured its third straight pennant by three and one-half games. Cobb and his teammates, however, failed in all three of those World Series, losing to the Cubs in 1907 and 1908 and to the Pirates in 1909. Throughout the rest of his career, Cobb would win a number of batting, slugging, RBI, and other offensive titles, but no more pennants. In fact, the Tigers didn't return to the pennant hunt until 1934, when the G-Men—Hank GREENBERG, Goose Goslin, and Charlie GEHRINGER—plus catcher/manager Mickey COCHRANE carried the team to the World Series. The Tigers suffered their fourth straight Series loss when the Cardinals won Game Seven by a score of 11–0, but a year later, they were back, this time beating the Cubs in six games to capture the team's first World Series championship. They split World Series in 1940 and 1945, losing to the Reds and beating the Cubs. The Tigers didn't win again until 1968—the "Year of the Pitcher." With 31-game winner Denny MCLAIN and 17-game winner Mickey Lolich, the team stormed to the pennant and squeezed past the Cardinals in a seven-game Series. Sixteen years later, the team dominated baseball again. They started that season 35–5 and never looked back on the way to 104 wins and a 4–1 World Series victory. Unlikely hero Willie Hernandez, with 32 saves in 33 opportunities, won the MVP and Cy Young Awards, and the middle infield tandem of Lou Whitaker and Alan Trammell showed why they'd been together since 1977. Today, the Tigers have distinguished themselves as perennially a great offensive team but also a terrible pitching one. Since they play in the close confines of TIGER

STADIUM—the league's oldest ballpark, which opened in 1912—it's not hard to understand why.

Double-A: Designation for the third level of minor league baseball, two steps ahead of rookie leagues and two steps below the majors. As with TRIPLE-A teams, each major league club is allowed to field one Double-A team. Representing cities from Portland, Maine, to Wichita, Kansas, Double-A leagues include the Texas, Eastern, and Southern leagues.

Eastern Division: One of three divisions in each league of major league baseball, the Eastern Division, as of the 1994 SEASON, is home to 10 teams: in the National League, Philadelphia, Montreal, New York, Atlanta, and Florida; in the American, Boston, New York, Toronto, Detroit, and Baltimore.

Federal League: A short-lived challenge to major league baseball's monopolistic two-league system, the Federal League set up operations in 1914 and lasted just two seasons. Federal League teams offered higher salaries but failed to attract enough stars or fans for the league to continue. Although then–Federal Judge Kenesaw Mountain LANDIS refused to hear its case, the Federal League mounted a legal challenge against major league baseball, alleging antitrust violations, that reached all the way to the U.S. Supreme Court. In a landmark 1922 ruling, the Court struck down the Federal League's challenge, illogically maintaining that major league baseball was a sport, *not* interstate commerce, and was thus immune from federal antitrust laws. This decision would be upheld three more times in history, including the famous *FLOOD V. KUHN* decision of 1972 that, despite the players' loss in court, opened the gates to free agency.

Florida Marlins: American League East team. Like the Colorado Rockies, the Marlins joined major league baseball for the 1993 season as part of the National League's third expansion. Blockbuster Video CEO Wayne Huizenga cajoled his way into favor with National League owners to secure the franchise for Miami in 1991, while St. Petersburg and other cities could only wait and hope for another chance. During the expansion draft, Marlins officials selected mostly minor league prospects, hoping to build a contender for the future, not the present. In 1993, the Marlins did manage to finish ahead of one team in their division—the pathetic Mets. With good ownership, star outfielder Gary Sheffield, and potential stars Jeff Conine and Kurt Abbott, the Marlins have a chance of becoming good in the next five to 10 years.

Grapefruit League: Nickname given to the SPRING TRAINING league that plays in Florida, as opposed to the CACTUS LEAGUE, which plays in Arizona. Twenty major league teams are members of the Grapefruit League: Red Sox, Yankees, Indians, Blue Jays, Orioles, Tigers, White Sox, Royals, Twins, Rangers, Marlins, Expos, Mets, Phillies, Pirates, Cardinals, Braves, Reds, Astros, and Dodgers.

Greatest Teams of All Time: The following chart lists 16 individual teams widely considered the greatest of all time. Each of them won the pennant, but some failed notably in the World Series.

Year/Team	Stars/Notes	Record	World Series
1902 Pirates	Wagner, Leach, Chesbro • Finished 27½ games in first place, led league in nearly every category	103–36	No World Series played
1906 Cubs	Evers, Chance, Brown • All-time record number of team victories.	116–36	L, 2–4 to White Sox
1911 A's	Baker, Collins, Plank • "$100,000 infield" at its peak.	101–50	W, 4–2 over Giants

Year/Team	Stars/Notes	Record	World Series
1912 Red Sox	Speaker, Wood • Wood's 34 victories won pennant in midst of Philadelphia's 4 titles in 5 seasons.	105–47	W, 4–3 over Giants
1927 Yankees	Ruth, Gehrig, Lazzeri, Hoyt • "Murderer's Row"	110–44	W, 4–0 over Pirates
1931 A's	Foxx, Grove, Cochrane • Power, pitching, defense; essentially same team as 1929 and 1930 pennant-winners.	107–45	L, 3–4 to Cardinals
1936 Yankees	DiMaggio, Gehrig • DiMaggio rookie, Gehrig won MVP.	102–51	W, 4–2 over Giants
1939 Yankees	DiMaggio, Gordon, Keller • DiMaggio won first of three MVPs.	106–45	W, 4–0 over Reds
1942 Cardinals	Musial, Slaughter • Musial rookie; 2nd-place Dodgers won 102.	106–48	W, 4–1 over Yankees
1953 Dodgers	Robinson, Snider, Campanella • Best all-around season for Boys of Summer.	105–49	L, 2–4 to Yankees
1954 Indians	Wynn, Feller, Lemon • AL record for team victories; four future Hall of Famers on pitching staff.	111–43	L, 0–4 to Giants
1961 Yankees	Mantle, Maris, Ford • Record number of home runs (240) and slugging pct. (.442) in expansion year.	109–53	W, 4–1 over Reds

Year/Team	Stars/Notes	Record	World Series
1962 Giants	Mays, McCovey, Marichal • Great offensive team beat Dodgers in thrilling 3-game playoff.	103–62	L, 3–4 to Yankees
1969 Orioles	F. & B. Robinson, Palmer • Dominant pitching, great fielding; same essential team as 1970 and 1971 pennant winners.	109–53	L, 1–4 to Mets
1975 Reds	Morgan, Bench, Rose • "Big Red Machine" dominated baseball.	108–54	W, 4–3 over Red Sox
1986 Mets	Strawberry, Carter, Gooden • Great pitching, powerful hitting.	108–54	W, 4–3 over Red Sox

Homestead Grays: The most famous of all NEGRO LEAGUES franchises, the Grays got their start as a group of black Pittsburgh steelworkers in 1910. Cumberland POSEY joined the team in 1911, took over the managerial reins in 1916, and owned the club by the 1920s. Initially an independent club, the Grays boasted such stars as future Hall of Famers Martin DIHIGO, Oscar CHARLESTON, "Cool Papa" BELL, and others. Beginning in 1929, the Grays, now based alternately in Washington, D.C., and Pittsburgh, moved from one Negro league to another until finally settling in the Negro National League in 1935. By 1937, with Josh GIBSON and Buck LEONARD leading the way, the Grays won nine straight NNL pennants. The deaths of Posey and Gibson in 1946 and 1947 sent the club into a slump, but they bounced back to win the 1948 and 1949 pennants. The integration of the major leagues, however, spelled doom for the Grays, as for most Negro league teams. They folded after the 1951 season.

Houston Astros: National League Central team. Originally created as an entry into the failed CONTINENTAL LEAGUE, the Houston Colt .45s (as they were then known) joined the NL during the expansion of 1962 and played home games in a hot, humid, bug-infested outdoor stadium. When the ASTRODOME opened in 1965, the club changed its name to honor the new home. Though they've never appeared in a World Series, the Astros have come close twice, losing in the final game of the 1980 NLCS and in the exciting GAME SIX of the 1986 playoffs. Poor ownership has been one of the team's flaws; in the summer of 1992, for example, the team's owner rented the Astrodome to the Republicans for their National Convention for an entire month—forcing the Astros to play 28 straight road games. Happily, that owner sold the team after the 1992 season, and with the advent of realignment for the 1994 SEASON, the club is ready to challenge for the pennant in the years ahead.

International League: A long-time minor league at the AAA level that includes teams from Maine, New York, Massachusetts, Virginia, and Ohio. There used to be franchises in Toronto and Montreal, but ever since major league baseball coopted those cities, there's actually nothing international about the I-League anymore.

Junior Circuit: Nickname for the American League, so called because the AL is 25 years younger than the NL (compare SENIOR CIRCUIT).

Kansas City Monarchs: This famed NEGRO LEAGUES team was founded in 1920 and, except for five seasons, fielded a team continuously until 1957, an impressive feat during the eras of the Depression and World War II. Owned by J. L. Wilkinson, who was one of the few white owners of Negro league clubs, the Monarchs were successful both on the field and at the ticket window. They won or challenged for pennants during almost every season of their existence, and their all-time team roster reads like a roll call of Negro league greats: Bullet Joe Rogan, Satchel PAIGE, Cristobal TORRIENTE, "Turkey" STEARNES, "Cool Papa" BELL, Willie WELLS, Buck O'NEIL, Jackie ROBINSON, Ernie BANKS, Elston Howard, and others.

Kansas City Royals: American League Central team. The Royals came to life during the 1969 expansion, partially as a way to quash the threats against baseball's antitrust exemption made by a Missouri senator, who was angry that Charlie FINLEY had moved the Athletics from Kansas City to Oakland a few years before. (Most of baseball's expansion, in fact, has come about because of Congressional threats or lawsuits.) Owned by Ewing Kauffman, a patent medicine magnate, the Royals drafted shrewdly and were able to field a winning team in just their third year of existence and a serious pennant contender in their fifth. Once Finley gutted the A's to break their string of five straight division titles, the Royals came to the forefront of the AL West, capturing division crowns from 1976 through 1978. The team could not, however, get past the Yankees in any League Championship Series. After a year off, the Royals returned to the postseason in 1980, this time defeating New York in the LCS to appear in their first World Series. That season, third baseman George BRETT, easily the greatest player in team history, came within five hits of batting .400, but an attack of hemorrhoids curtailed his hot hitting in the Series and the Royals lost to the Phillies in six games. They stayed in contention throughout the early 1980s, winning back to back division titles in 1984 and 1985. It was in 1985 that they finally captured a World Series, beating St. Louis in a Game Six that hinged on an umpire's blown call and a blowout Game Seven.

Little League: The organized baseball league for preteen boys and girls was established in 1939 by Carl E. Stotz in Williamsport, Pennsylvania, which is where the Little League World Series is now held every year. The league's motto of "Character, Courage, Loyalty" has come under scrutiny in recent years: in

1974, a court order had to force Little League teams to accept girls; in the late 1970s, when foreign teams began dominating LLWS competition, the governing body ruled that the final game had to pit a U.S. team against a foreign team rather than mixing all the teams randomly in one pool; and in 1992, the team from the Philippines was stripped of its title when it was discovered that many of its players were overage. Unfortunately for the children, many fathers consider Little League games to be the means for their sons and daughters to fulfill their dying dreams; they pressure their children to win at all costs—at the expense of the children. Still, for youngsters between the ages of 8 and 12, there is no better way to learn baseball than to play Little League.

Los Angeles Dodgers (formerly **Brooklyn**): National League West team. The Dodgers are, with the Yankees and Giants, among baseball's most storied teams; its exploits have been celebrated in books and movies, songs and poems. They went through a number of team nicknames—from Bridegrooms in the 1890s (because several of the team's players had married in the off-season) to Superbas (the name of a famous circus act) to Robins (in honor of manager/team president Wilbert ROBINSON)—before finally settling on Dodgers (short for Trolley Dodgers, which is what denizens of other New York boroughs derisively called Brooklynites) in the early 1930s. The franchise joined the National League in 1890 after starting out in the American Association, playing good ball throughout much of the decade. They didn't win a pennant until their owner, who co-owned the Baltimore Orioles, transferred all of Baltimore's best players to Brooklyn in 1899. After repeating their success in 1900, the club fell into turmoil. Charley Ebbets, who'd started his career with the team as a ticket seller, purchased majority ownership and clashed with his partners. They sank to last place in 1905 and remained in or around the cellar for most of the next dozen seasons. Meanwhile, the team moved into a new concrete and steel ballpark, EBBETS FIELD, to replace old, broken-down Washington Park. In 1916, now managed by Wilbert Robinson, the team made it to the World Series, only to lose to Babe RUTH's Red Sox. They won another pennant in 1920, this time losing to Cleveland in the Series. For the next 21 years, the team failed to qualify for the postseason, and club officials realized something drastic had to be done. They hired volatile general manager Larry MACPHAIL from Cincinnati and gave him free rein. Through deft trades and brilliant moneymaking schemes—such as installing lights at Ebbets Field and promoting games on the radio with announcer Red BARBER—MacPhail had built a pennant winner by 1941. The Dodgers lost that World Series to the Yankees, their third straight Series loss, and a year later, MacPhail was gone: off to war to fight the Germans. Certified baseball genius Branch RICKEY then came aboard and began to build a dynasty. Signed by Rickey, Jackie ROBINSON broke the COLOR BARRIER and returned the Dodgers to the World Series in 1947. Other great players followed Robinson to Brooklyn: Roy CAMPANELLA, Don NEWCOMBE, Duke SNIDER, Gil Hodges, and more. *THE BOYS OF SUMMER*, as they would come to be called in the title of a well-known book, won pennants in 1949, 1952, and 1953—losing to the Yankees each time in the Series—before winning everything in 1955. They followed that with another pennant, and another loss to the Yankees, in 1956. Meanwhile, a new man had taken over the club's reins: Walter O'MALLEY. O'Malley began his rise to head of the Dodgers franchise in 1941, when his employer, the Brooklyn Trust Company, took over partial ownership in bankruptcy proceedings. He invested his own money and became a part-owner by the mid-1940s, but he knew almost nothing about baseball. He let co-owner Rickey handle that. With O'Malley handling the business and Rickey the players, the club flourished and became a perennial pennant winner. But after years of fights, O'Malley forced Rickey out in a bitter power struggle. O'Malley would wield great influence over other team owners, so his biggest achievement received hardly any opposition in ownership circles: his transfer of the Dodgers from Brooklyn to Los

Angeles after the 1957 season to continue baseball's WEST-WARD EXPANSION. Fans in Brooklyn weren't as generous, however, branding O'Malley a traitor and worse. After one bad year, the Dodgers returned to the World Series in 1959, beating the White Sox—the first time the Dodgers had faced anybody in the Series but the Yankees in 39 years. Behind the great Sandy KOUFAX–Don DRYSDALE pitching staffs of the 1960s, the club captured three more pennants and two Series victories. They lost three more World Series in the 1970s but rebounded to become the only team to win two Series in the 1980s. Now and for the last two decades, the Dodgers regularly draw over three million fans per season and are among the top two or three most valuable sports franchises in America. They're known for their remarkable stability in the front office—they've had only two managers in the last 40 years—probably because their owner, Peter O'Malley, Walter's son, makes his money entirely from baseball (unlike most owners, for whom baseball is a hobby). That's why the Dodgers, who periodically post bad seasons, never remain bad for long.

major leagues: The self-defining term that refers to the country's best baseball leagues. In addition to the National and American Leagues, which received "major league" certification in 1876 and 1901, respectively, there have been a number of other major leagues in this country. The baseball establishment recognizes seven different leagues throughout history as "major":

League	Years
National Association	1871–1875
National League	1876–present
American Association	1882–1891
Union Association	1884
Players' League	1890
American League	1901–present
Federal League	1914–1915

Mexican League: The infamous Mexican League case occurred in 1946, but its ramifications were felt for decades.
That was the year Mexican League officials attempted to ele-
vate their league to "major league" status by luring American
players south of the border with the promise of higher salaries. During the off-season, the league enticed six players,
whose contracts had expired, including minor stars Vern
Stephens, Sal Maglie, and Mickey Owen, to play in Mexico, ig-
niting a firestorm of controversy that raged throughout team
and major league offices. Because baseball's powers considered the Mexican League a threat to their profit-making monopoly, Commissioner "Happy" CHANDLER issued a harsh
edict: Any player signing a Mexican League contract would be
barred from American baseball for five years. Such a threat, of
course, scared most ballplayers from leaving. As it turned out,
the Mexican League soon folded due to poor organization
and lack of funds—which, of course, left those players who
did sign with no place to go. One player, a youngster named
Danny Gardella, fought back. With the help of lawyer
Frederic Johnson, Gardella sued baseball on the grounds that
the RESERVE CLAUSE that supposedly bound him to a club for
life was "a conspiracy in restraint of trade." To the owners'
dismay, Gardella won a judgment from the federal Court of
Appeals. This threat to their monopoly forced baseball executives into action again, and Commissioner Chandler declared
amnesty toward all Mexican League players. Though Gardella's case was still valid, Danny needed to feed his family, so to
avoid a protracted court battle, he accepted a settlement
worth $60,000 and dropped the lawsuit. The next serious
challenge to the reserve clause would come just three decades
later, when Curt FLOOD and Marvin MILLER took the case all
the way to the Supreme Court.

Milwaukee Brewers (new): American League Central team
since 1970. The franchise was founded prior to the 1969 season as the Seattle Pilots, which lasted one horrible, nearly
bankrupt season. Current owner Bud SELIG then purchased

the team and moved it to Milwaukee, where fans were desperate for major league baseball after losing the Braves in 1965. It took only eight years to field a division contender and twelve years for a pennant winner. That came in 1982, when the slugging Brewers—known as "Harvey's Wallbangers" in honor of manager Harvey Kuenn—captured the AL pennant but lost to the St. Louis Cardinals in the famed "World Series of Suds." Today, the Brewers face the dilemma of most small-market teams: Low television and merchandising revenues translate to low payrolls, which hinders their ability to compete for high-priced free agents—thus, to compete for the pennant. Although I am skeptical whenever baseball owners shout poverty, I do believe this particular argument. Until baseball adopts some sort of revenue-sharing plan, it's likely that teams such as Milwaukee, Pittsburgh, and Seattle may never reach a point of sustained excellence; they may win a pennant now and then but will probably never contend year after year like the Dodgers and Blue Jays.

Milwaukee Brewers (old): The Brewers were originally a team in the American League's very first season, 1901. After finishing in last place, the franchise was immediately moved to St. Louis to become the Browns, which transferred to Baltimore in 1953 to become the Orioles.

Minnesota Twins (formerly the old **Washington Senators**): American League Central team. After 60 years in the nation's capital, Washington Senators owner Calvin Griffith bolted for the greener pastures of Minnesota. The Senators had been losing money, as well as a lot of games, and the people of Minneapolis–St. Paul were clamoring for a team. The change of scenery did wonders. A perennial also-ran in Washington, the Twins finished second and third in 1962 and 1963, then won the pennant in 1965, losing the World Series to Los Angeles. In 1967, the Twins led the AL until the last day of the season, when the "IMPOSSIBLE DREAM" Red Sox swept a doubleheader to beat the Twins by a single game. They followed with division titles in 1969 and 1970, led by slugger Harmon KILLEBREW and sweet-swinging Rod CAREW, but couldn't top the Orioles in the LCS. During the 1970s, the Twins finished third or fourth nearly every season, and owner Griffith was mostly responsible: He resisted the high salaries stars were making, and he traded away all his stars for low-cost alternatives. The team dropped to last place in 1982, the year the team moved into the HUBERT H. HUMPHREY METRODOME. Griffith finally sold the team in 1983 to banker Carl Pohlad. The most popular player in the history of the franchise, Kirby PUCKETT, joined the team a season later, and in 1987, the Twins won another division title. Despite the lowest winning percentage of any American League pennant winner, the Twins captured their first World Series, a seven-game victory over St. Louis in the first Series ever played indoors. By 1990, they were in last place again, but in 1991, they and the Atlanta Braves became the first teams ever to go from "worst to first" in a single season. In the 1991 WORLD SERIES, the Twins vanquished the Braves in one of the most thrilling championships in baseball history.

minor leagues: The story of the minor leagues is like the story of what happens to a small town when Big Business moves in. Since the founding of professional baseball, minor leagues have existed and flourished throughout the country, usually in small cities like Pocatello, Idaho, and Durham, North Carolina, but sometimes also in places as big as Detroit and Miami. At one time, thousands of players in dozens of minor leagues performed for fans who otherwise had no contact with professional baseball. In order to survive, minor league teams would sign young players right out of high school or a small college, usually local kids, and if they got good enough that major league scouts were interested, they'd sell the players to big league clubs. Attendance and player sales—that's how minor league owners made their money. But when major league owners began to realize that professional baseball could be a big moneymaker—and some owners realized it sooner than others—they started manipulating minor league teams to their advantage. Around the 1920s, the major leagues began to set limits on how much they would have to pay for minor league players. Then they set a hierarchy of leagues, depending mostly on sizes of the cities, like we see today; back then, however, there were class A, B, C, and D leagues, as well as AA and AAA. A player would work up the minor league ladder all the way to the majors. Meanwhile, savvy owners and general managers were following Branch RICKEY's lead: They began setting up "farm systems" of minor league teams owned by major league clubs. The big club would sign agreements that would give them the pick of the litter from their minor league affiliates. At this point, minor league owners found themselves in trouble. Profits were sagging because they couldn't sell their best players on the open market to the highest bidders. And fans stopped coming to games because they had no bonds with the local players; once a player became good and popular, he'd get called up by a major league club. Of course, this wasn't the case everywhere. In leagues with little major league affiliation, like the PACIFIC COAST LEAGUE in the 1930s, for example, a lot of players became local heroes and attendance flourished; Buzz Arlett, for example, smashed over 400 minor league home runs, more than half with the PCL's Oakland Oaks. But for the majority of teams, it was all they could do to survive financially. So major league clubs took the inevitable step: They started to buy out minor league teams. That's the system we have today for almost every minor league team. The big club pays all the player salaries and a stipend to the small club for operating expenses. The minor league team's profits depend on attendance, which is tough because meaningful pennant races usually don't exist at the minor league level. If a guy is hitting .350 with a bunch of home runs and his team is in first with two weeks to go, none of that matters to a big league club if it wants a player to come off the bench every six days to pinch-hit. Like the small town that used to have a dozen corner stores before the Wal-Mart moved in, the minor leagues were ruined by corporate greed. The minors have a great history in the United States, and it's a real shame that major league owners destroyed them.

Montreal Expos: National League East team. The Expos own probably the least exciting nickname in all of team sports, its source being the Expo '67 World's Fair. Born during the 1969 expansion, the Expos continued a strong tradition of baseball in Montreal, where the minor league Royals had established a large fan base. The club's first year was typical of an expansion team, as they finished in last with a miserable 52–110 record, 48 games out of first. They got as close as three and a half games behind the division leader in 1973, but they didn't break the .500 mark until 1979. Two years later, thanks to the players' strike that split the season in half, the Expos captured the second-half quarter-pennant and beat the Phillies to win the NL East title. They made it close against the Dodgers in the NLCS, but Rick Monday's home run in the top of the ninth in Game Five broke Montreal's hearts. That has been the closest they've gotten to the World Series, and it stands to reason that they may never reach a level of sustained excellence. The problem? They can't attract the high-profile free agents other clubs can because (1) they're not a major market, so they can't draw as many fans or make as much money from TV deals as other clubs; (2) they're located in French-speaking Quebec, where players have to deal with a whole different culture; (3) the fans are seemingly apathetic; and (4) the team doesn't have a distinct identity. They currently have lots of good young players, and they may soon challenge for the pennant, but we'll see if they can do it year after year.

National Association of Base Ball Players: The first professional baseball league, the Association was formed in 1871 but was so disorganized it lasted only a few years. As the name suggests, players rather than club owners had all the power. They could jump their contracts with ease, going wherever the money was. Teams could join just by paying a $10 entry fee, so clubs dropped out regularly. There was no set schedule; teams were expected to play each other five times per season, but they often did not. The volunteer umpires couldn't control the players, and the weak league office had little disciplinary power. Without proper financing, the league was doomed, and its demise in 1875 set the stage for the formation of the National League a year later.

National League: As with the birth of the American League, the National League was born in response to an outrageous season by the previously established league. With the AL, it was the 1899 season, which culminated in the disbanding of four National League clubs. For the NL, it was the NATIONAL ASSOCIATION's 1875 season, dominated by the 71–8 record posted by Harry WRIGHT's Boston Red Stockings, that got other club owners thinking about forming another, tightly controlled league. The brainchild of Chicago White Stockings owner William HULBERT, the National League of Base Ball Clubs would be an *owner's* league, not a *player's* league. The owners set limits on who could enter the league. They created a RESERVE CLAUSE to bind players to their clubs for life. They implemented regular schedules and paid independent umpires (though not full-time umpires; the AMERICAN ASSOCIATION started that). Compromise candidate Morgan Bulkeley was named the head of the League, but he really had nothing to do with anything; it was Hulbert's baby. In any case, when Bulkeley failed to show up for a meeting in 1877, he was ousted in favor of Hulbert, who ruled until his death in 1882. During the NL's first 25 seasons, the League vanquished three rivals—the AA, Union Association, and PLAYERS' LEAGUE. But League owners couldn't stop the American League from cutting into their monopoly beginning in 1901 (see AMERICAN LEAGUE WAR). The system of peaceful coexistence between the two leagues, which we take for granted today, was a hard-fought and bitter battle. Still, players and managers in each league take a lot of pride in beating the other in World Series and All-Star Games. One fact that gets trumpeted every year around July is that the NL once had a stranglehold on All-Star Games, winning the midsummer classic 21 out of 23 tries from 1963 through 1985. The reason for the dominance can almost certainly be traced to the fact that the NL was the first league to really embrace black and Latin players. Think of the stars from the 1950s through the 1970s: ROBINSON (both Jackie and Frank), SNIDER, MAYS, MANTLE, CAMPANELLA, AARON, BERRA, BANKS, CLEMENTE, MCCOVEY, MUSIAL, WILLIAMS, KOUFAX, GIBSON, MARICHAL, BROCK, KALINE, ROSE, MATHEWS, CEPEDA, BENCH, MORGAN, and so on. Most of those players are black or Latin, and most played in the National League. Over the last decade, however, the AL has gotten even; now the AL has most of the really exciting players, such as Frank THOMAS, Ken GRIFFEY, Jr., and Albert Belle. The AL and NL expanded in 1961 and 1962, respectively, then again in 1969, during the latter expansion splitting into two divisions each. In 1977, the AL placed franchises in Seattle and Toronto, and in 1993 the NL finally agreed to expand by adding teams in Denver and Miami. One thing the NL has never agreed to, however, is the implementation of that offensive abomination known as the DESIGNATED HITTER. The NL and Japan's Central League are the only two organized leagues in the entire world that haven't adopted the DH, a fact that ALers gleefully highlight to show how old-fashioned and hardheaded the NL is for not using the DH. (My thoughts on the DH should be clear.) The best thing about the current system, in which each league now plays a distinctly different style of baseball, is that NL fans get a perverse sense of retribution against the AL every year at World Series time, when both teams have to let pitchers bat when they play in NL stadiums. Watching an AL pitcher, who usually hasn't picked up a bat since high school, flail against a major league slider almost makes up for the damage the AL has done to the game.

Negro leagues: Negro leagues were born out of the desire for players of races other than white—mainly African-Americans and dark-skinned Latins—to play baseball in organized leagues. As the COLOR LINE became entrenched in white "organized" baseball in the 1880s and 1890s, nonwhite ballplayers led by such luminaries as Sol WHITE and, later, Rube FOSTER made it their life's work to create and maintain leagues for the 10 to 15 percent of the American population shut out from the mainstream by blatant racism. You may notice throughout this book that I refer to the "Negro leagues" with a lower-case "l," whereas a number of current books capitalize both words. "Negro league" is a generic term the same way "major league" is. Both terms encompass the numerous specific organizations that do deserve capital letters, like American League and National League, etc. I think capitalizing both words makes it seem as if there was only one single specific league called the "Negro League" when, in fact, there were more than half a dozen different ones. Some such leagues were the Negro National League, Negro American League, East-West League, Eastern Colored League, Negro Southern League, and others. The Negro American and Negro National Leagues were the most famous and most successful, annually pitting the pennant winners in a "Colored World Series." League seasons generally lasted only 70 or 80 games; the rest of a team's schedule was made up of exhibition games against barnstorming major leaguers, local semipro teams, and anybody else who wanted to challenge them. As you can tell, the leagues were loosely organized, subject to the whims of the national or local economies. During the Depression, for example, a number of teams and leagues folded. Clubs depended on gate receipts to make payrolls, and because of that, Negro league play was probably the most exciting baseball played in the country. From the 1920s until the 1960s, by contrast, major league baseball was stuck in a rut. Babe RUTH had taught players how to hit home runs, so managers didn't ask for anything else. With a few notable exceptions, the game was played station to station. Get a hit, draw a walk, wait for a home run. Boring! Negro league players, on the other hand, danced off bases, stole home, and used the bunt-and-run. The players considered themselves professional entertainers, paid to put on a show. Flamboyant players such as Satchel PAIGE would call in his outfielders while he struck out the side. "Cool Papa" BELL would score from second on an infield out. Josh GIBSON would hit mammoth home runs and throw out baserunners from his knees. It's no coincidence that major league baseball changed dramatically for the better in the 1960s and 1970s, after players such as Jackie ROBINSON, Minnie MINOSO, Willie MAYS, Maury WILLS, and dozens of others had made their impacts. It wasn't until 1972 that the Hall of Fame, after years of stalling, finally agreed to create a special committee to select Negro league players for enshrinement. After electing nine, the committee was disbanded; since then, four more Negro leaguers have been elected. But from the same era of white major league baseball, there are more than 160 players in the Hall of Fame. And since the proportion of blacks in the American population from that era remained steady at 10 percent, argued Robert B. Peterson in his landmark study of the Negro leagues called *ONLY THE BALL WAS WHITE*, "then it stands to reason that 10 percent of the Hall of Famers of that time should come from the Negro leagues" (Peterson, incidentally, wrote his book in 1968). That means that at least three more players should be added; some of the most popular candidates are Cristobal TORRIENTE and Willie WELLS. John B. Holway, in his book *Blackball Stars*, presents other interesting data: research showing that Negro leaguers and major leaguers played against each other 436 times, with the "non"–major leaguers winning 268 games. People often wonder how Negro leaguers would have done in the white major leagues. Holway wonders just the opposite: How would white major leaguers have fared in an integrated league? Ruth and Gehrig no doubt would have lost some homers, argues Holway, and Cobb and Hornsby would have lost some points off their batting averages if they'd had to face a Satchel PAIGE or Smoky Joe WILLIAMS on a regular basis. Alas, the sad consequences of breaking major league baseball's color line in 1947 were the death of the Negro leagues and the creation of another color line: the one keeping nonwhites from the ranks of major league team owners.

New York Knickerbockers: The first organized baseball club, created in part by Alexander CARTWRIGHT and "Doc" ADAMS in 1845. More of a social club than a sandlot or semipro team, the Knickerbockers influenced several significant rules changes, such as the diamond-shaped infield with bases 90 feet apart, three strikes per out, and three outs per inning. The Knickerbockers published and popularized these rules, and their version of baseball, known as the "New York game," was adopted by the other baseball clubs that soon appeared—many of which played and lost to the Knickerbockers. *See also* KNICKERBOCKER RULES.

New York Mets: National League East team. The exodus of the Dodgers and Giants from New York in the late 1950s left the nation's largest city void of National League baseball. To say that the 1962 Mets were able to fill that void would be generous. In losing a record 120 games, the Mets established a record for futility that has never been in danger of being broken (*see also* WORST TEAMS OF ALL TIME). For the next six seasons, the team pretty much stayed in the cellar of the NL, save for 1966 and 1968, when they vaulted up to ninth. The next year was different. Led by Tom SEAVER and a young Nolan RYAN, the 1969 "MIRACLE METS" have become part of baseball folklore. They captured the NL East title in the first year of divisional play by winning 38 of their final 49 games, beating a Cubs team that has been unjustifiably accused of choking. In the World Series against the mighty Baltimore Orioles, the underdog Mets parlayed strong pitching, timely hitting, and often-spectacular fielding into a 4 games to 1 victory. Four years later, the team posted an unimpressive 82–79 record—their worst since 1968—but it was good enough to win them the division title and pennant, although they lost the Series to the A's. The club finished between third and sixth for the next decade before gearing up for another serious pennant run. Meanwhile, they'd traded local hero Seaver, gotten him back, and then lost him via a clerical error in the front office. Lucky for the Mets, they had a young phenom named Dwight GOODEN who would make fans forget Seaver. Gooden stormed into the baseball world in 1984, wielding a blazing fastball and remarkable control. In 1985, when the Mets finished a close second to the Cardinals, Gooden had established himself as the best pitcher in baseball. The next season, with a stellar offense to go with the league's best pitching, the Mets were unstoppable. They won 108 games and finished 21½ games in front of second-place Philadelphia. In the playoffs, the Mets won a thrilling series against Houston in the LCS and Boston in the championship to bring home their second World Series title (*see also* GAME SIX; 1986 POSTSEASON). The team finished second in 1987, then won the division again in 1988, though losing to Los Angeles in the playoffs. Team owners refused to stand pat, however, and they began trading away or losing to free agency several of the players who'd played small but significant roles on the 1986 club, including, over a period of a few years, Darryl Strawberry, Gary CARTER, Keith HERNANDEZ, Len Dykstra, Mookie Wilson, Kevin Mitchell, and others. By 1991, the team had returned to the second division, and in 1993, despite a huge payroll, the Mets posted a wretched 59–103 record. Currently possessing a depleted farm system, it's unlikely the Mets will return to the pennant hunt anytime soon.

New York Yankees: American League East team. You can't argue with the numbers proving that the Yankees are American professional sports' most successful franchise: 33 pennants, 22 World Series titles, utter dominance of the league for 45 years, a host of baseball's greatest players. It wasn't always that way. When the Baltimore Orioles shifted to New York at the request of American League president "Ban" JOHNSON in 1903, the club—first known as the Highlanders because they played in a park in upper Manhattan—had trouble competing. They finished a close second in 1904, losing on the final day on a wild pitch by Jack Chesbro, and in 1906, and then a distant second in 1910. Otherwise, fifth to eighth place finishes were more likely. Then Babe RUTH came over from the Red Sox in the most celebrated trade in baseball history: Ruth for $100,000 and a mortgage on FENWAY PARK. Boston manager Ed BARROW soon rejoined Ruth in New York, and the dynasty had begun. Barrow knew the Red Sox system so well he was able to steal away half a dozen of its players to play for the Yankees. From 1921 through 1964, the Yankees finished lower than third only twice. During those 44 years, they captured 29 pennants and 20 World Series, including four in a row once and five in a row another time. Another significant achievement during the early years was the team's move into YANKEE STADIUM in 1923; they'd shared the POLO GROUNDS with the Giants for the previous 10 years. In the meantime, Barrow and, later, George WEISS produced most of the league's top players: Ruth, Lou GEHRIG, Bill DICKEY, Lefty Gomez, Joe DIMAGGIO, Joe Gordon, Yogi BERRA, Mickey MANTLE, Whitey FORD, and many more. According to Gordon, the reason for all the championships was simple: Yankees owner Colonel Jacob Ruppert paid some of the lowest salaries in the league, and players needed the Series bonuses to live. It's not easy to select which Yankee teams were the most dominant: were they the Ruth–Gehrig teams of the late 1920s, or the Gehrig–DiMaggio teams of the late 1930s, or the Mantle–Berra teams of the 1950s, or the Mantle–Maris teams of the early 1960s? In terms of sheer dominance, it's hard to argue with the selection of the postwar Yankees, as managed by Casey Stengel. During the Stengel era, 1949–60, the team won 10 pennants and seven World Series, plus four more pennants and two more championships after Stengel and Weiss were fired following the 1960 season. The 1964 season marked a turning point for the franchise. Yogi Berra managed the team through tough injuries and subpar performances, but they still won the pennant. Still, Berra was fired unceremoniously as owners Dan Topping and Del Webb sold the club to CBS. CBS also dumped popular broadcaster Mel ALLEN and generally ran the team into the ground. The team dropped to sixth in 1965, then 10th (last) in 1966—the club's first last-place finish since 1908. Slowly, they began to creep out of the second division, but it wasn't until the team's purchase by a group headed by George STEINBRENNER in 1973 that the team made any serious waves. Unlike the previous owners, Steinbrenner wasn't afraid of spending money. He dipped into the new free agent market and came away with Reggie JACKSON, "Catfish" HUNTER, and "Goose" GOSSAGE. The team captured three consecutive pennants, 1976 through 1978, and World Series victories the latter two years. But turmoil off the field was rocking the club. Over the next decade and a half, Steinbrenner would make 19 managerial changes; Billy MARTIN alone had five different stints as manager. Steinbrenner would engage in loud, public feuds with many of his star players, notably Jackson and Dave WINFIELD. And, after the 1981 pennant and subsequent loss to the Dodgers, the Yankees would go more than a dozen years without a league title—the longest drought in club history since the pre-Ruth days. Now, Steinbrenner is threatening to move out of New York City unless local government will finance a new ballpark somewhere besides the Bronx. The New York Yankees out of New York! If that happens, no one will ever be able to look at baseball as a sport ever again; as if it hasn't already, baseball will have crossed the line into the territory of ruthless business, never to return. And Steinbrenner will be to blame.

Oakland Athletics (formerly **Philadelphia**, **Kansas City**): American League West ball club. One of the AL's charter franchises in 1901, the Philadelphia A's were managed and partially owned by Connie MACK for the first 50 years of the franchise's history, until he retired at the age of 88. During his reign, Mack fielded some of baseball history's greatest teams, including the 1911–14 teams that featured the famed "$100,000 INFIELD" and the 1929–31 teams starring Jimmie Foxx, Lefty GROVE, and Mickey COCHRANE—clubs that won six pennants and four World Series between them. But Mack was equally famous for his periodic "housecleanings" that dismantled his teams through trades, sales, and cuts—often at the peak of a player's career. Consequently, A's history is replete with last-place finishes—a record 27 of them, to be exact. After 1951, when manager Mack was forced out of the dugout by his three co-owner sons, both player quality and attendance plummeted. So, in 1954, the team—which finished an astonishing 60 games out of first—was sold and moved to Kansas City. When that owner died in 1960, the team was still floundering in last place. New owner Charles O. FINLEY took over and began to infuse the team with young talent. In 1968, Finley moved the A's to Oakland, where they experienced a renaissance in the form of five straight AL West titles (1971–75) and three straight World Series victories (1972–74), led by such stars as Reggie JACKSON, Rollie FINGERS, and "Catfish" HUNTER. But Finley was a tough man to work for, and the clubhouse atmosphere reflected it: bickering, fights, and feuds were common. Finley was also very cheap. At one point in the late 1970s, Finley was angry at the deal he had with the local radio station that broadcast the team's games; to try to force a new contract, he awarded the team's exclusive broadcast rights to a 10-watt FM station owned by the University of California. That lasted about a month, but Finley's parsimony did not. Unwilling to succumb to the demands of the free agent era, Finley sold off or traded nearly all his stars, and by 1977 the team had returned to the cellar. He finally sold the team in 1981 to the Haas family, heirs to the Levi-Strauss company. By the end of the 1980s, excellence returned to Oakland as the Tony LA RUSSA–led A's won AL pennants from 1988 to 1990. Now, the Haas family has sold the club, claiming that it's impossible for the club to make a profit in a two-team area.

Pacific Coast League: A TRIPLE-A level minor league located throughout the western United States. Until the 1950s, when the Dodgers and Giants moved west, the PCL was the closest westerners got to big league baseball. The players were as celebrated locally as major leaguers were in their home cities. The PCL produced many baseball greats: Joe DiMaggio, Ted Williams, Billy Martin, Ernie Lombardi, and others. One of the PCL's greatest players, however, had only a brief major league career—Oakland's Buzz Arlett, who blasted a PCL-record 251 lifetime homers. (Actually, Arlett smashed 184 homers in other minor leagues, making him the all-time minor league home run champion.) During the golden age of the PCL (1920–57), some of the league's teams included the San Francisco Seals, Oakland Oaks, San Diego Padres, Portland Beavers, Los Angeles Angels, Seattle Rainiers, Hollywood Stars, and Sacramento Solons. Today, with major league baseball ubiquitous on the West Coast, the PCL is a misnomer. With teams in Albuquerque, Calgary, Colorado Springs, Edmonton, Las Vegas, Phoenix, Salt Lake City, Tacoma, and Tucson, most of the states represented don't touch the Pacific Ocean.

Philadelphia Phillies: National League East team. The Phillies represented the city of Philadelphia in the National League for almost 100 years before finally winning a World Series. (And Yankee fans bemoan the fact that they haven't won a championship since 1978!) This despite the fact that the Phils have had their share of great players: "Big Ed" Delahanty, Elmer Flick, Grover Cleveland Alexander, Gavvy Cravath, Chuck Klein, Robin Roberts, Richie Ashburn, Dick Allen, and many others. Philadelphia took part in the first game in National League history, a 6–5 loss to Boston on April 22, 1876. The loss typified a season in which the club went 14–45 and was expelled from the league for failing to play out their last western road trip. They returned to the league a few years later and posted a few second- and third-place finishes for the next 30 years, but didn't field a pennant winner until 1915. They lost that World Series 4–1 to the Red Sox and promptly returned to the ranks of also-rans in the National League. The blockbuster trade of Alexander to the Cubs before the 1919 season began an era that saw the Phillies finish dead last 16 times and second-to-last another eight times over the next 30 years. The club reached its absolute nadir in 1928 when it posted a 43–109 record, a winning percentage of .283. The problem was the pitching staff. Helped by the cozy BAKER BOWL, Philly pitchers boasted the league's worst ERA every year from 1918 through 1934. But it wasn't just the ballpark that contributed to those ERAs: Pete PALMER's book *The Hidden Game of Baseball* notes that the 1930 Phillies allowed 8.36 runs per game at home and 7.03 on the road, both the highest totals of all time. The Phils moved out of the antiquated Baker Bowl in 1938, but their march to respectability didn't begin until after the war. In 1950, a group of young players known as the "WHIZ KIDS," led by Ashburn, Roberts, Dick Sisler, and Curt Simmons, along with veterans such as reliever Jim Konstanty, Eddie WAITKUS, and Harry Walker, captured the National League pennant, only to get swept in the World Series by the Yankees. The Phils fell out of contention again until 1964, when the Gene Mauch-managed club led the NL for much of the season and were six and a half games in front of the Cardinals on September 21. In one of the greatest collapses in baseball history, the Phils dropped 10 straight games and lost the pennant. The 1970s, by contrast, were good to the Phillies. Behind the pitching of Steve CARLTON and the slugging of third baseman Mike SCHMIDT and outfielder Greg Luzinski, the team captured three straight NL East titles from 1976 to 1978 but couldn't make it past Cincinnati or Los Angeles to get to the Series. In 1980, everything went right. Carlton won his third of four Cy Young Awards and Schmidt his first of three MVPs as the team edged past the Astros to win Philly's first pennant in 30 years. In the Series against the Royals, Schmidt drove in seven runs and Carlton won two games in leading the Phillies to their first-ever championship. They returned to the Series in 1983 and again a decade later but couldn't bring home another championship; the 1993 Series turned on the Phillies' blowing a five-run, eighth-inning lead in Game Four, losing 15–14.

Pittsburgh Pirates: National League Central team. Known at first as the Pittsburgh "Alleghenies," then the "Innocents," the club has represented Pittsburgh since 1882, though not always with distinction. They became "Pirates" in 1891 after "pirating" a player from rival Philadelphia following the PLAYERS' LEAGUE revolt of 1890. Otherwise nondescript in the 19th century, the Pirates reached their apex around the turn of the century. They'd picked up a host of players from the disbanded Louisville club, including the immortal Honus WAGNER, and captured pennants in 1901, 1902, and 1903, shockingly losing the 1903 WORLD SERIES—the first ever played—to Boston. The Pirates won their first Series in 1909 as Wagner outplayed Detroit's Ty COBB in a battle of the best players in baseball at the time. They won another Series in 1925 and a pennant in 1927 but slumped for the next 30 years. After the war, the team dropped out of contention altogether. In 1952, despite having the game's best slugger in Ralph KINER, the team finished with a 42–112 record, 54½ games out of first place. Baseball genius Branch RICKEY joined the team and began to rebuild the sagging franchise. He signed Roberto CLEMENTE in 1954, laying the groundwork for future success, which came in 1960. The Pirates captured the pennant by seven games, and then beat the mighty Yankees in a thrilling World Series finally won on Bill MAZEROSKI's sudden home run in the final inning of the final game. They returned to the Series 11 years later to face the equally mighty Baltimore Orioles. This time, Clemente was the hero, using the national stage to remind fans that he'd been one of the best players in the game for over a decade. With additional contributions from slugger Willie STARGELL and a great pitching staff, the Pirates beat the Orioles in seven games. The Pirates never finished lower than third throughout the 1970s but couldn't return to the Series. So, in 1979, it was Stargell's turn to come to the fore. With the disco song "We Are Family" as the theme, "Pops" Stargell led the Pirates back to the World Series—a replay of the 1971 Series against the Orioles, which even ended the same way: a seven-game victory for Pittsburgh. The 1980s were less successful, as the small-market club found it couldn't compete for the high-priced free agents other clubs were signing. By 1990, deft trades and a good farm system—built by the high draft picks earned from its last-place finishes—had returned the club to the top of the division. Outfielder Barry BONDS won two MVP Awards and the Pirates won three straight division titles from 1990 through 1992. But they couldn't make it to the Series, and most of the team's expensive stars—Bonds, Bobby Bonilla, and Doug Drabek among them—have left for more fame and cash.

Players' League: By 1885, baseball owners had been angering ballplayers for nine years in the National League and three in the AMERICAN ASSOCIATION. The biggest sore point was the RESERVE CLAUSE, which bound a player to his team for life, but the leagues also set limits on salaries, fined players arbitrarily, blacklisted the players who complained or demanded higher salaries, and refused to allow for a fair grievance system. So some NL players formed a union, the Brotherhood of Professional Base Ball Players, with John Montgomery WARD as its president. They set out to negotiate a labor agreement with the NL, demanding more equitable treatment in terms of salaries (but not, it should be noted, an end to the already entrenched reserve clause). The owners, however, rejected all negotiations and, in 1888, even introduced a plan to limit salaries based on skill level. Dismissing the idea of a strike, the Brotherhood tried to open the negotiations with the owners again. The League stalled, so the Brotherhood tried a different approach: They found some investors and created their own league, called the Players' League, in which both player and investor agreed to share in the administration and profits. To begin play in 1890, the Players' League rejected the reserve clause, making every player sign a three-year contract instead, which had the effect of the clause without its harsh side effects. Numerous stars defected to the league, including King KELLY, Buck EWING, "Ol' Hoss" RADBOURN, Pete BROWNING,

Dan BROUTHERS, and others. NL owners screamed and called the new venture an "outlaw" league; rather than negotiate with it, they set out to destroy it. Heading the NL's "War Committee" was Albert G. SPALDING, the most influential person in all of baseball. He set out on a massive public relations campaign, pointing out the weaknesses in the PL's setup. He even got Henry CHADWICK, the most influential sportswriter of his day, to speak out against it, calling the Brotherhood "revolutionaries" and "secessionists." The owners even appealed to the courts to compel players back to the NL, which failed. Aside from those judges, *The Sporting News* and *The Sporting Life*, both popular weeklies, supported the players. But it wasn't enough. To entice the players to return, NL had repealed its salary limitation plan and introduced other reforms. And fans were beginning to rebel against the chaotic state of the game, with three leagues now vying for attention on the field, in the papers, and in the courthouse. No league made money that year, but the Players' League, with the most to both gain and lose, lost bigger. Typically grandiose, Spalding said, "Not in the 20 years' history of professional club organizations was there recorded such an exceptional season of financial disaster and general demoralization as characterized in the professional season of 1890." The PL folded after the 1890 season, and the American Association disbanded a year later. Peace was declared, and the National League had regained its monopoly over the game. It would last only a decade. *See* AMERICAN LEAGUE WAR.

rookie leagues: The rookie leagues are usually where major league clubs send the players they've just drafted out of high school; college draftees, by contrast, usually bypass rookie leagues and go to SINGLE-A or DOUBLE-A leagues, sometimes even TRIPLE-A. Rookie leagues usually play a shortened season, since most of their players are just getting out of school and aren't used to playing more than 30 or 40 games in a year. The Arizona and Gulf Coast Leagues are "low rookie" leagues, while the Pioneer and Appalachian leagues are called "advanced rookie" leagues.

St. Louis Browns: American League team, 1901–52; now the Baltimore Orioles. St. Louis was the most hapless franchise in American League history, winning only one pennant during its entire existence—and that coming during World War II when baseball's best players were in the military. Only a few great players were ever members of the Browns; George SISLER is clearly their best. Among the others on the team's all-time roster: a one-armed outfielder (Pete GRAY) and a midget (Eddie GAEDEL).

St. Louis Cardinals: National League Central team. One of baseball's oldest and proudest franchises, the Cardinals were founded in 1882 by a beer magnate who hoped to use the club to promote sales of his ale. Also called the Browns, Perfectos, Maroons, Red Hats, and Red Socks, St. Louis joined the National League when the AMERICAN ASSOCIATION folded in 1891. They didn't become good, however, until after General Manager Branch RICKEY instituted baseball's first farm system in 1918. With the big league club getting the top players from dozens of minor league affiliates throughout the country, the Cardinals became a National League powerhouse, winning five pennants from 1926 to 1934—the last few with the Dizzy DEAN "GAS HOUSE GANG"—and then four more with the Stan MUSIAL–led teams from 1942 to 1946. But Rickey's firing in 1942 marked the beginning of a down period for the team. Slow to integrate after the COLOR LINE was broken, the club didn't appear in another postseason game until the 1960s, when new owner August Busch Jr.—another beer magnate—rejuvenated the team. World Series victories in 1964 and 1967 and a seven-game Series loss in 1968 were due largely to the strong play of All-Stars Bob GIBSON, Orlando CEPEDA, Curt FLOOD, and Lou BROCK, none of whom would have seen action before the color line was broken. Over the next decade, the club lost several close pennant races but didn't see postseason action again until 1982 during the "World Series of Suds" against the nation's other beer capital, Milwaukee. A St. Louis victory that year preceded close losses in the 1985 and 1987 Series, and although recent seasons have produced only mediocre teams, St. Louis is one of those franchises (like the Dodgers and Yankees) that will never remain out of contention for very long.

San Diego Padres: National League West team. The dogged efforts of sportswriter Jack Murphy were responsible for bringing major league baseball to San Diego in 1969—although "major league" was a term applied loosely to the team during its early years. They finished last for their first six seasons and didn't post a winning season until 1978. In 1974, with attendance foundering, club owner C. Arnholt Smith decided to sell the club to investors from Washington, D.C., which had been recently abandoned by the team that became the Texas Rangers. At the last minute, McDonald's founder Ray Kroc bought the team to keep them in San Diego. For the next decade, the team made some ill-advised forays into the free agent market and never mounted serious competition for the pennant. In 1984, with some good free agent pickups—including Steve Garvey, Graig Nettles, and "Goose" GOSSAGE, each of whom had won a number of pennants in the 1970s—and batting champion Tony GWYNN, the Padres made it to the World Series. The powerful Tigers walloped them four games to one, and the Padres haven't been able to return. In 1993, new owner Tom Werner, responding to declining revenues and a small fan base, traded away most of the team's high-priced stars in return for cheap youngsters. If the Padres compete for the pennant by the end of the century, I'll be surprised.

San Francisco Giants (formerly **New York**): National League West team. Some 48 men who wore Giants uniforms have been inducted into the Hall of Fame as of 1994—the most of any team in major league baseball. Included in that group are men who can arguably be called the greatest manager of all time (John McGRAW), the greatest pitcher (Christy MATHEWSON), and the greatest overall player (Willie MAYS). Yet somehow, the Giants, who captured 15 pennants in their first 55 years of existence, have won just four in their last 55. The team came into being in 1883, when tobacco merchant John Day acquired several players from the recently defunct Troy Haymakers and started a new National League team in New York. He also owned the successful New York Metropolitans of the AMERICAN ASSOCIATION, and soon it became clear to him that the National League was the more profitable league. So he shifted his best players from the Mets to the "Nationals," laying the groundwork for a team that would capture the 1888 and 1889 pennants. After a dry spell in the 1890s, the Giants, as they became known, hired "Little Napoleon" McGraw to manage the team. For the next four decades, the team flourished. McGraw won his first pennant in 1904 but refused to play in a World Series against the rival American League. In 1905, tempers had subsided as the Giants remained at the top of the National League. Behind three shutouts by the amazing Mathewson, New York beat the Athletics for the franchise's first World Series championship. They lost the thrilling 1908 PENNANT RACE by a single game to the Cubs, then finished second and third in 1909 and 1910 before winning three straight league titles from 1911 through 1913 and another in 1917. None of those pennants brought Series victories, however, and the team went into the 1920s having won six 20th-century pennants—more than any other team—but only a single World Series. That changed in the next two decades. Led by fiery second baseman Frankie Frisch, the Giants began a string of four straight pennants in 1921, the first three of which pitted them in the World Series against their tenants in the POLO GROUNDS, the Yankees. The Giants won two of those four Series, then waited until 1933 before they made it back. Now the Giants had a new crop of stars— including Mel OTT and Carl HUBBELL—and a new manager, Bill TERRY, who'd taken over for McGraw after his retirement in 1932. Terry led the team to three pennants and two World Series wins before stepping down in 1941. Ott took over in the 1940s, playing and managing, but the teams didn't go anywhere. According to Brooklyn Dodger manager Leo DUROCHER, the Giants players were all too nice, and, of course, "Nice guys finish last." Durocher, in fact, replaced the ousted Ott in 1948 and three years later, after apparently teaching the players the benefits of being mean, led them on one of baseball's greatest-ever pennant chases, which culminated with Bobby THOMSON's "SHOT HEARD 'ROUND THE WORLD." They lost to the Yankees juggernaut in the Series, but with Willie Mays, their rookie center fielder that season, the team had promise. Mays would lead them to a 1954 Series victory, a 4–0 sweep of the powerful Indians. Five years after moving to California with the Dodgers in the infamous WESTWARD EXPANSION, the Giants won the 1962 pennant, which followed another legendary pennant race against the Dodgers. Over the next 30 years, the team would capture two Western Division titles and one pennant but no more World Series. The 1993 season—following the arrival of three-time MVP Barry BONDS—proved to be their biggest heartbreak. In the final year each league had just two divisions, the Giants posted 103 wins but saw no postseason action because the rival Braves won 104. With the new divisional setup (*see* 1994 SEASON), which includes a wild card team, such a disappointment will never happen again.

Seattle Mariners: American League West team. Until 1994 the Mariners were the only expansion team (other than the new Rockies and Marlins) who never made a serious challenge at the division title. The team came into being in the 1977 American League expansion to settle a long-standing lawsuit against major league baseball for the loss of the Seattle Pilots after the 1969 season. Bad ownership and a small fan base were mostly responsible for the team's performance. They had trouble paying high salaries to free agents and potential free agents both because the owners were cheap and because they didn't make much money from gate receipts or local TV revenues. Bought by a group headed by the Japanese company Nintendo, the Mariners' front office became committed to winning, even if the team's play seemed to indicate otherwise at first, and they reached the playoffs in 1995. (Superstar Ken GRIFFEY, Jr., the best player in Seattle history, had suggested that he'd leave Seattle when he became a free agent because of his teammates' apathetic attitude toward winning.)

Senior Circuit: Other name for the National League, as distinguished from the American League, known as the JUNIOR CIRCUIT. The names are based simply on chronology: The NL was created in 1876, the AL in 1901.

Single-A: The second-lowest level of minor leagues, just above the rookie leagues. Teams in Single-A leagues represent mostly small cities, such as Appleton, Wisconsin, and Durham, North Carolina. Seven Single-A leagues are around today: the California, Carolina, Florida State, Midwest, New York-Penn, Northwest, and South Atlantic Leagues.

Texas Rangers (formerly the new **Washington Senators**): American League West team. Like the Seattle Mariners, the Rangers have never won a division title. The Rangers joined the American League in the 1961 expansion as the new Washington Senators, who'd taken the place of the old Washington Senators, who'd just moved to Minnesota to become the Twins. Before the 1972 season, team owner Bob Short decided to get out of Washington, and the league's owners approved the move to Arlington, Texas. Two years later, with volatile Billy MARTIN at the helm, the Rangers finished in second place, five games out of first, the closest to the top they've ever finished (excepting the 1981 and 1994 strike-shortened seasons). From the late 1980s through the early 1990s, experts kept predicting that Texas's offense would eventually carry them to the division title. Now that they're in the weakened AL West, with only four teams, the Rangers may finally fulfill that promise.

Toronto Blue Jays: American League East team. In the 1977 American League expansion, the city received the Blue Jays franchise after failing to lure the Giants away from San Francisco. The Blue Jays are one of baseball's most profitable franchises and play in one of the game's most luxurious stadiums, the SKYDOME. After only a few lean years, the Blue Jays parlayed comprehensive scouting and excellent ownership— headed by the Labatt's Beer Company—to become one of baseball's best teams by the mid-1980s on the way to consecutive World Series victories in 1992–93. The best trade they ever made was the one that brought Roberto Alomar and Joe Carter to the Jays in exchange for Fred McGRIFF and Tony Fernandez. Alomar became baseball's best second baseman, Carter kept driving in 100 runs per season, and sweet-swinging John Olerud took McGriff's place at first base and challenged the .400 mark in 1993.

Triple-A: Designation for the highest level of minor league baseball, just a step below the majors. Today, three Triple-A leagues featuring 28 clubs in cities as large as Phoenix and as small as Pawtucket feed players to the majors: the AMERICAN ASSOCIATION, INTERNATIONAL LEAGUE, and PACIFIC COAST LEAGUE.

Veterans Committee: The group of 12 men responsible for selecting players for the Hall of Fame who had earlier been shunned (or were ineligible for selection) by the BASEBALL WRITERS ASSOCIATION OF AMERICA (BBWAA). Veterans Committee membership changes every few years and is usually made up of former players, executives, and journalists; right now, for example, the committee has six former players: in chronological order of membership, Stan MUSIAL, Al Lopez, Birdie Tebbetts, Buck O'NEIL, Monte IRVIN, and Ted WILLIAMS. The committee has a checkered voting history, making

some good and some bad moves. Among the best were the selections of Harry WRIGHT, "Goose" Goslin, "Home Run"
BAKER, John Montgomery WARD, Casey STENGEL, and several
others, especially ones from the early days of the committee
when there were still a great many top players from the early
days of baseball who weren't eligible for election by the
BBWAA. Among the worst selections have been Waite Hoyt,
Jesse Haines, Chick Hafey, Lloyd Waner, and a few others. Actually, to document all the selections of the committee here is
pointless; if you're interested, I would suggest reading the definitive book on the Hall of Fame, Bill JAMES's *Whatever Happened to the Hall of Fame?* Often, the committee is unduly
influenced by a couple of members who are able to push
through the selection of an old teammate or friend. As
pointed out in James's book, such eminently unqualified players as Haines, Hafey, Dave Bancroft, Freddie Lindstrom, Ross
Youngs, and George Kelly were chosen chiefly because they
were teammates of Frankie Frisch and Bill TERRY, who were
able to dominate the committee in the early 1970s. The recent selections of Phil RIZZUTO, Bobby Doerr, and Red Scho-
endienst—while *not* the committee's worst-ever choices—also
illustrate how players with friends on the board can receive
the honor while players with better credentials have to wait
outside.

Washington Senators (old): American League team, 1901–60;
now the Minnesota Twins. "First in war, first in peace, and last
in the American League" went the saying about the Senators.
But for all the talk about how bad the Senators were, they in
fact finished last only 10 times in their 60-year history, a better
ratio than the Athletics, Browns, or Phillies. One of the.char-
ter members of "Ban" JOHNSON's American League, the Senators did start out poorly. In their first 11 seasons, they never
finished higher than sixth. Walter JOHNSON, arguably the
greatest pitcher of all time, came aboard in 1907, but it wasn't
until the 1920s that they were able to seriously compete for
the pennant. In 1924, with 27-year-old boy wonder Bucky Har-

ris playing and managing, the Senators captured their only World Series victory, a thrilling seven-game affair in which four games were decided by one run. Game Seven was legendary: with the score tied 3–3, the 36-year-old Johnson entered in the ninth against the Giants and shut them down until the Senators could score in the 12th. Johnson wouldn't be so lucky the following year, when his Game Seven performance cost the Senators the World Series. They made it to the Series again in 1933, this time losing to the Giants in five games. Over their last 27 years in the nation's capital, the club challenged for a pennant just once and finished last six times. It was after World War II that the previously quoted expression came into popular use. In the late 1950s, owner Calvin Griffith believed a change of venue would help the struggling franchise. After the 1960 season, he got his wish: the team moved to Minnesota, where it would win a number of pennants and division titles and two World Series.

Washington Senators (new): American League team, 1961–71; now the TEXAS RANGERS. Baseball men let the old Washington Senators leave to become the Minnesota Twins only because the 1961 expansion put a new team in the nation's capital. The new Senators were not, however, any better than their predecessors. They lost 100 games in each of their first four seasons, then improved by a few games for the next three years before returning to the cellar in 1968. In 1969, baseball immortal Ted WILLIAMS joined the team as manager, and he went about teaching the players as much as he could about hitting. It worked. Nearly every offensive player had a career season at the plate, and the team jumped to fourth place, posting its first winning record. The magic somehow disappeared after the season ended, however, and the team returned to the cellar. After a fifth-place finish in 1971, team owner Bob Short received the permission of his fellow owners to shift the club to Arlington, Texas, where they've been ever since.

Western Division: The smallest of the three divisions, the Western Division, as of the 1994 SEASON, contains just four teams in each league. In the AL: California Angels, Oakland A's, Seattle Mariners, and Texas Rangers. In the NL: Colorado Rockies, Los Angeles Dodgers, San Diego Padres, and San Francisco Giants.

Worst Teams of All Time: The following table lists some of the worst teams in baseball history, along with their records and how far back in the standings they finished. Although there might be a few teams that might be worse than the ones named here, some of the teams on this list are notable for their dubious achievements more than their won-loss record. Further explanatory notes follow the table.

Year/Team	Notes	Record	W%	GB
1899 Spiders	*See page 199.*	20–134	.130	84
1904 Senators	Pre–Walter Johnson team had league-worst .227 BA, .288 slugging percentage, and 3.62 ERA.	38–113	.252	55½
1916 Athletics	Team won pennant two years earlier; owner Connie Mack had sold the team's best players in cost-cutting move.	36–117	.235	54½
1930 Phillies	*See page 199.*	52–102	.338	40
1932 Red Sox	Philadelphia's Jimmie Foxx hit more homers (58) than this Red Sox team (53).	43–111	.279	64
1935 Braves	Following this horrendous season, the team changed its name to "Bees," but the new name was so unpopular that "Braves" returned four years later.	38–115	.248	61½

Year/Team	Notes	Record	W%	GB
1939 Browns	No regular pitcher had ERA below 5.00.	43–111	.279	64½
1952 Pirates	Pittsburgh's Ralph Kiner tied for league lead in HRs; he was only Pirate with more than 500 at bats	42–112	.273	54½
1961 Phillies	Gene Mauch's second season as manager. In '62, Phillies finished over .500; in '64, vied for pennant.	47–107	.305	46
1962 Mets	*See page 200.*	40–120	.250	60½
1969 Expos	First season of expansion club; Gene Mauch (see '61 Phillies) was manager.	52–110	.321	48
1969 Padres	In first year of existence, team drew only 512,000 fans, making officials wonder why they bothered.	52–110	.321	41
1993 Mets	In season with two NL expansion teams, high-priced Mets had worst record in baseball.	59–103	.364	38

1899 Cleveland Spiders: Why was this team so pathetic? Cleveland was owned by the same group that owned the St. Louis Cardinals, so the Spiders' best players were scuttled to St. Louis to assist in a pennant race with Brooklyn—which, not coincidentally, was also a "syndicate" team. (Imagine such a practice occurring today!) After the farcical season, National League officials mercifully eliminated Cleveland and three other clubs to form an eight-team league. The owners' shenanigans eased the formation of the rival American League. *See also* 1901 SEASON; AMERICAN LEAGUE WAR.

1930 Philadelphia Phillies: While this team's won-loss record isn't on par with some of the other teams on this list, these Phillies deserve mention because they had the worst pitching staff of all time. Playing in tiny BAKER

Bowl during the peak season of the LIVELY BALL ERA, their team ERA was an all-time record 6.71. The defense was no better, committing a league-high 239 errors. Outfielder Chuck KLEIN, meanwhile, led an offensive attack that batted .315 as a team, second in the league.

1962 New York Mets: This expansion team, which recorded a modern-baseball record 120 losses, is probably the worst of the 20th century. Casey STENGEL, who'd just won 10 pennants with the Yankees before getting fired for being too old, had the pleasure of managing a team that consisted of a modest collection of low-talent rookies and over-the-hill veterans. The very first run scored against the Mets came ignominiously: a balk by pitcher Roger Craig when the ball slipped out of his hand. In their final game, they hit into a triple play. *See also* "AMAZIN' METS."

DATES AND EVENTS

1876: Inaugural year of the National League of Base Ball Clubs, today known simply as the National League. On April 22, the League played its first game ever, a 6–5 victory by Boston over Philadelphia. The Chicago White Stockings, led by pitcher Albert G. SPALDING and owned by NL co-founder William HULBERT, captured the League's first pennant.

1884 World Series: The first sanctioned postseason series between the champions of the rival National League and AMERICAN ASSOCIATION. In earlier seasons, pennant winners had met informally to play exhibition games, but the 1884 Series was the first to be officially approved and scheduled by league offices. In it, the NL's Providence Grays, behind the pitching of Charles "Old Hoss" RADBOURN, swept all three games from the AA's New York Metropolitans. Postseason championships continued until the AA folded in 1891, then reappeared as the Temple Cup Series that pitted the top two National League finishers against each other. Lack of fan interest killed the Temple Cup after four years of lopsided series. Then, two years after the American League's formation in 1901, baseball's czars reestablished interleague championships with what most fans considered the first "modern" World Series in 1903. *See also* 1903 WORLD SERIES.

1894 season: The pitching mound was moved to 60 feet, 6 inches from home plate in 1893. Amos RUSIE, "the Hoosier Thunderbolt," was partially responsible for the shift, because at the previous 50-foot distance, his fastballs were unhittable. A year later, as pitchers were still getting used to the new distance, batting totals soared to a level they wouldn't reach again until the introduction of the cork-centered baseball in 1911. In 1894, "Sliding Billy" HAMILTON scored 192 runs and Hugh Duffy batted .440—both still all-time single-season records. In addition, four players hit .400, three players recorded on-base percentages of over .500, and the entire league batted .309.

1903 World Series: The first World Series between the American and National leagues, in which the AL's Boston Pilgrims (now Red Sox) upset the haughty Pittsburgh Pirates five games to three in a best-of-nine series. The idea of a postseason series was proposed by Pirates owner Barney Dreyfuss, who challenged Pilgrims owner Henry Killilea near the end of the season. All it took to seal the deal was a handshake. The victory by the American League upset the peace that had ended the AMERICAN LEAGUE WAR. And the following season, manager John McGRAW of the pennant-winning New York Giants, whose ownership did not recognize the "treaty" between the two leagues and was angry at the AL for having placed a rival franchise in New York, refused to entertain any notions of staging another postseason contest. By 1905, tempers had subsided and the Series was allowed to continue—which it did uninterrupted until 1994, when a bonfire of greed and power conspired to take the Series away from the public. *See also* 1994 STRIKE; SEPTEMBER 14, 1994.

1910 batting race: At the beginning of the 1910 season, the Chalmers Automobile Company announced it would award a new car to the major league player with the highest batting average; since few people owned cars, this was a coveted prize. As the season wore on, it became a two-man race: the Tigers' much-hated Ty COBB versus Cleveland's beloved Napoleon LAJOIE. Both played the final weeks of the season at a sizzling pace—Cobb 25 for 47, Lajoie 30 for 54—but Cobb had the upper hand on the season's final day, .383 to .376. Cobb sat out the Tigers' last game to protect the batting title, knowing that Lajoie would have to go 8 for 8 during his team's double-header against St. Louis—a near-impossibility. Cobb was wrong, and the impossible happened: Lajoie went 8 for 8, including 7 bunt hits, which aroused suspicion since Lajoie possessed little speed. A scandal soon erupted when it was discovered that the Browns' manager had instructed his third baseman to play extra deep on Lajoie and allow him to drop in those bunts. The incident forced the St. Louis manager from his job, and AL President "Ban" JOHNSON declared that a "discrepancy" had been discovered in the batting records and credited Cobb with an extra 2 for 3 and, consequently, the batting title. (It is this 2 for 3 which modern baseball historians have subtracted from Cobb's batting record, thus giving him 4,189 career hits and a career .366 batting average instead of the previously established 4,191 and .367.) To avert the controversy, Chalmers awarded automobiles to both Cobb and Lajoie, but thereafter decided to give the cars to league MVPs as determined by a panel of baseball writers rather than by simple mathematics. *See also* CHALMERS AWARD.

1918 season: Baseball's first shortened season since the establishment of the two-league system in 1901. Because of World War I, government officials had ordered a military draft of all able-bodied men not involved in "essential" work; baseball, somehow, had been classified as nonessential. The government gave the leagues until Labor Day to finish the season, plus two more weeks to play the World Series—in effect canceling 25 regular season games. The government's 1918 policy contrasts sharply with its policy during World War II, when President Roosevelt asked baseball to continue to play its games in order to maintain the morale of the country and the troops (*see* "GREEN-LIGHT" LETTER).

1919 World Series: The World Series that was fixed by gamblers, ultimately won by Cincinnati over Chicago five games to three in a best-of-nine Series. Eight members of the heavily favored White Sox were offered money by gamblers to throw the Series to the Reds. The players accepted the offer—although they didn't receive all the money that was promised—and played poorly in the first few games: hitting batters with pitches, making errors and poor baserunning judgments. But as recounted in Eliot Asinof's landmark book *EIGHT MEN OUT* (and the movie of the same name), after Game Five, the gamblers seemed to renege on the deal and refused to pay up. The players then tried to salvage the Series, but the gamblers threatened to kill pitcher Lefty Williams and his family, forcing Williams to pitch poorly in the deciding game. *Eight Men Out*, which was the first book to give a complete account of this story, places much of the blame on White Sox owner Charles COMISKEY, who paid his players the lowest salaries in the league and practically forced them to seek money from other sources. And why didn't the players demand a trade or hold out for more legitimate money? Because baseball players of Comiskey's time were bound by the unethical, illegal RESERVE CLAUSE that forced a player to play ball for his current employer or *not play ball at all*. The White Sox were grossly underpaid compared to what other players were making. But if they quit, they couldn't play for *anyone*. If you thought you were underpaid by your employer, you could find another job. The White Sox, and every other player until free agency came in 1975, did not have your freedom. If you had to work for your employer or else *not work at all*, wouldn't you be tempted to resist in some way? None of this *excuses* the actions of the Black Sox; it merely tries to explain them. *See* *also* BLACK SOX SCANDAL; Arnold ROTHSTEIN; JACKSON, "SHOELESS" JOE; "SAY IT AIN'T SO, JOE."

1930 season: "The Year of the Hitter." 1930 was the peak season of the LIVELY BALL ERA, during which batting averages and slugging totals reached all-time highs. In 1930, Hack WILSON of the Cubs smacked 56 home runs with a record 190 RBIs, Bill TERRY batted .401, Chuck KLEIN had 445 total bases, the Phillies had a league-worst 6.87 ERA, and six *teams* had composite batting averages over .300. And that was just the National League.

1941 season: The season of two of baseball's most famous feats—Ted WILLIAMS's .406 batting average and Joe DIMAGGIO's 56-game hitting streak. DiMaggio's feat helped lead the Yankees to the pennant, while the perennially underachieving Red Sox finished seven games out despite Williams's heroics. Although Williams led DiMaggio in batting average by 49 points, DiMaggio won the MVP. Oddly, however, Williams actually outbatted DiMaggio .410 to .408 during DiMaggio's streak. *See also* 56; .406; STREAK, THE.

1955 World Series: The only World Series won by the Brooklyn Dodgers, a seven-game victory over the Yankees. Dodgers pitching hero Johnny Podres won two games, including an eight-hit shutout in the final, and Brooklyn center fielder Duke SNIDER belted four homers.

1956 World Series: The Series that produced the only no-hitter in postseason baseball history. The Yankees' Don Larsen actually did even better than a no-hitter—he tossed a perfect game. It came on October 8, in Game Five against the Dodgers. Larsen couldn't have been feeling good when the game began, since his wife had filed for divorce that very day. And because the Dodgers had roughed up Larsen in Game Two, he was a surprise choice to pitch Game Five with the Series tied at two games apiece. But his no-windup delivery stumped the Dodgers all day long. Only one batter reached a three-ball count, and only a few balls even came close to falling for hits. The last batter, pinch hitter Dale Mitchell, took a called strike three to end the game on a pitch that was probably high and outside. But umpire Babe Pinelli, who was going to retire right after the Series, didn't want to let the game go any further. As catcher Yogi BERRA and the rest of the Yankees ran to hug Larsen, Pinelli wept. "Sometimes a week might go by when I don't think about that game," says Larsen today, "but I don't remember when it happened last."

1960 World Series: One of the all-time great World Series, won by the Pirates over the Yankees in seven games. Although the Yankees had outscored the Pirates in the first six games 46 to 17—including scores of 16–3, 10–0, and 12–0—the scrappy Pirates hung on till the end. Game Seven was an immensely thrilling contest, perhaps the most exciting game in Series history: A total of 10 runs were scored in the final two innings, including a bottom-of-the-ninth, game-winning home run by Bill MAZEROSKI to give the Pirates a 10–9 victory.

1961 season: The season of baseball's first expansion since the American League's inception in 1901. In 1961, two teams were added to the AL: the Los Angeles (now California) Angels and the Washington Senators (which took the place of the old Senators, who had just moved to Minnesota to become the Twins; a decade later, those new Senators would themselves move out of Washington to begin life anew as the Texas Rangers—got all that?). The National League would expand in 1962, adding the New York Mets and the Houston Colt .45s (soon to become the Astros). As happens in most expansion seasons, pitchers suffered and hitters flourished. Roger MARIS set the major league record with 61 home runs while teammate Mickey MANTLE slugged 54. And first baseman Norm Cash of the Tigers recorded his greatest season: a

.361 average with 41 homers and 132 RBIs. He later admitted he used a corked bat all season—as if the weakened pitching weren't enough of an advantage.

1968 season: "The Year of the Pitcher." 1968 was the peak season of the pitcher's era, during which strikeouts were high and ERAs low. In 1968, Denny McLAIN won 31 games, Bob GIBSON had a 1.12 ERA in 304 innings pitched, Carl YASTRZEMSKI led the AL with a paltry .301 batting average, Don DRYSDALE fashioned his streak of 58⅔ scoreless innings, and both leagues had composite ERAs under 3.00. In another unlikely event typifying the strange season, Gaylord PERRY of the Giants no-hit St. Louis one day, and the Cardinals' Ray Washburn followed suit with a no-hitter of his own against San Francisco the very next day. Following that year, the strike zone was reduced and pitching mounds were lowered.

1969 season: The year of baseball's third expansion, which added four more teams: the Montreal Expos and San Diego Padres in the NL, the Kansas City Royals and Seattle Pilots (which became the Milwaukee Brewers) in the AL. To accommodate what had just become 12-team leagues, Eastern and Western divisions were formed and a round of postseason playoffs were added. The AL would increase by two more teams in 1977—with Seattle and Toronto—while the NL would wait until 1993 to reach 14 teams by adding Colorado and Florida. For the 1994 SEASON, the two leagues split anew, adding a Central Division and yet another round of playoffs.

1972 strike: Baseball's first players' strike, which lasted 13 days and forced the cancellation of a week's worth of games. 1972 was also the year the Supreme Court rejected Curt FLOOD's lawsuit challenging baseball's RESERVE CLAUSE. Though seemingly unrelated, the two events were parts of the same whole. *See also FLOOD V. KUHN*; MILLER, MARVIN; FREE AGENCY.

1973 season: The first season of the DESIGNATED HITTER in the American League, when Ron Blomberg of the Yankees became the first-ever DH to bat. League officials instituted the change hoping that it would increase attendance, and it did—but only briefly. In 1972, the average AL team drew 953,000 fans; in 1973, that total grew to 1.1 million—a substantial increase of 15 percent. But the next year, attendance dropped by 3 percent, followed by a year of zero growth. It took the 1975 WORLD SERIES—in which no designated hitter batted—for baseball to become really popular again.

1975 World Series: Reds over Red Sox, 4 games to 3, in a Series considered the greatest of all time. Five games were decided by one run and two went into extra innings, including the legendary GAME SIX. A lot of baseball historians credit the 1975 World Series with rescuing baseball from the foundering attendance that had plagued the sport for the previous two decades. Yearly attendance figures seem to support that conclusion. From 1960 through 1975, major league attendance per team actually dropped by one quarter of one percent (although overall attendance increased by 10 million because of the addition of eight new clubs). After the spectacular Game Six, 75 million fans watched Game Seven on TV, the highest total to watch any sporting event in American history up to that time. And over the next five years, attendance per team rose by an average of 5 percent per year—the largest sustained period of growth since the war. The sport hasn't looked back.

1981 strike: Baseball's first prolonged players' strike, when more than 50 games per team were canceled. The main issue of the strike was FREE AGENCY. The owners wanted compensation whenever one of their free agents signed with another team; the Major League Baseball Players' Association felt that such a policy would gut the whole concept of free agency. The confrontation came down to a battle of wills. Owners, thinking the players weren't strong enough to maintain their unity, failed to realize that the players were unified by their anger at ownership's arrogance. The owners did have a trump card: they'd secured a strike insurance policy from Lloyd's of London and could afford to lose some money. But once the insurance ran out, the owners caved in. With tough Marvin MILLER as their chief negotiator, the players retained their unrestricted free agency and other concessions earned during earlier negotiations. The real losers were the Cincinnati Reds and St. Louis Cardinals. Commissioner Bowie KUHN had decided to split the season in half, with the first-half "quarter-pennant" winners facing the second-half winners in each division to determine the participants for the League Championship Series. The Reds and Cardinals had baseball's two best overall records but saw no postseason action because they hadn't won either of the quarter-pennants. Instead, the Dodgers, Astros, Expos, and Phillies made it to the postseason. Because of that stupid decision, and because he was viewed as unhelpful in resolving the labor stoppage, Kuhn's days in office were numbered.

1986 postseason: Three of the most exciting postseason series of all time, all occurring within one calendar month. In the NL playoffs, the Mets defeated the Astros 4 games to 2 in a series that included: a 1–0 opening game; a 2–1, 12-inning contest; and a series-deciding, 16-inning game in which seven runs scored after the 13th inning (*see* GAME SIX, 1986 NLCS). The ALCS was just as exciting: the Red Sox were one strike away from elimination in Game Five but won that game and the next two to beat the Angels. In the World Series, it was the Mets who were one strike away from elimination only to miraculously come back in the bottom of the twelfth in the sixth game (*see* GAME SIX, 1986 WORLD SERIES). The Mets then came back again in Game Seven to ruin Boston's hopes of winning its first World Series since 1918.

1989 World Series: The Oakland A's swept the San Francisco Giants 4–0 in a World Series that will be forever remembered for the 7.1-magnitude earthquake that struck just before the start of Game Three. The quake would kill 63 people, and many sportswriters and others urged the cancellation of the Series. Cooler heads prevailed, however, and after a delay of 12 days, the A's finished off the Giants.

1991 World Series: A Series considered among the most exciting of all time, in which the Twins prevailed over the Braves 4 games to 3. Game Seven went 10 innings with venerable Jack Morris notching a complete-game, 1–0 victory. Game Six was just as thrilling, decided by a game-winning homer by Twins center fielder Kirby PUCKETT in the bottom of the 11th.

1994 season: The first year of baseball's three-division system with expanded playoffs, which would have been played if the 1994 STRIKE hadn't interfered. With 28 teams now in two leagues, baseball executives decided to realign each league into Eastern, Central, and Western divisions and add a second tier of playoffs: a best-of-five first round that would include the three division winners plus a wild-card team with the best record. The realignment also corrected some of baseball's stupidest decisions, such as the one in 1969 that put Atlanta and Cincinnati in the NL's Western Division while Chicago and St. Louis played in the East. Beginning in 1994, the divisions are now geographically correct. Of course, nothing this big could have been enacted without some controversy. The extra playoffs were added ostensibly to give more teams a chance to participate in a pennant race and to end the "injustice" of a qualified team not advancing to the playoffs, such as occurred at the end of the 1993 season, when the Giants won 103 games but didn't see any postseason action because the Braves won 104. But we all know what it was really about: money. So be it. If it means more baseball, who cares? Some believe the changes cheapen the pennant races and are the first step toward turning major league baseball into professional hockey. I say it enhances intradivisional rivalries and increases fan interest. But owners should take a few more steps:

shorten the regular season to 154 games; increase the number of games played between intradivisional foes from 13 to 18 or 24, so that the rivalries can get really intense; continue to study the idea of interleague play; and resist any attempts to add another tier of playoffs—two is enough.

1994 strike: The latest melee between owners and players, the 1994 strike canceled hundreds of games and wiped out the entire postseason (*see* SEPTEMBER 14, 1994). It was as close to a tragedy as anything baseball-related could get, for the 1994 season was shaping up to be one of the greatest ever. In the first year of the new divisional setup, the Cleveland Indians were marching toward the playoffs for the first time since the 1950s. Two storied teams—the Yankees and Dodgers—were leading their divisions. Greg MADDUX had sewn up his third straight Cy Young Award. Matt Williams and Ken GRIFFEY, Jr., were making runs at Roger MARIS's single-season home run record. And Frank THOMAS, Albert Belle, and Jeff Bagwell were vying for baseball's Triple Crown. But even though the players were the ones who went on strike, it's hard to side with the owners. This issue—surprise!—was money. The owners were claiming that at least 10 teams were losing money, even though 1993 attendance had been the highest in history—by a wide margin. It's hard to trust owners' claims of poverty, since most of the teams refuse to show their books to the players. The solution to the owners' problems, they believed, lay in a revenue-sharing agreement that included a salary cap limiting players to 50 percent of the clubs' revenues. The players, who were already earning 58 percent of the revenue, disputed the owners' claims, and they did not want their salaries artificially restricted; in all honesty, what self-respecting employee would? The existing collective bargaining agreement said that if no new agreement was reached by the end of the 1994 season, then the owners could unilaterally institute whatever plan they wanted. Even though they *knew* the players would never agree to a salary cap, the owners took a year and a half to develop their plan and presented it to the players in

June. The players had no choice but to strike. They struck in August, but they could have hurt the owners even more by striking in late September, just before the playoffs and after they'd received all their paychecks. Instead, they picked a date that could have saved the postseason if the owners hadn't been so adamant in their demand for a salary cap. Making matters worse, the owners inexplicably reneged on a scheduled pension payment. Then in December, they declared an impasse in the negotiations and imposed a labor system that included not a salary cap (which they had fought so hard for earlier) but rather a luxury tax, in addition to an end to AR- BITRATION and a restricted form of FREE AGENCY. The players would have none of it and challenged the owners' action in court. The strike dragged on through spring training with owners willing to use replacement players in real major league games. Bargaining was going nowhere; even an attempt by President Clinton proved fruitless. Two days before the season was set to begin, a federal court handed down its ruling: The owners had broken labor law by implementing its labor sys- tem. Owners were ordered to re-institute the old labor agree- ment, and the major leaguers returned for a season that began three weeks later than usual. Fans struck back by boy- cotting major league baseball. And as the season wore on, the prospect of labor peace still seemed a distant hope.

All-Star Game: Interleague exhibition game between the best players of each league, managed by the skippers of the previ- ous season's pennant winners. *Chicago Tribune* sports editor Arch Ward implemented the idea in 1933, just in time for an aging Babe RUTH to hit the first All-Star home run in a 4–2 AL victory played at COMISKEY PARK. Baseball's version is, I think, the best of all major sports' all-star games, but it has had its share of controversy, most of which has involved the selection of players. For the first 14 years, all players were cho- sen in a poll of major league managers. In 1947, league offi- cials decided to let the fans select the eight-man starting lineup (excluding pitchers) in league-wide balloting. But in

1957, a Cincinnati newspaper printed an all-star ballot with Reds players marked at every position and encouraged fans to mail it in, which resulted in the selection of seven Reds to the lineup (the other player was Stan MUSIAL). Incensed at the abuse of a system that *it had created and had failed to place controls over*, the commissioner's office replaced two of those Reds with Hank AARON and Willie MAYS and thereafter decided to hand over the selection of the all-stars to a poll of players, managers, and coaches. Finally, in 1970, the league decided to return the vote to the group to whom the game is supposedly dedicated: the fans. Even so, every year complaints arise that "deserving" players have been left off the team while popular stars who have been injured, slumping, or otherwise "unworthy" are annually selected. Although the games are sometimes boring or one-sided, I think the All-Star gala is a great showcase.

American League war: Headed by "Ban" JOHNSON, the American League had been a minor league called the Western League prior to 1900. But with the 1901 expiration of baseball's NATIONAL AGREEMENT, which regulated player contracts and franchise locations and allowed the National League to monopolize major league baseball, Johnson declared the AL a "major" league and touched off a bitter war between the two organizations. He encouraged his franchise owners to raid existing National League ballclubs for players. Since NL owners kept a tight rein on player salaries, the AL had little trouble getting many NL veterans to jump leagues. The most conspicuous defector was Phillies star second baseman Napoleon LAJOIE, who broke his contract to join Connie MACK's Philadelphia Athletics. The NL took legal steps to regain Lajoie's services, taking their case all the way to the Pennsylvania Supreme Court. And although the Court ruled against the AL and ordered Lajoie returned to the Phillies, Johnson wouldn't be defeated so easily. He simply transferred Lajoie to the AL's Cleveland franchise and forbade Lajoie from entering or playing in Pennsylvania, where Lajoie would have been arrested. This victory exemplified the AL's persistence, and in the fall of 1902, the war-weary NL called a truce, and the two leagues signed a revised National Agreement.

April 8, 1974: The day Henry AARON broke Babe RUTH's all-time record for career home runs. He'd hit 40 homers in 1973 to finish the season with 713, just one shy of Ruth's mark. He hit Number 714 on Opening Day in Cincinnati, and, to capitalize on the promotional value, Braves management wanted to keep him out of the next games so that Aaron would break the record at home. Commissioner Bowie KUHN intervened and ordered the Braves to put him in the lineup, but Aaron gamely waited until he made it home to break the mark. Every pitcher in the league dreaded facing Aaron; nobody wanted to be *the one*. Fate smiled upon Al Downing of the Dodgers. Aaron faced Downing in the fourth inning of a 3–1 game, with a runner on first. Fifty-two thousand fans greeted Downing's first pitch—a changeup in the dirt—with a chorus of boos. Downing's next pitch was supposed to be a tailing fastball, but it didn't tail. Aaron swung and ripped it over the left field wall, and just like that, the chase was over. He rounded the bases quickly and meaningfully, barely giving Braves' announcer Milo Hamilton a chance to describe the scene. Aaron's mother and father, as well as the whole Braves team, mobbed him at home plate. Atlanta relief pitcher Tom House, who'd been in the Braves bullpen in left field, handed the baseball to Aaron. It was a generous move, since at least two people were offering $25,000 for the home run ball. But it was the right one.

April 15, 1947: The date of Jackie ROBINSON's major league debut, the first time a black player appeared in a big league game in the 20th century. In the game, played at Brooklyn's EBBETS FIELD, Robinson sparked his Dodgers to a 5–3 victory over the Boston Braves. *See also* WALKER, MOSES FLEETWOOD; COLOR LINE; RICKEY, BRANCH.

August 16, 1920: The day Ray CHAPMAN was killed by a pitched ball, the only on-field death in major league history. On a 1–1 count, Carl MAYS of the Yankees threw a high fastball to Chapman, Cleveland's star shortstop. "Chapman seemed rooted to the spot," wrote Joe Vila of the *New York Sun.* "He made no move either with his head or feet to get out of the way and the ball, pitched with all of Mays' strength, struck him squarely on the left temple." Chapman slumped to the ground, then, like a well-trained batter, got up and took two steps toward first base. Reporters said they could see Chapman's left eye hanging from its socket. The shortstop collapsed again and was rushed to a hospital but died in a few hours. Back in Cleveland a few days later, newspaper accounts described Chapman's funeral as "the largest in years." In the wake of the shocking death, the league ordered umpires to keep fresh baseballs in play at all times, to make it easier for batters to see the ball. Although spitballs, which had been banned a year earlier, weren't a factor in Chapman's death, it was these two changes—*not* a new "lively" ball—that were most responsible for the increase in batting totals in the early 1920s. For batters, it was the difference between hitting a gray, discolored ball with a loose cover that had been used for the last five innings and hitting a new, white ball that had just been put into play. August 16, 1920, in effect, marked the end of the DEAD BALL ERA.

Black Sox scandal: The name given to what ensued when eight Chicago White Sox were charged with accepting money from gamblers to throw the 1919 WORLD SERIES to the Reds. Allegations and rumors of fixed games actually permeated the entire decade, and there was even some talk that the Reds had won the 1919 pennant because of the suspicious play of Giants players Hal CHASE and Heinie Zimmerman, who allegedly "laid down" for second-place New York. Throughout the decade, players consorted openly with gamblers and supplemented their incomes handsomely. The baseball powers did little to stop it, apparently fearing the publicity might hurt gate receipts. That was the environment that spawned the BLACK SOX: greed supported by quiet tolerance. Near the end of the 1919 season, gamblers including former major leaguer Bill Burns and former boxing champion Abe Attell— supported by gambling heavyweight Arnold ROTHSTEIN— conspired to fix the Series by promising $100,000 to eight Sox players: pitchers Eddie CICOTTE and Lefty Williams; infielders Buck WEAVER, Chick Gandil, Swede Risberg, and Fred McMullen; and outfielders Happy Felsch and "Shoeless" Joe JACKSON. Weaver never took any money and played his best, Jackson took the money but seemed to play his best, and McMullen barely played at all. But the others were enough to tip the scales away from Chicago as Cincinnati took the best-of-nine Series. Throughout the off-season and into the 1920 season, the rumors and accusations swirled against the Sox, much of it dismissed as grumblings by the losing team. Then, late in the season, as the Sox battled Cleveland and New York for the pennant, a Chicago grand jury convened to investigate the charges. In September, Cicotte, Jackson, and others con-fessed to the grand jury; they were coerced into confessing with empty promises that no action would be taken against them. Immediately suspended by the league, the players sat out the final week of the season as the decimated Sox lost the pennant to the Indians by two games. In June 1921, just be-fore the jury trial was to begin, the players' grand jury testi-mony mysteriously disappeared, and the Sox were acquitted due to lack of evidence. Meanwhile, in the wake of the scan-dal, major league baseball searched frantically for ways to re-store public confidence in the game—and to keep ballparks filled. The result: the installation of all-powerful commis-sioner Kenesaw Mountain LANDIS, a former federal court judge who'd made his name earlier in the decade with some popular antitrust cases. One of Landis's first official rulings was to uphold the suspensions of the eight players: "Regard-less of the verdict of juries," wrote Landis, "no player who throws a ballgame, no player that undertakes or promises to throw a ballgame, no player that sits in conference with a bunch of crooked players and gamblers where the ways and means of throwing the game are discussed and does not promptly tell his club about it, will ever play professional baseball!" That last part covered the suspension of Weaver, whose "guilty knowledge" doomed him. It seems unthinkable that such an event could occur today, with the big money the players are making. But is it? In 1994, Jim BOUTON (author of *BALL FOUR*) and Eliot Asinof (*EIGHT MEN OUT*) co-wrote a fascinating novel called *Strike Zone* suggesting the possibility that a crooked umpire could fix an important game. Legal and illegal gambling is a multibillion-dollar industry in this country, and greed will always remain high on the list of American sins. It is therefore imperative that baseball, and other sports, keep gamblers as far as possible from the game. That means meting out harsh punishment to those who are proven to have bet on baseball. If Pete ROSE is an unfortunate victim of the zeal in which baseball prosecutes such offenders, then maybe the Hall of Fame is a better place without him in it. The integrity of the sport, of all professional sports, is at stake.

Boston Massacre: The name given to the four-game series between the Red Sox and Yankees in the midst of the great 1978 pennant race. Boston led New York in the standings by as much as 14 games as late as July 17. But when the Yankees entered FENWAY PARK on September 7 to begin a four-game series, Boston's lead was down to four. With just 24 games to play, the Red Sox had a chance to get rid of the Yankees once and for all; the Yankees could pull even with a sweep. Then the massacre began: 15–3 in the first game, 13–2 in the second, 7–0 in the third, and 7–4 in the finale—all Yankee victories. It wasn't just the home runs and doubles that killed the Red Sox; it was also the 11 errors. The Yankees would go on to lead the division by 3½ in mid-September, but the Sox went on a tear with 12 wins in their last 14 games to tie the division race on the final day, setting up a one-game PLAYOFF in Boston. Weak-hitting shortstop Bucky DENT proved the hero for New York as he slugged a three-run homer to give the Yankees a 3–2 lead on the way to a 5–4 victory—giving Sox fans yet another reason to cry.

Called Shot, The: One of the most famous moments in baseball history. Babe RUTH came to bat in the fifth inning of Game Three of the 1932 World Series having already hit one home run in the game. But he had misjudged a fly ball the previous inning to allow the tying run to score, and the Cubs players and fans were really letting him have it. When he took the first two pitches for called strikes, the razzing got louder and more abusive. Ruth stepped out of the box. What happened next is the stuff of legend. Ruth either (a) pointed his index finger at pitcher Charley Root and the Cubs dugout to indicate he still had one strike remaining, (b) pointed his *middle* finger at the Cubs players to let them know what he thought of their abuse, or (c) pointed to center field to indicate where he was going to slug Root's next pitch. Whatever the truth, Ruth slammed Root's next pitch over the outfield fence in the general area where he did or did not point, helping the Yankees to victory in that game before finishing the Series sweep in Game Four. But did he really call his shot? The Associated Press thought not; its story the next day was headlined "Ruth Enjoys Razzing Cubs / Raises His Fingers To Show Strike Count, Then Hits Homer." Cubs pitcher Burleigh Grimes agreed, saying Ruth "[held] up his finger as if to say, 'I've got one left.' " But Hall of Fame sportswriter Fred LIEB wrote that Lou GEHRIG, who'd been on deck when it happened, had told him, "What do you think of the nerve of that big monkey calling his shot and taking those two strikes and then hitting the ball exactly where he pointed?" Meanwhile, Ruth, ever the showman, liked to claim he did call his shot, but former Dodgers outfielder Babe Herman once said he heard Ruth say to Root years later, "I know I didn't [point], but it made a hell of a story, didn't it?" It sure did, because more than 60 years later, people still believe Ruth called his shot. Let them.

Catch, The: What baseball fans call Willie MAYS's legendary grab of Vic Wertz's 460-foot blast in the 1954 World Series. With the score tied and two Indians on base in the eighth inning of Game One, Wertz sent a Don Liddle pitch to the deepest part of center field. In any park other than New York's POLO GROUNDS, it would have been an easy home run, giving the Indians a 5–3 lead. Instead, Mays made a running, over-the-shoulder, back-to-home-plate catch that has been preserved on countless highlight reels and works of art. The Giants went on to win that game in extra innings on the way to a four-game Series sweep.

Flood v. Kuhn: The famed court case that challenged baseball's infamous RESERVE CLAUSE. Thirty-one-year-old Curt FLOOD, a three-time All-Star, had filed suit against baseball after refusing a trade from St. Louis to Philadelphia in 1969. "After 12 years in the major leagues," Flood wrote to commissioner Bowie KUHN, "I do not feel that I am a piece of property to be bought and sold irrespective of my wishes. I believe that any system that produces that result violates my basic right as a citizen and is inconsistent with the laws of the United States." He later wrote that he challenged baseball to "stop 24 millionaire owners from playing God with thousands of ballplayers' lives." With the backing of the Major League Baseball Players' Association and its head, Marvin MILLER, Flood took his case all the way to the Supreme Court, knowing that he would be blacklisted from baseball and would almost certainly never play again. In handling Flood's case, former Supreme Court Justice Arthur Goldberg argued that baseball's reserve clause violated federal antitrust laws. Supreme Court history was against them: In 1922, the FEDERAL LEAGUE challenged major league baseball on antitrust grounds and lost; then in

1953 a player named George Toolson lost his challenge to baseball when the Court refused to hear his case. In both instances, the Court had ruled that baseball was a sport, *not* interstate commerce, and therefore not subject to antitrust laws—even though the Court had in the past ruled that football and other sports *were* subject to those laws. Resistance to the lawsuit came from all sides: from the owners, of course, but also from other players and the media. All believed that the reserve system was the "backbone" of baseball. The fact that it treated players as "property to be bought and sold" made little difference to them. Goldberg called a number of witnesses, including former (and future) owner Bill VEECK, Hall of Famers Jackie ROBINSON and Hank GREENBERG, and former major league pitcher Jim Brosnan. Flood today is convinced that if active major league stars such as Tom SEAVER, Pete ROSE, Reggie JACKSON, and others had testified on his behalf, they would have demonstrated the solidarity of the players and helped the case immeasurably. But in the end, the illogical 1972 decision by Justice Harry Blackmun came out against Flood, upholding the Federal League case by saying that Congress had jurisdiction over the matter: "Remedial legislation has been introduced repeatedly in Congress but none has ever been enacted. The Court, accordingly, has concluded that Congress as yet has had no intention to subject baseball's reserve system to the reach of antitrust statutes." Basically, the Court passed the buck. Although Flood had lost, his case became a great consciousness-raiser for players and media members who had blindly accepted the reserve system. And in 1975, arbitrator Peter Seitz's ruling in the MESSERSMITH–MCNALLY case disbanded the reserve clause—thanks in no small part to the courage of Curt Flood.

Game Six, 1975 World Series: Perhaps the greatest game ever played, Game Six of the 1975 WORLD SERIES introduced a whole new generation of fans to baseball. Three days of rain in Boston interrupted the World Series with the Reds leading the Red Sox three games to two. With each day's delay, fans and players grew more excited with anticipation, and in the end, nobody was disappointed. Boston took a 3–0 lead on a Fred LYNN home run in the bottom of the first. Cincinnati tied it in the fifth on a walk and three hits, then took the lead in the seventh when George FOSTER doubled home two runs. Cesar Geronimo slammed a home run to pad the lead to 6–3, but in the bottom of the seventh, Boston pinch hitter Bernie Carbo, little known before the Series, came to the plate with two on and two out. Earlier in the Series, Carbo had banged a home run in a losing effort, and here in Game Six, he did it again—this one a three-run shot to tie the game. The Sox loaded the bases in both the 9th and 10th innings to no avail, and in the top of the 11th, Dwight EVANS made a spectacular game-saving catch of Joe MORGAN's potential home run. Then, in the bottom of the 12th, catcher Carlton FISK blasted one of the most memorable home runs in Series history to win the game for the Sox. It was a high fly down the left field line, over the GREEN MONSTER; the only question was whether it would stay fair or hook foul. In one of the most widely seen baseball highlights, television cameras captured Fisk waving his hands to body-English the ball into staying fair. Unfortunately for Boston, Game Seven proved the ultimate anticlimax. The Sox took a 3–0 advantage but lost the lead, the game, and the Series when Morgan blooped a single to drive Ken Griffey home with the winning run in the ninth inning. As had happened in 1946 and 1967—and would occur again in 1986—the Sox had lost a thrilling seven-game World Series. The CURSE OF THE BAMBINO lived on in Boston.

Game Six, 1986 NLCS: Game Six of any playoff series always contains a special drama. One team is always on the verge of elimination, the other wants to avoid losing its one-game advantage. GAME SIX of the 1975 WORLD SERIES remains one of the greatest ever played, and the year 1986 produced two equally famous Game Sixes—first in the National League

Championship Series between the Mets and Astros, then in the World Series between New York and Boston (see below). The NLCS pitted the Mets against the Astros, a pair of teams with excellent pitching: eventual Cy Young Award winner Mike Scott and all-time strikeout leader Nolan RYAN anchored the Astros, and 1985 Cy Young winner Dwight GOODEN headed a deep Mets staff. In Game Six, pitching would be at a premium. The Mets led the series 3–2, but Astros lefty Bob Knepper shut down the Mets on two hits and took a 3–0 lead into the ninth inning. Then things fell apart as Knepper allowed two runs and relief ace Dave Smith allowed another, sending the game to extra innings. Both relief corps did their jobs until the 13th, when the Mets tagged Aurelio Lopez for a run on two singles and a walk. In the bottom of the 13th, though, Billy Hatcher hit the biggest home run of his life to prolong the game. Three innings later, the Mets tagged Lopez and another Houston pitcher for three more runs, giving them a seemingly insurmountable 7–4 lead going to the bottom of the 16th. But Houston showed remarkable resilience: A one-out walk to pinch hitter Davey Lopes. A single by Bill Doran. Another single by Hatcher, scoring Lopes. Then, with two outs, Glenn Davis brought the Astros to within a run with an RBI single. Two on base, one run down, Houston an out away from elimination. Ready to pitch Game Seven, if Houston could win Game Six, was Mike Scott, who'd already shut down the Mets twice before. "I really don't want to see Scott until April," thought Mets manager Davey Johnson. Johnson got his wish. Mets reliever Jesse Orosco struck out Kevin Bass for his third win of the series, and the Mets were on their way to their first World Series since 1973.

Game Six, 1986 World Series: The Red Sox led the Mets three games to two going into Game Six at SHEA STADUIM—one victory away from their first World Series championship since the days of Babe RUTH. With Roger CLEMENS on the mound, the Sox held a 2–0 lead until the fifth, when a walk, a steal, an error, and a ground ball double play brought home two Mets runs. Each team scored single runs later and the game went to the 10th inning tied, 3–3. Then the fireworks happened. First, Dave Henderson slammed an 0–1 pitch into the left field stands, giving the Sox a 4–3 lead. Then, with two out, Wade Boggs doubled and scored on a single to pad Boston's advantage. After the first two New York batters flied out to start the bottom of the 10th, reporters began to make their way to Boston's clubhouse for postgame interviews. The champagne was chilled and ready. Pitcher Bruce Hurst was about to be named the Series MVP. Sox owner Jean Yawkey, aging and frail, stood with commissioner Peter Ueberroth, ready to receive the championship trophy. But on the field, catcher Gary Carter singled to left. Pinch hitter Kevin Mitchell banged a hit to center. Ray Knight blooped a single to drive home Carter, sending Mitchell to third. Pitcher Bob Stanley replaced Calvin Schiraldi and promptly threw a wild pitch, bringing home Mitchell with the tying run. With millions of disbelieving Red Sox fans watching, center fielder Mookie Wilson banged a soft ground ball to first baseman Bill Buckner, the ostensible third out that would send the game to the 11th. But gimpy Buckner, with bad knees and sore ankles, couldn't make the play! The ball bounced between his legs, Ray Knight scored, the Mets won, and Boston's frustration was prolonged yet again. Buckner was immediately blamed for the loss, but it was Stanley who wild-pitched the tying run home, and it was Schiraldi who couldn't get the final out, and it was manager John McNamara who failed to put in a defensive replacement for Buckner and left Schiraldi in for 2⅔ innings, and it was the whole Boston lineup that left 14 runners on base during the game. Two days later, the Sox lost a tense Game Seven, and the Curse of the Bambino continued.

League Championship Series: The games played between baseball's division winners to determine each league's pennant winner. Prior to 1969, the team with the best regular-season record would win the league's pennant. But with baseball's 1969 expansion (*see* 1969 SEASON), the leagues decided to split into two separate divisions, effectively doubling the number of pennant races. From 1969 through 1984, the LCS pitted winners of the Eastern and Western divisions in a best-of-five series. In 1985, the owners instituted a best-of-seven format, which lasted until the 1994 SEASON, when baseball's realignment added a second round of playoffs. To owners, the LCS has always been about one thing: money—more TV revenue, higher gate receipts, increased fan interest. To fans, on the other hand, the LCS has been about fun. Some of the greatest games in recent times have taken place in the LCS: NLCS Game Seven in 1992; GAME SIX, 1986 NLCS; ALCS Game Five in 1976; and a bunch more. For thrills and drama, the LCS often betters the World Series.

longest games: The longest baseball game in major league history lasted 26 innings, occurring on May 1, 1920, between the Boston Braves and Brooklyn Superbas (later the Dodgers). Opposing pitchers Leon Cadore and Joe Oeschger actually *went the distance* for their teams, although you have to wonder why they bothered: the game was finally called due to darkness with the score tied 1–1. Brooklyn would lose a 13-inning contest to the Phillies the following day, thus playing the equivalent of 4⅓ games but finishing only one of them. The longest game in *professional* baseball history, meanwhile, lasted 33 innings, with the TRIPLE-A Pawtucket Red Sox defeating the Rochester Red Wings 3–2 in a 1981 game that was completed 35 days after it started. The two teams began playing on the evening of April 18th and continued for 32 innings locked in a 2–2 tie until 4:00 A.M., when the INTERNATIONAL LEAGUE president halted the game. On June 23rd, when the two teams met again, the marathon mercifully ended on an RBI single by Pawtucket's Dave Koza in the bottom of the 33rd.

Lou Gehrig's Farewell Speech: Most people know only one line of the famous speech Lou Gehrig made on July 4, 1939, Lou Gehrig Day, when he said goodbye to over 61,000 fans at YANKEE STADIUM. He had already been diagnosed with amyotrophic lateral sclerosis and had taken himself out of the lineup on MAY 2, 1939. Here are some of the highlights of the speech, which went on for about five minutes: "Fans, for the past two weeks you've been reading about a bad break. Yet today, I consider myself the luckiest man on the face of the earth. . . . When you look around, wouldn't you consider it a privilege to associate yourself with such fine looking men as are standing in uniform here today? Sure I'm lucky. . . . When you have a father and a mother who work all their lives so you can have an education and build your body—it's a blessing. When you have a wife who has been a tower of strength and shown more courage than you dreamed existed—that's the finest I know. So I close in saying that I might've been given a bad break, but I've got an awful lot to live for. Thank you." Gehrig's biographer, Ray Robinson, called the speech "baseball's Gettysburg Address."

May 2, 1939: The day Lou GEHRIG took himself out of the New York Yankees' lineup, ending his record-setting streak of 2,130 consecutive games played (*see also* 2,130). On that day in Detroit, Gehrig was batting just .143 in 28 at bats, and he seemed to know his playing days were numbered. "I haven't been a bit of good to the team since the season started," he told reporter James P. Dawson. "It would not be fair to the boys, to Joe [McCARTHY, New York's manager], or to the baseball public for me to try going on. . . . Maybe a rest will do me some good. Maybe it won't. Who knows? Who can tell? I'm just hoping." There was speculation at the time that Gehrig was simply tired, that he might return when the weather turned warm. But weeks later, the news from the Mayo Clinic ended all conjecture, ruined all hope: Gehrig suffered from amyotrophic lateral sclerosis, a debilitating disease that robs muscles of their strength. He would be dead two years later. *See also* LOU GEHRIG'S FAREWELL SPEECH.

Merkle's Boner: One of the most famous gaffes that affected one of the greatest pennant races of all time. The Pirates, Cubs, and Giants were neck-and-neck-and-neck through most of the 1908 season, leading up to a September 23 game between New York and Chicago at the POLO GROUNDS. With the score tied 1–1 and darkness falling in the bottom of the ninth, the Giants had runners on first and third with two out. Shortstop Al Bridwell singled to center to score what everybody thought was the winning run. Believing the game was won and trying to avoid the onslaught of screaming fans onto the field, the runner on first—poor Fred Merkle—ran straight to the dugout without touching second base, a common practice in those days. Alert Cubs second baseman Johnny EVERS, who knew the rule book, retrieved a ball (though it probably wasn't the actual *game* ball, which was lost in the melee of swarming fans), got the attention of umpire Hank O'Day, and tagged second base. O'Day ruled Merkle out on the force play, but because it was dark and the field was overrun with fans, the game was called a tie. The Giants protested the decision, and NL president Harry Pulliam ruled that the game would be replayed at the end of the season if it affected the pennant race. It did. The two teams met again in the final game of the season in an epic battle between Christy MATHEWSON of the Giants and Chicago's "Three-Finger" BROWN, won by the Cubs 4–2. For the rest of his playing days, Merkle would be reminded of his bonehead play and accused by ignorant fans of blowing the pennant for the Giants. In fact, Merkle was simply following baseball tradition, and Giants manager John MCGRAW never blamed Merkle. What most fans didn't (and don't) know was that Evers had tried to capitalize on the same kind of blunder in an earlier game, but umpire O'Day had disallowed his protest; when it came up again, O'Day was ready to rule correctly.

Old-Timers Game: An exhibition game featuring retired players, usually benefiting a cause such as baseball's pension fund. Major league clubs sometimes stage games between members of past teams to remember famous historical events such as pennant races or playoff games; in San Francisco a few years ago, for example, retired players from the 1962 Giants and Dodgers, including Willie MAYS, Willie McCOVEY, and others, relived their famous pennant race for three innings. Before each year's All-Star Game, past all-stars take the field for a few innings in what's called the "Legends of Baseball Classic." It's great fun for the fans because we get to see greats like Gaylord PERRY, Ernie BANKS, and Luke APPLING, who at 77 slugged a home run off Warren SPAHN in one such game. But sometimes recently retired players who are still in their thirties dominate the game. It's not fair to make a 70-year-old Bob FELLER pitch to a 38-year-old Johnny BENCH, or something like that, but it happens.

Opening Day: The day millions of fans wait all winter for, when baseball begins its season. It used to happen around mid-April, but now that teams don't schedule doubleheaders, the season is longer than ever and begins around the third of April. Because Cincinnati is the alleged birthplace of professional baseball (*see* CINCINNATI RED STOCKINGS), that city traditionally hosts the season's very first game.

Pine Tar Incident: Probably the weirdest mini-scandal in recent major league history, replete with late-inning heroics, allegations of cheating, a near brawl, and Billy MARTIN. What would a minor scandal be without Billy Martin? It was July 24, 1983, New York versus Kansas City at YANKEE STADIUM. Relief ace "Goose" GOSSAGE was on the mound for the Yankees, protecting a 4–3 lead in the top of the ninth. With two outs and a runner on, third baseman George BRETT smashed a Gossage fastball over the fence to give the Royals an apparent 5–4 lead. To everyone's surprise, Yankee manager Billy Martin ran out of his dugout carrying a rule book, trying to contain his glee. He had known for weeks that Brett was putting pine tar—a sticky black substance that helps a batter's grip—higher on his bat than the 18 inches the rules allowed. He was waiting for the right moment to spring the news on an umpiring crew, and this was it. After measuring the pine tar on Brett's bat using the width of home plate, umpire Tim McClelland ruled the home run illegal and called Brett out, the apparent third out of the inning, giving the Yankees an apparent victory. Now here comes Brett, storming out of his dugout! Anybody who has seen the video footage of Brett in a wild rage, restrained by players and coaches, knows what pure, unadulterated anger is all about. Even though the game was supposedly over, the umpires tossed Brett, manager Dick Howser, coach Rocky Colavito, and pitcher Gaylord PERRY, who tried to hide the bat, out of the game. The umpires were able to confiscate the bat only because, as it was getting passed from Royals player to player, the last man in the line didn't have anybody to give it to. The Royals, of course, protested to the league office: "Broadway wouldn't buy that script . . . it's so unbelievable," huffed Howser. Four days later, AL President Lee MacPhail agreed with Howser. He overruled his umpiring crew, a rare occurrence, and allowed the home run. He declared that even though the pine tar was technically illegal, it didn't violate the "spirit of the rules." The Yankees were outraged. "It sure tests our faith in leadership," moaned Yankee czar George STEINBRENNER (of all people). Martin howled that the rule book was "only good for when you go deer hunting and run out of toilet paper." But MacPhail had the power, and his decision stood. Now there was the matter of completing the game, which was still in the ninth inning. The completion was scheduled for August 18, and the Yankees decided they would charge regular admission, even for fans who had tickets to the first game! Enraged fans protested, and two lawsuits were filed declaring the team's policy illegal. In response, the club changed its policy but forgot to announce it, so only 1,200 fans showed up to watch nine minutes and 41 seconds of baseball. Hal McRae struck out to end the ninth, and the Yankees went down in order in the bottom of the inning, giving the Royals a hard-fought 5–4 victory.

playoff: Major league baseball has held few playoff games and series, which occur when two teams are tied at the end of the regular season. The Dodgers, first in Brooklyn and then in Los Angeles, somehow were involved in baseball's first four playoff series: losing in 1946 to the Cardinals and in 1951 (*see* "SHOT HEARD 'ROUND THE WORLD") and 1962 to the Giants and winning in 1959 over the Braves. Since the advent of divisional play, teams that are tied at the end of the season play a one-game playoff. Such a scenario has happened just twice: in 1978, between the Yankees and Red Sox (*see also* BOSTON MASSACRE), and 1980, when the Astros beat the Dodgers (again the Dodgers!). Every year when there's a tight pennant race in the final weeks, the league office flips a coin to determine which team will get the home field advantage if a playoff is necessary.

September 14, 1994: The day the World Series died. On August 12, 1994, the major league players went on strike to protest the owners' proposed collective bargaining agreement that included a salary cap (*see* 1994 STRIKE). The players chose that date because they hoped they could settle the dispute in time to resume the regular season and play the postseason. But the two sides got nowhere during their so-called bargaining sessions, and by mid-September, the owners decided that it was too late. On September 14, acting commissioner Bud SELIG issued a statement that did the unthinkable: cancel the World Series. Here's part of that decree:

> WHEREAS, the MLBPA has consistently been unwilling to respond in any meaningful way to the Clubs' need to contain costs and has consistently refused to bargain with the Clubs concerning a division of industry revenues with the players or any other method of establishing aggregate player compensation; . . .

> NOW THEREFORE, BE IT RESOLVED that:

In order to protect the integrity of the Championship Season, the Division Series, the League Championship Series and the World Series, the 28 Clubs have concluded with enormous regret that the remainder of the 1994 season, the Division Series, the League Championship Series and the World Series must be canceled and that the Clubs will explore all avenues to achieve a meaningful, structural reform of Baseball's player compensation system in an effort to ensure that the 1995 and future Championship seasons can occur as scheduled and uninterrupted.

Several interesting things about that statement. Two owners refused to sign it: Cincinnati owner Marge Schott didn't sign because she felt the season should have gone on with replacement players from the minor leagues; and Baltimore owner Peter Angelos, a former labor lawyer, wouldn't sign because he objected to the negative wording of that first paragraph. Angelos was right. That paragraph shifts all the blame to the players when it is a fact that the owners were just as hard-line as the players about the salary cap. For most of the strike, the two sides didn't even meet, but Players' Union chief Donald FEHR said repeatedly that he would have met anytime, anywhere, but that the owners rarely called him. It was a big joke—a big, sad joke.

"Shot Heard 'Round the World": The name given to Bobby THOMSON's famous home run that captured the 1951 National League title for the Giants in one of the greatest pennant races of all time that culminated in one of the greatest games of all time between two of baseball's greatest rivals. The Brooklyn Dodgers had led the Giants most of the season, by as much as 13½ games as late as August 12. But the Giants, led by manager Leo DUROCHER and rookie Willie MAYS, rallied for the next six weeks with an amazing run of victories. And by the time the dust settled on the season, the two teams were tied atop the league standings, forcing a three-game PLAYOFF to determine the league champion. The clubs split the first two games, with the deciding Game Three to be

played at New York's POLO GROUNDS. With intimidating Don
NEWCOMBE on the mound, the Dodgers took a 4–1 lead to
the bottom of the ninth. Alvin Dark and Don Mueller
bounced singles through the infield to put two aboard and
bring the tying run to the plate. Monte IRVIN popped out, but
Whitey Lockman doubled in a run to make it 4–2. Dodgers
manager Charley Dressen had seen enough of Newcombe. He
signaled to the bullpen for Ralph BRANCA to come in. Maybe
if the game were being played today, when statistical analysis
in all forms is available to anybody who wants it, the game
would have ended differently; instead, Dressen chose the one
Dodger pitcher with the greatest chance of losing the game—
for Branca had already allowed one home run to Thomson
two days earlier and another during the regular season, and
all told, Branca had lost five other games to the Giants in
1951. Even so, the Dodgers could have avoided pitching to
Thomson because first base was open and slumping Mays was
on deck. But because conventional baseball wisdom says never
to put the winning run on base, Thomson saw two fastballs.
The first was right over the plate, a called strike. The next one
was a little higher and a little more inside, but Thomson
swung anyway. Here's what the Giants' radio audience heard
from announcer Russ Hodges: "Branca throws . . . There's a
long fly, it's gonna be, I believe . . . the Giants win the pennant! The Giants win the pennant! The Giants win the
pennant! The Giants win the pennant! Bobby Thomson hits
into the lower deck of the left field stands . . . The Giants win
the pennant! They're going crazy! They're going crazy!"
Watch the film of the event and you can see that Hodges is
right: the whole ballpark went crazy, including all of the
Giants players. Pandemonium ensued as Thomson rounded
the bases, with alert Jackie ROBINSON watching carefully to
make sure he touched them all. He did, and the Giants won
5–4. Reality returned when the Giants lost the World Series to
the Yankees a few weeks later, but for Thomson, fame and joy
would be everlasting.

spring training: The two-month tune-up players go through every year before the season starts. Spring training actually starts in February, when pitchers and catchers are asked to report. Other players arrive at their teams' camps in Florida or Arizona over the next few weeks, although there are always a few holdouts unhappy with their contracts. For some players, like Rickey HENDERSON, spring holdouts are practically an annual occurrence. Florida, where spring training originated, hosts the lion's share of major league clubs—20 to be exact, playing in what's called the GRAPEFRUIT LEAGUE. More recently, eight teams call Arizona's CACTUS LEAGUE their spring home. Spring training traces its roots to 1870, when, according to Harold SEYMOUR's *Baseball: The Early Years*, the Chicago and Cincinnati clubs started formal camps in Louisiana. Florida hosted its first spring training in 1888. Once it was just a way for players to get warmed up for the season. Now, spring training has become a real moneymaking tool for clubs, and cities have been constructing new ballparks to entice clubs to shift their home base. In simpler days, spring training used to be the place where kids and kids at heart could go to meet their favorite players face to face and get autographs. That has become harder now, what with the sports memorabilia craze booming and the number of rich spoiled athletes booming as well. Still, it's a great place to take the family, but don't *expect* to get Ken GRIFFEY, Jr.'s autograph.

Streak, The: Joe DiMAGGIO's famous 56-game hitting streak in 1941. There are countless kinds of consecutive-game streaks—games played, games with a home run, team and pitcher wins, at bats with a hit, etc.—but there's only one Streak with a capital "S." *See also* 56; 1941 SEASON; "JOLTIN' JOE DiMAGGIO."

Subway Series: A World Series played between New York teams, so that travel could theoretically be done by subway. There have been 13 Subway Series and three other World Series between teams from the same metropolitan area, also called City Series or, in the case of the Giants and A's in 1989, the Bay Bridge Series. The following table lists the teams and winners:

Year	Winner	Loser
1906	White Sox	Cubs
1921	Giants	Yankees
1922	Giants	Yankees
1923	Yankees	Giants
1936	Yankees	Giants
1937	Yankees	Giants
1941	Yankees	Dodgers
1944	Cardinals	Browns
1947	Yankees	Dodgers
1949	Yankees	Dodgers
1951	Yankees	Dodgers
1952	Yankees	Dodgers
1953	Yankees	Dodgers
1955	Dodgers	Yankees
1956	Yankees	Dodgers
1989	Athletics	Giants

"Subway Series" also describes the preseason exhibition series between the two New York teams. Most other teams that have nearby neighbors have similar series; in Los Angeles, for example, the games between the Dodgers and Angels are called the Freeway Series.

westward expansion: Following the 1957 season, in which the Brooklyn Dodgers finished third and the New York Giants sixth, Dodgers owner Walter O'MALLEY and Giants boss Horace Stoneham relocated their teams to Los Angeles and San Francisco, respectively. O'Malley had begun making plans years earlier when Brooklyn officials refused to build him a new ballpark; he had little trouble convincing Stoneham, whose club had been suffering from poor attendance in a rickety ballpark, to join him. Brooklyn fans have never forgotten O'Malley for uprooting their beloved team, since the move was obviously driven by greed—*unjustified* greed, in their minds, since the Dodgers franchise was already among the league's most profitable. Contrary to what a lot of people remember, this westward expansion was not baseball's first: The Boston Braves had relocated to Milwaukee four years earlier.

World Series: Also known as the Fall Classic, the World Series is, of course, the yearly postseason series to determine the championship of major league baseball. The 1884 WORLD SERIES is technically professional baseball's first-ever postseason championship to be known by that name. But the first one between the American and National Leagues took place in 1903 (*see* 1903 WORLD SERIES). Right now (when a strike isn't interfering), the championship is decided on a best-of-seven basis, but from 1919 through 1921, baseball staged a best-of-nine competition. Thankfully, that didn't catch on, and I hope no marketing flunky decides to reinstitute the best-of-nine idea. Seven is perfect. The Yankees have won the most World Series—22—followed by the A's and Cardinals with 9 and the Dodgers with 6. Some of the greatest and most memorable games in baseball history have happened in the Series, such as GAME SIX, 1975, and GAME SIX, 1986, among others. (For other great or significant World Series, see other entries in this chapter.) In fact, it seems like Game Six is often the most exciting game of a Series, but an analysis of all the World Series from 1903 through 1992 doesn't support that theory. In the 50 Game Sixes in Series history (excluding the best-of-nine Series), the average margin of victory was 3.8 runs; in the 34 Game Sevens, the average margin is 3.2 runs. Twenty-five of those Game Sixes (50 percent) were decided by one or two runs, while 19 of those Game Sevens (56 percent) had that margin. Another theory I tested is whether, in a seven-game Series, the winner of Game Six most often wins Game Seven, too. I wanted to see if "momentum" and "psychology" really do help determine the eventual winner, as broadcasters sometimes like to say. Not surprisingly, that theory is wrong. Of the 34 Series that went seven games, 17 were won by the Game Six winner, 17 by the Game Six loser. At the professional level, psychology should not affect how a player approaches his work, and thankfully, in this instance at least, it does not.

PLACES

Anaheim Stadium: Home of the California Angels since 1965, the "Big A" doubled as the home of the Los Angeles Rams during football season, until the Rams bolted in 1995. During the Angels' first few years of existence, the team was known as the Los Angeles Angels and played in DODGER STADIUM, which was called Chavez Ravine when the Angels were in town. In 1980, when the Rams moved in, 24,000 new seats were added by enclosing the outfield with a triple deck. Sixty-four thousand fans can now squeeze into the Big A. For Angels games, however, they never do. Now, Angels ownership is trying to build a new park. If they do, no one will shed a tear for the Big A.

artificial turf: Generic term for the fake grass first put into use in 1965 as sod for the first domed stadium, the ASTRO-DOME, and now used in 10 other major league ballparks and countless other college and pro stadiums. Controversy surrounds the fake stuff. Critics argue that it increases injuries and adulterates the game with sky-high bounces and ground ball triples. Supporters argue that it's good for the game because it requires less maintenance than natural grass. Hardly a convincing reason. As Dick ALLEN said, "If a horse won't eat it, I don't want to play on it." Alas, artificial turf is here to stay.

Astrodome: Baseball's first domed stadium, called the Eighth Wonder of the World when it opened in 1965. The roof was originally made of clear glass and the turf of *natural* grass. But outfielders complained that the glare from the sun through the roof hampered their ability to catch flies, so part of it was painted white—which killed the grass, of course, leading to the introduction of ASTROTURF the following season. Masterminded by Judge Roy Hofheinz, the 'Dome also introduced to American sport the luxury box—now a moneymaking staple of every new ballpark—and electronic scoreboards. Mickey MANTLE hit the first indoor home run during an exhibition game in 1965, and Maury WILLS of the Dodgers was the first man to bat on ARTIFICIAL TURF the following year. Contrary to popular belief, the Astrodome was *not* the world's first covered stadium. That honor goes to the ancient Colosseum in Rome, which was enclosed by an awning back in the days of gladiators and emperors.

AstroTurf: Brand name for the first ARTIFICIAL TURF used in professional sports. As its name suggests, it was introduced for use in the Houston ASTRODOME, the first indoor ballpark. We have two men to thank for this abomination: Judge Roy Hofheinz and Dr. Harold Gores. Hofheinz, owner of the Astros and the Astrodome, hired the chemicals manufacturer Monsanto to create fake grass to replace the real stuff that kept dying inside the 'Dome. Dr. Gores actually invented it, but he didn't intend it to be used in today's stadiums. Gores was a New York educator who wanted to create an artificial surface to be used on the playgrounds of New York City. As chairman of the Educational Facilities Laboratories, Gores helped Monsanto develop the turf, which Monsanto marketed as ChemGrass in 1964. Because of its high cost, ChemGrass/ AstroTurf never did fulfill its original purpose. Today, a number of different brands of turf adorn both professional and amateur stadiums—most of them perfectly good outdoor parks where grass could grow if only the park owners wanted to spend the money to maintain it.

Atlanta-Fulton County Stadium: Home of the Atlanta Braves since 1966, to be replaced by a new stadium sometime in the mid-1990s. Because of its 1,000-foot altitude, home runs come early and often, giving rise to the park's nickname: "The Launching Pad," which is a well-deserved moniker. From 1966 to 1992, Braves and opponents hit 4,056 home runs in Atlanta and just 2,940 on the road—a 38 percent difference. Outside the stadium, the team honors three famous players: Phil NIEKRO and Hank AARON, who played for the Braves, and Ty COBB, who hailed from the state of Georgia.

Baker Bowl: The fabulous Baker Bowl, as it was never called, housed the Phillies from 1895 until 1938, but to call it a major league ballpark would be an overstatement. It was so small that at its peak, it seated about 23,000 fans and featured some of the shortest outfield fences in baseball. Gavvy Cravath, for example, fashioned a pretty good career in the Baker Bowl as a DEAD BALL ERA power hitter; from 1913 to 1915, he hit 51 of his 62 home runs in Philadelphia. But its small size isn't really what separates it from a typical major league stadium—it's the fact that the park was so poorly made that on two separate occasions, sections of the stands collapsed during games, killing a dozen people and injuring hundreds. That Philadelphia management didn't shut the place down after the first collapse is unconscionable.

Ballpark in Arlington, The: One of the first in a new crop of beautiful baseball-only stadiums being built these days, The Ballpark in Arlington opened in 1994 to replace ARLINGTON STADIUM, which had been the home of the Texas Rangers since 1972, when the team moved to Texas from its previous incarnation as the expansion Washington Senators. Following the lead of CAMDEN YARDS in Baltimore, The Ballpark features lush green grass, quirky outfield fences, and gorgeous landscaping. Its success in 1994, however, was marred by a number of "unfortunate circumstances," as Texas's PR department might have put it. First, on Opening Day, a 26-year-old female fan seriously injured herself when she fell over a second-deck security rail and landed in the lower deck; it turns out that the front rail around all the sections is quite low and there were no warning signs on the railings. Second, the outfield fences and wind currents seem to discriminate against right-handed power hitters, with which the Rangers are stocked, and people wondered why the team would build a park that hurt their stars such as Juan Gonzalez and Jose CANSECO. Third, as the summer grew hotter, fans began complaining about a foul stench permeating the lower deck—it was the residue of the hot dog, beer, and other ingestibles that got washed into a nearby storm drain, where they rotted in the Texas heat. Basically, a PR disaster for the Rangers.

Busch Stadium: Named for the late August Busch, former owner of the Cardinals and founder of the Busch Brewing Company (which makes Budweiser and other beers), Busch Stadium has been home to the St. Louis Cardinals since 1966. It's a spacious pitchers' park with ARTIFICIAL TURF, giving rise to a brand of baseball practiced by the Cardinals based on pitching, speed, and good defense. As one of the strange benefits of artificial turf, Busch Stadium's pitching mound lowers into the field at the push of a button. Outside the stadium is a large statue of Cardinals great Stan MUSIAL. Other than that, there's really not much special about this modern ballpark, unless you count as special all the times a fan gets to hear the Budweiser theme played during a game.

Camden Yards: The home of the Baltimore Orioles since 1992, this is the first in what promises to be a long line of architecturally spectacular, baseball-only ballparks. Oriole Park at Camden Yards (its official title) is a throwback to an earlier generation of stadiums with all the amenities of modern ballparks such as luxury boxes and sufficient parking. Built with $105 million in lottery and bond money, the whole thing covers 85 acres near the city's waterfront. Along the right field side sits the old warehouse for the Baltimore & Ohio railway company, now the Orioles' offices. Only Ken GRIFFEY, Jr., has hit the warehouse's brick facade on the fly, some 430 feet from home plate, but it's a tempting goal for left-handed batters. Unlike the ballparks built from the 1960s to the 1980s, Camden Yards features asymmetrical outfield distances and emerald-green natural grass. It's the proud uncle of The BALLPARK IN ARLINGTON, JACOBS FIELD, and COORS FIELD— the other beautiful parks that have followed Camden Yards's lead. And there's no doubting its success: Baltimore has sold out most of its games since the park's opening in 1992, and the Indians, Rangers, and Rockies are reporting similar results.

Candlestick Park: It's really hard to judge which is the worst ballpark in the major leagues today, especially now that the CLEVELAND STADIUM is out of the running. Some might argue that those faceless multipurpose parks such as RIVERFRONT, THREE RIVERS, BUSCH, and VETERANS STADIUMS are the worst because they have no personality, nothing special about them. Others might say that the worst ballparks are the domed stadiums in Minneapolis, Seattle, and Houston, because of what their use has done to the game. But in any discussion of the worst field, Candlestick Park, home of the Giants since 1960, always gets mentioned. Why? It's ugly. It's inconvenient. When the fog rolls in, you can't see well. And being right next to the Bay, the howling wind makes it freezing. Pitcher Stu Miller was called for a wind-aided balk in the 1961 All-Star Game (he was *not* blown off the mound, as you sometimes read). Routine pop flies are anything but routine when they reach the Candlestick jet stream. Staying the length of a night game is a real feat, and the team even hands out special buttons to fans who weather a night extra-inning game; called a Croix de Candlestick, the button reads, "I came. I saw. I survived." In the last decade, voters in both San Francisco and nearby San Jose have on several occasions turned down ballot initiatives to finance a new baseball-only ballpark for the team. New Giants ownership is taking some strides toward reforming Candlestick's image, with better food and a better-looking outfield fence among the top new amenities. But the instant somebody coughs up a couple hundred million dollars, the Giants will take off faster than the Candlestick wind. And good riddance.

Cleveland Stadium: Certainly among baseball's worst stadiums, the park is now closed to baseball, thankfully—replaced in 1994 by beautiful JACOBS FIELD. "Cavernous" is probably the best way to describe Cleveland Stadium. The park seats around 70,000, which, for a short time around the late 1940s and early 1950s, was a boon to the club. By fielding some of the league's best teams outside the Bronx, the Indians were able to finish first or second in attendance six times between 1947 and 1954. But as soon as the talent stopped arriving, so did the fans. And by the 1970s, Cleveland Stadium lay empty way more often than not. So even if they drew a very good crowd of 40,000 (a rarity), the place still looked almost half-empty. That's demoralizing to a team. Unlike when EBBETS FIELD or old COMISKEY PARK or Baltimore's Memorial Stadium closed down, no tears were shed when the Indians left "The Mistake by the Lake."

Comiskey Park: The original Comiskey Park stood for 81 years as the home of the White Sox until local politicians bowed to the Sox ownership's request—blackmail is more accurate—to build a modern facility with luxury boxes and such; the owners threatened to bolt to Tampa–St. Petersburg if their demand wasn't met. Never mind that old Comiskey was still a serviceable park with plenty of history, natural grass, 43,000 seats, and foul lines made of crushed, painted water hoses. Never mind that the public money from a new hotel tax spent on the new park could have been put to better use—like fighting crime, educating schoolchildren, or another trivial thing. The owners wanted their luxury box money, so old Comiskey Park was turned into a parking lot across the street from new Comiskey. If the money *had* to be spent, it at least should have been spent wisely. They could have built a classic-looking park such as CAMDEN YARDS or JACOBS FIELD or The BALLPARK IN ARLINGTON, where old meets new to great success. Instead, the builders constructed a cookie-cutter park with a perfectly symmetrical outfield and front row upper-deck seats that are farther from home plate than the last row at old Comiskey. And they call that progress.

Cooperstown: Upstate New York home of the Baseball HALL OF FAME Museum and Library, supposedly where Abner DOUBLEDAY invented the game in 1839. We know now that the DOUBLEDAY MYTH is a lie, but that shouldn't detract from a fan's appreciation of Cooperstown as a tourist attraction. The place is named after its most famous resident, James Fenimore Cooper, author of *The Last of the Mohicans* and some stuff nobody's heard of. The story of how Cooperstown got the Hall of Fame is interesting because it illustrates once again (as if such illustration is necessary anymore) how the simple desire for money can affect history. The idea belonged to a man named Alexander Cleland, who worked for a non-profit foundation established by the heirs to the Singer Sewing Machine Company. Cooperstown had long been a resort community, but it, like the rest of the world, was hit hard by the Great Depression. Cleland suggested to the Clark Foundation, whose namesake lived in the town, that a museum based on baseball history would be a great way to attract tourists and spice up the local economy. As author Bill JAMES points out in his *Politics of Glory*, Cleland projected that such an establishment could draw "hundreds of visitors a year." He was only off by a factor of a thousand. With the backing of major league baseball and some money from the Clark Foundation, the Hall of Fame opened in 1939, steadily gaining in popularity so that today 400,000 fans (well, about 300,000 fans and 100,000 bored spouses and children) pass through its gates. Which is no easy task, by the way, because the town is in a remote part of New York. One good way to get there is to fly to Utica, watch a Blue Sox minor league game, and rent a car for the two-hour drive south to Cooperstown.

Coors Field: The fourth in what's proving to be a successful line of classic baseball-only ballparks, Coors Field opened in Denver in 1995. Like CAMDEN YARDS, JACOBS FIELD, and The BALLPARK IN ARLINGTON before it, Coors Field combines old and new with spectacular results. It's a 42,000-seat park with striking red-brick architecture and comfortable seats that are angled to face the pitching mound. While most of the seats are painted green, one row in the upper deck is Rockies purple, an indication that the row is exactly 5,280 feet in the air—truly mile-high seats. Right next door to the field, a restored Depression-era gasoline station acts as a ticket booth and souvenir shop. With a full set of luxury boxes and an entire city of baseball-crazy fans, Coors Field is a moneymaking machine for Rockies ownership. And the selling of the park's name to a beer company doesn't hurt the team's bottom line, either. It's only a matter of time before the Rockies buy themselves a pennant to hang up in their shiny new ballpark.

Crosley Field: Long-time home of the Cincinnati Reds until they abandoned it in 1970 for horrifically plain RIVERFRONT STADIUM. Named after Reds owner Powel Crosley, who made his fortune with the Crosley automobile, the park is most famous for having hosted the first night game in major league history, on May 24, 1935.

Dodger Stadium: Built in 1962, "Taj O'Malley" resides on a plot of land handed to Dodgers owner Walter O'MALLEY by city officials when he was moving the team from Brooklyn in

1957. Chavez Ravine, as it was known, previously had housed some families of squatters, one of whom bit and bruised the police when they came to evict them. Despite the meek protests, O'Malley built the stadium with his own money, and unlike most of today's parks, the stadium still belongs to that family. It's now the third oldest in the National League, behind WRIGLEY FIELD and CANDLESTICK PARK, but it looks like one of the newest because the team keeps the place immaculate. Some call it the best park in the majors, and one reason might be that it's refreshingly free of annoying billboards. It's not like SHEA STADIUM, which has that gigantic beer ad next to the scoreboard in the outfield, so every time you see a home run on the highlight reels on the news, it begs you to pour yourself a cold one. The Dodgers realized from day one that there's money to be made in encouraging families to visit the park, so they've priced their tickets below most other teams'. Consequently, they almost always draw more than three million fans every year, most of whom pay for parking and buy Dodger Dogs. In fact, according to a story from the 1960s, even if the team had charged no admission, they still would have made a good profit because of all the concessions and parking money. *That's* how to run a baseball team.

Ebbets Field: The home of the Dodgers when they played in Brooklyn, Ebbets Field is one of the most storied old ballparks. The site, on the corner of Flatbush and Bedford avenues, was once a slum, four and a half acres of shanties and garbage pits in a section of Brooklyn called Pigtown because local farmers often brought their pigs there to feed. Charley Ebbets, the first owner of the Dodgers, purchased the land in 1912 and built a ballpark when the team's previous one, Washington Park, began to crumble. Ebbets built the new one out of iron and brick and concrete, and named it after himself. It was a classic urban park, tucked into the neighborhood as if it belonged there, unlike modern parks that stick out like giant cysts. The fans there practically became part of the game. One famous fan, "Howling" Hilda Chester, sat in center field and rang a cowbell incessantly. The Dodger Sym-Phoney sat in Section 8 and led fans in a Brooklyn-made song: "Leave Us Go Root for the Dodgers, Rodgers / That's the team for me. / Leave us make noise for the boist'rous boys / On the B.M.T. / Summer or winter or any season, / Flatbush fanatics don't need no reason." When they tore it down in 1960, three years after the Dodgers moved to Los Angeles, a whole town wept.

Fenway Park: Conventional wisdom has it that Fenway Park in Boston is the absolute epitome of major league fields. Nestled into the neighborhood between Ted WILLIAMS Way and Yawkey Way, Fenway features some of the strangest outfield distances in baseball history. The right field foul pole lies just 302 feet from home, but the fence slopes out so that the wall in straightaway right is about 380 feet from the plate. Deepest center field has a 420-foot measurement, but straightaway center is 388 feet. And left field ... home of the fabled GREEN MONSTER. The sign on the 37-foot-high wall reads 315 feet, but Red Sox officials have refused to grant anyone the opportunity to independently measure it. Two rebel authors ran onto the field in 1975 and came up with 309 feet, five inches. With aerial photography, the *Boston Globe* calculated the distance as 304.8 feet. By any measurement, it's the shortest left field in baseball. And since Fenway also boasts the league's smallest foul territory, it's a classic hitter's park. Both built in 1912, Fenway and Detroit's TIGER STADIUM are baseball's two oldest ballparks, and in 1995, Fenway joined Tiger on the list of ballparks marked for shameful extinction because of its small seating capacity.

Forbes Field: A classic old ballpark, Forbes Field served as the home of the Pittsburgh Pirates from 1909 until 1970, when the team moved to THREE RIVERS STADIUM. The park was torn down but home plate is still there: It has been encased in glass and preserved in almost its exact location, which is now the University of Pittsburgh's Forbes Quadrangle (*almost* *exact* because the exact location is now a ladies room). Like most of the old parks, Forbes Field had character. When Hank GREENBERG played there in 1947, the team built a short fence in front of the left field scoreboard and "planted" it with chicken wire to increase home run production. Calling it "Greenberg Gardens" that season, fans dubbed that area "Kiner's Korner" when Ralph KINER began dominating the league's power hitting in 1948.

Green Monster: FENWAY PARK's 37-foot-high wall in left field, painted green since 1947. Before that, the wall featured a number of giant billboards, the most famous being a Gem razor blade sign reading "Avoid 5 O'Clock Shadow" and a Lifebuoy soap sign saying "The Red Sox Use It." The Green Monster is baseball's most famous wall (which is more of a distinction than it sounds), and it's obviously one of Fenway's greatest charms. But it has probably cost the Sox a number of pennants. Here's why: With such an inviting home run target, the team has traditionally stacked its lineup with power hitters, forsaking the all-around players who are the real keys to winning baseball. Additionally, left-handed pitchers are said to be intimidated by the Wall, so the Sox have trouble developing them. To Sox fans, the Green Monster really is a monster.

Griffith Stadium: The 50-year home of the Washington Senators, Griffith Stadium was where U.S. presidents traditionally threw out the first ball on Opening Day to inaugurate the season. Clark Griffith, the longtime owner of the Senators, humbly named the park after himself. The funniest thing that ever happened there—aside from the sorry play of the often last-place Senators—occurred during the park's first night game in 1941. According to author Philip J. Lowry in *Green Cathedrals*, the stadium's lights went out as the pitcher began his windup. When the lights came on again moments later, every outfielder and infielder, the batter, the catcher, and the umpire were lying flat on the ground, protecting themselves. The pitcher remained standing because only he knew he hadn't actually thrown the ball.

Hall of Fame: In the 1930s, baseball was in trouble. The Depression was cutting sharply into attendance, and the Babe RUTH juggernaut, which saved baseball in the 1920s, was winding down. Baseball needed something else. In 1931, the BASEBALL WRITERS ASSOCIATION institutionalized the MVP award, and two years later, sportswriter Arch Ward created the ALL-STAR GAME. Then some people from COOPERSTOWN, New York, the alleged birthplace of baseball, approached the commissioner with an idea: a museum honoring baseball's great players and innovators. The commissioner liked it, and so did the rest of baseball. When it opened in 1939, it was a single-room exhibit with plaques and pictures. Thanks to curator Lee ALLEN, who presided over the shrine from 1948 until his death in 1969, the Hall added an extensive library and expanded the museum, so that today the Hall features three stories and 50,000 square feet of exhibits to entertain and enthrall. When you go there, you can start in the Hall of Fame Gallery, where bronze plaques of the game's immortals stand in tribute to their accomplishments. The Great Moments Room features artifacts and photographs from the game's top events. There's a screening room that shows baseball movies continuously. And other parts give detailed histories about the game's origins, ballparks, and innovations. Ultimately, you can visit the Hall of Fame Library for the greatest collection of baseball books and papers in existence. The place is open year-round except on Christmas and Thanksgiving, but don't go in the summertime because it'll be jammed with people like you.

"House That Ruth Built, The": One of the nicknames for YANKEE STADIUM. The Yankees shared the POLO GROUNDS with the more popular and successful Giants until Babe RUTH joined the club. Once the Yanks became better than the Giants, John MCGRAW's club kicked out the American Leaguers. If it weren't for Ruth, there's no telling where the Yankees would be playing.

Hubert H. Humphrey Metrodome: The Metrodome, home of the Twins since 1982, is the only major league stadium that has a giant Hefty bag along one outfield wall, hockey rink–like Plexiglas along another, and a curved backstop so that wild pitches bounce toward first or third base instead of right back to the plate. Until 1986, when they installed a new carpet, the ARTIFICIAL TURF was so bouncy that manager Billy MARTIN once protested a game because he claimed the turf was making doubles out of pop-fly singles. They used to call it the "Homerdome" because people claimed home runs were easy to hit. That's not really the case. From 1991 to 1993, the Twins and their opponents hit 375 home runs in Minnesota and 398 on the road. The real home run parks in the American League are TIGER STADIUM (581 at home, 479 on the road) and the SKYDOME (457, 377). A more accurate nickname for the Metrodome is the "Tripledome": over that same time, Minnesota and opponents hit 52 percent more triples at home (120) than on the road (79), the second-highest differential in baseball behind Kansas City, where teams hit nearly twice as many triples as in road parks, 142–74. The lesson about park nicknames: Don't believe everything you read, unless you read it here.

Jack Murphy Stadium: A plain, blah, nondescript ballpark for a plain, blah, nondescript team, the Padres. Like most parks built in the 1960s and 1970s, the Murph doubles as a football stadium, but even though two big-league teams have played there for over 20 years, not a single championship flag flies over the ballpark. Probably the most interesting thing about the stadium is the name on the front: Jack Murphy. Just about every baseball fan can name where the Padres play their home games, but almost no one knows who Jack Murphy was. I'll tell you: He was a San Diego sportswriter who was instrumental in securing an expansion team for the city in 1969. If the ballpark owners had really been on the ball, they might have named it after the town's favorite son, Ted WILLIAMS. Wouldn't that have been nice, Williams Field?

Jacobs Field: The beautiful new home of the Cleveland Indians, who celebrated their move in 1994 with a team record 18-game home winning streak. In addition to providing the team with one of baseball's most attractive homes, Jacobs Field also sparked the Indians to their first first-place finish in 30 years—before the 1994 STRIKE hit. "This is the perfect case study of an environment improving employee production," said one team official. The result? A phenomenon not experienced in Cleveland in several generations: Indians Fever. The combination of a winning team, a new ballpark, and new uniforms helped the Indians sell more tickets in 1994 than in any season in the team's history. The strike put a damper on the celebration, but Jacobs Field is going to be around for a long time.

Joe Robbie Stadium: The all-purpose sports stadium that acts as home to the Florida Marlins during the baseball season and the Miami Dolphins during football. Named for the late owner of the Dolphins, JRS seats 48,000 and opened in 1987. It has a hand-operated, teal-colored scoreboard in left field, which is the only really distinguishing feature. Baseball parks that double as all-purpose stadiums never have much personality.

Kingdome: Baseball's worst dome, the Kingdome was constructed in the 1970s to lure a major league expansion team. The plan was a success, but the resulting stadium is not. In 1994, a number of ceiling tiles collapsed onto the seats, closing the park for several months until all 40,000 tiles could be replaced (the Mariners were about the only team happy about the 1994 STRIKE). But that's only the latest problem. From the beginning, the Kingdome was built on a shoestring budget of public money. The builders cut corners in the design and construction, scrimped on amenities such as comfortable seats, and basically created baseball's ugliest dome. If they had the money and desire, they *could* build a nice *outdoor* stadium because, despite the city's reputation, Seattle gets fewer inches of rainfall annually than New York City and as many days of rain as Cleveland. They don't need a dome!

Kauffman Stadium: Formerly known as Royals Stadium, this beautiful baseball-only park was renamed for late owner Ewing Kauffman before the 1994 season. From its construction in 1973 until 1995, it featured deep power alleys that made it a tough home run park and ARTIFICIAL TURF that made it great for speedsters. But after years of hearing from critics, Royals ownership replaced the turf with real grass and moved the fences in an average of 10 feet around the outfield. Former Royals great George BRETT, now a club vice president, crowed, "With this grass, it's going to look like a brand-new stadium and it's—what?—23 years old." Fans also love it. They come from all over Missouri, Kansas, and other neighboring states to see the immaculate landscaping and flowing waterfall in the outfield.

Metrodome. *See* HUBERT H. HUMPHREY METRODOME.

Milwaukee County Stadium: Currently in use by the Brewers, County Stadium was initially built in 1953 for the Braves. It's pretty nondescript visually, a natural grass park with a symmetrical outfield. But the place has a great atmosphere, exuding simply *baseball.* Fans there are loyal and knowledgeable, brought up for generations on both minor and major league ball. And the stadium's bratwurst is legendary. Brewers owner Bud SELIG, however, wants to replace the park with one that has luxury boxes. As soon as he can find enough investors, County Stadium will disappear.

Negro Leagues Hall of Fame: Like the one in COOPERSTOWN, another important museum for all baseball fans to see is the

Negro Leagues Hall of Fame, which opened in the summer of 1994 in Kansas City, Missouri. It's smaller than its Cooperstown brother but no less impressive. There, you can see pictures of and read about all the NEGRO LEAGUES greats who haven't been elected to that other Hall: Buck O'NEIL, Double-Duty Radcliffe, Lou Dials, Smoky Joe WILLIAMS, and countless others (O'Neil is, in fact, the museum's chairman). The museum isn't just about the hostile racism the players faced, although that's a part of it. It's also about the passion they felt for baseball, the sacrifices they made, and the fun they had. "Baseball fulfilled me like music," says O'Neil. "I played most of my life and loved it. I wasn't born too early. I was right on time."

Oakland Coliseum: Bowl-shaped home of the A's, the Coliseum is a pretty good-looking park—once you get inside— with a nice family atmosphere in most areas of the park. But if you have children with you, don't sit in the outfield bleachers; every time I've been there, a fight has broken out between drunk fans. I suppose it's like that everywhere. What really distinguishes the Coliseum from other parks in the American League is its vast amount of foul territory, which shaves about 10 points off hitters' batting averages. Also, Jose CANSECO used to complain about how hard it was to hit home runs there, and he's right about that: from 1968 to 1992, the A's and their opponents hit 12 percent more home runs on the road than at home.

Olympic Stadium: Built initially for the 1976 Summer Olympics, Montreal's *Stade Olympique* is perhaps the biggest ballpark fiasco in North American sports history. Because of internal Montreal politics, the park went horrendously over budget and wasn't even completed until more than a decade after the Olympics. Locals cynically call the stadium "The Big Owe," because as of 1994, the province of Quebec still owed $304 million in Olympics-related costs, including the stadium. And the costs seem to keep going up—and bad things keep happening. The retractable Kevlar roof that went up in 1987 is no longer retractable because constant rips in the material proved too costly to mend. Now there's talk of building a permanent metal roof at a cost of $37 million. And in September 1991, a 55-ton concrete beam fell off the structure, closing the stadium for the last weeks of the season. It's no wonder Montreal fans are renowned for their baseball apathy.

Polo Grounds: A truly unique ballpark, the Polo Grounds known to most fans was actually the fifth version of the park. The other four existed between 1883 and 1911 but didn't survive for various reasons; Polo Grounds number 1, for example, was unexpectedly leveled in 1889 so the city could build on 111th Street between 5th and 6th Avenues, and Polo Grounds number 3 burned to the ground in 1911. Polo Grounds number 5—the storied one—housed the Giants from 1911 through 1957, the Yankees from 1913 through 1922, and the Mets in 1962 and 1963. The park was perhaps most famous for its strange outfield distances: 279 and 258 feet down the left and right field lines, respectively; 447 and 440 to the alleys; and 483 to deep center. These distances made possible two of baseball history's greatest moments: Bobby THOMSON's "SHOT HEARD 'ROUND THE WORLD" in 1951, which was really just a medium fly to left that went about 280 feet; and The CATCH, Willie MAYS's running, back-to-the-plate grab of Vic Wertz's 440-foot drive to center in the 1954 World Series, which almost anywhere else would have been a home run. Even Dodgers and Indians fans would have to admit that these kinds of oddities account for most of baseball's charm. The same wrecking ball that leveled EBBETS FIELD in 1960 demolished the Polo Grounds four years later.

Riverfront Stadium: In 1970 and 1971, three National League ballparks opened, ushering in a new age of grass-free, multipurpose stadiums, following the lead set by BUSCH STADIUM in 1966. Riverfront Stadium, home of the Cincinnati Reds, replaced old CROSLEY FIELD on June 30, 1970, just weeks before Pittsburgh's THREE RIVERS STADIUM opened, and a year ahead of VETERANS STADIUM in Philadelphia. A big painted circle in left-center field commemorates the landing spot of Pete ROSE's 4,192nd career hit, which broke Ty COBB's all-time record.

Shea Stadium: William Shea, Shea Stadium's namesake, helped bring National League baseball back to New York City by helping to organize the CONTINENTAL LEAGUE; the pressure the CL placed on major league baseball forced the game's first expansion since 1901, creating the New York Mets and three other franchises. The Mets actually played in the decrepit POLO GROUNDS for their first two seasons, then moved to Shea in 1964. Located in Queens, the stadium lies right under La Guardia Airport's flight pattern, making Shea easily baseball's noisiest stadium if you don't count the METRODOME in Minneapolis, where crazed fans can create a deafening din. One of the most interesting things about the park is the huge black top hat past the outfield fence, out of which rises a big apple when a Met smacks a homer. Shea is a slight pitcher's park, even though it has standard outfield distances and below-average foul territory—mainly because hitters have the worst visibility of any other stadium. Look toward the outfield during any TV game and you'll see that the advertising and scoreboard create a terrible background to hit against.

Shibe Park: Also known as Connie MACK Stadium, Shibe served as home for the Athletics from 1909 to 1954 and for the Phillies from 1938 to 1970. When it was built in 1909, it was the first concrete and steel ballpark in the majors; the others were made of wood. Just about all parks built immediately after Shibe followed its example, since, through fire and collapse, rickety wooden stadiums had claimed countless lives in both the majors and minors—the most egregious example being Shibe's crosstown neighbor, the BAKER BOWL, where the grandstands collapsed two separate times. Like DODGER STADIUM in its early days, Shibe featured a big built-up pitching mound from which pitching greats such as Lefty GROVE, Robin ROBERTS, and others could dominate batters. Yet owing to its minute foul territory and short foul lines, it was a slight hitters' park, which makes the accomplishments of Grove and Roberts all that much more impressive. The Athletics vacated the park in 1955 for Kansas City, and the Phillies bailed out after the 1970 season for VETERANS STADIUM. Both teams traded down.

SkyDome: Toronto's huge $495 million colossus, the Sky-Dome is a triumph of modern architecture. It features the world's largest television screen, a 348-room hotel, a Hard Rock Cafe, a couple of other restaurants, a fitness club, 161 private luxury boxes, and an 11,000-ton retractable roof that uses $500 in electricity just to open or close. It's certainly a great spectacle. But it's a terrible baseball park, for two reasons: (1) Baseball should be played on grass; SkyDome has the fake stuff, even though grass could theoretically grow, since it could be exposed to direct sunlight when the roof is retracted. And, most importantly, (2) baseball is a game steeped in tradition, not modern accoutrements; the Sky-Dome is all about high technology and futuristic gadgets. However, there are four million fans in Toronto who prove me wrong every single season, and in so doing, they are making the Blue Jays baseball's most profitable franchise. One *good* thing about the SkyDome: Since it's the pinnacle of dome technology and it seems impossible to top it, maybe no new dome will ever be built.

Sportsman's Park: A quirky, oddly shaped ballpark in the old baseball tradition, Sportsman's Park housed the St. Louis Browns from 1909 to 1953 and the Cardinals from 1920 to 1966. It was another casualty of the shift in the 1960s from the classic hometown parks to the coliseum-sized general-purpose stadiums when the Cardinals moved to BUSCH STADIUM in 1966.

Three Rivers Stadium: Like VETERANS and RIVERFRONT stadiums, Three Rivers was born out of the need for team owners and major league cities to construct giant monuments to the latest and greatest technology. The results: cookie-cutter ballparks that have no character, no personality, and therefore are baseball stadiums in name only. Three Rivers is located in Pittsburgh and has been the home of the Pirates since 1971. Some people have called it "The House That Clemente Built," because it was Roberto CLEMENTE who returned the Pirates to glory and, supposedly, into the new park. But I think that to associate a ballplayer known for his passion and panache with a boring stadium known for ARTIFICIAL TURF and big blue outfield walls is unfair to Clemente's memory.

Tiger Stadium: For any number of decades, the city of Detroit has been involved in a weighty issue: to tear down or not to tear down venerable Tiger Stadium. Even though the team is leasing the ballpark rent-free from the city, owner Mike Ilitch wants to build a new park along the order of CAMDEN YARDS and JACOBS FIELD. He's even willing to pay the $175 million the park is supposed to cost, although the city must fork over the estimated $220 million in land acquisition and preparation costs. And in 1994, he threatened to move the team out of Detroit if he didn't get his wish. Tiger fans and taxpayers, however, want no part of it. Ilitch, in fact, is bound to Tiger Stadium by the strict lease that runs through the year 2008. If the taxpayers lose that battle, it will mean the end of a grand old park with heaping mounds of tradition dating back to Ty COBB, cozy outfield distances, and the closest seating in the majors. The Tiger Stadium Fan Club has kept pressure on the city to stand up to Ilitch's threats, and so far it has worked. But politicians are notorious for capitulating to the demands of rich guys.

Veterans Stadium: See THREE RIVERS and RIVERFRONT stadiums, except insert Philadelphia wherever you see Pittsburgh or Cincinnati. The only other thing to add is that Veterans

Stadium, which is owned by the city of Philadelphia, has the worst ARTIFICIAL TURF in all of professional sports and has been responsible for myriad football- and baseball-related injuries. The city refuses to rip out the turf—they say it would cost too much.

Wrigley Field: The grandest of the old-time ballparks, Wrigley Field belongs to the people of Chicago. At least it should. The park brims with charm and character—amazing for an inanimate object. But you can almost feel it! It starts when you get off the El at the Addison St. exit. On game day (and most games still take place under the sun, despite the installation of lights in 1988), the whole area is primed for baseball: T-shirt and newspaper vendors, locals, out-of-towners. There's not a bad seat in the house, from the third deck to the bleachers. If you're lucky, the wind is blowing out to center field and the home runs fly. When home run balls go out of the park and onto the street, there's a mad dash among the waiting kids to recover the ball. It's the only park where a ball can get stuck in the ivy-covered outfield walls—ivy planted originally by the young Bill VEECK in the 1930s. Across the street on Waveland and Sheffield avenues, the rooftops have makeshift bleachers so homeowners and their (sometimes paid) guests can watch the action. Even though the Tribune Company, which owns the team, doesn't have any luxury boxes to rake in the millions, they've never seriously tried to demolish the ballpark. It would be like the Catholics destroying Notre Dame.

Yankee Stadium: Today we take for granted the big concrete and steel, 60,000-capacity sports facilities. We call them stadiums, of course. But in the 1920s, they didn't exist. There were 30,000-seat ballparks, yes, but no gigantic *stadiums* as we know them today. Think of the old-time ballparks: WRIGLEY FIELD, FENWAY PARK, SHIBE PARK, EBBETS FIELD, POLO GROUNDS. Not a *stadium* among them. Yankee Stadium—the "HOUSE THAT RUTH BUILT"—changed all that. It was fitting that the

nation's largest city should serve as home for the most innovative entertainment facility of its time, and even more fitting
that the country's most larger-than-life sports figure should
have something to do with it. For it was Babe RUTH who put
the Yankees on the baseball map by making them a good
enough team to draw more fans than the rival Giants, to
whom the Yankees had always played second fiddle. As a reward, the Yankees designed the Stadium for him, building a
right field fence just 294 feet down the line so his clouts
wouldn't have to travel too far to go out of the park. Meanwhile, left-center and center field were cavernous—490 to
dead center, 395 to left center—a fact that cost the right-
handed-hitting Joe DiMAGGIO countless home runs. Yankee
Stadium seated more than 70,000 fans when it opened,
around twice as much as any other existing ballpark, and en-
abled the team to become the first club to draw more than
two million fans. Like all great ballparks, the Stadium had
some pretty amazing quirks. From the 1930s until the extensive remodeling in 1974–75, three marble monuments honoring Ruth, Lou GEHRIG, and legendary manager Miller
HUGGINS stood in deep center field—*in play.* Once, while
watching a long fly bounce around out of reach of his fielders, an exasperated Casey STENGEL is purported to have
shouted, "Ruth, Gehrig, Huggins, someone throw that ball in
here NOW!" During the $100 million renovation, builders
placed an inner fence in front of the monuments, shortening
the outfield distance but also removing one of baseball's cool-
est quirks. In the 1990s, team owner George STEINBRENNER
began threatening to move the team out of Yankee Stadium
unless the city built him a new park. Steinbrenner believes the
Stadium's Bronx location is hurting attendance, but more
likely it was the lack of a winning team between 1981 and
1994 that was responsible. In any case, it'll be interesting to
see how the situation plays out. With old COMISKEY PARK
gone and TIGER STADIUM on the way out, baseball can't afford to lose another great classic ballpark.

FOLKLORE, LITERATURE, AND DIVERSIONS

"Alibi Ike": A hilarious short story written by Ring Lardner in 1915 about a ballplayer who has an excuse for every situation. "His right name was Frank X. Farrell," begins the story, "and I guess the X stood for 'Excuse me.' Because he never pulled a play, good or bad, on or off the field, without apologizin' for it." They made a pretty funny movie out of the story in the 1930s starring Joe E. Brown and Olivia de Havilland.

APBA: A classic, much-imitated baseball board game invented in 1932 that uses real players and statistics; it's now also a computer game. Some of its competitors include Pursue the Pennant, Strat-O-Matic, Statis Pro, and others, and each of those games has its true followers. Incidentally, although APBA stands for American Professional Baseball Association, loyalists pronounce it "ap-bah."

"Amazin' Mets": Nickname for the New York Mets ballclub at its inception in 1962, first applied by Casey STENGEL during the team's first spring training. The team's 120 losses—an all-time record—should indicate that it's an ironic nickname. *See also* WORST TEAMS OF ALL TIME.

asterisk (*): The metaphoric symbol that Commissioner Ford FRICK placed in the record books next to Roger MARIS's single-season record of 61 home runs. Because the 1961 season consisted of 162 games—8 more than the season in which Babe RUTH established the previous record of 60 homers—Frick decreed that for the record to stand on its own, Maris would have to break it in 154 games. Unfortunately for Maris, he slammed his 61st homer in the season's final game, prompting Frick's infamous asterisk. Even though Frick never actually uttered the word "asterisk," the little star followed both Maris and Frick for the rest of their lives; Frick even titled his autobiography *Games, Asterisks, and People. See also* 61.

Babe: The Legend Comes to Life (New York: Simon & Schuster, 1974): The definitive biography of Babe RUTH, written by Robert Creamer and first published in 1974. Almost universally acclaimed as the greatest sports biography ever written, it was the first book on Ruth to dig past the myths and folklore, presenting a complete portrait of an extraordinary human being.

Ball Four (New York: Stein & Day, 1971; rev. 1981): The great baseball book written by Jim BOUTON recounting the first season of the 1969 Seattle Pilots expansion team. It gives an inside account of things such as contract negotiations and the off-field habits of players—both considered off-limits to the public in those days. In trying to tell the truth about everything, Bouton succeeded in angering the baseball establishment. The book jacket even brags that commissioner Bowie KUHN told Bouton, "You've done this game a grave disservice." These days, tell-all books are common, and the media seem to be all-knowing. But in the late 1960s, people didn't know that some players cheated on their wives, that every other word out of their mouths was profane, and that drinking was their second favorite sport. *Ball Four* is still in print, and even though some of the parts that were scandalous at the time might seem tame now, it's definitely worth reading.

Bang the Drum Slowly (New York: Alfred A. Knopf, 1956): Mark Harris's great baseball novel—a sequel to another great novel, *The Southpaw*—about left-handed pitcher Henry Wiggen, who throws the baseball "with his arm and his brain and his memory and his bluff for the sake of his pocket and his family." The 1973 movie version, starring Michael Moriarty and a young Robert De Niro, remains one of the best baseball movies ever.

***Baseball,* Ken Burns's:** The 18½ hour PBS documentary that provided fans with their only baseball-related entertainment during the fall of 1994. With labor unrest having canceled the World Series (*see* 1994 STRIKE), *Baseball* garnered some of the highest ratings in the history of public television. *Baseball* was a nearly unqualified success: comprehensive, engaging, sometimes funny, and always uncompromising. Purists quibbled with some of its historical inaccuracies; as one example, the miniseries cited the 1869 CINCINNATI RED STOCKINGS as the first team to play for money, but it has long been established that professional players existed nearly a decade earlier. Other critics knocked the documentary's often languorous pace. But even they would have to admit that such pacing suited its subject matter perfectly. Burns, whose previous documentary effort, *The Civil War*, earned equally strong accolades, divided 150 years of baseball history into nine episodes, or "innings." Among several recurring themes, the documentary continually explores baseball's tumultuous labor relations and its transcendent problems of race, and almost an entire "inning" is devoted to the NEGRO LEAGUES and the breaking of the COLOR BARRIER. Interspersed throughout are commentaries from writers (such as Roger ANGELL and Dan Okrent), former players (e.g., Buck O'NEIL and Bill Lee), and other noteworthy baseball fans (from Billy Crystal to Steven Jay Gould). The information is presented so effectively, and the style is so effortless, that, warts and all, it can quite simply be called the *Citizen Kane* of sports documentaries.

baseball Annie: Baseball slang for a female baseball groupie. Several examples of such women appear in the movie BULL DURHAM.

Baseball Encyclopedia (New York: Macmillan, published every three years, with annual updates): The first comprehensive reference book on baseball history, first published in 1969. Updated yearly, it contains the statistics of every player who ever played major league ball, plus many NEGRO LEAGUES players. Once a one-of-a-kind item, it now receives competition from several other books, the best of which is TOTAL BASEBALL. Until 1995, the *Encyclopedia* was officially sanctioned by major league baseball. Now, *Total Baseball* claims that honor.

baseball card: A cardboard-backed card featuring photographs or paintings of ballplayers. The first baseball cards were packaged with cigar and cigarette boxes and received limited distribution. In 1951, the TOPPS Co. began selling the cards in packages of 10 to 15 with a stick of bubble gum. The hobby grew only gradually for 30 years, then exploded in 1981 when two more companies, Fleer and Donruss, began selling similar cards. In the late 1980s, several more companies flooded the market; this glut has caused a massive devaluation of all post-1980 cards while also increasing the value of earlier cards. The world's most valuable card is a 1909 tobacco card of Honus WAGNER, of which there are about a dozen in existence; one was sold at auction recently to hockey great Wayne Gretzky and L.A. Kings owner Bruce McNall for $451,000. The story behind that card has become part of baseball folklore, but recent research has debunked much of the tale. Legend has it that after the cards came out, Wagner ordered them removed from circulation because he didn't want his name associated with tobacco products. But in 1993, *Sportslook* magazine published an article saying that Wagner actually smoked cigars and chewed tobacco. In addition, Wagner's face can be seen on four other tobacco company cards from around the same time. What seems most likely, according to the article, was that Wagner threatened legal action against the tobacco company for using his picture without paying him any money.

Baseball's Great Experiment: Jackie Robinson and His Legacy (New York: Oxford University Press, 1983): The definitive historical treatise, written by Jules Tygiel, on the breaking of the COLOR LINE by Jackie ROBINSON. Still in print, Tygiel's learned study presents a full history of African-Americans in baseball, from Moses Fleetwood WALKER to Robinson and beyond in a readable, enjoyable style.

"Baseball's Sad Lexicon": Baseball history's second most popular poem, written by Giants fan/newspaper columnist Franklin P. Adams. Appearing in the *New York Globe* in 1908, the poem laments the excellent work of the double play combination of the Chicago Cubs, who won consecutive pennants over the Giants from 1906 through 1908 (the word "double" in line 6 refers to double play, not two-base hit):

> These are the saddest of possible words,
>   "Tinker to Evers to Chance."
> Trio of bear cubs, and fleeter than birds,
>   "Tinker to Evers to Chance."
> Ruthlessly pricking our gonfalon bubble,
>   Making a Giant hit into a double—
>   Words that are heavy with nothing but trouble:
>   "Tinker to Evers to Chance."

Mostly because of this poem, Joe TINKER, Johnny EVERS, and Frank CHANCE were inducted into the Hall of Fame as a group in 1946. (Baseball's *most* popular poem, by the way, is "CASEY AT THE BAT.")

"Big Bang" Theory: The managing style popularized by the Baltimore Orioles' Earl WEAVER. In leading his team to four pennants, Weaver disdained the sacrifice bunt and hit-and-run, choosing instead to let his batters hit away, get runners on base, and wait for a three-run homer. The thinking is that in the majority of ball games, the winning team scores more runs in one inning than the loser scores in the entire game (the daily box scores will bear this out). As Weaver liked to say, "If you play for one run, that's all you're gonna get!"

"Big Red Machine": Nickname given to the Cincinnati Reds teams of the early- to mid-1970s. Featuring Hall of Famers Johnny BENCH and Joe MORGAN and career hits leader Pete ROSE, the Reds won five division titles, four pennants, and two World Series from 1970 through 1976.

Black Sox: Ignominious nickname given to the Chicago White Sox team that accepted money from gamblers to throw the 1919 WORLD SERIES. Something people forget is that the team had earned that nickname even before the scandal. Club owner Charlie COMISKEY was so cheap that at one point during the season, he began to make his players pay for the cleaning of their uniforms. Outraged, the players protested by not washing them, so they became known around the league as the Black Sox—not metaphorically but physically. *See also* BLACK SOX SCANDAL; ROTHSTEIN, ARNOLD; CICOTTE, EDDIE; WEAVER, BUCK; JACKSON, "SHOELESS" JOE; "SAY IT AIN'T SO, JOE."

bleacher bums: Fans who sit in the BLEACHERS, drink beer, get into fights, taunt opposing outfielders, throw back visiting team home run balls, and support the home team vehemently and loudly. While almost every team can claim its own group, baseball's quintessential bleacher bums reside in Chicago's WRIGLEY FIELD.

bonus baby: A young prospect who gets a large sum of money as an incentive to sign with a major league team. Because of the high amount of money invested in them, bonus babies are treated more gingerly than non–bonus babies as they move up the minor league ladder. When this term first came into popular use, a $100,000 bonus was rare and noteworthy; today, million-dollar bonuses for the top few picks in the yearly AMATEUR DRAFT are commonplace.

Boys of Summer, The (New York: Harper & Row, 1972): Poignant bestseller by Roger Kahn about the Brooklyn Dodgers of the 1950s, who included, among others, Jackie ROBINSON, Roy CAMPANELLA, and Duke SNIDER and won five pennants in eight years. It examines the players' lives both in and out of baseball—the challenges, successes, and heartbreaks of not just a group of players but a group of men.

Bronx Bombers: Nickname given to the NEW YORK YANKEES, first applied to the oft-pennant-winning teams of the RUTH–GEHRIG era, because YANKEE STADIUM is located in the Bronx. In 1993, owner George STEINBRENNER began threatening New York City officials that he would move the team out of that location—*out of Yankee Stadium!*—because of lackluster attendance. So much for the nickname.

bubblegum cards: Cardboard-backed cards featuring photographs—paintings in the early days—of baseball players. They used to come in packs of 10 to 15 along with a stick of bubble gum, but during the 1980s and 1990s, when card collecting became more a business than a hobby, "collectors" complained that the gum was soiling the cards. There's more to the story. *See also* TOPPS CO.; BASEBALL CARD.

Bull Durham: Excellent, extremely funny baseball movie that came out in 1988, starring Kevin Costner and Susan Sarandon, about minor league life with the Durham Bulls of the SINGLE-A Carolina League.

"Casey at the Bat": The greatest and most popular baseball poem ever written, "Casey" first appeared on page 4 of the Sunday, June 3, 1888, edition of the *San Francisco Examiner*. Ernest L. Thayer, a Harvard friend of *Examiner* publisher William Randolph Hearst, penned the ballad under the pseudonym "Phin," and it was the only thing noteworthy he ever wrote. More than two dozen sequels and homages have appeared in the years since "Casey's" publication, including "Casey's Revenge," "Casey the Comeback," "Mrs. Casey at the Bat," "Casey's Son," "Casey's Daughter at the Bat," and others. But none is as good as the original. Here it is, in its entirety:

CASEY AT THE BAT
A Ballad of the Republic, Sung in the Year 1888

The outlook wasn't brilliant for the Mudville nine that day:
The score stood four to two, with but one inning more to play,
And then when Cooney died at first, and Barrows did the same,
A sickly silence fell upon the patrons of the game.

A straggling few got up to go in deep despair. The rest
Clung to that hope which springs eternal in the human breast;
They thought, "If only Casey could but get a whack at that—
We'd put up even money now with Casey at the bat."

But Flynn preceded Casey, as did also Jimmy Blake,
And the former was a lulu, and the latter was a cake;
So upon that stricken multitude grim melancholy sat,
For there seemed but little chance of Casey getting to the bat.

But Flynn let drive a single, to the wonderment of all,
And Blake, the much despised, tore the cover off the ball;
And when the dust had lifted, and men saw what had occurred,
There was Jimmy safe at second and Flynn a-hugging third.

Then from five thousand throats and more there rose a lusty yell;
It rumbled through the valley, it rattled in the dell;
It pounded on the mountain and recoiled upon the flat,
For Casey, mighty Casey, was advancing to the bat.

There was ease in Casey's manner as he stepped into his place;
There was pride in Casey's bearing and a smile on Casey's face.
And when responding to the cheers, he lightly doffed his hat,
No stranger in the crowd could doubt 'twas Casey at the bat.

Ten thousand eyes were on him as he rubbed his hands with dirt;
Five thousand tongues applauded when he wiped them on his shirt;
Then while the writhing pitcher ground the ball into his hip,
Defiance gleamed in Casey's eye, a sneer curled Casey's lip.

And now the leather-covered sphere came hurtling through the air,
And Casey stood a-watching it in haughty grandeur there.
Close by the sturdy batsman the ball unheeded sped—
"That ain't my style," said Casey. "Strike one!" the umpire said.

From the benches, black with people, there went up a muffled roar,
Like the beating of the storm-waves on a stern and distant shore;
"Kill him! Kill the umpire!" shouted someone on the stand;
And it's likely they'd have killed him had not Casey raised his hand.

With a smile of Christian charity great Casey's visage shone;
He stilled the rising tumult; he bade the game go on;
He signaled to the pitcher, and once more the spheroid flew;
But Casey still ignored it, and the umpire said, "Strike two!"

"Fraud!" cried the maddened thousands, and echo answered "Fraud!"
But one scornful look from Casey and the audience was awed.
They saw his face grow stern and cold, they saw his muscles strain,
And they knew that Casey wouldn't let that ball go by again.

The sneer is gone from Casey's lip, his teeth are clenched in hate;
He pounds with cruel violence his bat upon the plate.
And now the pitcher holds the ball, and now he lets it go,
And now the air is shattered by the force of Casey's blow.

Oh, somewhere in this favored land the sun is shining bright;
The band is playing somewhere, and somewhere hearts are light,
And somewhere men are laughing, and somewhere children shout;
But there is no joy in Mudville—mighty Casey has struck out.

color line, color barrier: Just as slavery is part of America's shameful past, so is the color line part of baseball's. In the early days of professional baseball, blacks played alongside whites in professional leagues throughout the country. Brothers Welday and Moses Fleetwood WALKER even made it to the majors, albeit for a single season. The practice reached a turning point in 1887, however, following an incident in which Chicago White Stockings' manager Adrian "Cap" ANSON, one of baseball's first superstars, threatened to forfeit an exhibition game unless the opposing team's black pitcher was removed. Anson backed down when he learned that he'd lose his game money, but similar threats began to come from other managers, and teams began to drop their black players. By 1895, baseball's color line had become entrenched, and blacks wishing to play professional ball were forced to join the loosely organized NEGRO LEAGUES and play for substantially lower salaries and prestige. To hear baseball executives put it, however, no color line had *ever* existed. Just before his death in 1944, commissioner Kenesaw Mountain LANDIS, who had ruled baseball with czarlike authority since 1921, declared: "There is no rule, formal or informal, no understanding subterranean or otherwise, against black ball players in the majors." As explanation for the absence of black players from major league rosters, owners claimed that they could find none who were qualified, and thus shifted the blame to the minor leagues: "Colored players have never been discriminated against in the major leagues," said Indians owner Alva Bradley. "They have simply never been able to get into the minor leagues to get the proper training for major league competition." The fact that the majors controlled the minor leagues shows just how hypocritical and illogical Bradley's argument was. And in any case, there are dozens of anecdotal incidents of baseball owners and managers blocked, either by the league office or the other owners, from signing black men to play "organized" baseball. Bill VEECK, for instance, was barred from purchasing the Philadelphia Phillies in the early 1940s when the league found that he planned to sell off all the team's regulars and restock the club with players from the Negro leagues. In the 1940s, Jackie ROBINSON and Branch RICKEY changed everything. But even after Rickey signed Robinson to play for the Dodgers' Montreal farm team, doubters still existed. To mask their racism, however, they looked for other reasons to denigrate Robinson. In 1945, *The SPORTING NEWS* reported: "Robinson, at 26, is reported to possess baseball abilities which, were he white, would make him eligible for a trial with, let us say, the Brooklyn Dodgers Class B farm at Newport News, if he were six years younger." Of course, if Robinson had been white, he would have made it to the majors years earlier. Other doubters did not hide their racism. Before Robinson's first year in the majors, a number of Dodger players signed a petition asking Rickey not to promote Robinson to the big league club. Rickey ignored it. Then, during the 1947 season, rumors spread that the St. Louis Cardinals were threatening to strike rather than play against Robinson. National League president Ford FRICK threatened back: Anybody who refuses to play against Robinson, he wrote, will be banned from baseball. They didn't strike, and they have denied ever discussing a strike. Either way, Frick's threat and Robinson's determination made the "great experiment" a success. The most complete study on the breaking of the color line is *BASEBALL'S GREAT EXPERIMENT* by Jules Tygiel.

cricket: One of the three British games on which baseball is based, cricket resembles baseball only in the sense that both sports use a bat and a ball. Cricket originated in England before 1700 and is now played around the world, mostly in former British colonies. In it, two 11-player teams take turns defending a wicket with a bat. A "bowler" throws the ball at the wicket, and the batsman swings at the ball to prevent it from striking the wicket. When he hits the ball, he scores runs for his team by running from wicket to wicket while the fielders retrieve the ball. If the ball strikes his wicket either directly or while he's running, he's out, and then the next batsman on his team takes his turn. Play continues until all 11 men are retired, and then the two teams switch sides; that's an inning. A game lasts just two innings, but sometimes it can go on for days. Baseball's much better.

Curse of the Bambino: The mythological curse that has befallen the Boston Red Sox, explaining why they haven't won a World Series since they traded Babe RUTH to the Yankees in 1919. The Sox had won the championship a year before that, and they have come within a single game of winning it in 1946, 1967, 1975, and 1986. But then Ruth's curse has struck them down.

Damn Yankees: A 1955 Broadway musical, then a 1958 movie, based on Douglass Wallop's entertaining novel *The Year the Yankees Lost the Pennant.* Legendary choreographer Bob Fosse arranged the dance numbers, with lyrics and music by Richard Adler and Jerry Ross. The story concerns a Washington Senators fan who sells his soul to the Devil so that the Senators can beat the Yankees for the pennant. It was successfully revived on Broadway in 1994.

dead ball era: The era of baseball history from the turn of the century until the 1920s, characterized by low batting averages, low run totals, and little power. The reason the dead ball era begins around 1901 or 1902 is that both leagues had just changed the rules to count foul balls as strikes and pitchers began to throw spitballs and other trick pitches in earnest. Before that, .400 seasons were common. After 1903, there were only two seasons when batters topped the .400 mark—both coming after a new cork-center baseball was introduced in 1911. Overall, league batting averages hovered around .240 to .250 (vs. .265 today), league slugging percentages stayed around .320 (vs. .390 today), and league ERAs were below 3.00. Strikeout totals were also low, and so were home run totals; a typical league-leading home run season would be 10 or 11. Along with the foul strike rule, there were some other factors that created the dead ball era. First, batters were trained to just make contact with the ball, not swing for the seats. That was the dominant strategy: bunt, beat out a single, sacrifice, steal, hit behind the runner, force an error. Most of the players could run well, and the majority of teams would steal more than 200 bases a year (vs. 125 today). Why risk a strikeout when you can claw your way onto first base and usually steal the next one? The second, and probably most important, reason for the dead ball era has to do with the ball. The spitball, tobacco ball, emery ball, and all other ways to doctor a baseball were legal. Pitchers could do whatever they wanted with it, and their teammates could help out by spitting on the ball themselves. Additionally, umpires would usually only use one or two baseballs per game. If the ball went into the stands, the fans would toss it back and play would resume using that same ball. So even in broad daylight, the ball could be hard to see when it came out of the pitcher's hand. It's no wonder players concerned themselves with just putting bat on ball. The dead ball era ended because of three unrelated events: the coming of Babe RUTH, the BLACK SOX SCANDAL, and the death of Ray CHAPMAN. *See also* LIVELY BALL ERA.

"Dem Bums": Loving nickname Brooklyn Dodger fans bestowed upon their hometown team in both print and speech. And the Dodgers earned it. From the 1920s through the 1930s, the team finished in the second division more often than not, and then from 1941 through 1954, the Dodgers won five pennants, came nightmarishly close to four others, and lost all five World Series to the Yankees.

Doubleday Myth: In 1905, famed sportsman and entrepreneur Albert G. SPALDING decided to commission a study on the origins of baseball. Fervently patriotic, Spalding set out to prove that baseball was a uniquely American invention, not a descendant of the British games ROUNDERS and CRICKET, as was asserted by the legendary sportswriter Henry CHADWICK. Instead of considering all the facts—including the obvious similarities between baseball and those much older British games—the MILLS COMMISSION REPORT relied almost exclusively on the dubious testimony of an elderly mining engineer named Albert Graves, who claimed to have witnessed the day Abner DOUBLEDAY created the first baseball diamond in 1839 in COOPERSTOWN, New York. Never mind the fact that Doubleday, a famous Union general during the Civil War, had never discussed the sport he had supposedly invented in any of his diaries. Spalding wanted an American genesis, and he got one. Even today, the Doubleday Myth remains so pervasive that many fans, broadcasters, and players believe it to be true. The HALL OF FAME, to its discredit, does little to discourage such thinking.

Eight Men Out (New York: Holt, Rinehart & Winston, 1961): Eliot Asinof's marvelous recounting of the BLACK SOX SCANDAL and its legacy—the first book that attempted to tell the full story. John Sayles made a movie out of it in 1988, a film that has some flaws but pretty much does what it set out to do: re-create the 1919 baseball scene and try to explain why the players did what they did. In their retelling, Asinof and the filmmakers shift most of the blame for the scandal onto White Sox owner Charles COMISKEY, who treated his players like poorly paid slaves. Certainly the players were greedy, too, in placing cash above integrity. Asinof's book strikes a good balance. *See also* 1919 WORLD SERIES.

Elias Sports Bureau: The official statisticians of major league baseball, the Elias Bureau is responsible for verifying the accuracy of all baseball statistics. For many years, they also published a statistical analysis every season called *The Elias Baseball Analyst*, but they ceased publication in 1994.

fantasy league: A fictitious "league" in which players act as general manager/owners of "virtual teams," accruing points based on how their teams' major leaguers perform in real life.

(They're also known as ROTISSERIE leagues, for reasons explained at that entry.) Over the last decade, the popularity of fantasy leagues has grown exponentially. I think the growth has had something to do with the explosion of personal computers during the same time period. In most leagues, the teams compete for supremacy in categories such as team batting average, home runs, RBIs, stolen bases, pitcher strikeouts, ERA, wins, and a category called *ratio*—the ratio of hits and walks to innings pitched; many leagues offer some other categories, too. It's a fun game to play, but it really changes the way you follow baseball, and a lot of critics argue that it's ruining fans. They have a point. Fantasy league players are only interested in individual stats, not team victories, which detracts from what baseball is: a *team* sport. Many fantasy league players don't root for *teams* anymore; they root for *players.* If Barry BONDS hits three home runs but the Giants lose 11–7, Giants fans go home sad—but the fantasy league guy who has Bonds and doesn't care what the score is goes home happy. Some people think that's bad for baseball. I don't think it's necessarily *good* for the sport, but I think baseball will survive.

Field of Dreams: A great baseball film—for my money, the best ever—*Field of Dreams* is one of those sports movies that is so good people say things like, "It's not *about* baseball. It's about life." But those people are wrong. *Of course* it's about baseball. *And* it's about some other things, such as love and dreams and relationships and growing up and passion. I still get chills when Burt Lancaster's character tells Ray (played by Kevin Costner) what he would want with a single wish. And I often fast-forward my tape to watch the part in which James Earl Jones's character gives a moving speech about baseball's role in American culture to convince Ray that "people will come." When you're done watching the movie, go out and buy the novel *Field of Dreams* is based on, *SHOELESS JOE* by W. P. Kinsella.

"Gas House Gang": The nickname for the Cardinals teams in the 1930s, featuring such colorful characters as Frankie Frisch, Leo DUROCHER, Dizzy DEAN, Pepper Martin, and Joe Medwick. With Durocher as the ringleader and Martin as the clown, the Cardinals made themselves famous for scrappy play and childish pranks. Once, after a tough loss, player-manager Frisch called a team meeting during which he lambasted his players with insults and profanity, then asked if anyone had any questions. Martin broke the heavy silence: "I was just wondering," he asked Frisch innocently, "whether I ought to paint my midget auto racer red with white wheels or white with red wheels." Even Frisch smiled. The first Gas House Gang, according to author Paul Dickson, was a band of thugs who prowled the Lower East Side of Manhattan near a number of large gas tanks in the 19th century. The term came to be applied to the Cardinals because, according to one legend, they were a notoriously rough team that once played a game against the Giants in soiled uniforms, reminding a New York writer of the famed thugs.

Glory of Their Times, The (New York: Macmillan, 1966): A landmark book, the first of its kind: the baseball oral history. Lawrence Ritter's book is a collection of interviews with more than two dozen ballplayers from the first third of the century, including Hall of Famers Edd Roush, "Goose" Goslin, and Paul WANER. It's a great insight into the early days of baseball, full of terrific stories and honest opinions. It's also a wonderful place to learn about the legendary ballplayers who died before their stories could be told. In *The Glory of Their Times*, Sam Crawford talks about Ty COBB, Tommy Leach about Honus WAGNER, Chief Meyers about Christy MATHEWSON. Ritter says he got the idea for the book in 1961, when Cobb died at the age of 74, and he decided that somebody should, before it was too late, tell the stories of some of the men who influenced the game that has affected American society so much. Ritter's book succeeded so well that there have been dozens of imitators, with more coming out each year. Whenever you see a new baseball oral history, remember that it's there because of Lawrence Ritter.

"Good field, no hit": Scout Mike Gonzalez's famous assessment of catcher Moe BERG in a terse telegram to his superiors. The phrase now gets used all the time, usually to pass judgment over a middle infielder with an invisible bat.

Great American Novel, The (New York: Holt, Rinehart & Winston, 1973): One of the greatest novels about baseball, this work by mega-bestselling author/baseball fan Philip Roth takes you on a surreal and hilarious trip through the Pioneer League, the fictional third major league that enthralled fans before World War II. Definitely worth spending time with.

"Green-light" letter: The letter written by President Franklin Roosevelt to the baseball commissioner, Kenesaw Mountain LANDIS, in 1942 urging professional baseball to continue despite America's involvement in World War II. During World War I, by contrast, President Wilson had ordered all nonessential industries halted, and because baseball fell under that category, the 1918 season was cut short. Roosevelt felt differently: "I honestly feel that it would be best for the country to try to keep baseball going," he wrote in the letter. "There will be fewer people unemployed and everybody will work longer hours and harder than ever before. And that means that they ought to have a chance for recreation and for taking their minds off their work even more than before. . . . Here is another way of looking at it—if 300 teams use 5,000 or 6,000 players, these players are a definite recreational asset to at least 20,000,000 of their fellow citizens—and that in my judgment is thoroughly worthwhile." Nobody has ever said it better.

"Hit 'em where they ain't": Wee Willie KEELER's famous proclamation describing the secret of his success as a hitter. Keeler was the king of the 19th-century slap hitters, a five-foot-four, one-half-inch outfielder who choked way up on the bat. Consequently, 86 percent of his 2,932 hits went for singles.

Hot Stove League: A term for a mythical league that's in season during the winter months, consisting not of athletes but of regular folks who like to sit around a hot stove and talk baseball.

"Hub Fans Bid Kid Adieu": Written in 1960 originally for *The New Yorker* magazine, this great essay by John Updike gets reprinted in almost every baseball anthology. As well it should. It describes the last game in Ted WILLIAMS's career, a day that was "overcast, chill, and uninspirational" but that nevertheless produced one of baseball's most remarkable moments: the home run hit by Williams, aka "The Kid," in his last major league at bat. Updike viewed the action from a box seat with the eyes of a loving fan, not as a cynical sportswriter sitting in press row. The result is a piece full of beautiful prose and surprising turns. I can't recommend it more highly.

"Impossible Dream": The term applied to the 1967 Red Sox's miraculous season, in which they advanced from a ninth-place finish in 1966 to capture the American League pennant. Carl YASTRZEMSKI got most of the credit for the team's surge—and deservedly so. In winning the majors' last Triple Crown, Yaz dominated the month of September: In the final two weeks, with the Sox in a tight pennant race with the Twins and Tigers, he batted .523. And on the final day, against those Twins, he went seven for eight as the Sox eked out a one-game pennant victory. Against St. Louis in the World Series, he batted .400 with three homers, but he couldn't stop Bob GIBSON's Cardinals by himself. In a fitting end, Yaz singled to lead off the ninth inning of Game Seven with the Cards ahead 7–2. The next batter, Ken Harrelson, erased Yastrzemski on a double play grounder. Thus the city of Boston awoke from their dream, and the CURSE OF THE BAMBINO struck again.

"If you build it, he will come.": The opening line of the great baseball movie *FIELD OF DREAMS*, taken from W. P. Kinsella's novel *SHOELESS JOE*. It's spoken by a disembodied voice that only the main character, Ray, can hear. The "it" is a ballpark, which the voice asks Ray to build out of his cornfield. The "he" is something for viewers and readers to find out.

"Is Brooklyn still in the league?": Giants first baseman/manager Bill TERRY's fateful response to a reporter's question during spring training 1934. The reporter had asked Terry what he thought of Brooklyn's chances in the pennant race. Since the Dodgers had finished twenty-six and one-half games behind pennant-winning New York the previous season, Terry gave his now-infamous snide answer. The quote got lots of play in the local media, and the Dodgers took it seriously. On the final weekend of the 1934 season, Brooklyn eliminated the Giants from the pennant race.

jersey numbers: Here's a listing of some of baseball's most famous jersey numbers, all of which have been retired by the players' teams:

No.	Player/Manager	Team(s)
1	Billy Martin	Yankees
1	Pee Wee Reese	Dodgers
3	Babe Ruth	Yankees
3	Harmon Killebrew	Twins
4	Lou Gehrig	Yankees
4	Mel Ott	Giants
5	Joe DiMaggio	Yankees
5	Brooks Robinson	Orioles
5	Johnny Bench	Reds
5	Hank Greenberg	Tigers
5	George Brett	Royals
6	Al Kaline	Tigers
6	Stan Musial	Cardinals
7	Mickey Mantle	Yankees

No.	Player/Manager	Team(s)
8	Yogi Berra	Yankees
8	Carl Yastrzemski	Red Sox
9	Ted Williams	Red Sox
14	Ernie Banks	Cubs
19	Bob Feller	Indians
20	Mike Schmidt	Phillies
21	Roberto Clemente	Pirates
21	Warren Spahn	Braves
24	Willie Mays	Giants
30	Nolan Ryan	Angels
32	Sandy Koufax	Dodgers
32	Steve Carlton	Phillies
37	Casey Stengel	Yankees, Mets
39	Roy Campanella	Dodgers
41	Tom Seaver	Mets
42	Jackie Robinson	Dodgers
44	Hank Aaron	Braves
44	Willie McCovey	Giants
45	Bob Gibson	Cardinals

One interesting thing about this list is that it offers insights into the choices of jersey numbers for some current players. For example, many young power hitters choose number 44 (such as Darryl Strawberry and Eric Davis) because of Hank AARON. Steve CARLTON may have selected 32 because of that other talented left-hander, Sandy KOUFAX. Ruben Sierra and several other Puerto Rican players have worn number 21 to honor their fallen hero, Roberto CLEMENTE. And speedy outfielders with power often wear number 24 in honor of Willie MAYS—just look at Ken GRIFFEY, Jr., and Barry BONDS when he was with Pittsburgh.

"Joltin' Joe DiMaggio": A popular song, circa 1941, celebrating the man who captivated the nation with his 56-game hitting streak (*see* STREAK, THE; 56; 1941 SEASON). The tune, written by Alan Courtney and performed by Les Brown and his Orchestra with Betty Bonney on vocals, streaked to number 12 on the pop charts just weeks after DiMaggio's streak ended.

Knickerbocker Rules: The rules created by the NEW YORK KNICKERBOCKERS Baseball Club of 1845, led by Alexander CARTWRIGHT and Daniel "Doc" ADAMS. For his part, Cartwright is in the Hall of Fame, where his plaque says that he was responsible for setting the bases 90 feet apart and establishing 9 men per team and 9 innings per game. I have no idea where they made that up, because the actual Knickerbocker rules don't say anything about 90, 9, or 9. Rule 8 says that the game will "consist of 21 counts, or aces"—that means the first team to 21 runs. Rule 6 discusses the size of each team, but it doesn't give any actual numbers; it just says, "If there should not be sufficient number of members of the Club present at the time agreed upon to commence exercise, gentlemen not members may be chosen in to make up the match"—basically, ringers are allowed if needed. And the part about 90 feet? Rule 4 does say that the distances from home to second and first to third should be 42 paces. If you assume three feet per pace, that calculates to 30 yards between bases, or 90 feet. At last! Something that's accurate about Cartwright's Hall of Fame plaque! Sorry, no. As author John Thorn has pointed out while debunking the Cartwright story in TOTAL BASEBALL, a "pace" in 1845 was defined as two and one-half feet, not three. Thorn quotes Webster's 1832 and 1853 dictionaries to prove it: "Pace: The space between the two feet in walking, estimated at two feet and a half." Three feet per pace didn't get established until well into the 20th century, which means that the base paths under the Knickerbocker Rules were actually about 75 feet long. Some things that the Knickerbocker Rules did establish were the idea of foul territory, three strikes per out, and three outs per inning. Over the next 17 years, while Doc Adams presided over the Knickerbocker Club, he changed the rules to create a 9-inning game, 90 feet between bases, and a pitcher's box 45 feet from home. For more on the propaganda that we've been

fed about the origins of baseball, *see* DOUBLEDAY, ABNER;
DOUBLEDAY MYTH; MILLS COMMISSION REPORT.

lively ball era: An oft-told baseball story is that sometime
around 1920, major league executives acted in concert with
baseball manufacturers to "liven up" the ball. Their supposed
aim was to increase flagging attendance in the wake of the
BLACK SOX SCANDAL. With the alleged new ball, Babe RUTH
slammed 54, then 59 home runs, shattering the major league
record, and for the rest of the decade, batters went wild and
attendance soared. It's almost impossible to find a baseball
history book that does *not* tell this story as if it were
uncontroverted truth. There's only one thing wrong: It's a lie.
No writer who espouses this theory has any evidence to prove
it. That's because no evidence has ever existed that the ball
used from 1920 to 1926 was in any substantial way different
from that used from 1911 to 1919. The REACH COMPANY,
which manufactured balls for both leagues (although SPAL-
DING SPORTING GOODS put its name on the NL's balls), did
use a higher-quality yarn after World War I, but it had little,
if anything, to do with the inflated averages. (*See also* "RABBIT
BALL.") Traditional baseball history blames the "rabbit ball"
based on the simple fact that offensive totals increased. But
that's like accusing somebody of murder when the only evidence you have is the dead body. Actually, three important
factors were responsible for the outrageous hitting totals of
what became known as the "lively ball era": the banning of
the spitball; the death of Ray CHAPMAN on AUGUST 16, 1920;
and the coming of Babe Ruth. The outlawing of the spitball
came before the 1919 season because there was a fear that a
pitcher might lose control of the ball and kill someone. Well,
someone did die the following season, but it wasn't because of
the spitball. Chapman's death from an underhand fastball by
Carl MAYS inspired major league executives to order that umpires keep fresh white balls in play at all times; prior to that,
the same one or two balls were used throughout the game,
and by the later innings, that ball would get spit on and cov-

ered with dirt and mud. Ruth, who had already broken the home run record before Chapman's death, helped usher in the new era by showing the baseball world that home runs were possible. Before he became a full-time hitter, baseball games were won with "scientific" spray hitting and stolen bases (*see* DEAD BALL ERA). Ruth and his uppercut swing became so popular that legions of baseball players started copying him. Add to that the small size of most ballparks, and of course you're going to have an increase in home runs. What proof is there that no lively ball was introduced? A lot more than the proof that a lively ball *was* introduced. Throughout the 1920s, journalists and league offices launched any number of investigations into the alleged "rabbit ball" theories, and all of them came to the same conclusion: that the balls used after 1920 had the same weight and size and bounce and used the same materials (except for the yarn, which didn't make much of a difference) as the ball that had been used in the past decade. In addition, the manufacturer and league officials gave sworn depositions to that effect. Much-respected NL president John Heydler said, "At no time have the club owners ordered the manufacturer to make the ball livelier. The only stipulation the club owners have made about the ball is that it be the very best that could be made." The *Reach Baseball Guide* ran a full-page ad announcing, "We never experiment with our patrons. There has been no change in the construction of the CORK CENTER BALL since we introduced it in 1910." In the mid-1920s, pitcher Vean Gregg, who'd also played during the 1910s, asserted that the ball was, indeed, the same. And the United States Bureau of Standards conducted extensive tests that came to the same conclusion. So what we have is an easy-to-understand *effect*—the inflated batting numbers—without an easy-to-understand *cause*. In such instances of uncertainty, many people find it reassuring to believe that somebody, somewhere, no matter how manipulative and secretive, is in control of things. Certainly, batting totals zoomed out of sight, and at just about any other time in the game's history, such an explosion would have been met with some kind of official attempt to get control of things. Instead, what the league found was that fans loved it. Attendance per game increased by 21 percent in both leagues in 1920, and though it fluctuated for the next decade, the owners let their bottom lines do their talking, and the home run was there to stay. In 1926, Reach introduced the "cushioned cork center" to replace the plain old "cork center," but that change actually *hurt* the batters: league batting, on base, and slugging averages went down in 1926. By 1930, however, an entire generation of players had honed the art of power hitting using thin-handled bats, and batting totals reached their peak (*see* 1930 SEASON). Technically, I suppose, the "lively ball era" is still with us because teams are still hitting home runs at levels well above the dead ball era. But the *de facto* end of the lively ball era is the beginning of World War II. Throughout the 1930s, batting and slugging averages were still really high, but after the war, they seemed to go down to more "normal" levels. There's really no easy explanation for that change except to note that it was gradual and probably due to evolutionary forces rather than Babe Ruth's *revolutionary* force. (An excellent study of 1920s baseball, from which much of my information comes, is William Curran's *Big Sticks*.)

Long Season, The (New York: Harper & Brothers, 1960): Jim Brosnan's epochal book about the life of a baseball player, *The Long Season* created a minor scandal at its publication because it discussed such taboos as drinking and sexual activity among ballplayers. Like its successor in that genre, Jim BOUTON's *BALL FOUR*, Brosnan's book seems tame by today's standards. But you have to remember that in 1960, the press hadn't yet insinuated itself into every element of celebrity life. And in any case, *The Long Season* made its real impact not because of any sordid escapades, but rather because Brosnan is a smart thinker who had a lot to say about the game.

Lou Gehrig's Disease: Amyotrophic lateral sclerosis (ALS), the deadly disease that slowly but inevitably robs muscles of their strength. Lou GEHRIG, its most famous but not its only victim, succumbed to the illness on June 2, 1941.

Louisville Slugger: The name of the most famous bats in baseball, manufactured by the Hillerich & Bradsby Company. Pete Browning, a 19th-century slugger who played for Louisville of the AMERICAN ASSOCIATION, was known to be fond of his bats, and when one of them broke during a game in the 1880s, John Hillerich, the son of a local woodworker, approached Browning with the offer of making a bat for him. Browning was so successful and happy with his new bat that other players started requesting them. H&B rode that success to become the king of bat manufacturers, a position they hold today. Although there are six other bat companies in the United States, H&B has contracts with 70 percent of all major leaguers. To keep up with the demand, a big factory in Jeffersonville, Indiana, across the Ohio River from Louisville, puts out 1.4 million bats per year, 10 to 15 percent of which go to the professionals. If you're in the vicinity, you can take a tour of the plant. You can see all the lathes working, and you'll be amazed that it takes as little as eight seconds to mold a bat. They'll even custom-make one for you with your own brand on it.

Mills Commission Report: In 1907, powerful sporting goods magnate Albert G. SPALDING created the Mills Commission ostensibly to examine the origins of baseball. In fact, the patriotic Spalding really just wanted to end all the "rumors" to the effect that baseball was not truly an American game. As he wrote, "While it is true that ball playing in many forms has been engaged in by most nations from time immemorial, it is a proven fact that the game now designated 'Base Ball' is of modern and purely American origin." Now that Spalding's mind had been made up, there was the little matter of those pesky "facts." So the commission, headed by A. G. Mills, who had succeeded William HULBERT as president of the National League in 1882, scoured the land for someone who could provide them. They found an elderly mining engineer named Abner Graves who claimed he was on hand the day a West Point cadet named Abner DOUBLEDAY laid out the bases and positioned the fielders in a configuration like that of baseball. The many holes in Graves's claim can be found elsewhere in this book. Despite the obvious falsehoods, here is what the report found, in part:

> First—That Base Ball had its origin in the United States;
> Second—That the first scheme for playing it, according to the best evidence obtainable to date, was devised by Abner Doubleday, at Cooperstown, New York, in 1839.

After these findings went public, the son of Alexander CARTWRIGHT protested to Spalding that his father, who headed the NEW YORK KNICKERBOCKERS, should receive credit for the invention of the game. The young Cartwright was so successful that today almost all modern fans who give it any thought believe the Cartwright story (although a few still think Doubleday had something to do with it). But as author John Thorn demonstrated in a chapter from *TOTAL BASEBALL* called "The True Father of Baseball," the Cartwright story is also incorrect. Thorn gives the lion's share of the credit to Daniel "Doc" ADAMS.

"Miracle Braves": One of the first "miracle teams," the Braves of 1914 were a ragtag bunch of aging veterans and unknown kids. They'd finished thirty-one and one-half games out of first place in 1913, and were languishing in last place on July 18 the following season. But then they won 60 of their last 76 games (!)—one of the most amazing runs in the history of baseball—and captured the pennant by ten and one-half games. In the World Series, they faced the mighty Athletics, winners of four AL titles in the previous five years. True to the fairy tale finish, the Braves swept the stunned A's in four straight. Their biggest star, Johnny EVERS, captured the league's CHALMERS AWARD, and the team rewarded itself with a new ballpark the following season. Alas, despite the new home, the magic had disappeared. The Braves finished second in 1915, then third—a position in the standings they wouldn't reach again until after World War II.

"Miracle Mets": Like the "MIRACLE BRAVES," the 1969 "Miracle Mets" shocked the baseball world with an amazing pennant run. The Mets had been born in 1962 as the worst team of the 20th century, losing a record 120 games. Their next six seasons weren't much better, but in 1968 they did show some promise by climbing out of the cellar to finish ninth out of ten. Nobody expected the Mets to go anywhere in 1969, the first year of divisional play. But pitching ace Tom SEAVER won 25 games to lead the league, and the team's pitching staff as a whole finished tops in the NL with a 2.99 ERA. Though just ordinary offensively, they had enough clutch performers that the Mets won 38 of their final 49 games and notched exactly 100 victories. They beat the Braves in the League Championship Series, and then faced the Baltimore Orioles in the World Series. Those Orioles—with Jim PALMER, Dave McNALLY, Mike Cuellar, Frank ROBINSON, Paul Blair, Boog Powell, and others—were regarded as the greatest team in recent years. But they couldn't stop the miracle. Thanks to some big fielding plays and timely hitting, the Mets beat the O's in five games—cementing the '69 Mets' position in baseball folklore.

"Murderer's Row": Nickname for the 1927 Yankees, who featured power up and down the lineup: Babe RUTH, Lou GEHRIG, Tony Lazzeri, Earle Combs—all of whom made it to the Hall of Fame—as well as a deadly pitching staff featuring Hall of Famers Waite Hoyt and Herb Pennock. The '27 team won 110 games in the regular season, then demolished Pittsburgh in the World Series in four straight games. Interestingly, the term "Murderer's Row"—which comes from the mythical death row in a prison filled with murderers awaiting execution—had been applied to a number of teams before

1927. But once Babe Ruth stepped in, the term became his team's alone.

"Mustache Gang": One of Charlie FINLEY's greatest strengths as an owner and businessman was his ability to generate publicity out of nothing. The "Mustache Gang" was an example. In the early 1970s, he gave bonuses to any A's players who would grow mustaches. In almost any other line of work, it wouldn't have been a big deal, but at the time, most teams forbade players to grow facial hair as a matter of policy; the Reds still do. Rollie FINGERS, "Catfish" HUNTER, Reggie JACKSON, Joe Rudi, and most of the team took Finley's money, and the team became known as the "Mustache Gang." They would be forgotten today if they hadn't won three straight World Series from 1972 to 1974.

national pastime, the: Although baseball evolved in the mid-19th century from the British games CRICKET and ROUNDERS, people almost immediately bestowed upon the sport the mantle of "America's national pastime"; probably the first journalist to do so was William Trotter Porter, who ran *Spirit of the Times*, a leading sports journal. Poet Walt Whitman would say, "I see great things in baseball. It's our game—the American game. It will take our people out of doors, fill them with oxygen, give them a larger physical stoicism. Tend to relieve us from being a nervous, dyspeptic set. Repair losses and be a blessing to us." Famed historian Jacques Barzun had this to say: "Whoever would understand the hearts and minds of America had better learn baseball." And President Herbert Hoover said, "Next to religion, baseball has had a greater impact on the American people than any other institution." It's hard to argue.

Natural, The (New York: Harcourt, 1952): Bernard Malamud's classic baseball novel was made into an Oscar-nominated film starring Robert Redford back in 1984. It's about the fairy tale life of Roy Hobbs, an aging outfielder with a sweet swing who

makes it to the majors for one glorious season. If you've seen
the movie, you can still read the book, because the two works
have very little in common except the title. If you've read the
book and liked it, however, it's almost a certainty that you
won't like the movie. The movie version of *The Natural,* to me,
is a great work, full of sentiment and schmaltz, but fun
throughout. Not all viewers share my opinion.

Nice Guys Finish Last (New York: Simon & Schuster, 1975):
Generally regarded as one of the best baseball autobiographies, this work by Leo DUROCHER (with Ed Linn) remains a
classic. In it, you can read Leo's side of 50 years of chaos and
controversies, including his explanation of the title; in this
book, you can read the explanation under the Durocher
entry.

nicknames: Even though hardly any players have nicknames
today, baseball history is brimming with great ones. Throughout this book I've included a nickname next to a player's
name if it's appropriate. Here's a sampling of some nicknames for some other players:

"Sudden" Sam McDowell
"Smiling" Mickey Welch
"Bollicky" Billy Taylor
"Laughing" Larry Doyle
"Grunting" Jim Shaw
"Poosh 'Em Up" Tony Lazzeri
"Daffy" Dean (Dizzy's brother)
Bob Ferguson, "Death to Flying Things"
Pepper Martin, "The Wild Horse of the Osage"
Arlie Latham, "The Freshest Man on Earth"
Red Lucas, "The Nashville Narcissus"
Lou Novikoff, "The Mad Russian"
Russ Meyer, "The Mad Monk"
Eddie Yost, "The Walking Man" (check out his yearly walk
    totals)

Sal Maglie, "The Barber"
Camilo Pascual, "The Little Potato"
Lou Skizas, "The Nervous Greek"
Jimmie Wynn, "The Toy Cannon"
Dick Radatz, "The Monster"
Phil Regan, "The Vulture"
Hughie "Ee-Yah" Jennings
Odell "Bad News" Hale
Jim "Bad News" Galloway
Hazen "Kiki" Cuyler (pronounced "kai-kai," not "kee-kee")
George "Twinkletoes" Selkirk
Joe "Ducky Wucky" Medwick (modern fans incorrectly call
 him just "Ducky")
Eric "Boob" McNair
Hugh "Losing Pitcher" Mulcahy
Walter "Boom Boom" Beck (one "boom" for the sound of
 a batter connecting with one of Beck's fat pitches, the
 other "boom" for the sound of the ball hitting the out-
 field wall)
Lynn "Line Drive" Nelson (a pitcher, not a hitter)
Johnny "Grandma" Murphy
Eddie "The Brat" Stanky
Jim "Abba Dabba" Tobin
Walter "No-Neck" Williams
Frank "Hondo" Howard
Jim "Mudcat" Grant
Jack "The Ripper" Clark
Ray Schalk, "Cracker"
Ernie Lombardi, "Schnozz"
Mike Epstein, "Superjew"
Many Native Americans were nicknamed "Chief"

"$100,000 Infield": The Philadelphia Athletics' famed infield
from 1911 to 1914, consisting of 1st baseman Stuffy McInnis,
2nd baseman Eddie COLLINS, shortstop Jack Barry, and 3rd
baseman "Home Run" BAKER. Together, they helped Connie
MACK's A's to three pennants and two championships in four

years. The $100,000 referred not to what they were paid in those days of the oppressive RESERVE CLAUSE, but rather what they would have been worth to A's ownership if they had been sold on the open market (and don't think that idea hadn't occurred to Mack, who was notorious for periodic "housecleanings" where he would dismantle a team to raise quick cash). Much later, Baker and Collins—as well as Mack—would be reunited in the Hall of Fame.

Only the Ball Was White (Englewood Cliffs, NJ: Prentice-Hall, 1970): Robert Peterson's influential work on the NEGRO LEAGUES. When Peterson published this book, the Negro leagues were a part of baseball history that, like its great players, had been shunted to the fringes. Peterson succeeded in raising awareness about black baseball, and he helped get the Hall of Fame to start including Negro leaguers. Today, Peterson's book is out of date in many places, and other books—notably the ones by John B. Holway—have done more to set the record straight. But as an introduction to the players and the time, you can't go wrong with *Only the Ball Was White*.

Pride of the Yankees: The famous 1942 movie about Lou GEHRIG starring Gary Cooper as Gehrig and Teresa Wright as his wife, Eleanor. It's a great piece of Hollywood, and most of it is accurate, telling the emotional story of the son of immigrants who makes it big in New York, then is struck down by a horrible, debilitating disease. Like most movies of that period, it's overdramatic and overacted at times, but it's great entertainment.

"rabbit ball": The conspiracy theory that tries to explain why batting and home run totals go up in a given year. Simply put, there is no evidence that the "rabbit ball" (so named because it hops off the bat) has ever existed. In 1987, for example, home run totals increased by 14.5 percent, and fans, players, and the media cried that the leagues had surreptitiously introduced a new "juiced" ball. But other than the batting totals, they had absolutely no evidence—no confession from a disgruntled RAWLINGS COMPANY employee, no leaks from the commissioner's office, no legitimate results from an investigation, no tests showing that the ball used in 1987 was any different from that used in 1986. The exact same allegations sprang up in the 1920s to explain the tremendous batting successes of Babe RUTH, Rogers HORNSBY, George SISLER, and others. And they've come up at various other times in baseball history, most recently in 1994. (*See* LIVELY BALL ERA for a discussion of the 1920s batting revolution.) The truth is, however, that only three times in this century has the ball been altered: in 1910 with the introduction of the cork center, in 1926 when the cushioned cork center was invented, and in 1974 when manufacturers switched from horsehide to cowhide. Only the first of those moves really affected major league batting totals. But in the absence of evidence, conspiracy theorists like to create some. They claim that the ball is being manufactured differently from year to year. Ridiculous, says Scott Smith of Rawlings. "The balls we manufacture are the most consistent baseballs ever manufactured," he says. "And test results prove it." The balls weigh the same and have the same measurements as always. One subtheory is that the ball is "wound tighter." But if you wind the yarn tighter, then it stands to reason that you either have to make the balls smaller or you have to add more yarn to fill the existing size, which would make the ball heavier and negate the whole purpose of the tighter winding. In either case, the whole design of the baseballs would have to change, as well as the manufacturing process. Rawlings has not done that. They've been asked so many times about the rabbit ball that they're tired of it; if you think about it, it's really an attack on the company's integrity. Some possible explanations for the increased batting totals include quality of pitching, especially in an expansion year, a smaller strike zone, and the predominant weather in league cities; home runs are easier to hit in hot weather than in cool weather. There are, in fact, quite a few legitimate theories for increased batting totals, many related to physics. But a "rabbit ball" isn't one of them.

Rawlings Company: The company that manufactures balls, gloves, uniforms, bats, helmets, and other equipment used by major league baseball teams as well as equipment for other sports. Founded by George and Alfred Rawlings, the company opened its doors in 1887 as a general sporting goods company, selling mainly hunting and fishing equipment. In 1906, the St. Louis Cardinals became the first team to contract with Rawlings for uniforms. In the 1910s, the company first began supplying major leaguers with gloves, and today, more major leaguers use Rawlings gloves than any other (see GLOVE for more). Capitalizing on its standing as the premier glove manufacturer, Rawlings began sponsoring the GOLD GLOVE award in 1957, the trophy for fielding excellence as selected by a panel of managers and coaches. Since 1977, Rawlings has supplied all the balls to major league baseball—totalling 60,000 dozen per year, all manufactured at a plant in Turrailba, Costa Rica. Now and again, the company is accused of "juicing" the baseball to help batting totals, but the idea that a $130 million company—which has to answer to its shareholders, customers, and the public at large—would engage in such a deception is patently ludicrous; *see* "RABBIT BALL" for more.

Reach Company: The first big baseball-related sporting goods company, Reach was founded by Ben Shibe, who went on to own the Philadelphia A's, and A. J. Reach, an English-born baseball star of the mid-19th century. Reach standardized the manufacture of baseballs and earned the first contract to supply balls to the National League in 1876. Interestingly, the contract called for Reach to provide the balls free of charge; the company was obviously banking that the title "official baseball of the National League" would give them some marketing clout over the competition. Then its biggest competitor, the SPALDING SPORTING GOODS COMPANY, began *paying* the league to use its baseballs, so Reach turned to the AMERICAN ASSOCIATION. Little did people know that Spalding had actually contracted with Reach to produce the balls with the

Spalding name on them. In 1892, Reach was bought out by Spalding. As a marketing ploy, Albert G. SPALDING insisted that the buyout be kept secret and that Reach continue to manufacture and market products under its own label in direct competition with Spalding. When the American League was founded in 1901, AL president "Ban" JOHNSON offered Reach's Ben Shibe the contract to supply their baseballs if Shibe would back a Philadelphia franchise. Johnson probably didn't know at the time that Reach and Spalding were one and the same. He also may not have known that both Reach and Spalding baseballs were manufactured by Reach. In any case, Reach began an affiliation with the American League that lasted until 1977, when the RAWLINGS COMPANY took over. The funny thing is that for baseball's first century, countless writers and players throughout the years swore the balls were different. Actually, the only difference was the name on the ball and the color of the stitching: Reach balls were red, Spalding blue. Reach introduced baseball's two most significant innovations: the cork center in 1910 and the cushioned-cork center in 1926. The first change increased batting totals significantly; the second had no effect (*see* LIVELY BALL ERA).

Rotisserie League: Name of the first FANTASY LEAGUE, invented in 1979 at a now-defunct New York restaurant called La Rotisserie Française. Six baseball fans, including authors Dan Okrent and Steve Wulf, invented the game that, over the next decade, would sweep America and infect every other professional team sport.

rounders: One of the games upon which baseball is based, rounders was invented in England and has been played for centuries. It's played with a bat, a soft, rubbery ball, and three "bases," which are actually four-foot sticks poking out of the ground, between two teams of eight or more players. There's no foul territory. Batters are put out when the defense catches the batted ball on the fly or on one bounce or when a defensive player hits a runner with the ball when he's running to a base. The team bats until all its members are retired, then they switch sides. It's a great game for people of all ages because it doesn't require loads of skill. Pitchers don't throw fast—they just toss it in—and batters are only expected to make contact, not drive the ball 350 feet.

"Say hey!": Willie MAYS's trademark saying. He had a personalized license plate with those words, and he titled his recent autobiography *Say Hey!*

"Say it ain't so, Joe": The alleged cry made by a youngster to "Shoeless" Joe JACKSON as Jackson made his way from the courthouse after testifying before a Chicago grand jury in the early stages of the BLACK SOX SCANDAL. Although it makes for a good story, this is probably apocryphal, probably never happened. It is well known that reporters of that time would embellish their stories, and maybe a child within earshot of a journalist shouted something—perhaps "It ain't true, is it, Joe?"—from the crowd, but Jackson said he never heard it. "I guess the biggest joke of all," he said later in life, "was that story that got out about 'Say it ain't so, Joe.' It was supposed to have happened ... when I came out of the courtroom. There weren't any words passed between anybody except me and a deputy sheriff. ... He asked me for a ride and we got in the car together and left. There was a big crowd hanging around in front of the building, but nobody else said anything to me."

Shoeless Joe (Boston: Houghton Mifflin, 1982): The magical, lyrical novel upon which the movie *FIELD OF DREAMS* is based, W. P. Kinsella's version is more expansive and powerful than the movie. The most interesting difference between the two is that in the book, the author that Ray is supposed to find is not the fictional Terence Mann but the very real J. D. Salinger. Marvelously written, *Shoeless Joe* is my favorite baseball novel. And I'm not alone.

Society for American Baseball Research (SABR): Founded in 1971 by Bob Davids, SABR (pronounced "saber") is baseball's premier research organization. Each year, they publish numerous research journals and other books containing articles about baseball history—usually a previously unknown or unremembered part of history. They also hold a yearly convention in a major league city with guest speakers, contests, and other big events. Clearly, SABR has significantly advanced the research of the game's history. Memberships cost just $35 a year, which includes a monthly newsletter, several yearly publications, discounts on baseball books, and more. If you want to join, write to SABR, PO Box 93183, Cleveland, OH 44101.

Spalding Sporting Goods Company: Founded by Albert G. SPALDING while still enjoying a successful and popular career in baseball—first as a pitcher, then as a manager—the Spalding Company ruled the American sporting goods market in the late 19th century. With Spalding's name, the company marketed bats, balls, uniforms, gloves, and equipment for every other sport. In fact, as William Curran makes clear in *Big Sticks*, Spalding licensed the manufacture of that equipment to other companies, putting his name on the finished product as a marketing gimmick. Then he began to buy out his competitors but let their products "compete" with his. Today, that might be grounds for an antitrust lawsuit. In the 1890s, it was good business. Spalding, of course, diversified the company into other sports, introducing the world's first basketball in 1894 as well as the first American football, golf club, golf ball, and tennis ball. Now affiliated with the Even-Flo baby products company, Chicopee, Massachusetts–based Spalding is a billion-dollar company.

Sporting News, The: Founded in 1886 by Canadian-born Al Spink, *TSN* became known as the "Bible of Baseball" because of its in-depth coverage of the sport, including editorials, feature stories, team notes, and complete box scores through much of the publication's history. As part owner of St. Louis's

SPORTSMAN'S PARK, Spink and his partners tried to lure a major league team to his city. They succeeded in getting the Browns of the AMERICAN ASSOCIATION to move in, then Spink set about to compete with baseball's other weekly publication, Francis Richter's *The Sporting Life*. After just three years, Spink's weekly surpassed *TSL* in both circulation and advertising dollars. It was a true family affair as brothers, sons, a sister-in-law, and, later, grandsons joined the organization. What really helped the paper succeed, however, was the reporting by such luminaries as Ring Lardner and Fred LIEB; many of America's best baseball writers worked for *TSN*, either full-time or per article. Even though *TSN* had always covered other sports, baseball was always its number one priority. But after World War II, as professional football and basketball gained popularity, *TSN* began devoting nearly equal time to a variety of activities under the direction of the publication's most illustrious and forward-thinking leader, J. G. Taylor Spink. He also helped create the GOLD GLOVE award. With Spink at the helm, *TSN* entered the book publishing business with yearly preseason guides, record books, and histories. Today, *TSN* is an all-purpose sports weekly that still offers comprehensive baseball coverage—without the box scores, which they eliminated a few years ago. The Hall of Fame even offers the J. G. Taylor Spink Award "for meritorious contributions to baseball writing," whose recipients include Jim Murray, Red SMITH, Damon Runyon, Grantland Rice, and 38 others. The Spink family's role in helping popularize baseball can't be ignored.

Stengelese: The peculiar brand of double-talk and hilarious verbiage uttered by Casey STENGEL, Hall of Fame manager and noted linguist. Casey wasn't a buffoon. He was a great storyteller who loved to make people laugh. Here's a sampling of his memorable words:

- "I don't know if he throws a spitball, but he sure spits on the ball."
- "I was pitching batting practice and they told me not to

throw so hard. I wanted to impress the manager, so I threw as hard as I could. Then hitters commenced hitting balls over buildings. Then I threw harder and they hit the ball harder. Then, I told the manager I was really an outfielder."

- "If we're going to win the pennant, we've got to start thinking we're not as good as we think we are."
- "The secret of managing is to keep the guys who hate you away from the guys who are undecided."
- "Most people my age are dead."
- "They say some of my stars drink whiskey, but I have found that the ones who drink milkshakes don't win many ballgames."
- "When a fielder gets a pitcher into trouble, the pitcher has to pitch himself out of a slump he isn't in."
- "There comes a time in every man's life, and I've had plenty of them." (A quote that also appears on his gravestone.)
- "You could look it up." (His most quoted line.)

stickball: A game played mostly in big cities using a stick or broom handle for a bat and a small rubber ball. Since it's played on the streets between big buildings, the players have to come up with a unique set of ground rules regarding foul ground and extra base hits. A lot of major leaguers grew up on stickball, and in more innocent times, some stars—Willie MAYS among them—were known to play the game with neighborhood kids even after they'd made the majors.

"Take Me Out to the Ball Game": Written by the same guy who wrote "Shine on Harvest Moon," "Take Me Out to the Ball Game" became baseball's anthem shortly after its publication in 1908. Here are the complete lyrics to Jack Norworth's classic, although I suspect you know them already:

> Take me out to the ball game.
> Take me out with the crowd.

Buy me some peanuts and cracker jack.
I don't care if I never get back.
Let me root, root, root for the home team.
If they don't win it's a shame.
For it's one, two, three strikes you're out
At the old ball game!

In Ken Burns's 1994 *BASEBALL* documentary on PBS, he played more than 200 versions of the song.

30–30 Club: A mythical club for any player who slugs 30 homers and steals 30 bases in one season. Ken Williams of the St. Louis Browns first earned the distinction in 1922, but nobody remembers him. It took Willie MAYS and Bobby BONDS to make 30–30 famous. Bonds achieved five 30–30 seasons, the most in history, although his son Barry BONDS may challenge the record. But because so many players—from Howard Johnson to Ron Gant—have entered the club since the mid-1980s, it has lost quite a bit of its exclusivity.

Tinker to Evers to Chance: The infield double play combination of the Chicago Cubs from 1903 to 1910. Made famous by Franklin P. Adams's poem "BASEBALL'S SAD LEXICON," the trio of Joe TINKER, Johnny EVERS, and Frank CHANCE (with Harry Steinfeldt at third base) led the Cubs to four pennants and one World Series victory. All three are in the Hall of Fame, but how good *were* they? Adams seems to have thought they were something special. But maybe it was just because the Cubs' pennants came at the expense of Adams's Giants. Let's look at the stats. From 1903 to 1910, the Cubs as a team never led the league in double plays, and only once did they lead the league in the percentage of double plays turned per baserunner allowed. Strong argument for calling T–E–C overrated—an opinion that many baseball fans now hold. However, let's look at the big picture. The Cubs' pitching staff was always or nearly always the best in the league. During that eight-year period, they led in team ERA six times (with a low of 1.73), in lowest opponents' batting average seven times (low of .207), and in lowest opponents' on base percentage six times (low of .272). Since batters rarely got on base, the double play combo got few chances to record a DP. And even when they did allow baserunners, the opposing team's manager knew he was going to have a tough time scoring them against such stingy pitchers. What would he do? Sacrifice. Steal a base. Hit and run. Anything he could do to get that man to second base *and avoid the double play*. That's the way baseball was played during the DEAD BALL ERA. You can't fault Tinker, Evers, and Chance for failing to turn the DP when they probably got so few opportunities. Tinker to Evers to Chance may not have been the world's greatest double play combination. But they won all those pennants—they had to be pretty damn good.

Topps Co.: The chewing gum company that grew into the nation's preeminent BASEBALL CARD manufacturer. Topps was founded in 1938 by Abram, Ira, Philip, and Joseph Shorin, first marketing regular gum and then, after the war, Bazooka bubble gum. In 1951, the company put out its first set of baseball cards—two individual 52-card sets designed to be used in some kind of game. The next year, they released a 407-card set with player stats and personal information similar to the cards sold today. That set, which contains rookie cards of both Mickey MANTLE and Willie MAYS, is today worth at least $65,000 in good condition; the Mantle card alone has fetched $45,000 at auction. Topps, however, wasn't the first card manufacturer. Tobacco companies sold cards with players' pictures on them for many years, and right after the war, the Bowman Company marketed baseball cards. In fact, Bowman competed with Topps until 1955, when Topps bought them out. For the next 25 years, Topps held a virtual monopoly on the product, as the company became synonymous with bubble-gum cards of all types, including other sports and even cards relating to movies and music groups. In 1981, two competitors entered the market: Fleer and Donruss. Their cards also included sticks of bubble gum inside their packs. Topps sued over patent infringement, claiming that other companies weren't allowed to sell sports cards with gum. Undaunted, Fleer and Donruss took the gum out of the packs and avoided the lawsuit. Over the next decade, several other card manufacturers—including Upper Deck, perhaps the most successful of the bunch—entered the market, and card collecting became a business rather than a quaint hobby. Where once there was only a single card set issued each year, there now are more than 30 sets and subsets from nearly a dozen manufacturers. In addition, there are numerous magazines devoted to sports cards, many of them published by card guru James BECKETT. Topps alone says that it distributes over a billion cards each year. I don't know how collectors can keep up.

Total Baseball (New York: Warner, 1988; HarperCollins, 1989, 1993; Viking, 1995): The first true baseball "encyclopedia," *Total Baseball* picks up where the misnamed BASEBALL ENCYCLOPEDIA leaves off. While the latter is strictly a records-and-statistics book, *Total Baseball* includes dozens of analytical and historical essays by some of the game's most astute writers: John Thorn, Pete PALMER, Jules Tygiel, David Q. Voigt, Frederick Ivor-Campbell. While the *Baseball Encyclopedia* lists the winners of each major award and Hall of Fame inductees, *Total Baseball* provides the complete voting history for those honors. While the *Baseball Encyclopedia* gives only the traditional statistics, *Total Baseball* gives SABERMETRICS stats such as RUNS CREATED, TOTAL AVERAGE, and Palmer's Linear Weights. Editors Palmer and Thorn have assembled a dedicated bunch of researchers to examine and verify the accuracy of every stat. And beginning with the 1995 edition, *Total Baseball*, not the *Baseball Encyclopedia*, has received the endorsement of major league baseball, meaning that all the statistics included there—such as Ty COBB's hit total of 4,189, rather than the traditional 4,191—carry MLB's official stamp of approval. *See also* .367.

Veeck as in Wreck (New York: G. P. Putnam, 1962): Bill VEECK's wonderful, critically acclaimed autobiography, *Veeck as in Wreck* tells the story of a master showman, perhaps the most innovative baseball executive ever. Unlike most owners of his day, Veeck set out to bring entertainment—not just baseball— to the masses. He loved to stage promotions and publicity stunts; his signing of midget Eddie GAEDEL is his most famous, but the book tells of a dozen more. His freewheeling attitude angered the Establishment, and you can read about that, too. After 30-plus years, the book is still worth owning.

"Wait till next year!": The perennial cry of an also-ran. Brooklyn Dodger fans are most famous for this wail because from 1941 through 1953, they lost five World Series to the mighty Yankees. The Dodgers finally beat the Yanks in 1955, but when they lost again a year later, Dodger fans could be heard chanting, "Wait till *last* year!"

"Whiz Kids": Nickname of the 1950 Phillies, who won the National League pennant with a starting lineup of players all around 30 years old or less. With Robin ROBERTS, Curt Simmons, and MVP Jim Konstanty on the mound and Richie ASHBURN, Del Ennis, and Eddie WAITKUS in the field, the Kids squeezed past the Dodgers by two games to win the pennant but lost to the Yankees in four straight. Years later, the 1983 Phillies marched to the pennant with a band of older players led by Pete ROSE, Joe MORGAN, Tony Perez, and Steve CARLTON. They were called the "Wheeze Kids."

"Who's on First?": The great comedy routine made famous by Abbott and Costello. If you've never heard it, there's no way this book can do it justice, because even after several listenings, it's still really funny. The premise is that Abbott is the manager of a team and Costello wants to join as a catcher, but before that, he has to learn the players' names. Here's the lineup:

First base: Who
Second base: What
Third base: I Don't Know
Shortstop: I Don't Care *or* I Don't Give a Damn
Left Field: Why
Center Field: Because
Right Field: (not mentioned)
Pitcher: Today
Catcher: Tomorrow

After Abbott and Costello popularized it on the radio, they included the skit in one of their movies, *The Naughty Nineties*.

"Willie, Mickey, or the Duke?": The oft-asked question popular among New York City baseball fans in the 1950s. Nobody ever had to ask the first part of the question: Who is the best center fielder? Based on both career stats and single-season highs, it's pretty clear that the real battle comes down to Willie MAYS or Mickey MANTLE, with Duke SNIDER out of the running. But when this argument reached its peak in the mid-1950s, the answer wasn't so simple. Here's a comparison of their stats for the years when they played against each other (**boldface** type indicates league-leading performance):

	Mays			
Year	HR	RBI	BA	SLG
1951	20	68	.274	.472
1954	41	110	**.345**	**.667**
1955	**51**	127	.319	**.659**
1956	36	84	.296	.557
1957	35	97	.333	**.626**
TOTALS	183	486	.315	.601

Mantle

Year	HR	RBI	BA	SLG
1951	13	65	.267	.443
1954	27	102	.300	.525
1955	**37**	99	.306	**.611**
1956	**52**	**130**	**.353**	.705
1957	34	94	.365	.665
TOTALS	163	490	.321	.599

Snider

Year	HR	RBI	BA	SLG
1951	29	101	.277	.483
1954	40	130	.341	.647
1955	42	**136**	.309	.628
1956	**43**	101	.292	**.598**
1957	40	92	.274	.587
TOTALS	194	560	.299	.587

As you can see, the choice of who was greater was not an easy one at the time. Although Mays and Mantle could steal bases, Snider led them all in homers and RBIs during their five-year competition. Defensively, Mays was spectacular but Mantle and Snider were near-perfect. In terms of pennants, Mantle won four, Snider three, and Mays two. In MVPs, Mantle captured two, Mays one, and Snider was shut out. The Willie-Mickey-Duke question is only one reason why New York City was the capital of baseball from the end of World War II until 1958.

Yogi-ism: A term for the various mangled sayings that purportedly came from the mouth of the great Yogi BERRA. For his baseball mind, the Hall of Fame catcher was a near genius. He played the most difficult defensive position flawlessly, and he managed several pennant winners. But as a thinker ... that's another story. Here are some choice quotes attributed to Mr. Berra:

- "Ninety percent of this game is half mental."
- "A nickel ain't worth a dime anymore."
- "If you can't imitate him, don't copy him."
- When asked his cap size in spring training: "I don't know. I'm not in shape yet."
- "You can observe a lot by watching."
- "We made too many wrong mistakes."
- "You've got to be careful if you don't know where you're going, because you might not get there."
- "It ain't over until it's over."

That last line is Berra's most famous, and he even titled his autobiography after it. But in *Yogi: It Ain't Over . . .*, he writes that he doesn't think he said "even 10 percent" of what has been attributed to him. But he does admit to "It ain't over until it's over."

RECORDS, STATISTICS, AND AWARDS

.367: Ty Cobb's career batting average at his retirement, the highest in baseball history. After examining the records of Cobb's era, researchers have determined that Cobb was wrongly credited with a 2-for-3 game, and so Cobb's lifetime hits total should be lowered from 4,191 to 4,189 and his batting average should be adjusted to .366 (*see* 1910 BATTING RACE). For many years, major league baseball resisted such statistical changes. "The passage of 70 years," said commissioner Bowie KUHN in 1981, ". . . constitutes a certain statute of limitation as to recognizing any changes in the records with confidence of the accuracy of such changes." In 1995, however, major league baseball changed its policy by endorsing the statistics book *TOTAL BASEBALL*, which lists 4,189 and .366 as Cobb's official totals, among other changes. Many "purists" continue to argue against such revisionism. "Some of these numbers acquire a kind of a poetry to them," says Hall of Fame librarian Tim Wiles. "When somebody takes them away or changes them and says we've improved baseball record-keeping, it's someone else's loss." But John Thorn, *Total Baseball*'s co-editor, believes historical accuracy is more important. "To me," he says, "that's the equivalent of saying that if we disinterred Napoleon and found that contrary to all written reports he was not five-foot-two but six-foot-two, we should keep this a secret." I agree with Thorn, that truth should win out over fiction. Nevertheless, I think it's great that a controversy so trivial can stir up such a bonfire of emotions. It just proves that we baseball fans are a special breed.

.406: Ted WILLIAMS's batting average in 1941, the last time a player has batted over .400 for a season. While impressive, that figure is not nearly as amazing as Williams's ON BASE PERCENTAGE that year: an all-time record .551.

.426: Highest single-season batting average in the 20th century, achieved by Napoleon LAJOIE in 1901. This figure has been discounted in three ways: First, 1901 was the inaugural season of the American League, which had been a minor league the previous year, so the caliber of pitching was below that of the National League. Second, the AL had not yet adopted the foul strike rule, making it easier to get a hit. And third, the Macmillan BASEBALL ENCYCLOPEDIA, based on their interpretation of the statistics, credits Lajoie with a .422 average. If you go by that source, Rogers HORNSBY has the century's highest batting mark, .424 in 1924.

.440: Highest single-season batting average in baseball history since the pitching mound was moved to its current distance of 60 feet 6 inches from home plate. Hugh Duffy achieved this mark in 1893, the second season after the mound was moved back from 50 feet. As the pitchers adapted to the new distance, the entire National League batted .309. Duffy's high average wasn't a fluke—he also led the league in RBIs with 145 and tied in homers with 18. For this stellar season, the Boston outfielder received a salary increase of $12.50 per month.

1.01: This was once the record for the lowest single-season ERA since the pitching mound was moved to its current distance. Lefthander Dutch Leonard achieved this mark in 1914 while pitching for the Red Sox; in addition to the amazing ERA, Leonard had a 19–5 record and allowed just 139 hits in 224 innings pitched. After researching the season stats, TOTAL BASEBALL discovered some statistical anomalies and credited Leonard with an even more amazing mark: 0.96.

1.12: Single-season ERA record for a pitcher with more than 300 innings, held by St. Louis's Bob GIBSON. In the 1968 SEASON, "The Year of the Pitcher," Gibson pitched the Cardinals to a pennant with a 22–9 won-loss record, only 7.4 baserunners per nine innings, and 268 strikeouts. It's easy to figure out how he won 22 games. The question is: How did he lose nine?

7: Record number of no-hitters thrown by Nolan RYAN, an unbreakable record if ever one existed. As if any more proof is needed that Ryan is not a normal human being, he tossed the last two no-nos when he was over 40 years old.

36: Single-season record for triples in one season, achieved by Owen "Chief" Wilson in 1912. This is one of baseball's oddest, least challenged records: Odd because Wilson never totaled more than 14 triples in any other season, least challenged because nobody this century has come within 10 of breaking the mark.

44: Number of games in Pete ROSE's 1978 hitting streak, which tied the National League record originally set in 1897 by Wee Willie KEELER but was 12 short of Joe DiMAGGIO's major league record (*see* 56).

56: Record number of consecutive games in Joe DiMAGGIO's famous 1941 hitting streak. DiMaggio batted .408 with 15 homers and 56 RBIs during The STREAK, which lasted from

May 15 to July 16. It was finally stopped in Cleveland by pitchers Al Smith and Jim Bagby in front of a crowd of 67,468, which at the time was the largest crowd ever to see a major league night game. Third baseman Ken Keltner made two great fielding plays to rob DiMaggio, and Bagby induced him to ground into an inning-ending double play in his last at bat. The failure cost DiMaggio a tidy sum of cash: He would have received a $10,000 endorsement deal from Heinz 57 if he had extended the streak one more game.

57: Single-season record for saves, set by Bobby Thigpen in 1990, when both Thigpen and Dennis ECKERSLEY (with 48) broke the previous record of 46. Surprisingly, neither won the league's Cy Young Award. Eckersley would go on to notch a 51-save season in 1992—winning both the Cy Young and MVP Awards—while Thigpen would fall victim to fatigue and would never again approach his phenomenal record. The way relief pitching is progressing, this seems like a breakable record, but a lot of variables would have to fall into place: a team that plays and wins a lot of close games, a good starting pitching staff, and a reliever at the top of his game. I would guess that this record will be broken by the turn of the century, but I can't imagine anybody ever totaling more than 65 saves.

59: Number of consecutive scoreless innings pitched by Orel Hershiser in 1988, breaking Don DRYSDALE's 20-year-old record of 58⅔ innings. Hershiser broke the mark during his last game of the season by pitching a 10-inning shutout. To give Hershiser the opportunity, the Dodger "offense" failed to score during the nine regulation innings.

61: Roger MARIS's single-season record for home runs, set in 1961, breaking Babe RUTH's 34-year-old record. Though the record will inexorably link Maris and Ruth, the contrast between the two players couldn't be more striking: Ruth was beloved and popular; Maris, private and brooding. Ruth dominated his league; Maris wasn't even the best player on his team. But because Maris, who had joined the Yankees only a year earlier, challenged the record while playing Ruth's very position, and then broke it by just a single home run in a season eight games longer than Ruth's, baseball fans found innumerable ways to denigrate Maris's achievement: He batted only .269. He had Mickey MANTLE protecting him in the batting order (never mind that Ruth had Lou GEHRIG batting behind him). He did it against the diluted pitching of baseball's first expansion year. And worst of all, he did it in baseball's first 162-game season. Yankee fans responded by alternately booing and cheering him, and the media became increasingly hostile—all of which drove Maris even further into his shell. But such criticism was unnecessarily hard, for Maris was already one of baseball's top players. He had won the 1960 MVP award with a 39-homer, 112-RBI season, and he would win the 1961 award not only for the 61 homers but also for his 142 RBIs and league-leading 132 runs. Maris lost much of his hair during that historic season; he admitted later that he also lost his spirit. *See also* ASTERISK.

190: Single-season record for RBIs, achieved by Hack WILSON in 1930, the peak year of the LIVELY BALL ERA. Unless the baseball powers decide they're not making enough money and extend the season by a few more games, this mark has almost no chance of being broken. Nobody has come within 35 of Wilson's record in the last 40 years.

383: Single-season record for strikeouts, achieved by Nolan RYAN while with the California Angels in 1973 to break Sandy KOUFAX's 1965 mark by a single strikeout. Currently considered another of baseball's unbreakable records, the mark could realistically be broken only by a pitcher reaching 320-plus innings—a figure that hasn't been touched since 1979. With the growing influence of relief pitching, you can consider this record untouchable.

511: All-time record for victories by a pitcher, held by "Cy" YOUNG. During his storied career, Young recorded 316 losses—also the highest total in history. Both records are absolutely unbreakable.

714: Babe RUTH's career home run total. When he retired, Ruth was more than 300 home runs ahead of the number two man, and for many years, nobody thought the record would ever be broken. Hank AARON changed that. *See also* APRIL 8, 1974.

755: Hank AARON's career home run total, tops among all American players (Japan's Sadaharu OH finished his career with 868 home runs). While definitely reachable, Aaron's amazing record could be broken only by a truly remarkable player. Think about it: a guy would have to average about 35 home runs for 22 consecutive seasons. In these days of multimillion-dollar guaranteed contracts, what ballplayer really wants to stay around for 22 seasons?

2,130: Number of consecutive games played by Lou GEHRIG over 14 seasons from May 31, 1925, until he removed himself from the lineup on MAY 2, 1939. Gehrig, who earned the nickname "Iron Horse" during the streak, remained in the Yankee lineup despite several injuries and periodic bouts of lumbago—and played at a level above 99 percent of other ballplayers for most of that time. This mark stood as one of baseball's "unbreakable" records until September 1995, when Cal RIPKEN, Jr., surpassed it. Nearly 50 years passed between Gehrig and Ripken. It's probable that at least that much time will pass before someone else approaches this amazing figure.

3,508: Walter JOHNSON's career strikeout total, the record that stood until Nolan RYAN broke it in 1986. *See* 5,714.

4,191: Ty COBB's career hit total at his retirement in 1928. Further research has credited Cobb with just 4,189 hits,

knocking his career average down to .366. *See* 1910 BATTING
RACE.

4,256: Pete ROSE's career hit total, tops in major league
history.

5,714: All-time record for strikeouts by a pitcher, achieved by
Nolan RYAN during his incredible 27-year career. Since Ryan's
career began in an era when pitchers completed most of their
starts and routinely notched 300-inning seasons, it is doubtful
that anyone will ever even approach Ryan's mark.

batting average (BA): The standard statistic by which batters
are judged, first used in 1880. It's calculated by dividing a
player's base hits by his at bats:

Hits / At Bats

Hugh DUFFY achieved the highest batting average in major
league history in 1894 with a .440 mark. The following chart
lists the 10 highest batting averages in the 20th century
(which is when the foul strike rule was enacted) as well as the
all-time career leaders in this category:

Career	BA	Single Season	BA
Ty Cobb	.366	Nap Lajoie, 1901	.426
Rogers Hornsby	.358	Rogers Hornsby, 1924	.424
Joe Jackson	.356	George Sisler, 1922	.420
Ed Delahanty	.346	Ty Cobb, 1911	.420
Tris Speaker	.345	Ty Cobb, 1912	.409
Ted Williams	.344	Joe Jackson, 1911	.408
Billy Hamilton	.344	George Sisler, 1920	.407
Dan Brouthers	.342	Ted Williams, 1941	.406
Babe Ruth	.342	Rogers Hornsby, 1925	.403
Harry Heilmann	.342	Harry Heilmann, 1923	.403

Batting average is actually a poor measure of a player's total
offensive performance, since it excludes all the other things

that score runs for a team—extra base hits, walks, stolen bases, and so forth. Everybody lionizes a .300 hitter, but if a player hits .300 with little power and few walks, that's an empty .300. A much better stat to judge a player is his ON BASE PERCENTAGE.

batting championship, batting title: The mythical award given to the league leader in BATTING AVERAGE. Ty COBB holds the major league record for the most batting titles: 11, including seven in a row (if you count the disputed 1910 BATTING RACE).

Chalmers Award: Baseball's earliest official most valuable player award, the Chalmers Award was originally instituted in 1910 to reward the major leagues' batting champion. But after the controversial 1910 BATTING RACE, Chalmers changed its policy and awarded the prize—a Chalmers automobile—to the player in each league selected most valuable by a vote of sportswriters. The winners were: 1911, Wildfire Schulte (NL) and Ty COBB (AL); 1912, Larry Doyle and Tris SPEAKER; 1913, Jake Daubert and Walter JOHNSON; 1914, Johnny EVERS and Eddie COLLINS. After those four years, the Chalmers Company had fulfilled its five-year commitment to the award, and the honor was discontinued. While Chalmers went out of business, the MVP idea regained steam in the 1920s and was institutionalized in the 1930s. *See also* MVP AWARD.

Cy Young Award: The Cy Young Award came out of the (good) idea that pitchers should be honored separately from position players. In one of his few positive accomplishments, commissioner Ford FRICK helped orchestrate the new award, which initially honored one pitcher in both leagues, as selected by the BASEBALL WRITERS ASSOCIATION OF AMERICA. Since Frick instituted the award because the pitchers received little representation in the MVP voting, it's ironic that the first Cy Young winner was the man who also won that year's MVP award: Brooklyn's Don NEWCOMBE in 1956. In fact, pitchers' eligibility for both awards has never been addressed by the BBWAA, and every time a guy wins both, griping can be heard all over the land. The gripers do have a point: Why should one group of players have the chance to win two awards, while everybody else can only win one? The BBWAA can resolve the issue pretty easily—by rendering pitchers ineligible for the MVP Award—but for some reason, they haven't. Anyway, after Newcombe won, his career pretty much fell apart, making him the first victim of the so-called Cy Young Jinx. Supposedly, the Jinx strikes pitchers the year after they win, and a cursory look at the record gives that theory some credence. Some not-so-notable Jinx victims include Bob Turley, Mike Marshall, Steve Stone, Pete Vuckovich, LaMarr Hoyt, and John Denny. However, superstitions aside, it's pretty easy to figure out why the Jinx struck these guys: they were above average pitchers who had one great season that was good enough to win them the award. It's hard enough to have a *good* season, let alone a *great* season, and it's unfair to expect these pitchers to have consecutive great seasons. Pitchers such as Sandy KOUFAX, Steve CARLTON, Jim PALMER, Tom SEAVER, Roger CLEMENS, and Greg MADDUX—all multiple award winners—were (or are) legitimately great pitchers from whom great seasons are expected. The Cy Young Jinx is, in fact, simply a matter of a pitcher returning to his old self. Back to the award history: At commissioner Frick's insistence, the first 11 awards were given to the best pitcher between both leagues. When he retired, the award was changed to honor one pitcher in each league, which is how we have it today; it never did make sense to have Koufax compete with Whitey FORD, but most of what Frick did made no sense, so we shouldn't be surprised. At first, the voting structure was kind of screwed up: one writer in each major league city placed a single name on the ballot, and the pitcher who got the most votes won. MVP Award voting, on the other hand, featured a weighted ballot on which writers placed 10 names in descending order. In 1969, the screwed-up voting system came back to bite the

BBWAA when Mike Cuellar and Denny McLAIN tied for the award with 10 votes apiece. After that, the voting changed to an MVP-like weighted system—voters placing three names on their ballots with five points going to the first-place pitcher, three to second place, and one to third place. That's how it is today, and it's a good system.

earned run average, ERA: The basic statistical measure of a pitcher that calculates the average number of earned runs (as opposed to unearned runs, which usually aren't the pitcher's fault) scored against a pitcher every nine innings. The ERA formula is simple, but you do need a calculator:

$$Earned\ Runs \times 9\ /\ Innings\ Pitched$$

So, for example, a pitcher with a 3.50 ERA is expected to allow three and a half earned runs whenever he pitches a complete game. To be eligible for the yearly ERA championship, a pitcher must have thrown at least one inning for every game his team played, usually 162. One thing about ERAs from a historical perspective is that baseball has changed so much that any listing of the top single-season and career leaders has no meaning. From 1876 through 1892, when the pitching box stood at between 45 and 50 feet from home, and again from the late 1890s through the 1910s, top ERAs lay in the mid-1.00s and an ERA over 3.00 was poor. In the LIVELY BALL ERA, from 1920 through the war, an ERA below 2.00 was a truly rare and phenomenal event. From the war until the 1960s, ERAs fell slightly, and in the mid- to late-1960s, they reached lows that hadn't been seen since the DEAD BALL ERA. Today, ERAs are pretty stable, with the league leader occasionally below 2.00 and the league average around the high 3.00s. Rather than listing the top 10 ERA leaders for single season and career, I'll list the top three single-season marks for each separate era of baseball (stats and time periods provided by *TOTAL BASEBALL*):

Years	Career	ERA	Single Season	ERA
1876–1892	John Ward	2.10	Tim Keefe, 1880	0.86
	Tommy Bond	2.25	Denny Driscoll, 1882	1.21
	Will White	2.28	George Bradley, 1876	1.23
1893–1919	Ed Walsh	1.82	Dutch Leonard, 1914	0.96
	Addie Joss	1.89	"Three-Finger"	
	"Three-Finger"		Brown, 1906	1.04
	Brown	2.06	Christy Mathewson,	
			1909	1.14
1920–1941	Wilber Cooper	2.89	Carl Hubbell, 1933	1.66
	Stan Coveleski	2.89	Pete Alexander, 1920	1.91
	Carl Mays	2.92	Dolf Luque, 1923	1.93
1942–1960	Hoyt Wilhelm	2.52	Spud Chandler, 1943	1.64
	Whitey Ford	2.75	Mort Cooper, 1942	1.78
	Harry Brecheen	2.92	Hal Newhouser, 1945	1.81
1961–present	Sandy Koufax	2.76	Bob Gibson, 1968	1.12
	Andy Messersmith	2.86	Dwight Gooden, 1985	1.53
	Jim Palmer	2.86	Greg Maddux, 1994*	1.56

*Even though the 1994 season was shortened by the strike, Maddux had already pitched 202 innings, more than enough to qualify him for the league ERA title in a regular-length season. In absolute terms, Maddux's ERA was the 50th best of all time.

fielding average: "There are three kinds of lies," said Disraeli. "Lies, damn lies, and statistics." Nowhere is that adage more applicable than to the statistic of fielding average. People can twist it to transform, say, Steve Garvey into a great-fielding first baseman and Ozzie Guillen into a terrible shortstop. To apply fielding average successfully, you have to look at it in conjunction with other fielding statistics. You can determine fielding average by dividing the number of clean fielding chances by the total number of plays a fielder makes:

$$(Total\ Chances - Errors)\ /\ Total\ Chances$$

The resulting number is the percentage of plays a fielder makes cleanly. For a first baseman, as an example, a fielding average below .990 is usually unacceptable unless he shows great range or has a great arm. And therein lies the fielding average dilemma: a poor fielder can actually have a great fielding average because he never takes enough risks to make errors. That's Steve Garvey in a nutshell. Meanwhile, a shortstop who gets to balls other shortstops don't can have a bad fielding average because he has more chances to make a mistake. That's Ozzie Guillen. To look at it another way: You or I can stand anchored atop second base, and on every ball hit directly to us, we could make the play cleanly. That would give us a 1.000 fielding average, but it wouldn't make us a good second baseman. On the other hand, sometimes people discount this statistic entirely, and they're wrong, too. When considered with other stats such as total chances per game, assists per game—and especially with actual game observations—fielding average can help give a complete assessment of a player's ability. So fielding average is neither meaningless nor omnipotent; like most things in life, the correct answer is somewhere in the middle.

Gold Glove: A yearly award sponsored by the RAWLINGS COMPANY that honors the best fielders in the league. Today, the awards winners are selected by a poll of managers and coaches, who aren't allowed to vote for anybody on their own teams. The voting isn't perfect; sometimes a player wins based on his reputation rather than his skills, and an above-average defensive player with a good bat can usually beat out a defensive wizard who can't hit his weight. But overall, it's a great award, and it honors a part of the game that is often overlooked. The following table lists the top Gold Glove winners at each position, based on the number of awards:

Position	Player	No. of Awards
Pitcher	Jim Kaat	14
	Bob Gibson	9

Position	Player	No. of Awards
Catcher	Johnny Bench	10
	Bob Boone	7
1st Base	Keith Hernandez	11
	Vic Power	7
	Bill White	7
	Don Mattingly	7
2nd Base	Ryne Sandberg	9
	Frank White	8
3rd Base	Brooks Robinson	16
	Mike Schmidt	10
Shortstop	Ozzie Smith	13
	Luis Aparicio	9
Outfield	Willie Mays	12
	Roberto Clemente	12
	Al Kaline	10
	Dwight Evans	8
	Paul Blair	8

It's interesting to look at some of the past selections. There are some players who we don't remember for their fielding skills but who nevertheless captured a Gold Glove or two—for example, Ernie BANKS, Hank AARON, Roger MARIS, Mickey MANTLE, Maury WILLS, and George BRETT come to mind. Because fielding is so hard to measure accurately with statistics, today's researchers must place a lot of stock in what contemporary observers thought about a player's defensive skills. Today, for example, people say that Ernie Banks played out of position at shortstop, that he was slow and should have moved to first base much earlier in his career. But the managers and coaches who saw him play thought so much of him that they awarded the 1960 Gold Glove to him. He had to be pretty good.

"Mendoza line": The mythical "line" that separates decent hitters from bad hitters. The *de facto* Mendoza line is .200, even though Mario Mendoza—the Mendoza in question—hit .215 over his nine-year career with the Pirates, Mariners, and Rangers. George BRETT gets credit for originating the term when he said, "The first thing I look for in the Sunday papers is who is below the Mendoza line." Exactly what Mendoza did to earn such notoriety remains a mystery. Thousands of other players have hit worse than the poor guy. If Brett had been a National Leaguer, for example, he might have named it the "LeMaster line."

MVP Award: Record books often list Frankie Frisch and Lefty GROVE as the first official MVP winners, both in 1931. But that's just the first BBWAA award; MVP awards as voted on by sportswriters actually date back to the CHALMERS AWARD. A few years after Chalmers stopped awarding his autos as prizes, the leagues picked up the idea. American League president "Ban" JOHNSON wanted his league's winners, selected by a poll of sportwriters, to have their names engraved on a monument to be built in the nation's capital. The National League, by contrast, offered $1,000 cash for its winners. These League Awards, as they were called, were handed out from 1922 to 1928 for the AL and 1925 to 1929 for the NL. They fell out of favor for a number of reasons: the AL's monument was never built; MVP winners started demanding more money from their teams; and the AL disallowed repeat winners, which made a sham of the award because it shut out the league's best players—Babe RUTH and Lou GEHRIG. In the absence of League Awards, *The SPORTING NEWS* began selecting MVPs. The BBWAA started up in 1931, with the previous voting problems fixed, and that's the award we recognize today. *TSN* continued to hand out its awards in direct competition with the BBWAA, and in the early years, the *TSN* award may have been more prestigious. For several years in the late 1930s and 1940s, the BBWAA and *TSN* unified their awards, but then they split again, and today the honors compete with each other—although now it's the BBWAA trophy that means more. With a few minor changes, the voting structure in the

1930s is basically what we have today: two writers in each city rank 10 players on their ballots, the first-place winner receiving 14 points, second place getting nine, third place eight, and so on. The record for MVP victories is three, held by Jimmie Foxx, Joe DiMaggio, Stan Musial, Yogi Berra, Roy Campanella, Mickey Mantle, Mike Schmidt, and Barry Bonds (who has an excellent chance of breaking the record). There has long been controversy about what constitutes an MVP winner. Is he the league's overall best performer? Or is he the player who was most valuable to his team? Does his team's position in the standings have any effect? How can a player be valuable to a last-place team when they could have finished last without him? MVP voters have never addressed these questions meaningfully. For example, in 1958–59, they selected Ernie Banks, even though his team never contended for the pennant, because he was the best player in the league. But in 1947, Bob Elliot of the second-place Braves captured the award over Ralph Kiner and Johnny Mize, who dominated the league's offensive categories but didn't play on pennant contenders. Ted Williams lost out on about three awards because his teams didn't win the pennant (and because many writers hated him). And Joe DiMaggio won at least one award when he didn't deserve it simply because his name was Joe DiMaggio. (There's also a controversy about pitchers winning MVP Awards; *see* Cy Young Award for more on that.) Every year, columnists who have to fill space in their newspapers bring up the idea of starting a new award to honor the best player in the league, regardless of his team's position in the standings. We don't need that.

on base percentage (OBP), on base average (OBA): The measure of the number of times a player gets on base via hit, walk, or hit by pitch, expressed as a percentage of his total number of plate appearances:

$$(Hits + Walks + Hit\ by\ Pitch)\ /\ (At\ Bats + Walks + Hit\ by\ Pitch +\ Sacrifice\ Flies)$$

This stat *should have* replaced batting average as the basic unit of measure for offensive players. A player can have a good batting average but be a lousy hitter, but a guy with a good on base percentage is *by definition* a good hitter. The reason: the player with the good OBP knows the strike zone, knows how to put himself into position to score a run or drive one in. What's considered a good OBP? The league average is usually around .330, and the league leader is usually around .420; good is about .370 or so. Ted WILLIAMS, who had the best batting eye in history, is the lifetime OBP leader, and he also had the highest single-season OBP. Here's a list of the top 10 single-season and career leaders in 20th century OBP (the reason I drew the line at the 20th century is that foul balls weren't called strikes until around 1901):

Career	OBP	Single Season	OBP
Ted Williams	.483	Ted Williams, 1941	.551
Babe Ruth	.474	Babe Ruth, 1923	.545
Lou Gehrig	.447	Babe Ruth, 1920	.530
Rogers Hornsby	.434	Ted Williams, 1957	.528
Ty Cobb	.433	Babe Ruth, 1926	.516
Jimmie Foxx	.428	Mickey Mantle, 1957	.515
Tris Speaker	.428	Babe Ruth, 1924	.513
Ferris Fain	.425	Babe Ruth, 1921	.512
Eddie Collins	.424	Rogers Hornsby, 1924	.507
Wade Boggs (thru 1994)	.429	Ted Williams, 1942	.499

What that means is that Williams got on base via hits (185) and walks (145) more than 55 percent of the time in 1941. Amazing. Also amazing is that when you look at this list, you realize what phenomenal seasons Barry BONDS (.463) and John Olerud (.473) had in 1993, and how great Frank THOMAS (.487) was doing in 1994 before the strike hit. Those three totals are among the 10 best OBP seasons in the last 30 years.

RBI: Abbreviation for run batted in, an official league statistic since 1920. A batter gets an RBI when he brings a runner home via a hit, walk, hit batsman, sacrifice bunt or fly, fielder's choice, and sometimes on an error if the official scorer believes the runner would have scored even without the error. A batter doesn't get an RBI when he drives a runner home on a ground ball double play. There's a (very) minor controversy going on today about how to pluralize the term RBI. Some people believe that since RBI stands for run batted in, and since the plural of run batted in is "runs batted in," then the plural of RBI is still RBI, as in "Mattingly notched 4 RBI last night." But I and many others think that's wrong. We pluralize RBI separately from runs batted in, as in "Hack WILSON had 190 RBIs in 1930." I think RBI has gained its own stature as a baseball term and deserves its own plural—just like the Oakland Athletics are usually known as the "A's," not the "A." Here's a list of the top 10 RBI seasons and careers:

Career	RBIs	Single Season	RBIs
Hank Aaron	2,297	Hack Wilson, 1930	190
Babe Ruth	2,213	Lou Gehrig, 1931	184
Lou Gehrig	1,995	Hank Greenberg, 1937	183
Stan Musial	1,951	Lou Gehrig, 1927	175
Ty Cobb	1,937	Jimmie Foxx, 1938	175
Jimmie Foxx	1,922	Lou Gehrig, 1930	174
Willie Mays	1,903	Babe Ruth, 1921	171
"Cap" Anson	1,879	Chuck Klein, 1930	170
Mel Ott	1,860	Hank Greenberg, 1935	170
Carl Yastrzemski	1,844	Jimmie Foxx, 1932	169

Note how many of the top 10 seasons occurred during the peak of the LIVELY BALL ERA: 100 percent. The ballparks were smaller, the pitching was worse, fielding was unscientific, relief pitching barely existed, and a substantial portion of the American population was still shut out of the game.

Rolaids Relief Man: The award given every year to each league's top relief pitcher, sponsored, of course, by the famous antacid company. It's a simple statistical assessment that considers all the pertinent information about relief pitchers:

Wins + Saves − Losses − Blown Saves

Rookie of the Year Award: The yearly honor awarded to each league's top rookie, as selected in a vote by the BASEBALL WRITERS ASSOCIATION OF AMERICA. To be eligible for the award, a player may not have totaled more than 130 at bats, 50 innings, or 45 days on a roster in any previous season(s). In 1987, commissioner Peter UEBERROTH changed the name of the award to the Jackie ROBINSON Award, paying homage to the award's first recognized winner in 1947. Even though Robinson is considered the first winner of the BBWAA's version of the award, the Chicago chapter of the BBWAA made separate selections beginning in 1940. *The SPORTING NEWS* got into the act in 1946, and the overall BBWAA finally woke up a year later. The Rookie of the Year is a fun award but it doesn't always portend greatness for a player. Sam Jethroe (1950), Harry Byrd (1952), and John Castino (1979) are three players who disappeared from baseball soon after copping the award, and a number of others never lived up to the expectations. On the other hand, dozens of great players—many of whom are in or headed for the Hall of Fame—have captured the ROY, including Willie MAYS (1951), Frank ROBINSON (1956), Luis APARICIO (1956), Willie McCOVEY (1959), Tom SEAVER (1967), and many others.

Runs Created: A statistic invented by author/sabermetrician Bill JAMES to measure the value of an offensive performer. Unlike BATTING, ON BASE, and SLUGGING averages, which each measure only part of a batter/baserunner's skills, Runs Created expresses the actual contribution of that performer to his team's offensive output. Its simplest form is:

(Hits + Walks) × *(Total Bases)* / *(At Bats + Walks)*

The stolen base version assigns a value of approximately ½ to each stolen base but also subtracts one for each caught stealing. James believes stolen bases add little to a team's offense.

$$[(Hits + Walks - Caught\ Stealing) \times (Total\ Bases + .55 \times Stolen\ Bases)] / (At\ Bats + Walks)$$

There are a couple of more technical versions that incorporate other events, such as hit by pitch, grounded into double plays, sacrifices, and so forth. For more on that subject, read James's *Historical Baseball Abstract* or Pete PALMER and John Thorn's *TOTAL BASEBALL*. Here are the single-season leaders in runs created (for the 20th century only because of the enactment of the foul strike rule) as well as three other statistics (**boldface** type signifies league-leading performance):

Player, Year	RC	BA	OBP	SLG
Babe Ruth, 1921	**238**	.378	**.512**	**.846**
Babe Ruth, 1923	**223**	.393	**.545**	**.764**
Babe Ruth, 1920	**211**	.376	**.530**	**.847**
Jimmie Foxx, 1932	**207**	**.364**	.469	**.749**
Ty Cobb, 1911	**207**	**.420**	.467	**.621**
Babe Ruth, 1924	**205**	.378	**.513**	**.739**
Lou Gehrig, 1927	**203**	.373	.474	.765
Ted Williams, 1941	**202**	**.406**	**.551**	**.735**
Rogers Hornsby, 1922	**200**	**.401**	.459	**.722**
Babe Ruth, 1927	200	.356	**.487**	**.772**

One way to test an offensive statistic is to see whether Babe Ruth overshadows the list of single-season leaders; if he does, then you know it's a good stat. As with every other offensive statistic, players from the LIVELY BALL ERA dominate this list.

sabermetrics: The study of baseball using advanced statistics to analyze the game. Today, Bill JAMES and Pete PALMER are baseball's foremost sabermetricians (although James would like to shed that label in favor of simply "author"). James, in fact, is the one who created the word "sabermetrics" in honor of the sport's first and finest research organization, the SOCIETY FOR AMERICAN BASEBALL RESEARCH (SABR). Here's an example of how sabermetrics works. We'll look at Nolan RYAN's career to examine how great a pitcher he really was. The biggest knock against Ryan always was that he was never much of a winner. He won 20 twice and 19 twice, but most of his career was filled with double-digit loss totals. He finished his career with 324 wins but also 292 losses, which rank 12th and 3rd all time, respectively, for a .526 winning percentage— not an impressive total. On the other hand, his teams were not world-beaters, so here's the question: How much was Ryan's won-lost total hurt by the teams he played with? To answer that question, we'll look at a stat called Wins Above Team. This is how it works. Nolan Ryan's teams, throughout his career, won 2,115 games and lost 2,048. We subtract Ryan's won-loss totals from that and get 1,781 wins and 1,757 losses, for a winning percentage of .503, which isn't as bad as people might have thought. If we then take that winning percentage and multiply it by Ryan's total of wins and losses—his decisions—we'll arrive at the number of wins an *average* pitcher would be expected to have gotten if he had pitched for those teams when Ryan did. That number is 309.6. Ryan won 324 games, which means he won 14.4 games more than the average pitcher would have won. Now let's compare Ryan's numbers with a few others. The table below lists the career won-lost stats of Ryan and four current Hall of Famers: Ferguson JENKINS, Ted Lyons, Walter JOHNSON, and Lefty GROVE. Included in the table is the won–loss record of the player's teams after subtracting his personal wins and losses. Three of the pitchers were chosen because they, like Ryan, weren't blessed with great teams; Grove did have good teams behind him, so I threw him in as a control. Here are the totals:

Player	W	L	W%	Active	Teams	Team W%	WAT
Ryan	324	292	.526	1966 –1993	Mets, Angels, Astros, Rangers	.503	+14.4

Player	W	L	W%	Active	Teams	Team W%	WAT
Jenkins	284	226	.557	1965 –1983	Phillies, Cubs, Rangers, Red Sox	.500	+30.0
Lyons	260	230	.531	1923 –1946	White Sox	.442	+43.3
Grove	300	141	.680	1925 –1941	Athletics, Red Sox	.561	+52.6
Johnson	417	279	.599	1907 –1927	Senators	.460	+96.0

What do the numbers show? Well, for one thing, they show that true greats such as Grove and Johnson are able to rise significantly above their teams, whereas Ryan was only slightly better than his teams. Grove and Johnson were arguably the greatest pitchers of all time, so maybe it's not fair to compare Ryan to them. So we'll focus on the other two. If you ask most fans who was better between Jenkins, Lyons, and Ryan, the nearly unanimous vote will be Ryan. But check the stats: Jenkins and Lyons had significantly more wins above their teams over the course of their careers *despite shorter careers than Ryan.* We can run the numbers for other pitchers, too: Steve CARLTON (44.9), Phil NIEKRO (42.3), Robin ROBERTS (36.5), and Gaylord PERRY (23.1). Sandy KOUFAX was 27 wins above the Dodgers—nearly twice as many as Ryan even though Koufax's career was half as long and his teams were much better. I know that winning percentage is not the only criterion to evaluate pitchers. But I also know that the object of baseball isn't to strike out the most batters or allow the fewest hits; the object is to *win* games, making winning percentage a very important statistic—one in which Ryan, despite his other fantastic numbers, falls significantly short. None of this is to imply that Ryan wasn't a great pitcher, because we all know he was. But when we're evaluating the greats, we have to look beyond reputation and glossy stats. That's what sabermetrics are all about.

slugging percentage, slugging average: A statistical measure of power hitting, determined by dividing the number of total bases into a player's total at bats:

$$[Singles + (2 \times Doubles) + (3 \times Triples) + (4 \times Home\ Runs)]\ /\ At\ Bats$$

The numerator of that formula is known as *total bases*, and there's an easier way to calculate it without duplicating your efforts by subtracting extra base hits from total hits. Here's the simpler formula that produces the same result:

Total Hits + Doubles + (2 × Triples) + (3 × Home Runs) / At Bats

Real power hitters have slugging percentages above .500, higher than .600 usually leads the league, more than .700 is Ted WILLIAMS territory, and above .800 is positively Ruthian. Not surprisingly, Babe RUTH is the slugging percentage leader, both career and single season. Here's a list of the top 10 in both categories for the 20th century:

Career	SLG	Single Season	SLG
Babe Ruth	.690	Babe Ruth, 1920	.847
Ted Williams	.634	Babe Ruth, 1921	.846
Lou Gehrig	.632	Babe Ruth, 1927	.772
Jimmie Foxx	.609	Lou Gehrig, 1927	.765
Hank Greenberg	.605	Babe Ruth, 1923	.764
Joe DiMaggio	.579	Rogers Hornsby, 1925	.756
Rogers Hornsby	.577	Jimmie Foxx, 1932	.749
Johnny Mize	.562	Babe Ruth, 1924	.739
Stan Musial	.559	Babe Ruth, 1926	.737
Willie Mays	.557	Ted Williams, 1941	.735

Barry BONDS truly placed his name in the history books with his .677 slugging percentage in 1993; it was the 36th best of all time, *the* highest since 1961 (for a full season), and better than any season put together by MAYS, AARON, McCOVEY, or DiMAGGIO. They should just enshrine him right now. And the numbers put up by Jeff Bagwell, Frank THOMAS, and Albert

Belle in strike-torn 1994 were even more amazing: .750 for Bagwell, .729 for Thomas, .704 for Belle. It's doubtful that they could have kept it up for the last two months of the season, but they're still amazing numbers.

Total Average: A statistic invented by *Washington Post* writer Thomas BOSWELL, designed to measure the total performance of an offensive player. Boswell calls Total Average "elementary, easy, and obvious." Based on the theory that "baseball's two fundamental units of measurement are the base and the out," TA calculates the total number of bases made and divides it by the total outs made:

$$(Total\ Bases + Steals + Walks + HBP)\ /\ (At\ Bats - Hits + Caught\ Stealing + GIDP)$$

Any TA above 1.000 is phenomenal because it means that a player has gotten more bases than outs. Boswell says that any TA above .900 makes you a star and above .800 is the "B" grade. The average grade is .667, which indicates that a player has achieved 50 percent more outs than bases. Here are the all-time greatest TAs, career and single season.

Career	TA	Single Season	TA
Babe Ruth	1.399	Babe Ruth, 1920	1.797
Ted Williams	1.320	Babe Ruth, 1921	1.745
Lou Gehrig	1.229	Ted Williams, 1941	1.688
Billy Hamilton	1.191	Babe Ruth, 1923	1.683
John McGraw	1.152	Hugh Duffy, 1894	1.619
Jimmie Foxx	1.143	Babe Ruth, 1926	1.606
Hank Greenberg	1.105	Billy Hamilton, 1894	1.605
Rogers Hornsby	1.105	John McGraw, 1899	1.601
Mickey Mantle	1.091	Ted Williams, 1957	1.599
Ty Cobb	1.066	Babe Ruth, 1927	1.571

Some of the surprising names on those lists include Billy HAMILTON and John MCGRAW, but they received help because for most of their careers, foul balls weren't counted as strikes.

A similar statistic to TA is Bill JAMES's RUNS CREATED. Unlike RC, TA gives the same weight to the stolen base as to the single or walk, but it should be pretty obvious that getting on base is more important than stealing a base; consequently, TA rewards players with high stolen base totals much better than RC does. Despite its drawbacks—which Boswell freely admits—TA does an excellent job of separating great performers from those whose superficial stats, such as batting average and home runs, appear good.

Triple Crown: A mythical crown awarded to a player who leads the league in BATTING AVERAGE, home runs, and RBIs. Because it takes a ballplayer with a truly unique blend of skills, only 14 players have won a Triple Crown:

Player, Year	HR	RBI	BA
Paul Hines, 1878	4	50	.358
Hugh Duffy, 1894	18	145	.440
Nap Lajoie, 1901	14	125	.426
Ty Cobb, 1909	9	115	.377
Heinie Zimmerman, 1912*	14	103	.372
Rogers Hornsby, 1922	42	152	.401
Rogers Hornsby, 1925	39	143	.403
Chuck Klein, 1933	28	120	.368
Jimmie Foxx, 1933	48	163	.356
Lou Gehrig, 1934	49	165	.363
Joe Medwick, 1937	31	154	.374
Ted Williams, 1942	36	137	.356
Ted Williams, 1947	32	114	.343
Mickey Mantle, 1956	52	130	.353
Frank Robinson, 1966	49	122	.316
Carl Yastrzemski, 1967	44	121	.326

Heinie Zimmerman gets an asterisk because researchers who checked the records discovered some anomalies and determined that he should have been credited with only 98 RBIs, which would have given the RBI title to Honus WAGNER. He's listed here because at the time, Zimmerman was believed to have won it. A recent issue of *Baseball Digest*, among other publications, has put forth the argument that the Triple Crown should be changed. Writer Jerry Coen believes no one will ever win another Triple Crown because the three Triple Crown stats are "remarkably incomplete measures" of a ball-player's offensive abilities. Coen argues in favor of a modified Triple Crown: ON BASE PERCENTAGE, SLUGGING AVERAGE, and runs produced (the combined total of runs and RBIs minus home runs, to avoid duplication). Although his argument makes some sense, I don't buy the notion that we should change the Triple Crown. First of all, the title itself is mythical, so it's not as if there's a crown in a basement somewhere waiting to be awarded. Second, the traditional Triple Crown comprises stats that are basic and obvious to even the most casual fan. Third, I like the fact that it's such an exclusive title, and so do thousands of other fans. Every year, one or two players make a run at the Triple Crown, and it's always a great story when somebody comes close in all three categories. Baseball has changed so much, there should be some things that stay the same.

RULES, GAME TERMS, AND BASEBALL BUSINESS

60 feet, 6 inches: The distance between the pitching rubber and home plate since 1893. In years prior, the distance was 45 or 50 feet, but as pitchers got stronger and learned trick pitches such as CURVEBALLS and SPITBALLS, they became nearly unhittable. Amos RUSIE, whose nickname—"The Hoosier Thunderbolt"—should give an idea of how great his fastball was, is acknowledged to have been most responsible for the rule change.

90 feet: The distance between the bases on a baseball diamond. Sportswriter Red SMITH once wrote, "Ninety feet between bases is the nearest to perfection that man has yet achieved."

ace: A team's best pitcher. Obviously the term comes from gambling parlance, where the ace is the best card a player can have. After the Atlanta Braves signed Greg MADDUX before the 1993 season, they had four aces: defending Cy Young winner Maddux, former Cy Young winner Tom Glavine, and Cy Young candidates John Smoltz and Steve Avery.

agent: The person or team of people—usually lawyers but often relatives or close friends—hired by a player to represent him in salary negotiations with owners and in endorsement deals with such companies as glove, shoe, and baseball card manufacturers. Agents generally take a 10 to 15 percent cut of all contracts negotiated. Owners forced players to negotiate for themselves until 1970, although Babe RUTH, baseball's preeminent revolutionary, was the first to hire an agent to handle his off-field activities and publicity. Baseball's first really powerful agent was Jerry Kapstein, a Harvard lawyer who worked for a while as the color commentator for Washington Bullets basketball games. He made his name in baseball handling salary arbitrations in the early 1970s, when he beat Charlie FINLEY in a number of high-profile cases. By the advent of free agency in 1976, Kapstein represented more than 60 players, including some of baseball's biggest stars: Steve Garvey, Rollie FINGERS, Tony Perez, and others. He has since left agenting.

alley: The parts of the outfield between the center fielder and the left and right fielders. Also called the *power alley* or the *gap.*

aluminum bat: A bat made of aluminum or other metal alloy, used by LITTLE LEAGUE, high school, and college baseball players as well as softball players; it's illegal in professional baseball. The primary functional difference between wood and aluminum bats, aside from the sound each produces when striking a ball ("knock" vs. "ping"), is the size of the ideal hitting area, or SWEET SPOT: it's larger on aluminum bats, which means a hitter can be fooled by a pitch and still make good contact. For this reason, the aluminum bat will probably never be used in the major leagues; many argue that a pitcher could get killed by a batted ball.

amateur draft: The yearly draft of high school, college, and, since 1990, Latin American ballplayers. A player is eligible for the draft when he has graduated from high school, has completed two years at a junior college, has completed three or more years at a university, or lives in Latin America and is at least 16 years old. Like drafts in other pro sports, teams draft in reverse order of the previous year's finish. *Un*like most other drafts, baseball teams continue to select players as long as they want, usually for at least 60 rounds.

appeal play: A fielding play that occurs when the defensive team contends that a runner missed a base or left a base early on a fly ball. Unlike most sports, baseball requires that the fielders appeal to the umpire to make the call; imagine if a football linebacker had to *ask* the referee to call a holding penalty.

arbitration: A concession won by the players in the 1973 Basic Agreement, arbitration is the method used to settle salary disputes between teams and players with between two and six years of major league experience. Under current rules, an independent arbitrator selects either the salary bid submitted by the player or the one by the owner; there is no compromise. To determine what the player deserves, the arbitrators use comparable players as reference points. For example if power-hitting outfielder A makes $3.3 million and power-hitting outfielder B, with similar or better stats, is up for arbitration, B's agent will argue that B should get at least as much as A. Club representatives will usually present a case that highlights all of the player's deficiencies—low clutch batting average, poor throwing skills, and so forth. It's up to the arbitrator to decide whose argument is most effective. The owners would like to do away with arbitration because they say it artificially inflates salaries. In the above example, if player A didn't "deserve" (in the owners' minds) the $3.3 million, then the arbitrator is merely compounding one mistake if he rules in favor of player B. The Major League Baseball Players' Association, however, believes that players operate in a system where a free market determines salaries. If a player is getting $3.3 million, then he is by definition *worth* $3.3 million, and there's nothing artificial about it. This chasm between the MLBPA and management over salary arbitration was one of the catalysts of the 1994 STRIKE.

around the horn: Baseball slang for a DOUBLE PLAY that goes third to second to first. It comes from the fact that until the opening of the Panama Canal, a ship could reach the Pacific Ocean from the Atlantic only by traveling around Cape Horn on the southern tip of South America. A strange source for a baseball term, if you ask me.

assist: A throw that puts out a runner. Every fielder makes assists, but shortstops get the most. Rabbit MARANVILLE holds the career (8,962) and Ozzie SMITH the single season (621) records for assists.

at bat, official at bat: A time at the plate by a batter in which he either gets a hit, makes an out, or reaches base via error or FIELDER'S CHOICE. A WALK, SACRIFICE, HIT BY PITCH, and CATCHER'S INTERFERENCE count as a PLATE APPEARANCE but not an at bat.

bad-ball hitter: A hitter who is known for swinging at—and getting hits from—balls outside the strike zone. Yogi BERRA is an example of someone who employed this "strategy" successfully; the minor leagues are filled with players who employ it unsuccessfully.

bad hop: A grounder that takes a strange bounce off the infield, usually causing a fielder to misplay the ball.

balk: A pitcher's motion considered by the umpire to be deliberately deceptive toward a baserunner, such as dropping the ball while on the rubber or faking a throw to first base.

The penalty is that all baserunners advance one base. Few balks are as obvious as the examples just listed; most are nearly undetectable except by instant replay cameras and umpires, who seem to have an inexplicable sixth sense for balks.

ball: A pitch out of the STRIKE ZONE. Four balls equal a WALK or BASE ON BALLS.

Baltimore chop: A batted ball that hits the ground just in front of home plate, then bounces high enough that the hitter reaches first before he can be thrown out. The name refers to the old Baltimore Orioles of the 1890s, whose groundskeepers kept the area in front of home plate especially hard so its players could get hits by swinging down on the ball. Although the term is still used today, nobody ever *tries* to hit a Baltimore chop like the old Orioles did. It's usually just accidental.

bandbox: A ballpark with small dimensions. In today's era of spacious stadiums, only WRIGLEY FIELD and FENWAY PARK qualify as bandboxes. The term comes from the "boxes" that musicians stand in while playing their instruments.

bang-bang play: A play in which a runner and the ball reach the base at almost the same instant, creating a difficult call for umpires. However, instant replay has shown that umpires call a surprisingly high percentage of bang-bang plays correctly.

barnstorming tour: An off-season tour in which teams play games against each other and against local players. In the first half of the century, major league and NEGRO LEAGUES teams would play in small towns and foreign countries that had no access to big league ball. The players would augment their salaries substantially, sometimes earning more on a barnstorming tour than from penny-pinching owners. Today, a team of major league all-stars "barnstorms" to Japan every year to play exhibition games against Japanese major leaguers; the U.S. team usually wins.

barrel: The thick part of a baseball bat, where the SWEET SPOT is.

base: The white marker at each of the four corners of a baseball infield. Each base is 90 feet from the others and is marked by a 15-inch square bag, with the exception of home plate, which is a pentagon-shaped slab of rubber.

base on balls: Also WALK; it's what occurs after a batter receives four pitches out of the STRIKE ZONE during his time at the plate; the reward is a free trip to first base. For the first 30 or so years of the game's history, the number of BALLS it took to earn a walk fluctuated from as high as nine to four, which became the rule in 1889.

baseball: The hard, white, round ball used in a baseball game. Made of a small cork core followed by layers of rubber, yarn, and cowhide with red stitches at the seams, the ball is between 9 and 9¼ inches in diameter and weighs between 5 and 5¼ ounces—dimensions that have ruled the manufacture of baseballs for more than 100 years. At various points in the game's history, when offensive totals would increase or decrease dramatically in one of the leagues, people would claim one league's ball was "juiced" while the other was deadened (*see* "RABBIT BALL"). In fact, the REACH COMPANY—owned by the SPALDING SPORTING GOODS COMPANY—manufactured all baseballs until 1976, even though American League balls carried the "Reach" label while National League balls said "Spalding." In 1977, the RAWLINGS COMPANY took over the contract to manufacture the balls, which is done now at a plant in Costa Rica.

baseball mud: The reddish-brown mud used by umpires to rub into new baseballs. The tradition began in the 1920s when, after the death of Ray CHAPMAN from an errant pitch, umpires were ordered to keep fresh new balls in play at all times. After pitchers complained of difficulty gripping the balls, league officials decided to institute a policy of "rubbing down" baseballs to remove the sheen from the leather. Today, umpires use Lena Blackburne's Baseball Rubbing Mud, named after the 1930s-era manager who discovered the secret location in the Delaware River that produced the exact consistency and color of mud to make a ball perfect.

basket catch: A method of catching a fly ball with your glove near your body at belt level. Generally accepted as a fundamentally poor way to field, it has nevertheless been used by many great fielders, including Willie MAYS and Roberto CLEMENTE (24 GOLD GLOVE awards between them). Rabbit MARANVILLE, a shortstop in the early part of the century, first popularized the basket catch.

bat speed: The time it takes for a hitter to move his bat from the "ready," upright position into the batting zone. Scouts use a player's bat speed to judge his potential ability to connect with a major league FASTBALL. You often hear broadcasters and managers refer to a player with a "quick bat"; this means, for one thing, that the hitter can misjudge a fastball and still make contact.

bat: The piece of sculpted pine used to hit the ball. They come in a variety of sizes, measured by both length and weight, and are manufactured in Indiana, upstate New York, Japan, and other locales. *See also* LOUISVILLE SLUGGER.

bat around: What occurs when the entire lineup bats during an inning, sending the first batter of an inning to the plate for a second time.

batboy: The boy or girl who takes care of the bats, balls, and helmets during a game. The batboy picks up the bat and helmet after a hitter's at bat is finished and delivers new balls to the umpires between pitches.

batter's box: The boxes on each side of home plate, outlined by white chalk, where a hitter must stand when at bat. If a hitter makes contact with the ball while standing outside the box, he is supposed to be called out, although this rule is rarely enforced. If the pitcher has an excellent CURVEBALL, hitters will often stand in the front of the box to try to catch the curve before it breaks; if the pitcher has a good FASTBALL, they'll stand at the back of the box. Next time you go to a game, watch the way the LEADOFF HITTER rubs out the back line of the box to gain a few extra inches.

battery: Term for the pitcher and catcher in a game, which probably comes from military lexicon. "Battery" has been used in the baseball sense since at least 1868.

batting cage: (a) The big cage placed behind home plate during batting practice to help keep foul balls from rocketing into the stands and at bystanders. (b) An indoor cage with a pitching machine standing 60 feet from home plate where hitters can practice. A lot of new businesses have appeared during the last decade that sell time in a batting cage. It's a good place to learn your stroke.

batting eye: Term for a player's ability to judge the strike zone. Ted WILLIAMS possessed probably the sport's greatest batting eye, amassing the second-highest WALK total in baseball history as well as the top ON BASE PERCENTAGE.

batting glove: Soft leather glove worn by hitters, usually on their bottom hand (left for a right-hand hitter, right for a lefty), to help maintain a good grip on the bat and prevent blisters.

batting helmet: The hard plastic headgear batters wear to protect themselves from errant pitches. The 1941 Dodgers experimented with plastic liners inside their hats, but helmets weren't put into common use until the 1950s and weren't mandatory until the 1960s. Following the fatal beaning of Ray CHAPMAN on AUGUST 16, 1920, many writers called for the league to make players wear the helmets. But those calls were largely ignored, and although Chapman's was the only on-field death in major league history, countless careers would have been saved (Mickey COCHRANE's, to name one) if helmets had been instituted earlier.

batting practice: Pregame hitting practice, usually two to three hours before game time. If you want to catch a foul ball at a major league game, BP offers your best chance.

beanball: A pitch that hits a batter, often as retaliation for a previous offense against the pitcher's team. Beanball is usually used to describe a pitch that purposely hits the batter. *See also* HIT BY PITCH.

bench jockey: A player who screams insults at umpires and opposing players in an effort to break their concentration. Umpires have little tolerance for a bench jockey who directs his taunts at them. Sometimes, in an effort to quiet a particularly annoying bench jockey, the umpire will eject a random player who may or may not be the culprit. Often the ejectee is a player, such as the previous night's starter, who has little chance of getting into the game. In September 1951, a DOUBLE-A player named Bill Sharman was called up to the Dodgers and was sitting on the bench for a game against the Braves. When the umpire made a call that went against the Dodgers, the whole Dodger dugout protested loudly, and the umpire responded by ejecting the entire bench, including Sharman. The young man never did get into a game that season, and he was released during the winter. He decided instead to try basketball. He played 11 seasons with the Boston Celtics to earn induction into the Basketball Hall of Fame in 1975.

big league: Synonym for major league. Also, The Bigs and THE SHOW.

bleachers: Cheap, backless, uncomfortable, hard metal or wooden seats in the outfield sections of most major league ballparks. *See also* BLEACHER BUMS.

bloop, blooper: A weakly hit ball that barely clears the infield on the fly, resulting in a pretty cheap hit for the batter. Other terms include *wounded duck, dying quail,* and TEXAS LEAGUER.

bonehead play/boner: A mistake, usually a mental error but sometimes a physical one. A player who commits a bonehead play that helps his team lose a game is called a goat, and baseball history boasts its share of famous goats: Fred Merkle (*see* MERKLE'S BONER), Fred Snodgrass, and Bill BUCKNER are among the most ignoble.

Book, The: Imaginary book of traditional "rules" that managers either follow or disdain. Some of The Book's rules include calling for a SACRIFICE with the pitcher at bat and a runner on base, PINCH-HITTING a left-handed batter against a right-handed pitcher (and vice versa), and playing for the win on the road and the tie at home. Some managers are known as "by-the-book" skippers, while others reject it freely.

boot: To commit a fielding error.

box score: Daily statistical record of a baseball game, recording data such as AT BATS, RUNS, HITS, RBIs, and complete pitching lines. Though Henry CHADWICK, "the Father of Baseball," was the first to devise a box score that looks like the one in use today, the *very* first one—which looks nothing like today's—actually appeared in the *New York Clipper* on July 16, 1853, reporting a 21–12 victory by the Knickerbockers over the Gothams. Strange fact: Early box scores often included a category called "fatal errors."

box seats: The seats closest to the field, down the foul lines or behind home plate, considered the best in the house.

breaking ball: Any pitch that is meant to curve or break in some manner. The term can refer to a CURVEBALL, SLIDER, SCREWBALL, or other breaking pitch, but broadcasters use "breaking ball" because it's hard to distinguish between them from the booth.

Bronx cheer: Also "raspberry," it's the sound made when you stick your tongue between your lips and blow hard. The term reputedly comes from a minor league outfielder named Doyle Raspberry, a player for the minor league Bronx Oilers in 1919, who responded to boos from the crowd by performing baseball's first Bronx cheer.

brushback: A pitch aimed at a hitter who's crowding the plate, intended to move him away. As Hall of Famer Don DRYSDALE once said, "You've got to keep the ball away from the sweet part of the bat. To do that the pitcher has to move the hitter off the plate." Brushbacks aren't meant to hit the batter, but they sometimes do.

bullpen: The place where pitchers warm up before they appear in a game. In some stadiums, the bullpen is located behind the outfield fence. In others, it's in foul territory along the left and right field lines. The origin of the term is unclear. Some say it's a reference to the Bull Durham tobacco signs that years ago adorned the outfield walls of hundreds of professional league ballparks, under which pitchers often warmed up. Casey STENGEL claimed the term came from the place where pitchers would sit and shoot the bull.

bunt: A batting play in which a hitter sticks his bat into the hitting zone just to make contact with a pitched ball. You can bunt both for a base hit (often a drag bunt) or to move a runner up a base (a SACRIFICE). Unlike a full-swing foul ball, a foul bunt with two strikes results in a STRIKEOUT.

bush, bush league: A derogatory term for an act or thing considered low class, crude, or amateurish. The term stems from the fact that the minor leagues are often called the bush leagues because they were once characterized by crude playing fields where bushes grew.

businessman's special (now often called "businesspersons' special"): A weekday day game, so called because teams hope to lure businesspeople from work to come to the ballpark.

butcher: A poor fielder who "butchers" even the routine plays. Classic butchers have included Dick Stuart, Lonnie Smith, and Harmon KILLEBREW.

catcher's interference: A play in which a catcher interferes with the batter, either inadvertently or on purpose, by touching the batter or his bat or some other way. The batter gets first base if it happens and is not charged with an official time AT BAT.

change-up: A pitch that looks like it might be a fastball but hurtles toward the plate at a much slower speed than expected. Even though a change-up doesn't break, it's effective because it keeps a hitter off-balance. Warren SPAHN once said, "Hitting is timing. Pitching is upsetting timing."

check(ed) swing: An aborted swing by a batter, sometimes called a STRIKE and sometimes not, based on how far around the hitter goes. Usually, if the hitter turns his wrists, it's a strike, but it's up to the umpire to decide. A hitter can also make contact on a check swing and, if he's lucky, beat out a ground ball for a hit or BLOOP it over the infield.

closer: A term for a RELIEF PITCHER who finishes, or closes out, games. Some of baseball history's premier closers have included Firpo Marberry (the very first acknowledged closer), Joe Page, Hugh Casey, Elroy Face, "Goose" GOSSAGE, Bruce Sutter, Lee SMITH, and Dennis ECKERSLEY.

clutch: An important or pressure-packed situation, often in the late innings of a ball game when the score is close. Reggie JACKSON is known as an impressive clutch performer based on his play in six World Series from 1972 to 1981.

commissioner: The top official of major league baseball, elected and paid by the team owners. For the first 20 years of the two-league system, the game was ruled by the three-man National Commission, made up of the two league presidents and one team owner. When the BLACK SOX SCANDAL hit in 1920, however, owners feared an erosion in public confidence—i. e., profits—and created a powerful commissioner's office to oversee all operations and provide the appearance of total propriety. To fill the post, they hired former federal judge Kenesaw Mountain LANDIS, who ruled baseball until his death in 1944. Throughout his tenure, owners regretted handing Landis czarlike authority—which allowed no appeal and no recourse—and when he died, they decided to make some changes. They restricted the powers of the office and elected Kentucky Senator A. B. "Happy" CHANDLER, whose nickname should suggest what the owners expected: a good-will ambassador. But what they got was a strong politician who believed that baseball belonged to America, not to a bunch of suits in a dozen major league cities. And in a set of circumstances that has typified the conflict between owners and the commissioner, Chandler was defeated for reelection when he came up for renewal in 1951 because of his refusal to bow to all of ownership's demands. Since then, the owners have searched for a commissioner who could accomplish several seemingly irreconcilable goals: preserve the game's integrity, increase profits, and placate the owners' requests. Since Chandler, six men have held the full-time commissioner's post— Ford C. FRICK, Gen. William D. ECKERT, Bowie KUHN, Peter

UEBERROTH, Bart GIAMATTI, and Fay VINCENT—each with varying degrees of success. Nearly all angered the owners in some way during their tenures, but none more than Vincent, who resigned in the middle of his term in 1992, claiming the owners had forced him out. Following Vincent's departure, owners stood without a full-time commissioner for several years, as Milwaukee Brewers owner Bud SELIG served as acting commissioner (and got paid a quarter of a million dollars more than Vincent). What the owners really want is a person to act as both CEO and errand boy to 28 rich bosses, and they've gotten few takers.

corked bat: A bat that's been illegally tampered with to give the hitter a slight edge. The way it works is, you drill a deep hole into the barrel of the bat and fill it with cork (or shredded rubber), then plug it with glue and sawdust so it looks normal. The benefit a hitter gets is that the bat maintains the size of, say, a 36-ounce bat but the weight of a 33-ouncer. The result: a faster swing. Norm Cash is one of the most infamous corked bat users; he won the 1961 American League batting title with a bat he later admitted was doctored. Every now and again, a hitter is accused of such chicanery and has his bat confiscated and X-rayed. I have no idea how an umpire or opposing manager can possibly tell—unless the bat breaks and the pieces of cork go flying, which happened to Astros outfielder Billy Hatcher a few years ago.

cup of coffee: Baseball slang for a short amount of time, usually used to refer to a minor leaguer who gets called up to the majors and sent back down just a few days or weeks later. He was only in the bigs long enough to have a cup of coffee.

curveball: A pitch that's thrown in such a way that it curves down and to the side on its way to the plate. Alternate terms for curveball include *hook, deuce, bender, breaking ball, Uncle Charlie* (or *Lord Charles* if it's a really good one), and there are probably others. The curveball has been the subject of perhaps more speculation and awe than any other single part of baseball. First of all, there's some question over the pitch's true inventor; see Candy CUMMINGS for more on that. Second, and most interestingly, a lot of baseball people throughout the years have claimed that the ball does not, in fact, really curve, that it's just an optical illusion. And many who believe that the ball does curve also think the ball travels along a straight line toward the plate, then breaks sharply at the last second. Here's the real story, according to Dr. Robert K. Adair, a physicist at Yale University: The ball does curve, but it does so along a smooth, constant arc. In his book *The Physics of Baseball*, Dr. Adair provides a technical yet reasonable explanation for the action. Translated to English, he says that when you increase the spin on the ball as you throw it, one side of it receives much more air resistance than the other side. This difference in air resistance forces the ball to one side. He asserts that the curve itself is "nearly constant" during the ball's flight but that most of the pitch's deviation from the original position occurs during the last half of the ball's flight. In other words, the ball's path does follow a constant arc, but it also "breaks" as it nears the plate. To understand it better, take a look at the following diagram of a constant arc with a tangential line:

Imagine that the pitcher is on the left side of the diagram and home plate is on the right side; the curved line is the path of an exaggerated curveball, and the hash mark splits the lines in half. As you can see, the first 50 percent of the throw results in about 20 percent of the break, while the final 50 percent contains 80 percent of the arc. In pitching terms: after the first 30 feet of a pitch toward the plate, the ball has "broken" only about 3 inches, but over the final 30 feet, it breaks about 12 inches—thus appearing to suddenly "fall off the table."

cycle: The term used when a player hits a SINGLE, DOUBLE, TRIPLE, and HOME RUN in a single game. Bob Meusel and Babe Herman are the only players to do the trick three times. Although it seems like it shouldn't be that rare, hitting for the cycle actually occurs much less often than a NO-HITTER.

designated hitter: The player in the lineup who bats permanently for the pitcher. Since its inception in 1973 (*see* 1973 SEASON), the DH has been adopted by nearly every single baseball league in the world—major and minor, professional and amateur, high school, college, even youth leagues. *Every league,* that is, except the National League and Japan's Central League, the only two leagues on the planet with the sense to resist such a radical change to the sport. A lot of people like the DH, their main argument being that the DH increases offensive totals. There is no disputing that contention: for the five-year period 1989–93, the AL averaged half a hit and half a run per game more than the National League. But is a fan's enjoyment of baseball really enhanced by seeing one more run scored every two games? I don't think so. On the other hand, is the game of baseball hurt by the adulteration of the game for the sole purpose of improving attendance and increasing revenue? I think so. The DH has been argued about for more than 20 years, so I'm not bringing up anything new. And there's no way the DH is going to go away. It's too entrenched in baseball now.

diamond: The layout of a baseball field. Some people describe the infield as diamond-shaped, but it is, of course, a perfect square.

double: A two-base hit. Tris SPEAKER holds the career doubles record with 792 doubles from 1907 to 1926. Boston Red Sox outfielder Earl Webb, meanwhile, set the single-season record for doubles with 67 in 1931. *Earl Webb?* He played only seven seasons in the majors and appeared in 140 games only twice, never hitting more than 30 doubles in any other season! But he lives on in the record books. Stories like Earl Webb's—and Owen Wilson's, who is the unlikely possessor of the record for TRIPLES—are part of baseball's unique charm.

doubleheader: A day in which teams play games back to back. Baseball used to schedule a number of doubleheaders every year, often on holidays or Sundays. Today, however, a doubleheader occurs only when a rainout necessitates a makeup game. For obvious reasons, owners would prefer us fans to buy two tickets rather than just one.

double play: A single defensive play that results in two outs made. It can be a ground ball that goes shortstop to second base to first, a line drive that doubles off a runner who has taken too big a lead, a strikeout/caught stealing on the same pitch, or even the strange play that happened to the Brooklyn Dodgers on August 15, 1926. With Hank DeBerry at third, Dazzy VANCE on second, Chick Fewster on first, and one out, Dodger outfielder Babe Herman turned on a fastball and sent it to the right field wall. DeBerry scored easily. Vance should have, too; instead, he rounded third and retreated to the bag, unaware that Fewster was racing there as well. Herman, meanwhile, never looked up as he chugged around second base and headed for now-crowded third base. One can only imagine the scene as the Boston catcher tagged out every Dodger he could find, including probably the third base coach. Since only Vance was entitled to the base, the umpires called Fewster and Herman out for perhaps the strangest double play in history. There's an old baseball myth saying that Babe Herman tripled into a triple play—impossible, since there was already one out. He merely doubled into a double-play, which, as writer John Lardner put it, is the next best thing. Years later, the story goes, a Brooklyn fan shouts out of his tenement asking for an update of a game. Somebody else shouts, "The Dodgers have three men on base." The first man's reply: "Which base?"

double steal: When two baserunners attempt to steal on the same pitch. A delayed steal is a variation of the play, an attempt to catch the defense off guard. With runners at first and third, the runner on first takes off on the pitch, hoping to draw a throw from the catcher. If the throw comes down, the guy on third can try for home to complete the double steal. Sometimes the catcher will fake the throw to second to prevent the runner on third from scoring, and sometimes he'll throw to third to try and catch the runner off base. It's always an exciting play.

dugout: The two enclosures along the first and third base lines where the teams sit during the game. Seats behind the dugout are the premium seats in the house. When building the ASTRODOME, former Astros owner Roy Hofheinz made the dugouts extra long so that more seats could reside behind the dugouts.

E: SCORECARD and box score symbol for fielding ERROR. When the shortstop makes an errant throw, for example, a scorer writes "E-6" on his scorecard.

earned run: A run that is deemed to be the pitcher's fault. That means a run that is scored without the help of an ERROR, interference, passed ball, or other defensive miscue; those kinds of runs are called unearned runs. There's a flaw to that guideline. Let's say the score is tied 0–0 and, with two outs, the batter lofts a weak fly ball to right that gets muffed by the outfielder. The batter ends up at second base. Rattled, the pitcher allows a hit, then walks a guy, then surrenders back-to-back home runs. Now it's 5–0 and the pitcher is pulled from the game. His team is losing big now, but none of those runs are considered earned. Why? Because the scoring guidelines say the inning should have been over, so the runs don't count against the pitcher. Sure, that original guy on second wasn't the pitcher's responsibility, but what about everybody else? It's the pitcher's job to keep his team in the game, and since errors are an inevitable part of baseball, a good pitcher should be able to overcome them and pitch out of it without any more damage done. A pitcher who allows a lot of unearned runs might be saddled with a poor defensive unit, but at the same time, he isn't helping his team much.

error: A defensive misplay, muff, fumble, or wild throw that either prolongs a batter's time at bat, helps a runner advance, or puts a runner on base. In the early days of baseball, when fielders used their bare hands, single-game error totals in the double digits were common. As glove technology advanced, fielding got much better and error totals went way down. Honus WAGNER, for example, was a great shortstop, probably the best of his era, but he never made fewer than 35 errors for a full season. Ozzie SMITH, meanwhile, is the best of our era, and he averaged 16 errors per year.

expansion team: Generic term for one of the 12 teams added to major league baseball since its first expansion in 1961. For the previous 60 years, baseball had survived with just 16 teams in mostly Eastern cities. But as the nation's population exploded, the owners saw few reasons *not* to expand into other cities. And although many believe expansion hurts the quality of play, the owners are more eager than ever to add major league franchises. A list of expansion teams reads like this: in the AL, the Angels, Blue Jays, Mariners, Rangers, Royals, and Twins; in the NL, the Astros, Expos, Marlins, Mets, Padres, and Rockies. By the end of the decade, two *more* teams will join major league baseball: the Tampa Bay Devil Rays and Arizona Diamondbacks.

farm system: The system of minor league teams affiliating themselves with major league clubs to supply players. Branch RICKEY is responsible for founding the farm system for the St. Louis Cardinals, an invention so successful that other teams copied it almost immediately. At its peak, the St. Louis farm system featured dozens of teams and hundreds of players throughout the nation; the cream of the human crop would go to St. Louis while the rest would either languish in Class D leagues or get sold to other clubs. Minor league baseball as a whole reached its peak in 1949, when 59 leagues included over 450 teams. By the 1980s, farm systems had diminished enough that every big league team owned or affiliated itself with just a half-dozen lower league clubs, and the number of minor leagues had dwindled to 17.

fastball: A pitch that's thrown at top speed. Who had baseball history's fastest fastball? Nolan RYAN boasted the highest measured speed, 101 miles per hour. But other contenders for the title are "Smoky" Joe Wood, Smoky Joe WILLIAMS, Walter JOHNSON, Lefty GROVE, Bob FELLER, "Goose" GOSSAGE, and J. R. Richard. Sometimes fastballs are thrown with such speed that they seem to "hop" or "rise" before they reach the catcher's mitt. In fact, the rising fastball travels on a continuous, smooth arc upward as it reaches the plate; it's the same principle as the CURVEBALL.

foul pole: The big yellow poles sticking up along the outfield lines that help the umpire decide whether a ball hit into the stands is foul or a home run. Nonsensically, a ball that hits the foul pole is ruled a fair ball.

free agent, free agency: A free agent is a player who is not under contract with any team and is free to negotiate with whoever wants to pay the right money. As of 1995, free agency is available to any player with an expired contract who has played six or more years in the majors. The Major League Baseball Players' Association, led by Marvin MILLER, won the right of free agency with the Andy MESSERSMITH–Dave McNALLY decision in 1975. Before that, the RESERVE CLAUSE in every player's standard contract bound a player to his team for as long as the club wanted him; during salary negotiations, players had absolutely no rights and had to accept whatever offer the team made or else not play baseball at all. Many people argue that free agency has torn apart the game because it has created a system of rent-a-players and mercenaries who go wherever the money is. But I like the fact that a favorite team has a chance to get a great player at any moment; ask Giants fans whether they like free agency in the wake of the Barry BONDS deal. Sure, free agency has driven salaries into the stratosphere, and sure, there have been a lot of bad free agent signings. The key is for teams to be smart when they hand out their money. In recent years, for example, there have been probably more good signings than bad ones: Bonds, Greg MADDUX, Bobby Bonilla, David Cone—they've all paid off handsomely for their respective clubs. Is it a coincidence that the beginning of free agency also marked the beginning of the baseball attendance boom? There were other factors, to be sure, but I think free agency has been good for baseball.

full count: A three-ball, two-strike count.

glove: The leather equipment worn to protect the hand. All fielders use gloves except the first baseman and catcher; they use mitts, which have more padding. The first gloves were the tight-fitting kind, worn on both hands, with the fingers cut off the player's throwing hand. Gloves were introduced around the early 1870s, and the few players who wore them were routinely ridiculed. When the great Albert G. SPALDING donned gloves in 1877, the jeering stopped. Gloves have gone through an amazing evolution in the past 100 years, the trend being toward larger, more comfortable gloves. Hall of Famer Buck EWING used the first heavily padded catcher's mitt in the mid-1880s, and padded, oversized fielder's gloves came into general use soon after. In 1912, the RAWLINGS COMPANY introduced the "Sure Catch" glove, the first one of its kind with sewn-in finger channels. The next significant advancement came nearly a decade later, when spitballing pitcher Bill Doak approached Rawlings with an idea: a piece of leather stitched between the thumb and forefinger to act as webbing. The company has improved upon that development over the years, adding a "Deep Well" pocket, "Basket Web," "Edge-U-Cated Heel"—all terms that should be familiar to people who have owned Rawlings gloves. Rawlings is rightly seen as the world's premier glove manufacturer, and nearly 60 percent of all major league players use the company's gloves and mitts.

grand slam: A home run with the bases loaded. I know people who get really mad when a broadcaster says a player has just hit "a grand slam home run," claiming the phrase is redundant.

green light: The manager's metaphorical sign allowing a baserunner to steal whenever he wants or giving a hitter the right to swing on a 3–0 or 3–1 count.

hanging curve: A CURVEBALL that doesn't break as much as it's supposed to—or not at all—giving the hitter an inviting target that often ends up in the seats.

heat: A term for an extremely fast FASTBALL. Other descriptions include *high heat, heater, smoke, high cheese, hummer, the high hard one, a pitch with a lot of mustard,* and *gas.*

hit: A ball struck so that the batter reaches base safely without benefit of an ERROR or fielder's choice. Hit in the generic sense refers to all kinds of hits, including extra-base hits, but it also can refer to a single, depending on the context.

hit by pitch, hit batsman: A pitch that hits a batter. These days, a hit batsman—whether accidental or not—usually results in a big fight that starts between hitter and pitcher and ends after both benches have emptied. Clever journalists and broadcasters like to call such a spectacle a "basebrawl" game. Don DRYSDALE is baseball's all-time leader in hit batsmen with 154.

hit-and-run: An offensive play involving a baserunner and the batter. During the pitcher's windup, the runner takes off for second base, and the batter is obligated to make contact with the pitch, in hope of sending the ball into right field so that the baserunner can take an extra base. A variation is the run-and-hit, where the runner attempts a steal but the batter doesn't have to swing. The hit-and-run is a good play when the manager wants to stay out of a ground ball DOUBLE PLAY; hitters who have good bat control are the best at executing the hit-and-run. John McGRAW liked to claim that his old Baltimore Orioles of the 1890s invented this strategy, but it's likely that the play was around much earlier. Bill JAMES, in his *Historical Baseball Abstract*, quotes the great John Montgomery WARD describing the play in 1893, which was McGraw's first full season in the majors—and it's hard to believe that a near-rookie would be able to introduce such a new strategy. Ward actually credits Hall of Famer Tommy McCarthy, an innovative player and manager who also developed on-field SIGNS, as the hit-and-run's real inventor.

home run: A fair ball that either goes over the outfield fence or eludes the fielder long enough so that the hitter can run all the way around the bases, which is called an inside-the-park home run. Other terms for home run include *homer, dinger, dial 8, downtown, long ball, four bagger, round-tripper,* and *tater*; the pitch is often called a *gopher ball.* Babe RUTH was the greatest home run hitter the game has ever seen, having slammed 714 in 8,399 at bats for a ratio of one home run every 11.8 at bats; Ralph KINER is next with a 14.1 ratio (369 in 5,205 at bats). Hank AARON slugged 755 dingers to rank him number one on the all-time career list, and Roger MARIS owns the single-season record with 61 in 1961.

hot dog: In addition to the fat-laden sausage people love to eat at ball games, "hot dog" also refers to a showoff, a player who likes to draw attention to his own actions. Pete ROSE, Willie MAYS, Barry BONDS, and Rickey HENDERSON are all well known for their hot doggery, but the hottest of all dogs has to be Reggie JACKSON. If he didn't *invent* the practice of admiring deep home run balls, he sure made it an art form. As one-time teammate Darold Knowles said, "There isn't enough mustard in the world to cover Reggie Jackson."

infield fly rule: Whenever people want to make a joke about how complicated baseball rules are, they always use the infield fly rule as exhibit A. But it really isn't complex, it just *sounds* like it. Simply put, the infield fly rule is invoked when a batter hits a fair fly ball that can be caught with ordinary effort by an infielder when first and second or first, second, and third are occupied and there are less than two outs. The batter is automatically out, regardless of whether the infielder actually catches the ball. It's important to understand why the rule was enacted: to prevent the defense from benefiting from its own deception. Imagine this situation: Bases loaded, one out. The batter hits a high pop fly in the infield, so the runners retreat to their bases. But instead of catching the ball, the third baseman lets the ball drop at his feet. Stunned, the runners try to advance, but the third baseman tags third for one out and guns it to the second baseman for a double play. The inning is over, and the defense has stolen two outs. The infield fly rule was enacted in the 1890s to prevent such underhanded play. When the umpire waves his arms and shouts "Infield fly!" the play is basically over; the runners may advance if they want, but they'll almost certainly be tagged out. It's a great rule, part of what makes baseball *baseball.*

inning: The units that divide a baseball game. There are nine innings in a regulation game, less if the contest gets shortened by rain and more if the teams are tied after nine. Some writers like to use the word *stanza* as a synonym for inning, but I don't. Baseball is a sport, not poetry.

junk: A term for an assortment of pitches that includes only non-fastballs such as slow CURVEBALLS, KNUCKLEBALLS, off-speed pitches, and the like. A pitcher who survives on such pitches is called a junkballer.

K: The SCORECARD symbol for STRIKEOUT; if it's a called strikeout, many people turn the K backwards. The symbol was originated either by *New York Herald* sportswriter M. J. Kelly or by "Father of Baseball" Henry CHADWICK in the 1860s—chosen because an "S" would confuse it with SINGLE or SACRIFICE and because "K" is the last letter of the word "struck."

knuckleball: A pitch that's thrown with little or no spin so that the ball moves erratically on the way to the plate. It's really not thrown with the knuckles, but rather with the tips of the fingers. Some famous knuckleballers include Phil NIEKRO and Hoyt WILHELM, both of whom had extremely long careers because the knuckler exacts very little toll on a pitcher's arm. The perfect knuckleball makes exactly one revolution on the way to the plate. Air currents strike the stitches on the ball wildly and the ball dances and weaves through the air, making it difficult to hit, catch, or umpire. Today, few pitchers take the time to master the art of the knuckler.

leadoff hitter: The hitter who bats in the number one spot in the batting order. The test of a good leadoff man is whether he regularly scores 100 runs for your team. To be able to achieve that milestone, he generally has to get on base around 40 percent of the time and be smart on the bases. Rickey HENDERSON is acknowledged as baseball's greatest leadoff hitter because of his deadly combination of speed and STRIKE ZONE judgment—in addition to his excellent power. "Sliding Billy" HAMILTON, who played around the turn of the century, could do everything Henderson could except hit home runs, thus qualifying as history's second best leadoff hitter. After that, it's a tough call. In the first part of the century, batters such as Honus WAGNER, Ty COBB, and Tris SPEAKER—who, like Henderson, could hit well and steal bases—batted third or fourth; Eddie COLLINS types batted second. From

1920 through the 1960s, few players stole many bases. Luis APARICIO led the league in steals for many years, but his career on base percentage was .313, so he didn't get on base enough to really help his team; Maury WILLS had the same problem. During that era, Richie ASHBURN, who didn't steal that much, probably dominated the leadoff men. By the 1970s, Lou BROCK had helped introduce the all-around player to the leadoff position; Brock could steal bases, draw some walks, and hit for power. We're now witnessing the golden age of leadoff hitters: Henderson, Tim Raines, Kenny Lofton, Len Dykstra, and Marquis Grissom, among others. Alas, MVP voters usually overlook the number one hitters when filling out their ballots: Of today's leadoff men, only Henderson has captured an award.

line drive: A batted ball that travels fast and straight and fairly low to the ground. Also called a *frozen rope, bullet,* or *clothesline.* Although every player hits line drives now and then, some batters are known for their frequent line drive hits. Roberto CLEMENTE and George BRETT are two famous ones.

lineup: The nine (or 10 with the DESIGNATED HITTER) players who start a given game. Managers are required to turn in their lineup cards, which include the batting order and defensive alignment, before first pitch. Some by-the-book managers examine lineup cards intently for any mistakes, hoping to catch the opposition in a costly error.

magic number: The combined number of wins by a first-place team and losses by a second-place team it would take for the top team to clinch the division title. Here's the formula:

$$[(Second\ Place\ Wins + Games\ Remaining) - First\ Place\ Team\ Wins] + 1$$

For example, if the Dodgers lead the Giants by five games with 10 remaining, then any combination of Dodger wins plus

Giant losses totaling six would hand the division to Los Angeles. Every September, the newspaper prints magic numbers for all the leading teams. And every April, some clever sportscaster announces that the hometown team's magic number, after an Opening Day victory, is 161.

manager: The guy who runs the team on the field, making the important decisions such as filling out the lineup card, changing pitchers, sending in pinch hitters, ordering steals, and sometimes calling pitches. Other terms include *skipper* and *field general.* One of the great things about baseball, as opposed to other sports, is that the head guy is the manager, not just the coach. One of the bad things about baseball is that the manager wears the same uniform as his players, so fans are treated to the sights of rumpled and bumpy old men in tight polyester knickers. I think it would be great if a manager would wear a suit and tie in the dugout like Connie MACK and Charlie Dressen did. Imagine if Pat Riley coached a basketball game in shorts and a tank top.

mascot: A costumed character who's supposed to bring good luck to a team. The San Diego Chicken (alias Ted Giannoulas) is one of our most famous mascots, and today the Philly Phanatic also entertains fans at the Vet. Does anyone remember the Crazy Crab (Krazy Krab?) of the San Francisco Giants? Around 1984, the team polled its fans about what kind of mascot they'd like to see representing the Giants. By a nearly 2–1 margin, the fans asserted that they didn't want any mascot. Undaunted, the team introduced one anyway: The Crazy Crab, a purposely pathetic-looking orange thing whose job was to absorb whatever abuse the fans of a last-place team could muster. When he came out during the game, fans would boo, dump beer, throw trash, and otherwise abuse it any way they could. For about a year, the team used that crab as a marketing gimmick to get fans out to CANDLESTICK. It didn't work, so they dumped it not long after.

National Agreement: First signed in 1883, the National Agreement governs organized professional baseball. In the early years, the Agreement established the RESERVE CLAUSE and provided for a "gentlemen's agreement" that allowed clubs in the National League and AMERICAN ASSOCIATION to blacklist any player who tried to jump his contract for more money. Later, the Agreement was revised to govern the dealings between major and minor league clubs. The Agreement has been tested in court on antitrust grounds, first by the FEDERAL LEAGUE, then by Curt FLOOD *(FLOOD V. KUHN)*. The major leagues ultimately won both cases. It took the 1994 STRIKE to pose a serious challenge to the sovereignty of the National Agreement.

night game: A game played at night under the lights. Major league baseball's first night game took place on May 24, 1935, at CROSLEY FIELD between the Reds and Phillies, won by Cincinnati 2–1. The reaction from the rest of baseball was decidedly negative: "There is no chance of night baseball ever becoming popular in the bigger cities," said Senators owner Clark Griffith, typical of his era. "People there are educated to see the best. High-class baseball cannot be played under artificial light." Alas, night baseball proved immensely popular everywhere, and despite wails of complaint from traditionalists, bottom-line concerns forced the rest of major league baseball to adopt lights within a few years—all except the Chicago Cubs, who resisted modernization until 1988. But the history of night baseball actually begins not in 1935 but rather in 1880. That was when two department store teams played a 16–16 night game as a publicity stunt put on by the local electric company. Over the next 50 years, various entrepreneurs and inventors scheduled amateur and semipro games under the lights, many attempting to lure baseball owners to invest in their equipment. In 1930, three teams, including the KANSAS CITY MONARCHS of the NEGRO LEAGUES, successfully implemented quality lighting systems and attracted big crowds, leading many minor league clubs around the country to follow suit. Larry MACPHAIL, just up from the minors, spearheaded the effort by the Reds to install lights.

no-hitter: A complete game in which the pitcher (or pitchers) does not allow the other team to get a hit; a PERFECT GAME is a stricter variation of the no-hitter. Joe Borden of Philadelphia's National Association club tossed major league baseball's first no-hitter in 1875. Since then, the majors have seen more than 220 no-hitters—seven by Nolan RYAN for the all-time record. Johnny VANDER MEER is the only pitcher to throw no-hitters in consecutive games, and Bobo Holloman is one of three men to pitch a no-hitter in their first major league start. Neither of them ever did much else in the league.

off-speed pitch: Another term for a CHANGE-UP, a pitch that doesn't curve or do anything funny but is designed simply to throw off a hitter's timing.

official scorer: The man or woman whose job it is to keep the official score of a ball game. The scorer decides, among other things, whether a play should be ruled a HIT or an ERROR—a decision that often prompts bitter disagreement from the fans or even the players. New York Mets third baseman Bobby Bonilla, for example, was once accused of telephoning the official scorer between innings after he'd been charged with an error on a play; he wanted the scorer to change the ruling, apparently to help his fielding stats.

on deck: A circle between home and the DUGOUT where a hitter stands while awaiting his turn AT BAT. The phrase comes from the nautical lexicon, where to be "on deck" means to be on the main deck of a ship, presumably awaiting orders.

out: You know what this means, don't make me explain it. There are three per half-inning, 27 per game.

out pitch: A pitcher's best pitch, the one he uses most often when he wants an OUT.

payoff pitch: A FULL-COUNT pitch—with 3 balls and 2 strikes. So-called because something will happen on the next pitch, there'll be some sort of payoff, even if it's just a foul ball.

pennant: The symbolic flag awarded to the champion of each league. Prior to the 1969 SEASON, the team with the best regular-season record won the league's pennant. But with the advent of divisional play, a team had to capture the league championship series. Then, beginning with the 1994 SEASON, the pennant moved a step further from the regular season when the league instituted a preliminary round of playoffs (although the strike postponed the first actual implementation of the plan until 1995). Although the leagues don't actually award a physical pennant to the champions, most teams have one made for them to fly in the stadium or hang in the team's offices.

pepper: A quick-moving bunting and fielding game that helps players improve their reflexes. A hitter stands about 20 or 30 feet from a fielder or group of fielders. One of the fielders tosses a ball to the hitter, who bunts the ball back to the fielders. Whoever picks it up pitches it right back immediately, and play continues quickly in that manner. It's a fun game that should be a staple of youth league practices.

perfect game: A no-hit game in which a pitcher goes a step further: he prevents the other team from reaching base in any way—HIT, WALK, or ERROR. Through 1994, there have been only 14 perfect games in major league history; they're listed here:

1. June 12, 1880: Lee Richmond, Worcester vs. Cleveland (NL), 1–0
2. June 17, 1880: Monte Ward, Providence vs. Buffalo (NL), 5–0

3. October 2, 1908: Addie Joss, Cleveland vs. White Sox, 1–0
4. June 23, 1917: Ernie Shore, Red Sox vs. Senators, 3–0*
5. April 30, 1922: Charlie Robertson, White Sox vs. Tigers, 2–0
6. October 8, 1956: Don Larsen, Yankees vs. Dodgers, 2–0 (World Series)*
7. May 26, 1959: Harvey Haddix, Pirates vs. Braves, 0–1*
8. September 9, 1965: Sandy Koufax, Dodgers vs. Cubs, 1–0
9. May 8, 1968: "Catfish" Hunter, A's vs. Twins, 4–0
10. May 15, 1981: Len Barker, Indians vs. Blue Jays, 3–0
11. September 30, 1984: Mike Witt, Angels vs. Rangers, 1–0
12. September 16, 1988: Tom Browning, Reds vs. Dodgers, 1–0
13. July 28, 1991: Dennis Martinez, Expos vs. Dodgers, 2–0
14. July 28, 1994: Kenny Rogers, Rangers vs. Angels, 4–0

Although all of those games were remarkable in some way, three in particular deserve extra comment. Perfect game number 4 technically shouldn't appear on this list. In it, starting pitcher Babe RUTH walked the first batter and then protested the calls to the umpire so badly that he was tossed from the game. Ernie Shore entered in relief, the runner was caught stealing, and Shore retired the next 26 batters. Number 6 is the only postseason no-hitter (see 1956 WORLD SERIES for more). And number 7 represents perhaps the greatest game ever pitched—which resulted in a loss for starter Harvey Haddix. Haddix had recorded 36 consecutive outs through 12 innings against a Braves team that, according to a recent admission by Braves catcher Del Crandall, had been stealing Haddix's signs all evening long! Even still, Haddix was masterful, mowing down the Braves hitters with barely a difficult chance for his fielders. The end came in the 13th. Felix Mantilla led off the inning with a ground ball to Pirates third baseman Don Hoak, who made a throwing error to break up the perfect game.

Eddie MATHEWS sacrificed Mantilla to second, and Haddix walked Hank AARON intentionally. The no-hitter was still intact, but not for long. First baseman Joe Adcock sent Haddix's second pitch over the right field fence for an apparent 3–0 victory. Mantilla crossed home, but in the misty evening, Aaron thought that the ball had landed short of the fence and that Mantilla's run ended the game. He trotted toward the clubhouse, and Adcock passed him on the bases. The umpires ruled Adcock out and only allowed one run, changing Adcock's home run into a game-winning RBI double and a 1–0 Braves victory—a peculiar end to a remarkable game. In 1994, league officials changed the definition of a perfect game to include only complete game no-hitters, thus removing Haddix and Shore from the official list. They won't be forgotten here.

pickoff: A throw by a pitcher or catcher to nail a runner off base. Some catchers like to show off their strong arms by attempting pickoff plays even when there's little chance of getting the runners. Of recent players, Benito Santiago falls under that category.

pinch hitter: A hitter who substitutes for another in the batting order, usually for just one AT BAT. It's called that because such a hitter is mostly used "in a pinch," when the game is on the line. Pinch-hitting wasn't officially sanctioned by the National League until 1891, when the rules were changed to allow substitutions for reasons other than injuries. Current Dodger coach Manny Mota holds the career record for pinch-hits with 150, while Expo Jose Morales set the single-season record with 25 pinch-hits in 1975.

pinch runner: Pinch runners are usually speedy runners who substitute for slow guys in the later stages of the game. Always innovative Charlie FINLEY even went a step further in 1974 by signing world-class sprinter Herb Washington to be baseball's first ever—and only—designated runner. In his first season with the A's, Washington appeared in 92 games, attempted 45 steals, succeeded on 29 of them, and scored 29 runs. He came back in 1975 but lasted just 13 more games before the experiment mercifully ended.

pine tar: The black sticky substance derived from tree goo that hitters use to maintain a good grip on their bat. Owing to one controversial event, pine tar has earned an ignominious place in baseball history; *see* PINE TAR INCIDENT.

pitcher's mound: The mound of dirt in the middle of the infield where the pitcher throws from. The rules say the mound can be no more than 10 inches in height, but that rule has historically been loosely enforced. DODGER STADIUM, for example, was known to feature a big, built-up mound in the 1960s, enabling Sandy KOUFAX and Don DRYSDALE to really bear down on opposing hitters (as if they really needed much help). Following the outrageous 1968 season, in which pitchers dominated hitters to an extent not seen since the DEAD BALL ERA, the leagues cracked down on the big mounds to restore hitting to its previous heights. Pitchers didn't always throw off mounds. Until 1893, pitchers threw from a rectangular box 45, then 50 feet from the plate. The mound was added after the league moved the pitching rubber back to its current distance of 60 feet 6 inches from home plate.

pitchout: In an attempt to catch a baserunner trying to steal, a pitcher can intentionally throw the ball way outside the STRIKE ZONE so that the catcher can get a better throw to the base. That's called a pitchout. Basically, the defense is trying to outsmart the offense by guessing when the offense is going to attempt a steal. The best counts on which to call a pitchout are 0–2 and 1–2 because the pitcher can afford to waste a ball. That being the case, however, the opposing team will rarely steal on those counts. Conversely, managers are reluctant to call pitchouts on two-ball counts since they don't want to put their pitchers in a hole. But a manager might make such a call to throw the other team off balance, especially if he has a pitcher with good control. Calling pitchouts is just one of the many mind games that occur during a game between opposing managers. It's part of what makes baseball fun to watch.

plate appearance: A trip to the plate by a hitter. For statistical purposes, plate appearance (PA) differs from AT BAT (AB) because AB only refers to a trip to the plate that results in a hit, out, or error, while a PA covers everything: hit, out, error, walk, sacrifice, interference, hit by pitch, and so forth. A player's PA total, which is used in the calculation of ON BASE PERCENTAGE, is always higher than his AB total.

platoon: A system of alternating players at a position in order to take advantage of their batting strengths. Traditionally, platoons occur between right- and left-handed batters because conventional wisdom says right-handers hit better against left-handed pitchers and vice versa. Casey STENGEL often gets the credit for developing platoons, but the practice far outdates even him. Stengel did it with the Yankees in the 1950s, but Tris SPEAKER platooned his Indians extensively beginning in 1920, and prior to that, isolated cases of platooning existed; as author Bill JAMES has reported, however, they're hard to track down. From about 1930 until Stengel came to New York, few managers platooned. Stengel's success returned the practice to favor, and later, managers like Earl WEAVER have taken it to new heights.

play-by-play: The verbal descriptions of a ball game by a radio or television broadcaster. Play-by-play can also refer to any kind of verbal or written account of each play of the game. One of baseball's great stories is the one about Potter Stewart, the Supreme Court justice and baseball fan, who was in the courthouse listening to oral arguments during a 1973 playoff game between the Mets and the Reds. Justice Stewart had asked one of his clerks to keep him apprised of the game through notes describing each play. It was a tumultuous time in American politics, as one such note revealed: "Kranepool flies to right. Agnew resigns."

player-manager: A team member who doubles as the team's manager, calling plays and changing pitchers from his position on the field. Teams rarely employ player-managers these days; the last one was Pete ROSE in the mid-1980s. Historically, some of baseball's best players also player-managed for part of their careers, including Eddie COLLINS, Ty COBB, Tris SPEAKER, Rogers HORNSBY, Lou BOUDREAU (who was only 24 when the Indians named him player-manager), Yogi BERRA, Frank ROBINSON, and many others. I don't know why teams don't hire player-managers more often anymore, since it would seem like a good cost-cutting move. My guess would be that teams don't believe that players would have enough experience to do both jobs. But if a player has a smart baseball mind, is recognized as a team leader, and is popular with the fans, it would seem to make smart business sense to promote the guy. I'd like to see the return of the player-manager.

protest: When a manager believes the umpire has made a call that contradicts the rule book—not a judgment call such as a ball/strike or out/safe call—the manager can file an official protest with the league office to have the results of the game overturned. He must announce to the umpire that he's playing the game under protest immediately, before the next play begins. If the protesting team wins the game, the protest is immediately dropped. But if it loses, the league office investigates and makes a ruling. Some grounds for protest include ending a game too quickly during a rain delay, incorrect interpretation of the interference rule, and use of an ineligible player. There are many others. League offices rarely rule in favor of the protesting teams, but one infamous protest that was upheld was the PINE TAR INCIDENT.

purpose pitch: A pitch that has a purpose: to move the hitter away from the plate. After his retirement, Hall of Famer Early Wynn was quoted in Roger Kahn's *A Season in the Sun* as saying, "I've got a right to knock down anybody holding a bat." Wynn had just knocked down his son.

radar gun: The high-tech gadget used by cops to nail motorists for speeding and by baseball scouts to measure the speed of pitches.

regular season: The 162-game season that determines the leagues' playoff participants. Before 1969, the team in each league with the best regular-season record would meet in the World Series. In 1969, baseball added an extra round of playoffs, then in 1994, the powers added another round. As the following table shows, the length of the regular season grew substantially in the first 30 years of major league history, then remained stagnant for the next 60:

Year	Reg. Season	Comment
1871	30 games	First season of National Association
1876	70	First season of National League
1881	85	
1886	125	
1891	140	Competition between NL and Players' League
1896	130	
1901	140	First season of American League
1906	154	
1961	162	First season of major league expansion

release: To cut a player from the roster. When a player is released, he's free to sign with any other team, but the original team is still obligated to pay him if he has a guaranteed contract. In 1994, for example, the Dodgers released Darryl Strawberry because of the outfielder's well-known drug and alcohol problems. They bought out the remaining two years of his contract for about $4 million. Two months later, Strawberry signed with the Giants for the major league minimum salary, and so even though he was performing for Los Angeles's hated rivals, the Dodgers were still paying the bulk of his salary. It's rare that a released player will return to post big numbers in the majors, but when it happens, you can bet the team that released him will hear about it.

relief pitcher: Generic term for a pitcher who doesn't start the game. Relief pitching breaks down into six indistinct roles, perhaps more:

Long reliever	Enters the game in the early innings, usually after the starter has been shelled or injured; expected to pitch four or five innings.
Middle reliever	Pitches the middle innings, often in relief of a battered starter when the score is close.
Mop-up man	Pitches any time the game is way out of hand.
Setup man	Keeps the game close in the seventh and eighth innings, setting up the closer.
Left-handed specialist	A left-handed pitcher whose job is to get out one or two tough left-handed hitters.
Closer	Pitches the final one or two innings of a close game, often garnering a save if he shuts down the opposition.

The history of relief pitching could fill its own book, or at least an entire chapter. Over 125 years of evolution, baseball has gradually shifted from a system demanding that a pitcher complete all of his starts to today's system of five-man STARTING ROTATIONS who complete less than 20 percent of their starts. Teams started adopting late-inning relief specialists in the 1920s, when "Firpo" Marberry became the first *good* pitcher who spent most of his time in the bullpen. Before him, a team's relief corps was made up of failed starters. The concept caught on after a while, so by the 1950s, most teams had a designated closer who was every bit as important as the starters; Jim Konstanty even won the 1950 National League

MVP Award. Since then, relief pitching seems to undergo decade-by-decade transformations: It wasn't the same in 1970 as 1960, nor in 1990 as 1980. The trend is toward fewer games and fewer innings pitched, using the top closer only in actual SAVE situations: when the team is leading by three or fewer runs in the ninth inning. As of 1995, there are only two relief specialists in the Hall of Fame: Rollie FINGERS and Hoyt WILHELM. That's going to change in the next decade as players like Dennis ECKERSLEY, "Goose" GOSSAGE, and Lee SMITH become eligible. But it's definitely not a position that's ever going to get much recognition in the shrine. Why? Mainly because few good relievers are able to sustain a high level of performance for more than a few years. The list of relief burnout cases is long and distinguished and includes such names as Bobby Thigpen, Bruce Sutter, Sparky Lyle, Mike Marshall, Elroy Face, and Dick Radatz. Eventually, baseball may discover a way for top relievers to remain healthy and effective longer.

reserve clause: The part of a player's contract that, until 1975, kept him bound to his club forever. In the 1880s, Chicago White Stockings owner Albert G. SPALDING helped institute the clause as a way to help owners control costs and keep player salaries down. For many years, the baseball establishment considered the reserve clause to be the backbone of baseball. What they really meant was that it was the backbone of their financial security—for the reserve clause, more than anything else, kept player salaries artificially, despicably low. With the reserve clause in place, a player had absolutely no rights. If he thought he was being underpaid, if he objected to his treatment by the owners, if he was stuck in the minor leagues because the team had a better player at his position, he had absolutely no recourse except to quit baseball entirely. Curt FLOOD challenged the reserve clause in his monumental case *FLOOD v. KUHN*—and lost. The owners claimed that without a reserve system, the richest teams would dominate baseball because only they could afford the high prices FREE AGENTS would charge. That was the argument that many players, media members, and fans believed. But as we all know after 20 years of free agency, it proved totally wrong. And it was wrong even at that time. What team dominated baseball for the 50 years *prior to the destruction of the reserve clause?* It was the richest team in baseball: the Yankees, who could afford to have the best scouting system and pay out the best bonuses to young players. The end of the reserve system—because of the MESSERSMITH–McNALLY arbitration decision—allowed *more* teams to compete, not fewer.

rookie: A first-year player. "Rookie" probably derives from the army word "recruit" and was first applied to ballplayers around 1908. Before that, such players were usually called "yannigans"—a quaint and distinctly 19th-century word.

rubber: The 6-by-24-inch rubber slab on top of the PITCHER'S MOUND. A pitcher must start his motion while standing on top of the rubber. In the early days of baseball, there was no mound or rubber, just a box. A pitcher would stand at the back of the box and take a running start, releasing the ball from the front line, then 45 feet from home. The rubber was added in 1890, followed by the mound in 1893.

run: Baseball's scoring unit, which occurs when a player has safely made it around all the bases and touched home plate. Though the term comes from CRICKET, the KNICKERBOCKER RULES called them "counts" or "aces," so the word "run" must have come into use sometime between 1845 and 1854, which is the first known printed reference to "runs."

sacrifice bunt: A BUNT in which the bunter's job is to advance the runner at the expense of himself. Sacrifices always come with less than two outs and usually are attempted by the team's weakest hitters. Sacrificing was big in the DEAD BALL

ERA, when runs were hard to come by. But as home runs became more frequent, sacrifices became less useful. Many players never even bothered to learn how to do it. Harmon KILLEBREW, for example, never in his entire career executed a successful sacrifice bunt. Today, few managers order sacrifices with much frequency; the last guy who really used it a lot was Gene Mauch. Earl WEAVER hated one-run strategies like the sac bunt, but even he used it in the late innings of close ball games.

sacrifice fly: A fly ball hit deep enough to score a runner from third base, giving the hitter credit for an RBI. It can be an exciting play on medium-deep fly balls when the outfielder has a good arm, but usually the outfielder doesn't even risk the throw home.

save: Statistical credit given to the RELIEF PITCHER who ensures a team's victory in a close game. There are several rules governing the awarding of a save to a reliever. Most importantly, he must finish the game on the winning team and not get credit for the victory. Aside from that, his appearance must come under one of the following game conditions:

- He enters the game with his team leading by three or fewer runs.
- He enters the game with the tying run on base, at bat, or on deck.
- He pitches three effective innings regardless of the score.

Bobby Thigpen holds the single-season record for saves with 57 in 1990; the next closest is Randy Myers, who notched 53 in 1993. The save didn't become an official league statistic until 1969, but researchers have recalculated save totals for all pitchers back through the 1870s. To illustrate the changing role of relief pitching, here's a list of the major league leaders in saves at 10-year intervals:

Year	Player	Team	Saves
1880	Lee Richmond	Worcester	3
1890	Kid Gleason	Philadelphia	2
1900	Frank Kitson	Brooklyn	4
1910	"Three-Finger" Brown	Chicago-NL	7
1920	Bill Sherdel	St. Louis-NL	6
1930	Lefty Grove	Philadelphia-AL	9
1940	Al Benton	Detroit	17
1950	Jim Konstanty	Philadelphia-NL	22
1960	Lindy McDaniel	St. Louis	26
1970	Wayne Granger	Cincinnati	35
1980	Dan Quisenberry	Kansas City	33
1990	Bobby Thigpen	Chicago-AL	57

What's interesting is that two of those guys—"Three-Finger" BROWN and Lefty GROVE—were also fantastic starting pitchers whose managers realized the importance of a fresh, quality arm late in the game. Any discussion of relief pitching isn't complete, however, without a mention of the first really good relief specialist: Fred "Firpo" Marberry, who saved 101 games and won 148 others, mostly for the Senators, from 1923 to 1936. Marberry actually started 187 games in his career and completed 86 of them, but it was as a reliever that he gained his greatest fame.

scorecard: The graphical representation of a baseball game. Using a scorecard, you can track a game play by play. The scoring system assigns numbers and letters to fielders and plays. Most people have their own system, but here's a listing of some of the most popular symbols:

1	Pitcher	7	Left fielder
2	Catcher	8	Center fielder
3	First baseman	9	Right fielder
4	Second baseman	F	Flyout
5	Third baseman	K	Strikeout
6	Shortstop		

G	Groundout	HBP	Hit by pitch
1B	Single	E	Error
2B	Double	DP	Double play
3B	Triple	TP	Triple play
HR	Home run		
BB	Walk		

For example, a ground ball out, shortstop to first, would be marked as G6–3, or just 6–3. A fly out to right would be F9. A dropped third strike that gets thrown to first base for the putout would be K2–3. An AROUND THE HORN double play would be 5–4–3 DP. Keeping score is the best way to really follow a baseball game, either on the radio, on TV, or especially at the ballpark.

scoring position: A runner on second or third base is said to be in scoring position because almost any hit to the outfield will bring him home. By the same token, some prolific home run hitters are said to be in scoring position when they're at the plate.

scout: A person whose job is to evaluate talent, usually for a major league team or for the Major League Scouting Bureau. Scouts search high school, college, and minor leagues to look for players in anticipation of the yearly AMATEUR DRAFT and possible trades. The job of an advance scout, meanwhile, is to watch other major league teams, noting players' strengths and weaknesses in preparation for a future series between those teams and the scout's employer.

screwball: A BREAKING BALL that's thrown exactly the opposite of a CURVEBALL so that, for example, a left-hander's screwball curves away from a right-handed batter. Lefties are, in fact, the best-known practitioners of scroogies because it gives them an advantage over right-handed hitters; Carl HUBBELL and Fernando Valenzuela are two lefties who rode the screwball to great success. The first popular use of a screwball, however, was by Christy MATHEWSON, a right-hander who called the pitch a "fadeaway."

season ticket: A ticket that entitles the buyer to attend an entire season's worth of home games. Teams also offer partial-season ticket packages. If a team makes the post season, season ticket holders get first dibs at playoff and World Series seats.

seventh-inning stretch: The break in the action between the top and bottom of the seventh inning, known as the "stretch" because fans traditionally stand up to stretch their legs. Most ballparks play "TAKE ME OUT TO THE BALL GAME" during the break, and in WRIGLEY FIELD, broadcaster Harry CAREY leads the fans in singing baseball's anthem. Legend has it that President William Howard Taft inaugurated the practice when he stood up in the middle of the seventh of a game in 1910. The fans thought he was leaving, and, ever respectful, they stood to honor him. Another oft-told story credits the students of Manhattan College with initiating the practice in 1882. Cincinnati Red Stocking Harry WRIGHT, however, wrote a letter to a friend saying, "The spectators all arise between halves of the seventh inning, extend their legs and arms and sometimes walk about. In so doing they enjoy the relief afforded by relaxation from a long posture upon hard benches." That was in 1869.

shift: A change in the position of the fielders to defend against a particular hitter's strength. Ted WILLIAMS was the victim of the famous "Williams shift" that positioned every infielder on the right side of the diamond to protect against the deadly left-handed pull hitter. People were angry that Williams stubbornly refused to drop in hits to left field, but Williams knew that he was paid to hit home runs, not singles. Even so, he won six batting titles. Today, the shift is employed rarely and only against the toughest pull hitters.

Show, The: A synonym for the major leagues, usually used by aspiring minor leaguers.

shutout: A complete game in which a pitcher holds the opposition scoreless. The single-season record for shutouts is 16 by Grover Cleveland ALEXANDER; career, Walter JOHNSON with 110. Today, since few pitchers complete their games, shutouts are much more rare. The highest single-season total since 1969 is 10, achieved by John Tudor in 1985.

sign: Developed by Hall of Famer Tommy McCarthy in the 1880s, signs are secret on-field signals that give instructions to the players. The catcher gives signs to the pitcher to determine the next pitch. The third base coach signals the batter whether to HIT, TAKE, BUNT, HIT-AND-RUN, and so forth; he also signals the baserunner whether to steal. A shortstop might signal the second baseman about who should cover the base on a steal attempt. Fans are accustomed to seeing the third base coach go through an array of signs: he touches his nose, chest, ears, elbow, knee, nose again, back of the head, cap, sleeve, ears again, and so on. Usually, only one of those "touches" means something, and the rest are there to confuse the other team.

single: A hit that allows the batter to reach first base safely; a one-base hit. Singles come in a variety of shapes and sizes: a dribbler that barely scoots past the pitcher, a ground ball deep in the hole at shortstop, a blooper that falls just behind the first baseman, a line drive that falls in front of the outfielder, a booming smash that caroms off the outfield wall so hard that it bounces back to the infield before the batter can make it to second base, and a hundred other possibilities. But they all look the same in the scorebook.

sinker: A pitch thrown so that it curves slightly downward, usually resulting in a ground ball. To be successful, sinkerball pitchers must have a good infield defense behind them to turn those grounders into outs.

slider: A type of CURVEBALL that's thrown faster and curves less; it's really a hybrid fastball-curveball. Steve CARLTON made the Hall of Fame on the strength of his deadly slider, universally called the best in baseball history. The pitch first came into popular use in the 1930s, featured prominently by George Uhle, who won 200 games in his 17-year career, and George Blaeholder, who posted a 104–125 record mostly with the Browns.

slugfest: A high-scoring game that features lots of extra-base hits, especially home runs.

slugger: A player who specializes in slamming home runs—to the exclusion of other offensive weapons. Today, Cecil Fielder ranks as a quintessential slugger, while Barry BONDS, who can do so many other things, does not.

softball: The baseball-like recreational sport played throughout the country. Although the basic rules are the same, there are a number of fundamental differences:

- The ball is larger and lighter, so it doesn't travel as far when hit.
- The bases are 60 feet apart instead of baseball's 90.
- The pitcher throws from 46 feet instead of 60.
- The ball is pitched underhand. In slow-pitch softball, the ball travels in a high, slow arc toward the plate. In fast-pitch, the ball can come as fast as 70 mph.
- Some leagues allow the use of a roving 10th fielder, the buck-short.
- The bat has a thinner barrel.
- Slow-pitch games are much higher-scoring contests compared to baseball, while fast-pitch games are usually pitchers' duels, won with bunts and sacrifices.

southpaw: A left-handed pitcher. The term comes from the early baseball practice of positioning home plate on a field so that the batter wouldn't have to look into the setting afternoon sun. Since the batter is facing east, a left-handed pitcher's arm is on the southern side. Like many other sports-related words, this is an example of a term that originated with baseball and has been applied to other sports. Left-handed boxers, quarterbacks, golfers, and people in general are called southpaws.

spitball: A pitched ball that has been moistened—by spit, sweat, petroleum jelly, or another method—causing it to behave erratically as it travels toward the plate. To understand how it works, try applying a spot of glue to a Ping-Pong ball; when you roll it across the table, it will roll asymmetrically and oddly. That's what happens when a doctored baseball flies through the air at 90 miles per hour. The first pitcher to throw the spitball with frequency in the majors was Elmer "Spitball" Stricklett, who lasted just four years. Stricklett taught the pitch to Ed WALSH, who fashioned a Hall of Fame career with it. Spitballs have been illegal in major league baseball since 1919, when the leagues cracked down in the fear that a spitball might get away from the pitcher and hurt somebody. They did install a grandfather clause that allowed 17 pitchers to continue using the pitch, and Burleigh Grimes, a Hall of Famer, used the doctored pitch until 1934. Throughout the years, a number of pitchers have been accused of throwing spitters. Gaylord PERRY practically made a career out of denying he ever threw a spitball even though the world knew what he was doing. Perry was caught just once, earning a 10-day suspension. Then he went on the television show *Lie Detector* and passed six different tests. In his book *Me and the Spitter*, however, he wrote that he always kept his stash of grease in at least two places, "in case the umpires would ask me to wipe off one. I never wanted to be caught out there without anything. It wouldn't be professional."

split-fingered fastball: A FASTBALL variation that sinks as it reaches the plate. It's very similar to a forkball in that the ball is held tightly between the forefinger and middle finger, but the split-finger is thrown a little harder. It caused a sensation and was called the "pitch of the 1980s" when it was featured by Jack MORRIS, Mike Scott, Bruce Sutter, and a number of other pitchers who came in contact with Tigers pitching coach/Giants manager/split-finger guru Roger Craig.

squeeze play: The squeeze comes when there's a runner on third and less than two outs. As the pitcher begins his windup, the runner on third breaks for home. The batter's job is to bunt the ball far enough from home plate that the runner can score the run. That's a suicide squeeze—"suicide" because if the batter doesn't make contact, the runner is dead. A variation is the "safety squeeze," in which the baserunner waits to see if the ball has been bunted effectively before charging down the line. The best defense against a successful squeeze is the PITCHOUT.

starting rotation: A team's rotating group of starting pitchers. Today's five-man rotation means starters will only get about 34 starts per season—all but ruling out the possibility that a pitcher will ever again notch 30 victories in a season. In fact, it's a rarity that pitchers ever get 30 *decisions* in a given year. What does that mean in the long term? Probably that no pitcher will reach the magical 300-victory plateau. As recently as 15 or 20 years ago, teams regularly employed four-man rotations, and in the DEAD BALL ERA, a rotation generally consisted of three men. Thus, those pitchers were able to compile lifetime stats that will be unreachable by today's stars.

stolen base: A legal maneuver where a runner advances, or "steals," a base while the pitcher is in his motion. A's and Yankees left fielder Rickey HENDERSON, the king of the stolen base, possesses both the single-season (130) and career (1,117 through 1994) records for steals. In the early days of baseball, players were credited with a steal when they advanced an extra base on a hit; for example, a runner who went from first to third on a single would get a steal. That's how Harry Stovey was able to "steal" 156 bases in 1888; today's researchers have lowered that total to 87. In 1898, those rules changed to reflect a true stolen base as we know it today.

strike: A pitch that either (a) is swung on and missed, (b) is hit foul, or (c) crosses the plate in the STRIKE ZONE. A foul ball can be called a strike only for the first two strikes; after that, it's nothing, unless the ball is foul tipped into the catcher's glove and he holds on to it.

strikeout: The result of a batter getting three STRIKES. Reggie JACKSON is the all-time leader in strikeouts by a batter with 2,687 for his career, which is more than 600 ahead of number-two man Willie STARGELL. Bobby BONDS holds the top two single-season strikeout marks, whiffing 189 times in 1970 and 187 times in 1969. As far as the best strikeout pitchers, who else? Nolan RYAN holds both the career (5,714) and single-season (383) records. Unlike the BASE ON BALLS, whose criteria fluctuated during baseball's early years from nine BALLS to the present-day four, three strikes have always been enough for a strikeout. It's even written into the KNICKERBOCKER RULES: "Three balls struck at and missed and the last one caught, is a hand out; if not caught is considered fair, and the striker bound to run." That's one of the unique rules in baseball, that if the catcher drops the third strike with first base open or two outs, the batter can try to make it to first before a throw or tag. It's like giving a wide receiver a second chance to catch an incomplete pass.

strike zone: According to the rule book, the strike zone is the rectangular area from the top of the knees to the letters on a batter's shirt and the width of home plate. In actual practice, it varies from umpire to umpire and usually goes from the bottom of the knees to the belt buckle. "The ever-shrinking strike zone" is what broadcasters, writers, fans, and pitchers call it—and it's getting blamed for the explosion of home runs in the last few years as well as the increasing length of ball games. There's really no explanation for the shrinking strike zone, and every year people complain that something has to be done about it. But all attempts to reform the strike zone have been met with complacency and decided lack of action. Recently, in fact, the commissioner's office actually *shrank* the rule book's strike zone (changing the top level from the armpits to the letters), hoping that the redefinition would cause umpires to start calling the high strike. And in 1995, the leagues ordered umpires to call the high strike. We'll see.

sweet spot: The best part of a bat to hit the ball, a few inches from the thick end. When you're hitting, you can't *see* the ball hit the sweet spot, but you can sure feel it. There's no feeling like it.

switch-hitter: A hitter who can bat from both sides of the plate. Such a player gains the PLATOON advantage of not having to face a pitcher whose CURVEBALL breaks away from him. Right-handed batters have a tougher time against right-handed throwers than against lefties, and, of course, left-handed batters hit better against righties. That's why platooning exists. A switch-hitter who bats equally well from both sides never has to worry about being benched against a particular group of pitchers—which is why Mickey MANTLE's father taught his son to switch-hit at a very early age. Baseball's first switch-hitter was Bob Ferguson, who played from 1871 through 1884 and compiled a not-so-spectacular .265 batting average. A starting lineup of the *best* switch hitters is given opposite.

take: To let a pitch go by without swinging at it. On 3–0 or 3–1 counts, managers often order their mediocre hitters to take the next pitch, no matter how enticing, to force the pitcher to throw STRIKES.

A "Team" of the Best Switch-Hitters

Pos.	Player	G	H	R	HR	RBI	AVG
C	Ted Simmons	2,546	2,472	1,074	248	1,389	.285
1B	Eddie Murray*	2,706	2,930	1,477	438	1,738	.288
2B	Frankie Frisch	2,311	2,880	1,532	105	1,244	.316
3B	Pete Rose	3,562	4,256	2,165	160	1,314	.303
SS	George Davis	2,368	2,660	1,539	73	1,437	.295
OF	Mickey Mantle	2,401	2,415	1,677	536	1,509	.298
OF	Reggie Smith	1,987	2,020	1,123	314	1,092	.287
OF	Max Carey	2,476	2,665	1,545	70	800	.285
P	Vida Blue						
Bench:	Red Schoendienst (IF), Maury Wills (SS), Ken Singleton (OF), Wally Schang (C), Tim Raines (OF)						

*Stats through 1994.

Texas Leaguer: A looping fly ball that lands for a single in the unoccupied space between the infielders and outfielders. The term is around a century old, with uncertain origins. Did it come from a famed Texas League team that featured a number of players who specialized in such hits? From Texas League veteran Arthur Sunday, who used many looping hits to bat .398 with Toledo in 1889? From the major league debut of former Texas Leaguer Ollie Pickering, whose first seven hits were bloopers? From the fact that Texas League ballparks were very large, forcing outfielders to play deep and leave a lot of space between them and the infielders? Or, finally, from the strong Gulf Stream winds that affected fly balls in most Texas League cities, forcing a seemingly catchable ball to land in front of outfielders? Take your pick.

trade: An exchange of players between two (or more) teams. Sometimes a team will make a trade for the ubiquitous "player to be named later." Twice in baseball history, it resulted in that player being traded for himself—the ultimate fair trade. In 1962, Harry Chiti batted .195 in 15 games for the lowly Mets after coming to New York in a deal with the Indians for a player to be named. Chiti's performance stunk so badly—even on *that* awful team—that the Mets named him as that player and sent him back to Cleveland. In 1987, the Cubs "traded" Dickie Noles to Detroit for the month of September, then got him back when the clubs couldn't agree on a fair deal. Players aren't the only people who can be involved in deals. Teams have traded managers for players 13 times, and in 1960, Detroit and Cleveland swapped managers straight up, Jimmy Dykes for Joe Gordon. I doubt we'll ever see *that* again.

triple: A three-base hit. Triples are the most exciting single play in baseball, usually resulting in a long relay from the outfield to third base and culminating in a slide, a tag, and a cloud of dust. The all-time single-season leader in triples is Owen "Chief" Wilson, the unlikeliest record-holder of the unlikeliest record in baseball history (*see* 36). In terms of career numbers, the triples champ is Sam CRAWFORD, who banged 312 in his 19-year career. That's an average of 16 per season, which is generally more than today's *league leaders* hit. In fact, the top 18 players on the all-time triples list played before World War II, and many played in the DEAD BALL ERA. I'd like to know why batters don't hit as many triples as before. Is it because they don't hustle as much? Because outfielders are better? Because players have less speed? Because ballparks have uniform outfield fences, so the ball doesn't take strange bounces? Because the hits that used to be triples in the dead ball days now go for home runs? I'm sure *somebody* has done a study on triples, maybe somebody on the SABR records committee.

triple play: A defensive play that results in three outs recorded. TPs happen only a couple of times a year, and the *unassisted* triple play—when the same fielder makes all three outs—ranks as one of baseball's rarest occurrences: UTPs have happened only 10 times in major league history, making them less frequent than a PERFECT GAME (13) but more frequent than a Chicago Cubs world championship (2). Mickey Morandini of the Phillies did the trick in 1992. With runners on first and second against the Pirates, second baseman Morandini made a diving catch of a line drive, then got up and ran to second base to double off Andy Van Slyke, then tagged the unsuspecting runner from first, Barry BONDS, for the third out. It was the first UTP in the bigs since Washington's Ron Hansen accomplished the feat in 1968. Before that, more than 40 years had passed since the last. Strangely, of the 10 UTPs in major league history, 6 occurred during the 1920s, and 2 happened on consecutive days—the Cubs' Jimmy Cooney on May 30, 1927, and Detroit's Johnny Neun a day later.

umpire: The person on the field who calls BALLS, STRIKES, and OUTS and interprets the rule book for other plays. Today, four umpires call the plays for regular season games: a home plate umpire and one at each base. For postseason and All-Star Games, extra umpires man the outfield foul lines. In the early days of the sport, only one umpire called a game, then two. And umpires had a really tough time of it. They often volunteered for the job, until the National League decided to pay them five dollars per game. The AMERICAN ASSOCIATION was the first league to pay umpires fixed salaries, and the American League, headed by "Ban" JOHNSON, was the first to give its umpires full and unwavering support. In the 1970s, as baseball players fought for labor equity, the umpires' union rose to powerful heights. They struck at the beginning of the 1979 season, demanding better pay and better working conditions. The leagues called up replacement umpires from the minor leagues, but many games proved farcical when the rookie umps couldn't keep control of the games; the leagues then settled the dispute. Today's umpires earn six-figure salaries and vacation time in the middle of the season. But they also have to pay their dues. Like ballplayers, umpires have to work their way up the minor league ladder, and most never make it to the big leagues. Pam Postema nearly became the first woman to umpire in the major leagues, but she never received the call and was released from TRIPLE-A after 13 years. She had more experience than many of her colleagues who made it to the majors, and, having endured the constant taunting and sexist remarks by obnoxious fans and players through her career, she had to have more guts. The fact that the American League refused to hire her showed that they had less guts than Postema.

uniforms: What players wear on the field. Major league teams wear different uniforms at home and on the road; usually, the home uniform is white and the road one is gray or light blue. The evolution of baseball uniforms—from dull flannels to today's colorful double-knit polyesters—is a fascinating subject worthy of its own book. The best one on the market is Marc Okkonen's *Baseball Uniforms of the Twentieth Century*, which includes full-color drawings of every uniform ever worn at the major league level.

utility player: A versatile player who can man more than one position. Pete ROSE was the ultimate utility player because he could play first, second, third, and any outfield spot while also performing well offensively. A good current utility man is Tony Phillips of the Angels, who can play any position and hit for average and power. Neither of them, however, typify the utility player. Most aren't good enough to be regulars, either at the plate or in the field, so they fill in for injured starters. Some utility players can make a decent career out of it. Jerry Royster, for just one example, played 634 games at third, 416 at second, 187 at short, and 153 games in the outfield over 16 years in the majors.

waivers: The system by which players can be claimed in trades during the period from August 1 until the end of the season. Team A wants to TRADE a player to Team B because Team B is in a pennant race with Team C. It's after July 31st, which is the trading deadline, so Team A first places the player on waivers, making him available to any team in reverse order of the standings. The way it's supposed to work is, all the teams except Team B are supposed to "waive" their right to that player. Team B claims the player, usually in exchange for a "player to be named later," and the deal is done. If another team makes a claim for the player, Team A can decide to keep the player. If Team C's record is worse than Team B's, Team C can block the deal. Usually waiver claims are kept secret until a deal is consummated, but every now and then, word leaks out that, say, Team A's star outfielder was on the trading block until Team C put a stop to it.

walk: When a batter gets four BALLS, he gets a free trip to first base, and all the other baserunners advance if they're forced to by the walk; it's also called a BASE ON BALLS. Pete ROSE became famous for sprinting to first base on walks.

warning track: The strip of dirt in front of the outfield fences, designed to warn outfielders of their proximity to the walls. Pete REISER, the Dodgers phenom whose career was ruined by his numerous run-ins with hard outfield walls, is partially responsible for warning tracks.

waste pitch: A pitch deliberately thrown outside the STRIKE ZONE in an attempt to get the batter to chase the bad ball. Waste pitches often come on 0–2 or 1–2 counts. A pitcher who gives up a home run on one of those counts probably didn't waste the pitch far enough from the plate.

wild pitch: A pitched ball that's thrown wildly enough to get past the catcher. If the catcher is at fault, it's called a passed ball. A wild pitch only gets charged to the pitcher—and a passed ball to the catcher—when a runner advances a base or on a third strike if the batter reaches base safely.

winter league: A baseball league that plays in Florida, Arizona, or Latin America during the winter months. Most players in winter leagues were assigned by their teams to improve their skills or learn a new position, although many Latin American ballplayers return to their homes to play for their local teams. After batting .203 in DOUBLE-A in 1994, Michael Jordan played in an Arizona winter league, but it didn't help much.

winter meetings: The conferences held every November or December among all the big league clubs to discuss trades and other business matters. These days, it's rare that any real action springs out of the winter meetings. Mainly, teams announce free agent signings and minor deals. A few years ago, when the Padres traded Joe Carter and Roberto Alomar to the Blue Jays for Fred McGRIFF and Tony Fernandez, it was the biggest trade to come out of the winter meetings in quite a while.